LONELY TEARDROPS

THE JACKIE WILSON STORY

Design: David Houghton
Printed by: Unwin Brothers Limited

Published by: Sanctuary Publishing Limited, The Colonnades, 82
Bishops Bridge Road, London W2 6BB

Photographs courtesy of Tony Douglas's Private Collection, Lynn
Ciccone, Lynn Crochet, Michael Ochs Archive, John Goddard, Jimmy
Smith, David Yellen, Sammy Ward, Nate Lee, Audrey Sherborne, Billy
Davis, Dickie Thompson, Brunswick Records, Guy Warren and The
Detroit News

ISBN: 1-86074-214-9

LONELY TEARDROPS
THE JACKIE WILSON STORY

TONY DOUGLAS

About The Author

Tony Douglas was born in Melbourne, Australia, in 1942. After leaving school he began a career spent mainly in newspapers, working with the Melbourne *Herald*, the Sydney *Sun-Herald*, Montreal *Gazette*, Syme Newspaper Group and for Reed Business Publications.

Douglas moved to Thailand where he worked on the English language Bangkok *Post* newspaper in 1968 and also wrote travel articles for magazines. Whilst there he opened a bar, the Mississippi Queen, which was used for scenes in 1978's Academy Award winning movie *The Deer Hunter*. The bar quickly built a reputation as a centre for soul music, which renewed Douglas's interest in black music, especially that of Jackie Wilson. Hearing of Wilson's death in January 1984, Douglas realised he had no idea of the tragedy which had befallen Wilson more than eight years previously. Early in 1994, having searched unsuccessfully for a biography of the star, Douglas decided he would undertake the task himself and write his first book.

This book is dedicated to the four women who loved him most: Eliza Mae Lee, Freda Wilson, Lennie "Lynn" (Crochet) Guidry and Lynn Ciccone

Why A Book On Jackie Wilson?

B etween 1957 and 1968 Jackie Wilson had fifty-five Top Hundred and twenty-four Top Forty hits. Compare this achievement to the nine and six Top Forty hits of Little Richard and Jerry Lee Lewis respectively. More importantly, Jackie was one of the most remarkable vocalists in contemporary music, who quite easily could have become an opera singer. His vocal range and unique, rapturous presentation ensured he could never be confused with anyone else.

As a stage performer, again, he was untouchable. He would appear to glide and his entrances sometimes involved sliding on his knees to the stage edge. Black and white audiences were under his spell the moment he stepped out. Other times he would dive into the audience where his clothing would be shredded by hysterical female fans. He loved every minute of it and it was a brave artist that would go on after him. When Jackie was finished, both he and the audience were drained; the show was over!

Jackie pushed everything he did to the extreme. He married three times, had untold extra-marital affairs and fathered numerous offspring throughout the nation. His generosity was like his alcohol consumption; unbounded. He developed chronic addiction to amphetamines and cocaine, yet was able to record around four hundred songs ranging from gospel and blues, where his roots were, to standard evergreens like 'Stardust' and light operatic classics like 'Night' and 'Alone At Last'.

Not content there, he could as easily do raunchy rock 'n' roll or soul. His hallmark was to have his voice soar from its normal rich tenor range to notes in the high female range with perfect control and pitch. He was said to have invented notes.

Like many artists of the period, Jackie was owned outright by the Mob. Frankly, as a black artist of the 1950s and 1960s, he needed them to gain entry to Las Vegas and plush cabaret night spots. Record promotion and distribution also required their "expertise".

Early in his career he was shot and critically wounded by a female admirer. Despite losing a kidney and the bullet remaining lodged next to his spine for the rest of his life, he recovered fully.

Jackie's earnings were unheard of at the time for all but a few black performers, yet he was constantly dogged by the tax man, and the courts for outstanding family maintenance payments. He eventually suffered the indignity of having his family home seized by the IRS and sold by auction.

The public weren't Jackie's only fans. He was greatly admired by his peers, among them Elvis Presley who saw Jackie perform in 1956 in Las Vegas as lead singer with The Dominoes while Elvis was just starting out. Elvis was in awe of Jackie and remained one of his biggest fans, and later one of his friends. Likewise the young Michael Jackson would study Jackie and emulate his stage moves. In every way Jackie was a pioneer for the "crossover" of black artists into the broad appeal of the more lucrative white audience market – the Pop charts.

Throughout his career Jackie was dogged by legal hassles, some of which involved associations with white women that a still segregated southern United States would not tolerate. He had the indignity of having to perform to fully segregated audiences and despite being a worldwide star was unable to stay in the major hotels of his own country.

In 1975 Jackie suffered a heart attack on stage in New Jersey. For the next eight years he survived in a state between life and death, unable to communicate for the entire period. He died in January 1984 and was buried in an unmarked grave in his home city of Detroit.

Jackie's charisma was so huge that he would instantly be the focus of attention when he entered a room and today, twenty-two years since he collapsed on stage in New Jersey, and thirteen years since his death, he remains firmly focused in the minds of all those who knew and loved him.

The main purpose of *Lonely Teardrops* is to ensure that this great man will not be forgotten and that people who have not heard of him will take the trouble to re-discover the fabulous talent that he was. Indeed, had his time come just a decade later he would have been one of music's true superstars.

Acknowledgments

When I embarked on my search for Jackie Wilson, the fact that I'd never seen or met either him, or anyone who had any association with him, presented me with special difficulties. Not only did I have to locate the people who knew him, but I then needed to persuade them to divulge details that were not always flattering.

My first break came from Rhino Records in California who had released a three CD boxed set of Jackie's recordings. The seventy-two songs in the set had been selected by Simon Rutberg who had known Jackie for thirteen years as a fan and friend. Rhino put me in touch with Simon who was a mine of information. My sincere thanks go to him.

Next I came to know a young Detroiter, David Yellen, a record collector and major fan of Jackie and Motown artists. Resourceful and helpful, David assisted me in Detroit and over the next couple of years we were in regular contact. It would have been much more difficult without him.

Former Brunswick producer, Carl Davis in Chicago, was unstinting in his knowledgeable contribution and clearly held Jackie in the highest regard.

Possibly reluctantly in the beginning, Jackie's first wife, Freda, welcomed me into her home. From her I learned the most intimate details of life with Jackie. To me Freda is an heroic figure who has suffered much more than most and yet speaks with no bitterness. To my mind she always had a special place in Jackie's life. I tried to be her friend.

Through a remarkable chance meeting I met with guitarist Billy Davis in his Highland Park home. Billy had grown up with Jackie, later becoming a guitarist in his band. Billy loves Jackie, considering him the world's greatest singer. He was there when Jackie was in an emotionally low state and contributed towards his overcoming it. Without doubt one of Jackie's true friends and, I think, mine as well.

Few are more knowledgeable about the black music industry than Roquel "Billy" Davis who co-wrote most of Jackie's major hits. I will always be indebted to him for inviting me into his home and giving me so much vital information concerning the industry and Jackie's early career.

It was through Jackie's third wife that I made contact with Lynn Ciccone who had known and loved Jackie over many years, largely unknown to all but a few insiders. Lynn had researched and started a book of her own concerning her relationship with Jackie, the father of her only child. In the most unselfish gesture she handed over all her considerable notes and recorded interviews with no thought of reward. Over the next few years we were in constant touch and she seemed never to lose faith that I would eventually come up with a book about the man she still loves. A very special thanks to Lynn.

On a more personal level, my mother encouraged my efforts and maintained a keen interest in my progress. Sadly, she died before my work was complete.

My wife, Seda, who put up with the most. The long hours and my heavy drawing upon family savings must have given her serious cause for concern, yet she didn't complain. Indeed she provided the sounding board that such an enterprise requires. Likewise my young son, Dion, often had to take second place to Jackie. He would often ask me when it would all be finished, and every time he did I was racked with guilt.

On a more personal level I am thankful to my good friend David Irvine who was forever coming up with suggestions and, especially, encouragement. So, too, Trevor Baverstock and Vince Peach who were ever willing to lend an ear or give of their wonderful knowledge of the genre. With such encouragement giving up was never an option.

One friendship I formed through my search was that of former music arranger with Motown, Gil Askey, who fortunately had the good sense to become domiciled not far from my home. Gil had worked with Jackie in his touring band before doing arrangements for him on his dance hit 'Baby Workout' and the *Somethin' Else* album. Our conversations probably totalled days. I am eternally thankful, besides holding Gil in the highest regard. When I "dropped" his name, doors opened. Everyone seemed to love and respect him.

Many wonderful photographs were supplied by numerous people for which I am indebted. Sadly no film clips of Jackie in concert could be found. It seems extraordinary that nobody took the trouble to film these marvellous events.

Listed below are the other people who co-operated to varying degrees with my search for "the real Jackie". Some had only an incident or two, while others could tell untold details. To all of them, my sincere thanks.

Abrams, Al	*Publicity manager for Motown, Toledo, Ohio.*
Abrams, Reginald Jnr	*Rap singer, grandson of Jackie, Detroit.*
Abrams, Reginald	*Singer, son-in-law of Jackie, Detroit.*
Acklin, Barbara	*Singer, songwriter, Chicago.*
Adourian, Edward "Ted"	*New Jersey attorney. First court appointed guardian of Jackie.*
Atkins, Cholly	*Choreographer/dancer Apollo Theatre, Las Vegas.*
Ballard, Hank	*Of Hank Ballard And The Midnighters, Los Angeles.*
Barge, Gene	*Horn player, producer. Did session work with Jackie, Chicago.*
Barksdale, Chuck	*Singer, friend of Jackie, member of The Dells group, New York.*
Bass, Ralph	*Chess Records, A&R man, Chicago.*
Bateman, Robert	*Motown producer, Detroit.*
Bennett, Irma "Mary"	*Cousin of Jackie, Columbus, Mississippi.*
Billingslea, Joe	*Member of Contours, Detroit.*
Blavat, Jerry "The Geator"	*Philadelphia DJ.*
Bolden, Sheila	*Cousin of Jackie, Atlanta.*
Bonner, Joel "Joey"	*Brunswick promotions man, New York.*
Bowen, Ruth	*Booking agent (Queens Booking) for Jackie, New York.*
Bowles, Thomas "Beans"	*Horn player/music arranger for Motown, Detroit.*
Bradford, Janie	*Motown songwriter, Los Angeles.*
Byndon, Molly	*Friend of Jackie, mother of his daughter Sabrina, Los Angeles.*
Byndon, Sabrina	*Daughter of Jackie-Molly, Los Angeles.*
Cannon, Linda	*Sister-in-law of Jackie, Atlanta.*
Ciccone, Lynn	*Former girlfriend of Jackie and mother of his daughter Gina.*
Clark, Dick	*Hosted American Bandstand, Los Angeles.*

Collins, Johnny — *Singer, brother-in-law of Jackie, Chicago.*

Day, Jacqui — *Wife of "Rockin' Robin" Bobby Day, Los Angeles.*

De Loach, Loretta — *Knew Jackie as a teenager, Detroit.*

Devenne, Walter — *DJ and session mixer, Boston*

Drake, Tony — *Singer on Brunswick, New York.*

Dunn, Ron — *Motown session drummer, Los Angeles.*

Edwards, Esther — *Motown executive; sister of Berry Gordy, Detroit.*

Fox, John "Peanut" — *Drummer with Jackie from 1970-1975, Chicago.*

Fuqua, Harvey — *Former singer with Moonglows. Motown executive, Las Vegas.*

Gaines, Grady — *Sax player with Upsetters, Houston, Texas.*

Gaines, Roy — *Blues singer/guitarist. Songwriter for Jackie, Los Angeles.*

Gallimore, Jonathan — *Went to school with Jackie, Highland Park, Michigan.*

Gibson, Jack "The Rapper" — *DJ and Motown PR man, Florida.*

Goodman, Gene — *Music publisher and former director of Brunswick, New York.*

Green, Cal — *Early guitarist with Midnighters, Los Angeles.*

Guidry, Lennie "Lynn" — *Jackie's third wife and mother of his two children, Atlanta.*

Harris, Jenny — *Jackie's maiden aunt, Columbus, Mississippi.*

Holland, Eddie — *Detroit songwriter/singer. Did early demos for Jackie, Los Angeles.*

Hopkins, Linda — *Gospel and blues singer. Did duet album with Jackie, Los Angeles.*

Hunt, Tommy — *Chicago singer and friend of Jackie, Netherlands.*

Hunter, Joe — *Pianist, arranger. Worked with Jackie on tour, Detroit.*

Jackson, Chuck — *Singer, friend of Jackie, New Jersey.*

Jerome, Henry — *Musician, organiser Decca. Worked with Dick Jacobs, New York.*

John, Mabel — *Early Detroit singer, later Atlantic Records, Los Angeles.*

Johnson, Trina "Cookie" — *Friend of Jackie. Dancer with James Brown, Los Angeles.*

	Detroit.
Robinson, Claudette	*Formerly of Miracles, Los Angeles.*
Ryan, Jack	*Former Detroit journalist, now manager of Contours, Detroit.*
Sanders, William "Sonny"	*Producer, and arranger for Brunswick, Chicago.*
Schiffman, Bobby	*Former owner of Apollo Theatre, Florida.*
Sherborne, Audrey	*"Angel Lee". Stripper, friend of Little Richard and Jackie, Los Angeles.*
Silverman, Isidore	*Former accountant for Jackie, Detroit.*
Singleton, Eddie	*Songwriter for Jackie, Los Angeles.*
Smith, Ernestine	*Knew Jackie as a child, Detroit.*
Smith, Jimmy	*Drummer and close friend of Jackie, Virginia.*
Spain, Horace	*Cousin of Jackie and his driver in 1970s, Detroit.*
Stubbs, Levi	*Friend of Jackie, member of Four Tops, Detroit.*
Sutton, Charles	*One of original Royals/Midnighters, Detroit.*
Tarnopol, Paul	*Son of Jackie's manager, Nat, New York.*
Tate, Marlean	*Member of Andantes back-up group, Detroit.*
Taylor, Zola	*Original Platters group member, Los Angeles.*
Terry, Mike	*Motown sax session man, Chicago.*
Thiele, Bob	*Producer with Decca, New York.*
Thompson, Dick "Dickie"	*Guitarist. On road with Jackie as band guitarist/arranger, Arizona.*
Toledo, Launa	*Jackie's long-time close friend, San Jose, California.*
Trudell, John	*Orchestra leader and horn player, Detroit.*
Van de Pitte, David	*Music arranger for Jackie's last album, Detroit.*
Ward, Singin' Sammy	*Pioneer Motown singer, Detroit.*
Ward, Billy	*Of Billy Ward And The Dominoes. Jackie's mentor, Los Angeles.*
Weatherspoon, William	*Early songwriter, Detroit.*
Weiss, Hy	*Owned Old Town Records, New York.*
West, Sonny	*Close friend of Elvis Presley, Nashville.*
Williams, Paul	*Band leader, sax player and songwriter, New York.*
Wilson, Brenda	*Daughter of Suzie-Jackie, Detroit.*
Wilson, Mary	*Former member of Supremes, Los Angeles.*
Wyne, Josie	*Cousin of Jackie, Kalamazoo, Michigan.*

CONTENTS

INTRODUCTION

"If I am dead, as I well may be,
you come and find the place where I am lying
and kneel and say an Ave there for me."

These fitting lyrics, written last century, accompany a traditional Irish tune ('Londonderry Air') that is centuries older. Known now as 'Danny Boy', it was Jackie Wilson's favourite song. At 11am on Saturday 21 January, 1984, the heart of one of the world's great entertainers stopped beating. Fourteen minutes later he was pronounced dead. This remarkable man had sung his heart out and the world was a sadder place. Jackie Wilson was just forty-nine years old.

Singing is a practice common to every culture and particularly strong vocal traditions have developed in the Afro-American community. Having been transported from Africa in the most degrading and inhuman conditions, and then subjected to generations of slavery, they had few ways of alleviating their life of toil and trouble except through religious faith and singing. Two vocal styles resulted from this: gospel and the blues.

One humanitarian who was aware of the degradation of slavery was Mark Twain (Samuel Clemens), one of America's best loved writers. Twain was born in Missouri in 1835 and used his pen and satire to expose hypocrisy, bigotry and injustice. As a child he spent a lot of time on his uncle's farm. Despite his uncle having fifteen to twenty slaves on the farm, Twain, in his autobiography, says, "I have not come across a better man than he was." Of his relationship with the slaves: "All the Negroes were friends of ours and with those of our own age we were in effect comrades. I say in effect, using the phrase as a modification. We were comrades and yet not comrades; colour and condition interposed a subtle line which both parties were conscious of and which rendered complete fusion impossible." With guilt born of retrospect, Twain says, "In my school-boy days I had no aversion to slavery. I was not aware there was anything wrong with it."

An incident related in Twain's autobiography sheds some light on the importance of singing in the lives of the slaves, and reflects on the fact that tormented individuals can mask their pain through singing, which then becomes an integral part of their self-expression. Twain had begun to question the moral position of slavery, but observed that the "Negroes didn't appear unhappy".

> There was, however, one small incident of my boyhood days which touched this matter and it must have meant a good deal to me or it would not have stayed in my memory, clear and sharp, vivid and shadowless, all these slow drifting years. We had a little slave boy whom we had hired from some one, there in Hannibal. He was from the Eastern Shore of Maryland and had been brought away from his family and his friends, halfway across the American continent, and sold. He was a cheery spirit, innocent and gentle, and the noisiest creature that ever was perhaps. All day long he was singing, whistling, yelling, whooping, laughing – it was maddening, devastating, unendurable. At last, one day, I lost all my temper and went raging to my mother and said Sandy had been singing for an hour without a single break, and I couldn't stand it, and wouldn't she please shut him up. The tears came into her eyes and her lip trembled, and she said something like this: "Poor thing, when he sings it shows that he is not remembering, and that comforts me; but when he is still I am afraid he is thinking and I cannot bear it. He will never see his mother again; if he can sing, I must not hinder it but be thankful for it. If you were older, you would understand me; then that friendless child's noise would make you glad."

The blues came from the tradition of slaves singing as they toiled. Part of that involved the "field holler", a shout or shriek, described as a single expression of loneliness. Without the experience of severe oppression it is not possible to sing with the feeling that would be called "soul".

Jackie Wilson didn't experience slavery; he experienced its offspring – bigotry, prejudice and the humiliation that stems from it. He also had an advantage over Sandy in having a loving mother, but quite possibly he did sing for the same reason as the slaves – to hide the pain in his heart for all the injustices he and his community suffered purely as a consequence of their race.

CHAPTER ONE

Danny Boy

Jackie Wilson was a lot more than a good singer, he was a complete entertainer. He was, as songwriter Jeffree Perry, who knew him well, said, "a singers' singer". As contemporary and fellow Detroit singer, Betty Lavette, relates, "Many singers achieved stardom through pure good luck, perhaps a timely hit or a pretty face. However some people seem to be on earth for one purpose only; to express human emotion through song." Jackie was one of these people.

Jackie Wilson, as Jack Leroy Wilson became known, was born at 5.30am on Saturday 9 June, 1934 at the Herman Kiefer Hospital, on Hamilton and Taylor Streets, in Highland Park, Michigan. The hospital specialised in the treatment of tuberculosis sufferers and was still operating in 1996. Jackie was the only surviving son of his black American parents: Jack Wilson, then aged thirty-eight, and Eliza Mae Wilson, aged thirty. Eliza Mae was born on 22 April, 1904 to Bill and Rebecca (née Cobb) Ranson of Columbus, Mississippi. Eliza had a brother, King, and two sisters: the eldest of the three, Cassie and the youngest, Jenny (in 1996 Jenny was the only Ranson survivor). Her half-sisters, all Sanders, were Edith, Rose, Ida and Lucy, from Rebecca Ranson's first marriage (Jackie was never short of relatives!).

The Ransons lived on a fair sized farm on what is known as "Cobbs' Hill", Motley, just outside Columbus. They were Methodists and gospel singing was a large part of family life – Eliza Mae was a powerful singer, with a large, smiling mouth – and the house shook with foot stomping and singing when the family got together. Moonshine liquor was brewed there and bootlegging helped supplement the family income.

Jack Wilson Snr, a farmer, was born in 1896, just across the border in Alabama. His mother Anna lived in the nearby town of Starksville, Mississippi. After he married Eliza Mae in 1922, Jack Snr worked for the railroad. They lived for about three years in Columbus before heading to Detroit prior to the Great Depression.

Other relatives also made the move "up north" to Michigan, where they settled in Kalamazoo, Muskegon, Pontiac and Detroit. They were helped to find work in the enormous car plants by Jackie's cousin, Tom Odneal, son of Cassie (nee Ranson) Odneal. Many Wilson relatives still live there and carry the names of Taylor, Brown and Gray as well as Odneal.

After the move to Detroit came children. Eliza Mae and Jack Snr had had two children previously, but they hadn't survived. Jackie's birth certificate lists his father as "unemployed" and his mother as a "housewife". While in Detroit, no one can recall Jackie's father holding a job. He is best remembered for his drinking: he was a chronic alcoholic who sought the company of similar men. Being the only child of the marriage to survive, Jackie became the apple of Eliza Mae's eye.

They lived at 1533 Lyman Street, in north-eastern Detroit, a black neighbourhood known as Northend, close to the former Ford foundry plant and the former Chrysler headquarters and assembly plant. That modest little weatherboard house still stands, albeit in a dilapidated state, and surrounded by the open space of a bus storage yard.

Jackie was baptised in the nearby Russell Street Baptist church, where he would sing as a child, and where his funeral service would be conducted. Eliza Mae had a photograph taken of the infant Jackie at the time of his baptism, attired in a dress, with his hair braided and only one shoe on. It became one of the many mementos that have disappeared since his death. To family and close friends Jackie quickly became known as "Sonny", and they used this name until his death.

When Jackie was born in 1934, the world was emerging from the Depression and many people, especially blacks, had headed north to the cities of Chicago, New York, Pittsburgh, Philadelphia and Detroit. All sought to better their situation in life through work in the factories, many of which involved automobile manufacture. Detroit was at the forefront of the automobile industry and opportunities for blacks there were infinitely better than in either Mississippi or Alabama.

In fact Detroit was a melting pot of social groups and, although not as segregated as in the south, racial barriers prevailed. Blacks and whites mostly lived a separate existence: blacks mainly lived on the east side of Woodward Avenue, rarely the west and for a member of the black community to become successful by "white" standards, he or she had to have exceptional abilities, otherwise the best they could aspire to was a life of manual labour in the vast automobile plants.

Jackie's cousin, Virginia Odneal, one year his senior, can recall "whooping" his behind and shutting him in the closet as a young child when he misbehaved. She was a regular playmate of Jackie's between the ages of three and ten. At this time the family lived on Kenilworth Street in northern Detroit and the first school Jackie attended was Alger Elementary, on Alger Street. Virginia says Jackie could sing from the age of six: "He always said he was going to become a star, and when he became a star and made twenty-five cents he'd give his mother fifteen and keep ten." Jackie's aunt, Rebecca "Hot" Smith, said: "Jack was beautiful. He had a God given voice. He got it from his mother and grandmother; both could sing real good."

Eliza Mae divorced in 1940 when Jackie was six, and began a common-law relationship with John Lee, a hard worker at the Ford auto plant. John Lee, who was younger than Eliza Mae, was "a big, quiet man" who enjoyed his root cigars and usually owned an impressive car such as a Cadillac. They were, however, never formally married, so Eliza Mae was still eligible for single parent welfare cheques when needed.

After a black man was severely beaten by a group of white men, race rioting broke out in 1943 between blacks in the northern Detroit neighbourhood and Poles in the adjacent Hamtramck section. The violence consisted mainly of hand-to-hand fighting and rock throwing, but anyone foolish enough to cross the Hastings Street boundary line ran the risk of being killed. When the rioting had finished, thirty-four people had died and another seven hundred were injured. Ironically, white families were often amicable neighbours of black rioters and they were generally unaffected. Although the rioting didn't directly affect his family, the nine-year-old Jackie lived right near the area and must have been influenced by it.

Around this time he moved with his family a short distance to 248 Cottage Grove, off Woodward Avenue, in Highland Park, an area of three square miles entirely surrounded by the city of Detroit. It was the site of Chrysler Corporation's international automotive headquarters and the original site of Henry Ford's first mass-production car plant.

Highland Park was a tree lined working-class neighbourhood of around thirty-five thousand people, with two storey family homes surrounded by well tended lawns and gardens, and was fondly referred to as "the city of trees". To the east was the black neighbourhood, known as the Bowery; to the west the white. The segregation was not clear cut, however. Quite a few black families lived to the west of Woodward without any problems. There were also numerous Arabs, Jews and Italians in the area. Highland Park was also the candy making capital of the country, being home to Fanny Farmer, Sanders, Very Best, and Sidney Boggs just north of the area.

During the same period Jackie befriended Don Hudson and was a constant visitor to their house on Delmar Avenue. Don Hudson would die at the age of twenty-nine after serving in the Korean War as a fifteen-year-old and winning the Bronze Star and Purple Heart. He was severely injured, with shrapnel in his head, and was repatriated. He was not supposed to drink alcohol, but did, and had a brain seizure around 1963. His sister, Freda, an attractive girl with long hair, was just one year older than Jackie. They soon became sweethearts. "He was nine when he told me he was going to marry me," said Freda. "He told my mother at ten. He'd stay with my brother so he could see me. When he got to ten years old – I thought he was older – he said, 'Can I kiss you?' He was like my shining knight, my everything."

Freda had moved to Detroit with her family from Georgia. Her mother Leathia remarried and the family name became Hood. "When he was little Jack told me he didn't want to do nothing else but sing," recalled Freda. "He said he was going to be an entertainer. That was it, he was not going to do no hard work. We didn't have no record player, and I don't think he had no record player at home; he probably listened to radio. His mother could sing, his father could sing. He'd sing...my goodness. Even in church; he did that on Russell Street, Holbrook, Oakland, all that. They all knew him.

"He knew a lot of people who sang – he also used to sing on the corner. In the neighbourhood on the Northend, he'd stand up there in front of the store from about ten or twelve years old; he'd say, 'Hey mama, what you wanna hear some church songs or some blues?', or 'Mama, I'm going to sing you a song, you wanna hear it?'. They'd be giving him money for singing for them. He was just born to sing."

Jackie was always older than his years, in part as a result of his mother's very liberal upbringing. "When I first knew him, he was ten, singing on the street corner," explained Freda. "He'd get this wine; his mother would buy him this Cadillac Club Sweet Red or corn whisky. That's why I thought he was so old. After you got to know him, he was really very soft – he always acted different. Jack started doing things early [sexually], before most kids even think about it. He was way ahead of himself mentally."

Jackie's stepfather John ("Johnny") Lee worked at the Ford plant for forty years. By all accounts he and Jack Jnr got along well, although Eliza Mae always put her son's well-being ahead of John's. In Freda's words, "She could do anything with his [Johnny's] money; she liked to play cards. Jack could have anything he wanted."

A childhood friend of Jackie's, Eddie Pride, knew his stepfather and mother well. "He was a very decent, nice man. His mother was a beautiful lady. I couldn't think of nothing but nice things about her. She was a big help to him – an inspiration."

Freda remembers that Jackie always had a sense of parental respect, even if deep down he resented an instruction. "I don't care how drunk he got or whatever; he never said nothing to his mother or Johnny. His daddy [Johnny] could be drunk and if his daddy said, 'The sky is purple,' then it was purple!"

On 15 June, 1945, when Jackie was eleven, Eliza Mae had her second and only other surviving child, Joyce Ann. Her birthday six days from Jackie's, some speculated that their both being Geminis was the reason the relationship later became strained. Nevertheless, Jackie always loved her and would do whatever he could to assist her.

The Lee home didn't have a record player, but it did have a radio. The singers that Jackie listened to and whom he most admired were Al Jolson, Mario Lanza, the rhythm and blues ("R&B") singer Roy Brown, big band baritone Al Hibbler and the gospel great Mahalia Jackson. A common pastime of black families was group singing, especially families who had moved up from the south: before the days of television, group singing was one of the main forms of home entertainment, and people generally sang without musical accompaniment.

In 1945, Jackie transferred to Thomson Elementary School on Brush Street in Highland Park. (The school has since been torn down and the area has become part of the Chrysler complex.) Jonathan Gallimore, who was two years older than Jackie, captained the Highland Park High School track team. It was the role of the older children to look out for the grade children from the nearby Thomson Elementary School and

Gallimore introduced Jackie to track sports. He remembered Jackie as being a fast runner with plenty of track potential: "He was a very active little kid, always in trouble," he recalls.

No doubt Jackie had gained plenty of running practice eluding the school authorities for he was an incorrigible truant. The truant officers took their jobs very seriously; they knew Jackie and his close friend, Freddy Pride, by name and these two, along with a few others who had also decided early on that their futures lay in careers as singers, regarded attendance at school as a waste of time. The authorities' solution to truancy was the Lansing Correctional Institute and at about the age of twelve Jackie served the first of two detentions there.

Despite this, in 1947 Jackie, aged thirteen, was enrolled at the respected Highland Park High School; quite an honour as the school was reputed to be one of the best in the nation. At Highland Park High the majority of students were white: of the four hundred students who graduated in 1949, twelve were black. Nevertheless, Jackie remained uninterested in school.

The Pride family lived on La Belle Avenue in west Highland Park, a predominantly white section. Eddie Pride, who also attended Jackie's school comments: "Highland Park was an excellent school; I was really proud. Highland Park at that time went up to the fourteenth grade. That way they got to give the kids a chance to do two years of college – free." Regarding racism, Eddie says, "You know, I didn't know nothing about no race shit until I got in the army. Everybody in the class was white. We used to have to go through the whole school looking for somebody black. We didn't get too involved in that race thing. My neighbours were white, and all the people on my paper route were white. I just happened to be black."

Freddy Pride, twin brother of Eddie and now deceased, was one of Jackie's closest friends as well as being a fine singer. Freddy, who was two years older than Jackie, became one of the original Midnighters group. Jackie was a regular and welcome visitor to the Pride home where they met to practise their singing. Eddie: "I knew Jack since high school. He lived fast. Even at fifteen he was singing at clubs. He was quite fabulous, even then, as a youngster. Way ahead of himself. 'Danny Boy', Jack did when he was in high school. I said, 'Man, that'd be a hell of a recording.' He could sing opera. At that time Mario Lanza was out and Jack imitated him a lot.

"Jack didn't hardly go to school at all, but he would come down for music and excelled at music. His mother had him in church; had him in the choir. She had a voice, too. She taught Jack all the things, falsetto, and all that stuff he could do. He was doing that at thirteen, fourteen, fifteen years old." Little Willie John, who later became a successful recording artist, was also a regular at their rehearsals.

Mr Pride was an industrious auto worker, with plenty of growing children to feed. However guests were always welcome to dine with the family. A frequent dinner guest was Jackie. Mr Pride would say, "Brother Jack, would you like to eat with us today?" Then he'd say to his wife, "Okay, Bessy, you can go heavy on the mashed potato and light on the meat. There's a lot of us here today." Although not large, Jackie was a big eater.

The school Glee Club also met at the Pride house and was under the tutelage of an elderly woman, Mrs Kent. Eddie Pride's sister, Alice, a year younger than Jack, was also a member of the Glee Club, which she recalls had about fifteen members. "She'd always tell him he was going to make it," said Alice. "The song she liked was 'Silent Night' and she told everybody, 'Everybody be quiet! Jack! Come up here. I want you to sing. Jack, you're going to be good.' She praised him so. We would be laughing. He was about fifteen then. She discovered him. She'd say, 'You're going to make it, you have the voice.' He could hit those high notes – even back then."

Jackie spent much of his time at Northern High, Freda's school. "He would go into Highland Park High School and straight out the back door," stated Freda. "He spent more time over at my school than he did at his. We'd be looking out the window at him: he'd be standing outside messing with the girls. I'd know to go to that window in the study hall and wait…" Jackie was a womaniser from an early age, and was usually to be found wherever there were girls. Freda had to compete against her friends to win his attention.

Martha Scott, who was at school with Jackie and became Highland Park mayor, always knew he was going to be a star. Once a month a student would sing at school assembly. She remembers how nobody would miss morning assembly on the days that Jackie sang.

In 1949 Jackie's teacher remarked on his report card: "Jack's story is a sad one. He has a voice *out of this world*, but can't get to school on time to do anything about it. He has talent without ambition and charm without responsibility. I have doubts as to his future in 9-B or in life."

Jackie went only as far as the ninth grade, dropping out in 1950 when he was sixteen. His ambitions lay outside anything he could learn in school and he loathed discipline. Ernestine Smith, a few years older and a near neighbour, stated, "I think he dropped out early and did all the things my dad said he was going to do; drink and get girls pregnant." Martha Scott recalls that Jackie had impregnated around fifteen girls before he left school. Freda confirmed this.

Another Highland Park student, Loretta Deloach, was a friend of Jackie's and the Pride family, living in the same apartment building. "He always had this lovely voice. He would always sing when somebody asked him to sing for church or school; or if the kids wanted to raise some money for a programme we'd have these talent shows and we'd ask him to sing and he always would sing for us. A delightful young man; not conceited like some.

"I lived in an apartment and we'd all sit out on the back porch and sing. There were eight families in this apartment building. Jack would come to visit Freddy Pride. He called my Mom, 'Mom' and she was the one who did all the cooking and made hominy biscuits and everything. He'd say, 'Mom, got any biscuits?'. If she knew he was coming, she always had biscuits for Jack. She just loved him.

"We had this Sanders candy store and bakery [nearby] and the guys would go there and kinda get this candy without paying for it. We girls would try to make ourselves look attractive so the guys would give us some candy. Jack he always held out, but he'd give you more than the other guys. He'd give you a pound of candy. He was outgoing and all people accepted him. As a youngster he was still good looking. The women were after him." Loretta recalls that after Jackie became famous he was still the same warm person, "He didn't forget his friends. He'd always come back to Highland Park. When he came back it was a big deal."

Detroit during that period was a boom town. The city's chronic drug problem wasn't yet evident, although alcohol abuse and marijuana smoking were prevalent. Roquel "Billy" Davis, was a close friend and neighbour of Jackie's and became one of his songwriters, co-writing most of his major hits. He recalls: "In Highland Park in those days there was a sense of community. Everyone looked out for one another; it was like a big family. We played together, we entertained together, we ate together, we shared everything together. Poor little rich kids; that's what

I called us."

At around the age of twelve, Jackie formed a small group he called The Ever Ready Gospel Singers. Naturally, he sang lead. Jackie's best friend throughout most of his life was a lanky fellow with a big jaw and a friendly smile, Johnny Jones. "JJ", as he was generally known, was three years Jackie's senior and lived nearby. They often spent the night at each other's homes and attended the same Russell Street Baptist Church. JJ was part of the gospel group and sang bass. Two brothers, Emmanuel and Lorenzo made up the quartet.

"Jack was the group," according to Freda. "They performed at all kinds of churches throughout the day. A collection would be taken for them – a quarter at least. They could tear up a church. In the evening, after church, they'd shoot craps, and he'd win all their money. Those people believed they were giving to God; these were children of God. They didn't know Jack was shooting craps. Jack was just smart from the street. He always knew what notes he could reach. He did his own stuff; nobody trained him, they didn't have to." They sang the church circuit around the Northend area of Detroit, remaining active until he was fifteen or sixteen.

Jonathan Gallimore recalls, "They formed a group and used to sing on all the corners: the corner of Oakland and Connecticut, then they was around the west side and on the playground at the Highland Park High School and at Northern High School and the Community Centre."

Ernestine Smith lived on Russell Street, close to where Jackie lived. Ernestine's father was strict, religious and hardworking. He discouraged Ernestine from any involvement with Jackie or his friends. The back porch of the Smith house looked out on the alley where Jackie and his group hung out. It was also the place where his father gathered with his "wino" cronies. "Jack was basically a good young man," said Ernestine. "He liked to drink that wine, though. My dad picked who I mixed with. For some reason he didn't like me to mix too much with Jack. He was good looking; I always admired him and liked him, but had a little fear in my heart because he could be a little demanding, 'Come here!', like that. The way he'd talk to you, 'When I tell you to come over here, I mean it.' He said, 'I like you. Do you wanna be my girl?' I said, 'No, no.' I figured he was younger than me. One night he was with the fellas and he called me. I ran, I beat OJ [Simpson] running.

"My daddy said, 'He's out there in the world, he's rough.' That's the way he grew up and survived. In winter they'd put on a heavy coat and gloves. Some had holes in the gloves, mittens. If it was cold, that wine would heat them up. There was a Standard gas station in the alley. He liked to shoot dice with the guys. Jack would come up the alley to be with his dad and those men. There was a store nearby where they'd buy their liquor. They'd drink and solve the world's problems. There'd be six, seven or eight men. But if the minister came down the street, they had respect for him.

"They'd buy the wine and pass the bottle; they'd be laughing. If Jack would come up, they'd sing. They seemed always to be having fun. My dad resented that; he worked hard and thought they should. He'd say, 'Get away from my porch.' They would get carried away and be cussing. Jack did have a split life. I had seen him in church and saw him sing, but he could cuss! My dad was a church goer and didn't like the cussing. They'd say, 'Here comes that man, he's going to give us a sermon.' They used to enjoy taunting him. They'd tell my dad, 'You don't own this street!' If it was too cold you wouldn't see 'em."

Eddie Pride also has stories of Jackie's drinking: "Jack drank, too, you know; I was with him. Cadillac Club and Mr Boston – cheap wine – about eighty-nine cents. We'd put our quarters together and sing on that wine, instead of being in school. Mostly we hung out on Fourth and Hamilton [streets] – there was a liquor store up there. We'd get the older guys to buy the wine and let them have the first drink: 'take the poison off the top', as we'd say. Then we'd have a ball." They generally sang blues-style numbers and often composed their own songs.

Freda recalls that it was through his group that Jackie first met the singer Sam Cooke. She explained, "Back then Jack's group hung around the radio station. That's how he met Sam Cooke. They went on the radio because Sam asked them to give them a break. WJLB or WJBK, I believe it was." Cooke, who was from Chicago, was seven months Jackie's junior, but had been in a family gospel group since the age of nine. With his exceptional good looks, charisma and unique, mellow vocal skills he quickly became a singing sensation; loved equally by black and white audiences, especially the female fans. It's ironic that Cooke and Jackie were to meet so early and become such good friends. Many consider them to have had the two greatest voices in popular music.

In the tough Detroit environment in which Jackie grew up, where the racial divide was wide and deep, blacks were generally the last to be hired.

While in his teens he became a member of the "Shaker" gang, known as "the 'baddest' gang around" and "a pretty tough bunch, always in trouble". The Shakers' territory was around Woodward Avenue. Gang leaders were Maurice Munson, Calvin "Clem" or "Bo Bo" Thomas, and Donald Penniman; other members included JJ, Charles Hardaway, Nelson Small, the four Pashae brothers (Fred, Jim, Mack, Robin), Leroy Munson, "Red" (whose real name could not be established) and Harry "Dale" Respess.

Otis Williams of The Temptations, in his autobiography, describes gang leader Munson as "truly frightening", a big ugly scar above his lip and long hair parted down the middle and tied in a "doo rag" (a kerchief-like cloth bound around the head and fashionable amongst certain black youths at the time). Maurice Munson was feared, while Calvin Thomas was described as being "bad news". Mack Pashae became a professional fighter and served time in jail. Later he was murdered.

Roquel Davis knew the Shakers well. "They were feared by the whole of Detroit, but Jack wasn't a running part of the gang. No more than a dozen guys made up the most prominent part, meanest, and vicious." Former Shakers member Respess said that although only a dozen or so strong, the group was "the scourge of the city. Everyone was scared to death of us. We were little thugs. We'd look for fights and punch people out. Jack was pretty tough. Johnny Jones was there, of course. JJ was almost his alter ego, his shadow."

Respess fondly remembers they'd sit in an alley off Oakland Avenue, drinking muscatel wine and listening to Jackie sing 'Danny Boy' for them, "just as though we'd paid twenty dollars for a ticket. Man, we really got off on that after drinking that wine. We always said one day he's going to make it, if he kept trying. That was our idol and we were his faithful followers."

The girls were known as Shaker Rats. Not surprisingly Freda Hood became a Shaker Rat: "I wanted to be a Shaker Rat. I didn't know what it was all about. They'd go over to Hamtramck and beat up this Polish gang, and they would go to the Northend and beat up this other gang that was supposed to be bad. We'd have these long skirts on and felt we were looking sharp."

Around five foot seven, Jackie was reasonably small, but "he was a street fighter", remembers Freda. "All we did was hot-wire cars and fight for territory. But Jack did that with his fists – he was really something. He never got his face hurt because the other guys would step in if he looked like getting his face hurt, and they'd catch the blows themselves."

Freda rationalises his macho behaviour today: "He would fight, but I don't think he really liked fighting all that much. He knew he had a lot of people to cover for him. He could go in and do his thing and somebody was going to interfere. I think Jack liked to 'scrap' to show he was a man. 'Hey, I'm a man and can take care of myself', you know, like his people would be interfering when he'd be going to hit someone or something. 'I've got it,' he'd say. He didn't have a bad temper. He could smile at you and his eyes would be saying 'get the heck away from me'."

Loretta Deloach knew the Shakers: "They were dangerous but not killing like today. They were into claiming their territory and their women and proving they were tough. They could smack you around a little bit. Jackie wasn't a dumb kid – he had skills. He could run fast – he had to!"

Mack Rice, one of the original Falcons R&B group, recalls, "Jack was adopted. He didn't have nothing to do with that stuff. They were mean but not like today. When you were a 'star' like Jack you were an honorary member; they looked out for him. They would boost him up there, boy."

Ernestine Smith remembers Jackie's gang involvement: "He got into his little mysteries – stealing and things. Jack had a temper too. The Shakers sort of ruled; I was afraid of the gang. They'd intimidate people. They used fists, maybe a chain. They'd 'whoop' your ass real good. I'd stay clear of them and I would walk fast coming home from school. My daddy said, 'That boy is a hoodlum.' Jack wasn't all that well dressed, but he dressed decent. I've seen him with holey pants on. Blue jeans wasn't that fashionable back then. His shoes might be a bit run over."

According to Freda, Jackie was returned to the Lansing Correctional Institute when he was sixteen. Freda remembers: "I didn't want him to go to jail – he'd been to jail when he was a juvenile. That was a lark to him anyway; he acted like he was going on a vacation." It's possible that this period of incarceration had more to do with juvenile delinquency than truancy, but Freda wasn't prepared to elaborate.

She went on: "He told his mother to bring me down. I said to him, 'Why haven't you got shoelaces?' He said, 'They don't let us have shoelaces.' He had blue jeans, T-shirt – that's it. Gym shoes, no shoelaces. I said, 'Well, that's silly.' The guard says, 'Jack, I know that's not your sister, I met your sister Joyce – so go ahead and kiss her.' So he kissed me through the bars. He told his mother to go buy him some wine sometime, 'cause he was sick – and she did – she did everything he said to."

At Lansing he took to boxing and may have considered this as a career option. Detroit was the home town of "the Brown Bomber", world heavyweight champion, Joe Louis. Louis was home town hero to Detroit's black youth. On his release Jackie became a regular at Brewster's Gym, where he worked out and trained to become a professional boxer. In 1961, when he'd become a star, Jackie was interviewed by Mary Akon for New York's *Sunday News* [22 October, 1961]: "My ma took me along regularly when she went to choir practice in church, but I wanted to be a prize fighter when I grew up. When I was sixteen I said I was eighteen so I could compete in the Detroit Golden Gloves. I won the welterweight championship and turned pro; which was a terrible mistake. I won only two fights out of ten. One time I got flattened in the fourth round. I was seventeen when I began thinking about another way to make a living, especially since I had married Freda who'd been my girl in Highland Park High School."

Jackie's reminiscences were not always accurate; the Golden Gloves title was a later fiction he perpetuated. His claim to have only thought of another career path at seventeen also seems unlikely, as Freda and many others believe he'd been planning a singing career since early childhood. But this wasn't the last time he embellished a story.

In the early 1970s Jackie did a radio interview with New York DJ Norman N Nite (on WCBS—FM). "Boxing, actually I didn't want to leave," he said. "My mother just grabbed me by the hair one day and told me, 'No more.' I was getting real good and she walked into the arena one night and I was boxing. I always looked for her in a certain seat and she wasn't there. All of a sudden she walked in. My nickname is Sonny and she hollers out real loud, 'Hey, Sonny.' And I turn around, and wop, wop, wop. She finally saw me beat to bits. So she told me, 'No more.'"

His mother never went to see him boxing being strongly opposed to it. Freda said Jackie's mother didn't know he'd been boxing and was furious on finding out. She forbade him from boxing again. "He liked boxing; that's the one thing I could never understand," says Freda. "I'm glad he gave it up, because of his face. His mother was very concerned and he did everything she told him."

Ironically, it was the close bond he had with his mother that would later see Jackie put his pugilist's skills to the test, as Harry Respess recalls. "I remember once at the Greystone in Detroit he was performing and his mother was in the crowd," he says. "She was trying to get backstage and they didn't know who she was and he fought through the crowd – man, he was punching them out – to get to her. He fought through the crowd in plain view of everybody – knocking cops all over the place – knocking them out. Someone had said a cop hit his mother and he went berserk. 'Nobody hits my mother.' He came off stage like a madman, right in the middle of an act, fighting like a wild tiger. It took a few cops to subdue him and they finally arrested him." Part of Eliza Mae's problem in convincing the security staff who she was may have been caused by the fact that she looked nothing like Jackie, being dark and heavy.

At the time an important arena for aspiring black singers was the amateur nights at the Paradise Theatre (also called The Orchestra Hall): Detroit's equivalent of Harlem's Apollo Theatre. As well as the Paradise, Jackie participated at amateur nights at the Park, State, Gold Coast, Grant, Booker T and Warfield theatres. These were movie theatres that charged only twenty-five cents entry and would feature fifteen to twenty acts. The competition was fierce and the enthusiastic black audiences took the outcome very seriously, so it was useful to have your own cheer squad.

Jackie was regularly up against the vocal talents of Little Willie John, Singin' Sammy Ward, Della Reese, his friends Ralph Peterson and Freddy Pride and Levi Stubbs, who went on to become lead singer of The Four Tops. More often than not, Little Willie John would win over Jackie and walk away with the first prize of twenty-five or fifty dollars.

As he did on the street corners, Jackie liked to perform 'Danny Boy' at these evenings, which he sang with the emotional passion that was to become his hallmark. Freda recalls, "He'd always win amateur nights doing 'Danny Boy', and when he recorded it he did it the same way." Music writer Don Waller later wrote of hearing him do 'Danny Boy': "By the time Wilson hit the final cadenza in which he wrings twenty-three – count 'em – notes out of the word 'for', I was convinced there wasn't a pop singer alive who could stretch such a thin piece of material into the aural equivalent of an Armani suit."

The contests provided the opportunity for young artists to be noticed by talent scouts from recording companies and tour promoters. Alice Pride remembers that Jackie was already developing the footwork and falling down splits that would later become part of his stage act.

Ernestine Smith saw Jackie perform at the Grant Theatre. "On Fridays and Saturdays neighbourhood people could come and perform. Jack had on nice pants, nice shoes, nice shirt. I thought he'd have been sixteen or seventeen. He won singing 'Danny Boy', and after that he became famous. He had that charisma and he could always dance; great body movements. He brought the house down, and those kids could be cruel, too. They were cheering and stood up and clapped."

His hair would have to look right as well. "He used to 'conk' his hair," she recounts. "He would process his hair" – referring to the style favoured by blacks at that time, which involved the quite painful practice of treating their hair with lye in order to straighten it. He would then use Brylcreem to ensure his hair remained in place.

Johnny Otis, born in 1921 to Greek parents, was from California but travelled all over the USA seeking out R&B talent. Otis, who discovered many artists during the 1950s, recalls Jackie came in third to Little Willie John and The Royals at an amateur night at the Paradise Theatre and credits himself with "discovering" the singer. However, there is no record of his assisting Jackie in any way. One story has it that Otis tried to sign Jackie to Syd Nathan's King/Federal record label in Cincinnati, but they weren't interested. Instead they signed up The Royals and Little Willie John.

Little Willie John came from the same neighbourhood as Jackie: the two were friends and often rehearsed together. Born in Arkansas in November 1937, he moved to Detroit with his family while young. Singing was part of his family life.

Cal Green, an early guitarist with The Midnighters, knew Little Willie John. "We used to hang out together. Willie and I were the same size [five foot four-and-a-half] and we used to trade clothes. He was a crazy little dude. He was the 'singingest' little sucker. Boy, he could sing; he was a natural." Green also knew Jackie. "Jack had perfect timing. He could sing anything with a lot of feeling. He was one of the great all-time singers. I'll put him right up there with the best of them."

John was to go on to have a successful, albeit brief, recording career on King Records, being best remembered for the hits 'Talk To Me' and 'Fever'. But he was just as well known for his wild behaviour. "Little Willie and Jack knew each other as they grew up and through music," says his sister, Mabel John.

A vicious temper and a drug habit contributed to John's killing of a man in a bar fight for which he was convicted of manslaughter in 1966. This incredibly talented singer died of pneumonia in 1968, aged thirty, while in Washington State Prison. Today Little Willie John is largely forgotten, although in 1996 he was finally inducted into America's Rock 'N' Roll Hall Of Fame.

Jackie, Little Willie John and Levi Stubbs would often get together at each other's homes to rehearse. "Little Willie John, Mabel John and Jack would always be over at Mrs Stubbs' house and they would be over at Jack's mother's singing and carrying on," says Freda. Stubbs admits modestly, "I used to perform at amateur nights at the Paradise and the Warfield theatre on Hastings Street. Little Willie John and Jackie would perform at the same time. It's not a question of trying to out-perform each other; it's a matter of doing what you do. I personally never put myself on the same level as Jack and Little Willie John."

Freda was a regular at the Paradise: "They had an amateur show on Tuesday night. They had a lot of amateur shows and shows with Sonny Til And The Orioles and Lionel Hampton. Jack, Ralph [Peterson] and Johnny [JJ] would win sometimes, then they would let Levi Stubbs and his people win the next time. Jack and Ralph were on it every week. They had it all worked out. They had it all set up. Jack said, 'You win tonight, I'll win next night.'" He was as confident of success in the professional world: "He kept saying – I was working in the kitchen at that time – 'Don't worry, it'll be all right.'"

Levi Stubbs recalls how "Jack had a terrific voice. Jack had an influence on me. When you won the amateur night you got either twenty-five or fifty dollars. That's the world to them [the winners], and you had the chance to work with professional shows that they brought in. All the big black acts were there." The black audiences were very boisterous, very vocal. You could get booed off the stage. It was a good training ground, but it was useful to have supporters in the audience."

The amateur night contests sometimes took Jackie over to Holbrook and Delmar Streets, the Herokies Gang's territory. He needed Shaker Gang muscle to ensure his safety and to give him some vocal and moral support. "Jack would mostly win the shows there," remembers former Shaker gang member Respess. "Not only because he had the audience stacked or packed, but because he was the best singer."

Singin' Sammy Ward, who often competed against Jackie, remembers the enjoyment his opponent took from performing: "He was the kind of guy who would like to sing anytime, anywhere – for money or no money. Mostly for no money. He sang all the amateur shows, Paradise, Warfield, and the council had something going at one time."

Eddie Pride, formed his own group, Eddie Pride And The Nightcaps. "I used to call myself a singer, but after listening to Jackie I gave up," says Eddie. "He could go high C and above – and do bass. I couldn't understand how he could do that." Brother Freddy Pride was so close to Jackie, many considered them brothers. Freddy went on to become one of the original Midnighters but died of a drug overdose before he was thirty.

Apart from singing in church or contests, the other outlet for black singers was the street corner. It was extremely commonplace for small groups of youths to sing vocal harmonies. These became known as "doo wop", because they couldn't afford to buy instruments and had to vocally improvise them. Around 1950 a doo wop group was formed called The Royals which included Levi Stubbs, Lawson Smith, Sonny Woods, Henry Booth and Charles Sutton, with Alonzo Tucker or Arthur Porter on guitar.

As well as playing guitar, Tucker also wrote many of their songs, despite his inability to read music. He later became Jackie's most prolific songwriter, co-writing numerous tunes with him. Twenty-five years older than Jackie and referred to as "the old man", he passed on a great deal of his musical expertise and was loved by one and all. "A songwriter from the old school," says fellow songwriter Roquel "Billy" Davis. "Tucker taught us a lot about R&B. To write a song, you come up with a concept. You create a phrase that becomes a title.

"Tucker's spirit was young and he always had a smile. He was missing a tooth or two in the front, so that every time he laughed or smiled, which he did a lot, he would hold his hand over his mouth. He was a wonderful guy."

Similarly, Cal Green, who became The Midnighters' lead guitarist, also fondly recalls Alonzo Tucker: "Alonzo would have all the youngsters out on the corner singing. He'd help people to put a song together and end up doing it and then teaching them how to sing it…the whole nine yards. He was a good guy, a nice guy."

One of the original Royals, Charles Sutton, lived in downtown Detroit where many of the rehearsals took place. Sutton recalls Tucker, Hank Ballard, Jackie and his group visiting in his home in 1952. "They came to our rehearsals. My wife and I had a couple of kids, but she'd tolerate it;

all the singing and stuff," says Sutton. "Alonzo and I were friends a long time before all this. He only lived three doors from me."

The Royals went on to have limited success on Syd Nathan's King label in Cincinnati but, because of ongoing confusion with The Five Royales, they changed their name to The Midnighters. R&B singer Johnny Otis wrote the ballad 'Every Beat Of My Heart', which The Royals recorded in 1952. Sutton sang the lead, however the song only became a hit when Gladys Knight recorded it years later. Levi Stubbs was with The Royals for a time although never recorded with them.

As The Midnighters, and with Hank Ballard as their lead, they became the first black group from Detroit to achieve national success. With Ballard's emotional style of delivery, success soon followed starting with the 1953 R&B Top Ten hit 'Get It'. In 1954 they reached the "big time" with three hits, 'Work With Me Annie', 'Sexy Ways' and 'Annie Had A Baby'. When word reached Ballard that he had a hit he didn't wait to collect his Ford factory pay cheque. He immediately threw off his overalls and left the job.

Singing with a group taught Jackie the importance of harmonising: singing without musical backing emphasised the primacy of his voice as a musical instrument. But Jackie wasn't alone in benefiting from the style of the era as Roquel Davis explains: "The 1950s gave birth to a lot of black 'bird' groups [eg Ravens, Orioles, Flamingos, Robins, Penguins], which gave birth to doo wop groups. Every kid on the corner thought, 'I can sing.'" It was the ideal way to sing harmoniously and spawned some incredible talent.

Davis formed a group called The Thrillers, but after only local success they disbanded, with Davis, who had singing aspirations of his own, forming another group called The Aims. He quickly realised that to be a singer he needed original songs, so he said to himself, "'Okay, I'll have to write songs.' I have always loved poetry, but only had elementary music training at school – trumpet and drums. The poetry helped with the singing; it came easy. To song-write you have to be inspired. You'd have to have an idea." Davis had many ideas, co-writing songs with Charles Sutton and Alonzo Tucker, and a friend of Tucker's, William Weatherspoon. An early success was the hit 'Seesaw', co-written with Sutton.

All the while the romance between Jackie and Freda was blossoming. "He used to spend the night with my brother, Don," says

Freda. "My mother found out he was saying those things [about Freda being cute] and said, 'You can't stay here no more; I don't know about you.' I didn't know how to speak to a boy. I liked Jack because he could sing and he was handsome. All the girls liked him; all my friends tried to take him from me. He liked someone soft, someone he could control."

He had a vain streak. "My mother had this big mirror over the buffet – he didn't say nothing to me; he walk straight past, look in the mirror, lick his lips, and come back and say, 'Hey, baby.' Jack always knew how to dress. He was handsome, and he knew it. He just knew how to put nothing together and look real good. He never wore blue jeans, he always wore suits then, even when he was fifteen or sixteen. He also wore Stacey Adams shoes – alligator shoes – and all that. His hat would be 'couched' over one eye."

Freda, who Jackie always referred to by the pet name of Pee Wee on account of her initially being taller than himself, soon became pregnant and a marriage was arranged at her home on 22 February, 1951. But as the time for the wedding drew near the groom disappeared. "Jack was already drunk when he went. The minister was there, I was there; everybody was sitting there looking stupid. I said, 'I know where he is.' It was amateur night at the Paradise Theatre. My stepfather finally took me down there. He said, 'I know. I'm going down there to get him.' I said, 'I'll have to go there with you.'

"We got there; it was [a contest] between Ralph Peterson, Levi Stubbs and Jack. Ralph and Jack were so drunk on stage. Ralph was jerking the microphone from Jack when he was trying to sing. Jack was jerking the microphone from him. Jack was just hollering, it was nothing – people were just booing. So we went backstage. He said, 'Baby, I was coming. I was getting my nerves up.' So we just picked him up and took him to our house and that's where we got married. All of Jack's buddies were at the wedding, including JJ and Ralph Peterson. My mother was there with her boyfriend, and my grandparents. We went back and got married and we had a party. They already had some liquor and they got some more. Jack was sixteen and I was seventeen. He used the name Richards; a friend Elija Richards loaned him the ID, as he was underage at the time. Jack used the same ID so he could perform at Lee's Club Sensation, a black club on nearby Owen Street."

Jackie's mother wasn't present. "His mother knew about it," says

Freda, "and that was the first time he did something his mother told him not to. He didn't hide anything from her. She just accepted it and she liked me after; we got along very well. The minister across the road from us performed the ceremony. Jack had some money because he had won some at an amateur night a few weeks before. He gave it to pay the minister."

After the wedding they lived together at Freda's family home on Delmar Street, on Detroit's northside. Later on they moved about a mile away to Cottage Grove, off Woodward Avenue, living with his mother and John Lee. Freda: "Johnny was good to us and helped raise us. Even though I couldn't cook. They didn't have no phone. Johnny was a nice man. He used to let Jack have his kind of [Cadillac] limo to take me to my little society things. We were the only ones who had a big car."

The big car wasn't the extent of Freda's aspirations, though. She had ambitions of her own. "I didn't want to get married in the first place, I wanted to be a doctor." She was a trainee nurse and none of her colleagues knew she was married, let alone pregnant. "In 1951 they were already throwing girls out of school that was pregnant. I felt if I didn't tell anybody, Denise would just appear. I graduated in January, got married in February and had Denise in March. And nobody at the college knew. My counsellor kept coming over and saying, 'Why hadn't I gone on to college?' because I had won a scholarship. He said, 'If it's money, I can arrange something.' I said, 'No.' He said, 'Whose cute little baby sitting on the couch?' I said, 'Mine.' He answered, 'That Jack Wilson, I told you to stay away from him; I told you I knew he was bad.'"

When their first child, Jacqueline Denise, was born on 24 March, the Wilson's family future looked uncertain. Jackie had dropped out of school and was unemployed and his wife was suffering: "The delivery room was the worst place I've ever seen, it was like a torture chamber. They put me on this table, my feet in this thing; I kept sliding back. I said, 'What is this? This is like hell.' Anyway, I had her. I don't know if Jack called the hospital or what, but he found out I had that baby. He'd been singing at Lee's Club Sensation to make a little money. Anyhow, he came in the hospital about three or four o'clock in the morning. How he got in, I'll never know. 'You had a girl, eh? What's her name.' I said, 'I ain't named her yet.' Jack said, 'Her name's Jacqui.' I said, 'You get away from me. All you want to do is do that thing; that's horrible and it hurts and I can't stand it.' Jack said, 'Be quiet, I ain't supposed to be in here.'"

But his late night presence was discovered. "They were trying to put him out. He said, 'Just do me a favour; just let me see my little baby one time and I'll go and come back tomorrow or whatever.' Then he left."

The pain of childbirth would not be soon forgotten and Freda became wary of Jackie's excessive sexual demands. "When he came to bed, I got up," she admits. "I was pregnant fifteen times before I was thirty. I was a baby factory! When Jack came near me I said, 'No, no, don't! Go away! Please go away.' For a long time I couldn't stand to see sausages, hot dogs, none of those things. Each time I became pregnant I'd say, 'Please don't let this one look like him.' I wanted girls."

All their children would carry the last name 'Richards', in accordance with the marriage certificate. But regardless of surname, Jackie was proud of his new daughter and took her to where his father "hung out" with the other winos on Holbrook Street. He loved his father despite the shortcomings; Freda did as well, but that wasn't what she had in mind for her child. "I liked Mr Jack too, but I didn't want Denise up there," she explains. "His father drank wine in the alley and pushed a push-cart. I figured there'd be germs and everything. So Jack told me he was taking her to the doctor; she had a cold. I said, 'I'll come, too.' He said, 'No, I can take her.' He knew I wouldn't want him taking her.

"He was gone so very long that day. I finally said, 'I wonder where he could be?' I said, 'I know, I'm going up to Holbrook.' It was off Russell Street. I walked down there; sure enough, there was my baby in the garage. Jack was singing, drinking wine. Mr Wilson was holding the baby and talking about his grand-daughter. That's the only one [of their four children] he saw before he died [in 1953]. He carried Denise around and held her out in front of him. I didn't like for him to hold her when he'd been drinking, 'cause I was scared he might drop her. Jack said, 'Leave him alone – he ain't going to drop her – he knows what he's doing.'"

Jackie's championing of his father didn't just upset Freda. John Lee was a quiet and tolerant man, but this tolerance was tested to the limit when Jackie would bring his father back home to Cottage Grove. Although John Lee never openly objected he wasn't pleased, either. In Freda's words, "That [Jack] was Eliza's husband until he died. She didn't care how many husbands you had, the first husband was your husband. Until one of them died, that's it. So he'd bring his daddy over there to get him cleaned up. She'd put in the tub, get him all cleaned up; wash his hair, take him and give him a haircut, or someone in the house would cut it. She'd put him in some of Johnny's clothes. Johnny would be walking around slamming doors; boom, boom, boom. But he didn't say nothing! After, Mr Wilson had a guitar and he'd be playing. He could sing, too. Then Jack and he would sing together. Jack loved Johnny too, but that was his daddy, and they was real tight. Your mom and your dad was family, that's it."

Freda, both attractive and intelligent, was a good anchor for Jackie. Whenever she was able Freda worked as a trainee nurse at the hospital, but times were tough. Jackie was never known for his reliability or ability to take care of details and it was not an easy time for them. "Eliza Mae kept Jack in clothes after we got married," said Freda. "Every time I had a baby he'd pawn his good suit to get the milk and stuff."

But everyone who knew Jackie then believed his success was just a matter of time and a little luck. Freda says, "Jack had a sort of driving personality. He was determined to succeed. He could do anything he wanted – and he could sing. Everyone knew he could sing." As with the baby food, when he needed clothes for his stage appearances "he'd go to the pawn shop – get what he needed – always stayed neat and everything. He could chew a pawn shop down; he could get what he wanted for less than they wanted to sell it."

Quite naturally Freda was concerned about their prospects. "He said, 'Don't worry, everything's going to be okay.' All my friends would say, 'If the man makes it, you can forget him, because he don't want to die with his shoes on,' and all this stuff. I wasn't worried about it 'cause I said, 'I think he loves me.' My mother told me, 'He's never going to be anything, I don't know why you went and got yourself pregnant by him. He ain't going to be nothing.' Guess who was down there counting his money from the Greystone Ballroom? My mother!"

In 1952, aged seventeen, Jackie had his first opportunity to record some songs. Not surprisingly 'Danny Boy' was his first recording and a regular blues number, 'Rainy Day Blues', the next. They were done at Joe Syracuse's United Sound Studios in Detroit where many of the great Motown recordings would be cut in later years. They were released under the name of Sonny Wilson as two seventy-eights on the Dee Gee (Dizzy Gillespie) label. The flip sides were mainly instrumentals with some male group vocals which included Jackie.

Detroit sax player and band leader, Billy Mitchell, who'd performed with Count Basie's and Dizzy Gillespie's bands, arranged the recording and his band was used as back-up. Mitchell remembers that Dave Usher, Dizzy Gillespie's partner on the small label, spotted Jackie performing around town and suggested the session. Mitchell says he put Jackie on a recording contract, but fortunately didn't hold him to it when, next year, he was given the opportunity to join The Dominoes.

Although Jackie's uniquely marvellous voice comes through on 'Danny Boy', he tries too hard to make it different, and the result is rather jerky. 'Rainy Day Blues' had a lot more promise as an R&B number, but the two singles didn't sell well when they were released, although there is an inkling of the incredible voice that was recorded the following year with The Dominoes.

Today Freda remembers nothing of the recording session, twice denying he ever recorded under the name of Sonny. When questioned about it nearly two decades later, Jackie himself denied it ever took place. He may have preferred the world to believe he had instant solo success with 'Reet Petite'.

Jack Snr died in January 1953 before Jackie had achieved real success. He was fifty-seven. Like many father-son relationships, Jackie and his father had sometimes clashed, but the love was always there. "While he was living in Highland Park they had some knock-down, drag-out fights when his dad got soused," explains Harry Respess. "They had a love-hate relationship." But, as Freda says, her husband lost one of his biggest fans: "Jack Snr thought his son was the greatest, anyhow."

They learned of his death in typically convoluted fashion. "Jack's mother had put him in the hospital," says Freda. "It rained that night. The doorbell rang; it hadn't never rang before. We were sitting in the kitchen at 248 Cottage Grove. At the time he died we didn't have a phone, so they had sent a telegram to my mother-in-law." The telegram had been sent by the hospital to inform them that Jack's prospects were not good. "That doorbell rang at the exact time he had died at the hospital. She [Eliza Mae] got up and went in the room."

After his father died, Jackie locked himself in his bedroom for a few days. Half-sister, Joyce, told Susan Morse of the *Detroit Free Press* (11 January, 1976), "He [Jackie] was a spiritual fanatic up to the time his father died. When his father died, he took every spiritual record in the house and broke them...He knew his father was weak and an alcoholic, but Jackie loved him."

Jackie didn't go to the funeral. He had someone take pictures of his father in the casket. In the 1960s he still carried around a photo of his father who looked a lot like him, but had a little pencil-line moustache. Jackie never came to terms with death. Friend Harry Respess recalls the time: "I went to his funeral. Jack didn't go. He went to see his body. He was mortified by his father's death, but he also had a guilt complex about it. He loved Mama more, you believe me."

Jack Snr was buried at Lincoln Memorial Park Cemetery on Fourteen Mile Road, north of Detroit. "Big Jack" would push his cart around Russell and Holbrook no longer. Eliza Mae had loved the man dearly and now that he was buried she could focus her love on John Lee and her only son, Jackie.

At the end of the month of Jack Snr's death, Freda gave birth to their second child, Sandra Kay. Prospects were grim, with money in short supply. Jackie had an underground following among the seedy bars of northern Detroit, but at nineteen had his eyes set on far bigger things. He was convinced that he could hold his own in the fiercely contested talent shows and of his own performing talent. All Jackie needed was a lucky break; he didn't have long to wait.

CHAPTER TWO

You Can't Keep A Good Man Down

Writer Jeff Beckman, in the music periodical *Big Town Review* (February-March 1972) wrote a detailed piece on Billy Ward uncovering much about his life and career: "Ward was born in Los Angeles of a preacher father and a choir singing mother. The Ward family moved to Philadelphia in Billy's earliest years, where his father presided over the Wayland Baptist Church. From the age of six Billy sang soprano as a member of the church choir and later became the church organist. Sometime during this period Billy began what was to be a long and illustrious career as a composer, although at this time he was composing gospel and classical works rather than the type of songs he would become famous for. But Billy was talented in these areas as well, for at the age of fourteen he won a New York City-wide contest for a classical piece [entitled 'Dejection'] he had composed."

Ward was born in 1921, making him thirteen years older than Jackie. Like Jackie he was interested in boxing. He spent the Second World War years in the army, being based for two years at Fort Eustis in Virginia. His musical training came to the fore in the Coast Artillery Choir which had a gospel leaning. After another three years as a non-commissioned officer he returned to civilian life, attending various schools including the Chicago Arts Institute and the Julliard School of Music in New York.

Ward settled in New York and worked for Robert Malane of Carnegie Hall as a voice coach for white males. He met Bobby Schiffman, the owner of the famous Apollo Theatre, and they arranged for Schiffman to recommend Amateur Night singers with potential to Ward for regular vocal training. Ward was impressed that most of the group he was coaching lived in Harlem yet would walk ten miles in the freezing cold to his apartment in Greenwich Village and he felt that if they were that dedicated the least he could do was impart his musical learning to them. He did it not for money, but out of obligation to people of his race who were less fortunate than he.

Ward was a strict disciplinarian, who believed in rehearsing again and again until the act was perfected: aspirants didn't last long if they missed a rehearsal or showed up late. From the ranks of his vocal students he formed a group he initially named The Ques, later changed to The Dominoes, which he decided to enter in the hugely popular Wednesday Amateur Night contest at the Apollo. One night, early in 1950, The Ques won. As a result they were given the opportunity to appear on the Arthur Godfrey Talent Scouts Show, where amateur acts competed. Broadcast out of Dallas, this radio show had a huge nationwide audience.

At that time, Arthur Godfrey had a quartet called The Mariners. Ward admired them, but believed his quintet sang even better and decided to perform his own arrangement of the Leadbelly song, which eventually became a standard, 'Goodnight Irene'. Ward's group won on the night and the rest is history.

During the day, Ward worked as a graphic artist for a Jewish woman, Mrs Rose Marks, in her New York advertising agency, while doing his vocal training after hours. He described Marks as "one of the finest women who ever lived". She recognised the remarkable talent Billy Ward and his group possessed and recommended that they should consider a professional career. Ward said that the forming of a permanent, professional group was purely coincidental, being entirely due to the success of their Arthur Godfrey appearance as well as the urging of Rose Marks. He had no intention of touring with the group, yet for many years that's what happened. They began as a gospel group, and later progressed to rhythm and blues. Ward did the arrangements himself and played piano, but rarely if ever sang lead. When, in 1951, Marks became the group's manager, their average age was twenty-two.

In Cincinnati Syd Nathan's King Record Company, founded in 1945, and having success recording black artists for the large and largely ignored black populations in the northern cities of the USA, offered Ward the opportunity to record. Ralph Bass had recently joined the King group with his Federal label, and Ward was one of the first to record for this subsidiary.

The Dominoes' first single record release, 'Do Something For Me', was recorded in December 1950, and followed early in 1951 with the popular ballad 'Harbour Lights'. Both achieved moderate success on the R&B charts. At first sixteen-year-old lead tenor Clyde McPhatter was billed as Clyde Ward, presumably to imply that he was the brother of Billy. Born in 1932, son of a preacher from North Carolina, McPhatter was raised in New York City and sang as a fourteen-year-old with the Mount Lebanon Singers. Other notable early Dominoes members were the second tenor James Van Loan, baritone William Joseph Lamont and bass David McNeil, but it was McPhatter's magnificent and unique voice that Jackie was in awe of.

Ward wrote many of The Dominoes' hits, claiming that one of the major reasons for the group's popularity was that he wrote the songs for the voices. Typical of the group's versatility was their very next release, the risque and catchy 'The Deacon Moves In', which featured the superb voice of fifteen-year-old "Little Esther" Phillips. Fine as it was, it was their next release, however, that gained the group nationwide fame.

'Sixty Minute Man', complete with suggestive lyrics by Ward, was arguably the forerunner to rock 'n' roll, a fact Ward thinks he and his group deserve more recognition for. The song's success led to concert appearances all over the northern States including a return to Harlem's famous Apollo Theatre in February 1951. The group received another accolade that year in the form of the Independent Press Service Annual Award for achievement and distinguished service in the field of music.

Whilst McPhatter was lead singer of The Dominoes, Gil Askey, who later became a major music arranger with Motown, was at Harlem's Apollo Theatre playing trumpet with Arnett Cobbs' band. He recalls: "Billy Ward was very big at the time. The Dominoes were having a meeting, and I was meandering up to our band room. While we were on stage they took all our band's stuff down to the basement. Our room was always the gambling room no matter where it was. We could hear the voice of Rose Marks: 'You will no longer refer to Mr Ward as "Billy". He will from now on be over here.'" Marks was moving the band to a lesser room and reserving the better room for "Mr Ward" thus raising his status above the rest of them. It did not impress Askey, or the others, one little bit.

In 1952, around the time Billy Ward and his Dominoes were having their remarkable success, Jackie was still performing in Detroit's black clubs and especially Lee's Club Sensation. Freda says that for some reason Jackie suggested that he and his close friend JJ should enlist in the US Army. When the time came for them to enter, however, Jackie thought better of it. "So when it come time to go JJ went on down there, Jack didn't go. So JJ was in the army. The MPs came and got Jack." He was now in a serious predicament, having signed up to join, but failing to report. There were serious penalties for the offence.

They were both instructed to appear before the Military Board: "I was pregnant with Sandy and already had Jacqueline," Freda says. "There was one lady on that board, too. I don't know what Jack said…why he joined the army. Anyway they believed the story and the fact they weren't at war and I already had a child and I was expecting, and that I did need him at home to take care of the children. I was the one that was taking care of the children. He was trying to make it [as a singer] and I was working. So they let him out of there. JJ was mad that Jack didn't come. He had to do two years, mandatory; he couldn't get out of there. Jack felt he owed him something for those years. JJ would never have went if Jack hadn't suggested it." It is interesting to consider what may have happened with Jackie's career had he been obliged to sign up with the army.

At eighteen Jackie had built up a big local following as a night club act. This nearly came to an end when he was stabbed by a prostitute. Freda recalls: "A white girl, she stabbed him. My mother-in-law went down there to stab her. Rebecca [Pitt, his cousin] and my mother-in-law saw Jack come home with stab wounds to his stomach. My mother-in-law grabbed a knife and said, 'Are you coming?' I said, 'No, ma'am, I'm staying right here in the house.' I had to take care of the children.

"They went walking down to Hastings Street. My mother-in-law was going to stab her, but the police got involved somehow. They came down and got Jack; they grabbed him and my mother-in-law. My mother-in-law dropped the knife. I guess the girl must have called them or something. They [Jack, Rebecca and his mother] were down there around [Mt] Vernon, that precinct."

Both Jackie and his mother were held by the police and it was to Freda that they turned to for help. "Jack didn't call; my mother-in-law called, and I went down to get 'em. Eliza said, 'Don't tell Sonny, there's some money in my bed; find it.' Joyce [Jackie's half-sister, who would have been around seven] was running around the house screaming and hollering. I go down there to her [Eliza Mae] and the police said, 'How many wives has he got? There's so many women coming down here.' My mother-in-law said, 'I'm his mother, and I know this is his wife!' So they brought Jack out for us to see him. They brought him out without his shirt on. He said, 'Wait a minute; show respect, that's my wife and mother; they're not street people. Let me put my shirt on; you can have it back when I go back.' The police came and hit him in the head. He said, 'I'll be out sometime today, because I didn't do nothing. They are just trying to check me out to see if they can prove some kind of scandal.' Anyway he got out of this one," relates Freda in the most blasé tone of voice, as though the episode was a common occurrence.

In 1953 Billy Ward sought a new singer for his group. It is believed that Jackie's friend Ralph Peterson first informed him of the opportunity. Dominoes member William Lamont was going to do military service and fellow member David McNeil would soon follow. Jackie did not audition for the lead-tenor role, but the replacement role for William Lamont. It is quite likely that at this stage McPhatter had no intention of leaving the group.

There are different versions of how Jackie came to be signed up with The Dominoes. They had an engagement at the Michigan State Fair in Detroit. Ward was in his room at the Gotham Hotel and just about to retire for the night. The hotel manager called and said there were some people downstairs who wanted to see him. Ward invited them up. It was Jackie, with his mother, wanting to audition.

Ward says he always travelled with a portable piano and had Jackie sing for him. Although he can't remember what was sung, he was impressed. In his words, "A diamond in the rough; had to be polished." To create a diamond from coal requires time and pressure. Jackie had put in the time from his early childhood. Ward would be the pressure that was needed to ensure the creation of the gem.

Jackie as usual had his own version of events. One was that he went to meet Ward with a girl on each arm. Another was that he told Ward, "I'm the *baddest* thing to happen to Detroit." Certainly, he could be quite brash, even cocky. Ward says that, after the audition Jackie's mother called him aside and, with tears streaming down her face, begged him to give Jackie a chance. She was in fear of his being killed on the streets.

The young singer had made a powerful impression, but he would have to compete in a public audition, after which Ward would make his choice. The big night was at the Paradise Theatre, a second home to Jackie. When he arrived at the audition he bragged, "I can sing much better than Clyde McPhatter." Alice Pride recalls the event vividly: "It was talent night. He was like in the family and he told my mother he wanted to go in the audition, but he didn't have anything to wear. My mother said, 'Here's a few things, you go and get ready.' He won singing 'Danny Boy'."

In an interview with *Melody Maker* in October 1972, Jackie gave his version of how it all happened: "I'd liked all their [Dominoes] records, particularly for their lead singer, so I went up to Ward and I told him I could outsing Clyde. Billy sent one of his fellows to listen to me at an amateur night at the Paradise Theatre in Detroit, and he said he'd try to help me. Four or five months [more likely weeks] later, when Clyde was leaving to form The Drifters, I got a call. I didn't dare tell my mother, though – I just packed up and left." In the interview he goes on to say that others to influence him were The Mills Brothers, The Ink Spots, The Soul Stirrers, particularly the group's lead singers, the Reverend Harris; and later Sam Cooke.

In the same interview Jackie gives great credit to his mentor, Billy Ward: "I learned just about everything I know from him. Breath control... and how to dance during one number and then come back and sing a ballad. That's hard, and they don't move too much on stage these days."

Freda wasn't able to go to the formal audition at the Paradise Theatre because she had just given birth to their second child, Sandra Kay (born 29 January, 1953). She recalls Jackie's colourful version of the event: "Jack went down to audition and, even though he didn't know the song, he said that he could sing better than Clyde. He sang in front of Clyde and he made up the words, so Billy told him that if he had so much nerve to do what he did he could use him."

Although Jackie won on the night Ward did not inform him immediately that he had a place in the group. Freda: "Billy Ward told him he 'may have something' for him. 'He may', that's what he said. Then a few weeks later he sent him a telegram telling him to call collect. So we went to a phone booth – his mother and I went with him – he called, and Ward told him to fly out to Las Vegas, someone will meet him and pick him up. He had actually fired Clyde, but the way the contract was he had to still sing with them until they got Jack ready. Jack got a chance to watch what Clyde did, although he didn't do exactly that. But he learned some of the mannerisms of how to work the song."

Former Shaker Respess remembers when Jackie won: "You'd think that Joe Louis had won a title fight the way the city just went up, when they heard Jack won and he was the new singer. The whole northside –

where we lived around Oakland [Avenue] – people hit the streets, jumping and singing and shouting and screaming that Jack was the singer of The Dominoes. Oh, man! It was a festive occasion, everyone was singing and shouting, 'cause everyone knew him from church [from his Ever Ready Gospel Group]. Everyone went bonkers."

Roquel Davis, too, remembers Jackie's audition and the contribution Ward made to his career: "Jack told us that he was challenged to outsing McPhatter. He told Billy Ward he could sing better than McPhatter. Jack said, 'Clyde is great, but I sing better.' After hearing Jack, Ward was so impressed he took him as a Domino."

Ward became like a father to the eighteen-year-old. "Billy Ward should get more credit than he probably has," says Davis. "He introduced discipline for the first time in his life. Jack didn't like discipline. Basically everything he had as a recording artist he had when he was fourteen years old. Billy Ward added discipline and polish. About who discovered Jack? I would say Billy Ward should have the credit. He gave him his first break, showcased him, took him on the road with him. That's what launched Jack. Billy Ward, a professional who was in a position to do something, recognised Jackie's ability. Without that he wouldn't have come to the notice of anyone."

Jackie's stepfather, John Lee, had just procured a job for him at the Ford foundry on Woodward Avenue, close to the family home. When he was selected to join The Dominoes he quit. Freda recollects: "Jack had got a job at Henry Ford's but only for two weeks. I picked up that pay cheque. He told me he was going to quit anyhow 'cause it was messing up his hands. He couldn't stand it. Jack told me when he was little he didn't want to do nothing else but sing; he was born to sing. He said he was going to be an entertainer – that was it. He wasn't going to do no hard work."

The stories differ, but it is most likely that McPhatter only decided to leave the group after Jackie joined and after he learnt that Ward intended Jackie to share the lead tenor role with him. McPhatter had already clashed with Ward over his punctuality and drinking and he had a reputation for unruliness. The singer complained that despite the popularity of the group and himself especially, when he returned home he hardly had enough money to afford a Coke. Ward was a hard taskmaster and disciplinarian and by his own admission ran the group very much as a business. He had a saying: "Two things destroy a man;

booze and broads."

Once Ward decided to sign Jackie up there was still one hurdle to be overcome. When Jackie had made the Dee Gee label recordings he had signed a management contract with Billy Mitchell whose band had backed him on that unsuccessful 1952 recording session. Mitchell, therefore, could have made it difficult for Jackie. "After Jack made the recordings with me, I had a contract on him," he reflects. "Billy Ward called me up. I said, 'Yeah, I've got a contract, but if you want to use him go ahead.'" Mitchell had a career of his own to pursue and showed no disappointment in letting a major talent slip through his fingers.

Regardless of his boasts, Jackie was captivated by Clyde McPhatter's expressive tenor voice. But Ward was adamant that despite the unabashed admiration "he was never jealous of Clyde. Jack wanted to be somebody and wasn't a dummy. Clyde had very bad diction, but Jack's was worse. I taught him how to pronounce syllables, how to appeal to an audience – soulfully. He was appreciative but had a temper that wouldn't wait." Ward taught Jackie voice projection and how to breathe while singing. From this point on Jackie's articulation would be impeccable. In something of an understatement Ward adds, "Jack was a fine singer. I taught him; he was as good as anyone." Jackie, using his nick-name of "Sonny", was at last receiving his big break under the influence of the strict disciplinarian and father figure he fondly referred to as "Pap".

Although McPhatter remained with the group for a while after Jackie joined, there are no recordings featuring their voices together. In May, McPhatter signed with Atlantic Records and formed The Drifters. Thereafter Jackie took over as lead vocalist of The Dominoes.

Ward must have been sorry that McPhatter had chosen to leave – he wasn't fired, as others suggest. "I ran my vocal group as a business, not a jail. 'If you want to leave the group just come and tell me; God bless you.'" Like a good student, McPhatter took a lot of what he learned and used it with The Drifters. "When I heard Clyde with The Drifters I heard my arrangements," Ward says, "especially in 'White Christmas'." It is even said that McPhatter retained the major piece of The Drifters' financial pie in exactly the same way he'd objected that Ward did with The Dominoes.

Later, after being drafted into the army, McPhatter would succeed, albeit briefly, as a solo singer. But he suffered from many emotional problems which he tried to smother with drugs and alcohol. He died prematurely, aged thirty-nine, in June 1972. Musical fashion had changed and left him out in the cold.

Following an engagement in Las Vegas, Jackie shared an apartment with Ward in Greenwich Village. This caused some people to question Ward's motives and he remains very sensitive about this period; Jackie was eighteen, he was thirty-one. "Some people thought we had a thing going," says Ward.

Joyce McRae, a friend of Jackie's, put it like this: "Ward taught him how to speak, how to walk, sit, chew, dress, eat, wash and everything else. Billy was the closest thing he had to a father, both as a young man and as an adult. Billy really did amazing things with him to transform him; it really was a Pygmalion transformation."

Among the changes Billy Ward decided that the name Sonny, as Jackie was known, belonged back in Uncle Tom's cabin. He gave him the stage name "Jackie", which wasn't immediately appreciated. According to Ward it was not until many years later that Jackie decided the name change was a wise one and thanked him for it. From now on in his career it would be Jackie, but to old friends and family he would always remain Sonny, or Jack.

The Dominoes were especially popular amongst young females. In New York City an active Dominoes fan club was headed by a vivacious and ambitious young girl, Harlean Harris. Harlean was born at White Plains, New York in 1939 (the true year may be 1937). She generally refuses interviews, but a lengthy one was conducted in 1979 by Al Duckett of *Sepia Magazine* in which she says: "I met him [Jackie] in 1953 when he became replacement for Clyde McPhatter, who had left Billy Ward And The Dominoes, and I started dating him in 1958. When we first met, I was the president of the Billy Ward And The Dominoes fan club – the New York chapter. I was fourteen and there were twenty-four other pre-teen girls in the club. We were all positively wild about Clyde McPhatter, Billy Ward's lead singer.

"The Dominoes were coming to the Apollo Theatre in Harlem. All of our members became terribly upset when we learned that Clyde McPhatter was no longer with the group. The rumour was he had been replaced by someone named Wilson. We decided to show our resentment by going to the show and just sitting there up front and not giving The Dominoes the enthusiastic applause we usually gave them. We had made up our minds to stonewall it all the way in protest against the dismissal of our idol. We were determined not to accept this replacement. Being true McPhatter fans, we were just that adamant about it all. Needless to say, Clyde truly was one of the great talents. But I have to admit that when Jackie burst forth upon that stage, we forgot about Clyde."

This incident was used in the fictional movie on black doo wop groups of the 1950s, *The Five Heartbeats*. Harlean described the first meeting with Jackie. "I was one thrilled fourteen-year-old. When we went backstage, he was quite nice to us." At this time she was having an affair with McPhatter. In Ward's own words, "Harlean was Clyde's lady." Her mother was ambitious that her beautiful daughter should achieve fame and fortune and if marriage to a famous entertainer helped her achieve this aim then so be it. It is difficult to ignore the element of exploitation involved in exposing her to the world at so tender an age. Harlean would come to play a big part in Jackie's tumultuous life.

Freda discovered that while Jackie was with The Dominoes, he and other entertainers were having affairs with under-age girls. "There was a lot of them out there," recalls Freda. "They were thirteen, fourteen or fifteen. Their mothers would give them to the entertainers, because they wanted the money. These girls were serious, they don't mind going to bed; they hope they get pregnant. They wanted the money. Their mothers know what they're about."

Jackie got involved with one by the name of Estelle, according to Freda. "Estelle was another girl, [and] Suzie was her mother. Estelle would fight with Harlean. Harlean would like to tear her face up. I met Suzie. Suzie said she didn't know Jack was married. Jack lived in New York, he was always in New York. So Suzie gave him Estelle when she was fourteen. She told me this to my face. Estelle was mixed Spanish or something, but her mother was real black. She had short hair, but she tied it up in a pony tail. He lived with Estelle before he liked Harlean. I had a whole bunch of pictures. [His half-sister] Joyce has probably got a whole bunch of pictures, too."

Of course, the movie industry was littered with similar stories. It was simply a matter of overly ambitious mothers trying to better their own economic and social positions by exploiting their daughters. As Freda puts it, "New York is that way – those girls there, they're serious. They all wanted money. To the girls, this is like a dream, that they touched somebody famous."

Of course Jackie was only one of the stars exposed to such

temptations. "They'd be with The Isley Brothers there and four of them had been made pregnant by Ronnie [Isley]," says Freda. The Isley Brothers first came to the attention of the world with their hit 'Shout' in 1959. Ronnie Isley was seven years younger than Jackie, but Jackie took an early liking to him and, for a while, they were friends.

On 27 June, 1953, a few weeks after his nineteenth birthday in New York City, Jackie recorded as lead tenor for The Dominoes for the first time with 'You Can't Keep A Good Man Down'. His next Dominoes session was at the King/Federal Studios in Cincinnati on 12 October, 1953, when eleven tracks were cut, five of which allowed him to display his phenomenal vocal range and phrasing.

In 1953 'Rags To Riches', written by Richard Adler and Jerry Ross, reached Number One for Tony Bennett. The Dominoes' version, made later that year, was a clear improvement on the original, reaching the Number Two spot on the R&B chart, but getting nowhere on the more lucrative, mainly white, Pop chart. Bennett had the advantage of being heard by a white audience listening to white radio stations which promoted white music.

Another from the same session, 'One Moment With You', is a slow ballad in which Jackie's voice sounds either like a young boy or a woman. Singing in the high female range was easy for him. The song is pure and powerful. 'Above Jacob's Ladder', 'Christmas In Heaven' and 'Until The Real Thing Comes Along', which had previously been recorded by Ella Fitzgerald, were other tracks he sang lead on. He'd proven he was not just a good singer, but a major talent. Jackie was on his way. All he really needed was some exposure – which meant radio airplay.

Ward's friend and manager Rose Marks died suddenly in 1953, which greatly saddened him and Harry Stein took over management of The Dominoes. Jay Warner reports in the *Billboard Book Of American Singing Groups* that in November 1953, The Dominoes were to perform at the Music Festival in Quincy, Illinois. At the time they were touring with ex-middleweight boxing champion, Sugar Ray Robinson. Robinson had turned to promoting and entertaining and displayed some fancy footwork on stage. The Dominoes showed up thirty minutes late so Robinson refused payment. The story has it that Ward's response was to pull a gun on him – unorthodox methods were sometimes resorted to in this rough and tumble industry.

In the early 1950s, white radio stations were generally not playing music by black artists, which was termed "race music". White groups and artists often made insipid cover versions of black artists' songs, but the audience had no opportunity to listen to the original music. However, musical "crossover" was not far away: whereby tunes that were successful on the R&B charts (ie sold well in black record stores) were able to crossover, or chart well, on the Pop charts (ie sold well in largely white record stores), where the real financial rewards lay.

While it is true that a few black artists and groups had achieved success with white audiences, in 1953 they were few and far between. The Ink Spots' tune 'Address Unknown' reached Number One in 1939, as did 'We Three (My Echo, My Shadow And Me)' in 1940. Prior to them, The Mills Brothers achieved enormous success, starting in 1930 with the Number One 'Tiger Rag', and then 'Dinah' in 1932. They went on to become one of the greatest vocal groups of all time, with seventy hit records between 1931 and 1968.

The most successful solo black artist, who achieved early appeal and lasting popularity with white audiences, was the smooth balladeer Nat "King" Cole. Cole had four number one hits, 'I Love You (For Sentimental Reasons)' in 1946, 'Nature Boy' in 1948, 'Mona Lisa' in 1950 and 'Too Young' in 1951. So while it wasn't unheard of for black artists to crossover and be successful with white audiences, it was the exception.

Joe Glasser, who managed Lionel Hampton and Billie Holiday, also booked The Dominoes and kept them very busy on the gruelling touring circuit. In 1953 Jackie collapsed on stage during a performance with The Dominoes in Charlotte, North Carolina. He was suffering from chronic tonsillitis and had to be rushed to hospital. Freda remembers him being petrified lest surgery destroy his vocal ability. "His tonsils were so bad we thought he wasn't going to be able to sing. They were ulcerated – puss and stuff. He would write notes instead of speaking to save his voice so he could sing and he'd be eating lemon and honey all day long. Show time comes, I said, 'You can't sing.' He just looked me and smiled. Mr Wilson would sing just like a bird. What he was doing was resting his voice; he wasn't going to make no money talking." They need not have feared; he sounded better than ever! "He got his tonsils out at Sinai Hospital, but his voice didn't change. He was a happy person."

Despite many recordings featuring Jackie's emotionally wracked vocal treatments, The Dominoes had no chart success during 1954. Success to them came in the form of a two-year contract to perform at the Sahara

Hotel in Las Vegas for an extraordinary five thousand dollars a week. They were supporting the popular Louis Prima and Keely Smith, and playing to packed houses, although not in the main room. They weren't permitted to enter the casino or restaurants and had to live on the west side of town. Also, being black, they weren't allowed to stay on The Strip.

Still The Dominoes were becoming big time, in Las Vegas and elsewhere. Ward billed them as "The World's Most Entertaining Vocal Attraction" and by all accounts they were a polished act with some very slick stage work and recordings, which ranged from the earliest rock 'n' roll to great evergreen standards like 'Tenderly'.

Ward ran a very tight ship and didn't fraternise with members of the group. He held himself above them believing that this was the best way to encourage respect and discipline. The group at this stage consisted of Jackie, first tenor, James Van Loan, second tenor, Milton Merle, baritone, and Clifford Givens, bass. Ward played the piano but rarely, if ever, sang lead. As Freda says,"Billy always looked after himself and tried to get the boys to do the same. If they disobeyed they had a court session."

That discipline didn't exist in Jackie's private life. Before joining The Dominoes, he had two children with Freda, Jacqueline (Denise) and Sandra Kay (Sandy). While with the group they had another child, Jack Jnr, otherwise known as Jackie Jnr or Sonny Jnr, born on 13 February, 1954. Another daughter, Brenda, was born to Suzie Johnson in the same year. Another, Sabrina was born in 1954 to Molly Byndon who was from St Louis.

Freda, generally with one or two of their children, lived for some time with Jackie in Las Vegas. "White people rented their nice houses out to black entertainers, and they would go and stay somewhere else," she recalls. "They had washers and dryers. Joe Louis lived down the street. Indians, all the different coloured people, stayed on the black side of town." Freda has pleasant memories of their time there and saw plenty of Dominoes performances. She recalls proudly: "When they came out they looked so pretty. They were wearing those suits with the long back jacket. Jack's eyes were sparkling. He was young and pretty. The girls were going crazy; they were screaming and screaming. Milton Merle and other Dominoes members were older than Jack. When Jack got through there wasn't a dry eye in the place; even the ones who were drinking the wine and talking. He was also excellent in the background. He sang first tenor-falsetto or second tenor; he could even sing a light bass, right down, if he wanted to. He was a good baritone and could blend in with the other guys. He learned a lot by looking and listening to other entertainers.

"We'd go to the Key Club. They'd be singing; Jackie'd be singing. First he'd do his thing, then Sammy Davis Jnr would do his thing. I was in Las Vegas when Sammy got hurt [in 1954 he had a car accident and lost an eye]: he was driving – he drove too fast – and he was drunk." When socialising with Jackie, Freda knew to remain in the background. If she did have any criticisms, she kept them to herself or made him aware of them when there was nobody around. "I didn't know the other entertainers personally. Jack didn't like me to run around. You just sat down and acted like a lady."

Ward correctly observes that "Jackie had a temper that wouldn't wait". He expected obedience and respect from his children and from Freda, as well. In 1955, when daughter Denise was only four, Jackie arrived home one morning after working at the Las Vegas Sahara all night. He'd learned something a little different and was anxious to practise it, but Denise interrupted him and he became angry. Freda recalls, "He told her to get out of there. He threw her across there to the couch; she was petrified."

Denise always maintained a deep love and fascination, to the point of obsession, for her father, but maintains he expected strict obedience from his children. A slap wasn't unusual. "He used to tell me Wilsons don't cry," says Denise. "He said, 'You can breathe, I just don't want to see tears.' He said, 'Not in front of anybody. Go in your bedroom, or whatever. But if someone is looking, just because you got hurt or embarrassed, don't show that you're weak. Wilsons are not weak!'" Jackie had a ton of pride, and that would be his life's philosophy, no matter what was going on around him.

Jackie's sexual demands were still occasionally too much for Freda. "When I just had Sandy, I was not going to let him. He said, 'I just want to bring you something for the baby.' He comes over there [to the hospital]; I tried to get rid of him." Freda also became tired of being pregnant on an almost full-time basis and sought advice from a woman claiming she knew how to terminate an unwanted pregnancy. "She told me to drink half a pint of turpentine, or sit on a hot pail of water – I did all of that – as hot as I could stand it. It made me get drunk and sick and throw up. The doctor said it would have killed me if I didn't throw up, but the baby probably would have been all right." It was bad advice and not repeated.

Their first son, Jack Jnr was born in February 1954. Freda recalls: "When Jack Jnr was born he had grey eyes and red hair and freckles. My mother-in-law called Jack and said, 'You'd better check this baby out.' She said, 'I think it's mixed.' Now, I didn't even know he was coming; I was upstairs. Someone said, 'There's a limousine outside.' He didn't stop downstairs to say hello to his mother or anything. He bounced up those steps. He said, 'Get out of my way.' He turned the baby over and looked at its hands and fingers." Apparently this convinced Jackie that the baby was indeed his.

While domineering at home, at work it was Ward who had strict rules about what group members could and couldn't do. But Jackie was never one for rules, as Freda knew. "There was nothing Jack could do. Billy Ward had been a lieutenant in the army and he kept The Dominoes on the army routine: they couldn't drink, they didn't socialise with people – only each other – they couldn't be seen with this person or that person, they couldn't be seen over in the black side of town carousing around, they couldn't be going up to clubs and things there. Jackie wanted to leave the motel, but couldn't." Marv Johnson, a hugely successful Motown singer in the 1960s, confirms this: "Billy Ward was the boss, he was in charge; he was the leader. Jackie wasn't aware of the power of his voice; the way he was able to electrify people. Youth is innocence. You just do your thing and you do it well. In The Dominoes' case, Jackie was just a member of The Dominoes who sang well."

Once Freda was staying in Las Vegas while The Dominoes were playing the Sahara Hotel on a six month engagement. The discipline must have become too much for Jackie and he became bored. "This particular time we were staying at a motel on The Strip," says Freda. "I had Jackie Jnr with us that year. Jack worked days then and alternative nights from six to twelve and twelve to six in the morning. He'd get off at night, he'd get up and put on black pants, black shirt, black hat, black shoes... black everything. One night I said, 'Where you going?' 'I'm going out!' That night he came back, I didn't say nothing. He jumped in the bed and he said, 'Get back in the bed and if anyone knocks on the door, I've been here all night.' Pretty soon there was a knock on the door. It was the police; they said, 'Jackie Wilson in here?' I said, 'Yeah.' They said, 'How long's he been here?' I said, 'Mr Wilson's been here all night.' Someone said they recognised him in their room; he was taking a few things off the dresser. They were chasing him, he jumped over some fences. He'd been taking cologne, combs, any kind of jewellery…it wasn't worth nothing." Freda became increasingly nervous about her husband's strange behaviour. "I was getting scared. I thought Jack was losing his mind. I didn't want him to get in bad trouble – get shot, or something. Those people had guns out there."

Ward wasn't fooled by Jackie's alibi because he soon came to the room and said he wanted to see the "black bandit". He was most annoyed at Jackie's prank and called a meeting. Jackie said to Freda, "Do you think I'm crazy? I'm not going to tell him I did it, and you better never tell him I did it." Jackie needed Freda as his alibi, but she was nothing like the practised liar he was. She recalls, "We had a meeting with Billy Ward; he was upset. Every answer Jack gave, Billy Ward was looking straight in my eyes. I was trying to look at his eyes, so my eyes were wavering. He said, 'You shut up.' So Jack shut up. 'I want the truth; just what's the truth?' That's what he told me and I gave it to him. Billy always knew when Jack was lying, but he didn't want him screwed up down there. He sent me back to Detroit." Ward believed that if Jackie didn't have his family around he could be kept under more careful scrutiny.

Ward wasn't able to completely eliminate Jackie's excesses; he continued to drink without Ward's knowledge. "They say you can't smell vodka," explains Freda. "He always knew how to do good oral hygiene. He'd gargle and scrape his tongue with the bread knife; he'd work and work. They never smelled it on him for a long time, neither. He'd sing better and better." This bizarre habit of scraping his tongue with a knife remained with him throughout his life. "He conformed as long as he was with Billy Ward," Freda continues. "They were primarily in Las Vegas six months of the year, the rest of the time they were in California, some place like that. They only came back to Chicago, or New York to the theatres, like the Brooklyn Fox, and they did a lot of clubs. There's a lot of Irish people there – that's when he'd sing 'When Irish Eyes Are Smiling' so pretty. He'd also do 'Danny Boy', but he'd been doing 'Danny Boy' all his life. They really loved him in New York."

Another incident, involving Jackie and Ward's fiancée, further tested the relationship between mentor and singer. Freda remembers it this way: "The time he went out with Billy's fiancée, Jack was so mad at him [Ward]. Billy went out to California on a business meeting. Billy really loved that lady. She went out with Jackie. I don't know how Billy knew it; I knew it, everyone knew it. Billy had a meeting that day; he interviewed Jack. Jack lied and lied. Billy got it out of her. Billy beat her up; he gave her some back-hand licks and said, 'And I was going to marry you – I can't even trust you with my own people. You let him [Jackie] talk you into it; something like this destroys our lives, and you let it!' He wasn't mad at Jack. He was just a little person [Freda is not referring to Jackie's physical stature but to his social position, compared with the famous Billy Ward]. Why'd she go out with this guy? With one of his men, his young guy. It really upset him. It hurt him; he really liked her. She had a ring and everything. Can't she close her legs for a few minutes?" Ward broke off with his fiancée after that.

The episode was an example of a situation where Jackie's desire to hurt Ward caused deep hurt to others. But despite everything, Ward did a lot to bring out Jackie's full potential, and even Jackie later came to appreciate this. Says Freda: "Billy gave Jackie an autographed photo after he got to Las Vegas and it said, 'For a rough hewn stone who I am polishing into a diamond.' He ran a very strict group and he did a good job with Jack. He cut out the drinking [well, to some extent]. He stopped everything. Jackie thanked Billy Ward for a lot of things even though, at the time, he didn't appreciate it, because he wanted to do what he wanted to do."

In later years, Jackie gave credit to Ward for grooming him into the performer he became. The four years he spent with The Dominoes were the best kind of apprenticeship he could have hoped for. In the New York radio interview with Norman N Nite, Jackie said, "I can give full credit for that [my vocal style], to Mr Billy Ward; he was a vocal coach at Carnegie Hall. I studied under him for two [in truth – four] years." The only catch was, Jackie was not yet earning big money. For example, despite the five thousand dollars per week contract with the Sahara Hotel in Las Vegas, Jackie's share of that was only about ninety dollars.

The Dominoes played Las Vegas for many years both with and without Jackie. They also sold millions of records, however only one song featuring Jackie made it into the Pop charts. 'St Therese Of The Roses', reached Number Thirteen in 1956, and remained in the charts for six weeks. Ward said it was written for them "by a guy at the Copacabana". It was Jackie's first hit and also the first single The Dominoes recorded on Decca, for whom he also sang lead on the 1930s Inkspots hit 'To Each His Own', after moving from King/Federal. They also had a short stint at Jubilee where Jackie recorded two more singles, 'Take Me Back To Heaven' and 'Stop You're Sending Me', which didn't chart.

Ward was not happy with the contractual arrangement with King Records in Cincinnati, but the contract didn't expire until 1955. Nevertheless some musical gems were recorded by them with Jackie singing lead. His vocal gymnastics dominate on the ballads 'Until The Real Thing Comes Along', 'Love Me Now Or Let Me Go', 'Tenderly' and an up-tempo 'St Louis Blues'. Although he does not sing lead on 'Tootsie Roll', his vocal range is evident with his female range backing vocals and his piercing high tenor soaring above the other voices. His sound was completely unique.

Freda tells of one unnamed recording Jackie sang lead on, for which he thought he had taken too much from the original version. "He wasn't too proud of that song, because he felt he was stealing the song. But that was the way they wanted it to be done." He may well have listened to and admired Al Jolson, Mario Lanza, Roy Hamilton and blues master "Good Rockin'" Roy Brown, but he didn't sound like any of them. There was no confusing Jackie's voice with anyone else. In Freda's words, "Jack liked anyone who could sing, but he knew he was the greatest."

Ward trained and rehearsed the group so well the recordings did not have to be over-dubbed. They were all recorded with the musical backing "live". Yet it is unclear why these excellent King/Federal recordings didn't chart better. Perhaps they didn't have enough bop to be danceable for black audiences and lacked exposure to whites. At that time the radio airwaves were dominated by white vocalists such as Guy Mitchell (who also grew up in Detroit) and Perry Como. Another possibility is that this was the beginning of the "payola" system which ensured that influential disc jockeys (DJs) were paid in order to push particular songs or artists. The year 1955 was also the time that a white singer from Jackie's home neighbourhood, Bill Haley, led the vanguard of the social revolution that went by the name of rock 'n' roll. His record, 'Rock Around The Clock', remained Number One for eight weeks. Haley was singing a form of music that, although new to whites, had been familiar to blacks for some time as rhythm and blues.

In the eyes of his friends and fans, Jackie was now the star they had always known he would be and his homecomings were a celebration. Distant relative, Lawrence Payton, later of The Four Tops, recalls, "I remember Jackie when he used to come into town, when he was with Billy Ward And The Dominoes. It was always the highlight of our year. He was sort of our mentor, besides being our best friend and family. He was the guy we were all impressed with and made us want to be in showbusiness. He came by the neighbourhood to get all of us, take us over to his mother's house on Cottage Grove and play all the things he was coming out with. He'd play his records for us and all that stuff. I remember the record 'Jacob's Ladder'. It was so amazing for us; it was more like a Pop hit. At that time everything was rhythm and blues, but that song had religious connotations. I thought, 'What are you guys trying to do, man?'"

Around the same time another major musical force was emerging. On 6 July, 1954, Elvis Presley made his first commercial recordings at Sam Phillips' Memphis Recording Service studios, although it was not until the next year that he started to gain national attention. Elvis was a poor white boy who sounded and moved like a black, and was greatly influenced by the black gospel and R&B music he listened to on the radio or in local clubs. Jackie was only seven months Elvis's senior, but had first recorded in 1952. He would have a somewhat harder slog on the road to success than Elvis.

At the Memphis Recording Service studios in December 1956, owner Sam Phillips kept the tape rolling while Carl Perkins, Jerry Lee Lewis, Johnny Cash and Elvis Presley – "The Million Dollar Quartet" – were fooling around and singing a few of their numbers. On this recording, Elvis talks about a group he'd seen in Las Vegas: Billy Ward and his Dominoes. Elvis first performed in Las Vegas in April 1956 and had bombed with the middle-aged audience. But he did find time to go to see The Dominoes perform.

On the Sun recording the impression that Jackie made on Elvis comes through not only in what he says about Jackie (although he has no idea of his name), but also in the excitement in his voice and the fact that he returns to the topic despite others in the studio trying to discuss different matters. In Elvis's own words: "I heard this guy in Las Vegas – Billy Ward and his Dominoes. There's a guy out there who's doin' a take-off of me – 'Don't Be Cruel'. He tried so hard, till he got much better, boy; much better than that record of mine." He goes on: "He was real slender – he was a coloured guy – he got up there. He had it a little slower than me…He got the backin', the whole quartet. They got the feelin' on it…Grabbed that microphone, went down to the last note, went all the way down to the floor, man, lookin' straight up at the ceiling. Man, he cut me…He had already done 'Hound Dog' an' another one or two, and he didn't do too well, y'know; he was trying too hard. But he hit that 'Don't Be Cruel' and he was tryin' so hard till he got better, boy. Wooh! Man, he sang that song. That quartet standin' in the background, y'know – *ba-domp ba-domp*. And he was out there cuttin' it, man, had all 'm goin' way up in the air. I went back four nights straight and heard that guy do that. Man, he sung hell outta that song, and I was under the table lookin' at him. Git him off! Git him off!"

Levi Stubbs, who has been lead singer of The Four Tops for more than forty years and has one of the greatest voices in contemporary music, recalls how "Elvis Presley used to watch Jackie in Vegas every night. Jackie was in the lounge at the Hilton, and Elvis would come down to watch. Jackie was one of greatest that ever did it. Vocally...it just won't come along again." Later Elvis was to get to know Jackie and they became good friends. Elvis went to see Jackie perform whenever he was able and used some of Jackie's stage techniques in his performances. Jackie would later say, "I took as much from Elvis as he took from me."

Another relationship based on mutual give and take was that of Jackie and his mentor. Late in 1957 he informed Ward that the time had come, after four years with the group, to go solo. He was getting restless for a career of his own. Although Ward claims that he didn't try to hold either McPhatter or Jackie back from leaving the group, it must have been disheartening for him to see them go.

Freda confirms that Ward didn't stand in Jackie's way: "Billy Ward said he'd help him at anything he wanted to do. Billy felt that it was time for him to go and do his thing. Jack was sort of a driving personality and he wanted to do something himself, but he didn't want the responsibility. He was determined to succeed. He could do anything he wanted." Ward was probably also losing control over Jackie. "Jack was going to do what he was going to do."

Ward nurtured a lot of talent, but for the individuals involved they were largely hidden among a group in which many believed Billy Ward to be the lead singer. In Jackie's case, Ward had polished a rough diamond and deserves full credit for his efforts and for his own talent. Hank Ballard, the originator of "The Twist", knew Ward well and believes he should receive greater recognition for his pioneering of contemporary music. "I cannot understand why they keep overlooking this genius," he says.

The Dominoes may well have been the first group in rock 'n' roll. Clyde McPhatter and Sonny Til, along with Jackie, should be recognised as having paved the way and set the standard for all the singers who followed them.

Jack Leroy Wilson

1533 Lyman Street, Detroit – Jackie's first home

Strathmore Street – Jackie's mother's home

Jackie's home on LaSalle, Detroit

Jackie's initials are still visible on the awning at LaSalle

Billy Johnson, Allan Abrams, Johnny Jones (JJ), Berry Gordy, Jackie Wilson, Robert Bateman and Little Willie John on his knees, Cleveland 1960

A young Jackie and a younger audience

A promotional shot from Jackie's time with The Dominoes

Jackie's mentor, Billy Ward, with Jackie and friend

The women who loved him most: (clockwise from top left) mother, Eliza Mae Lee, first wife Freda Wilson (with the author), lover and friend Lynn Ciccone and third wife Lynn Crochet

Promotional shot, with Nat Tarnopol credited with "direction"

Promotional shot for Epic Records

Jackie often took his children on stage. Sadly, none of those pictured are alive today

Jackie and children backstage, Cleveland 1960

Equal partners: Nat Tarnopol and Jackie

Jackie the artist

With arranger/producer Dick
Jacobs

Discussing playback – Jackie,
Harry and Gene Goodman,
Dick Jacobs and Nat Tarnopol

Lee's Club Sensation, Detroit, where Jackie started out in the fifties

The cramped stage inside Lee's Club Sensation

Jackie didn't need a stage to perform

Artists like Prince and Michael Jackson copied Jackie's animated performances

Promotional shot

Jackie could perform acrobatics and not miss a note

Singing 'Danny Boy'

CHAPTER THREE

Reet Petite

Interviewed in October 1972 by *Melody Maker* about his leaving The Dominoes in 1957, Jackie said, "I'd learned all I could, and it seemed that Billy [Ward] wasn't aiming to go out any further than Las Vegas, which was where we were spending most of our time. I hadn't had a chance to play in the black field at all." Las Vegas audiences were, in the main, white; as was much of the music performed by the group.

Leaving the success and security of The Dominoes was risky. He had been part of a well known group, yet was barely known outside the Detroit night club circuit. Solo, there was no guarantee he would achieve the fame he sought. Freda explains some of the difficulties: "When Jack got back from The Dominoes, he thought he was going to sing with Levi Stubbs, but his voice was too similar to Levi's and they were already established. So he couldn't sing with them, and the guys he used to sing with couldn't sing any more, except JJ [Johnny Jones]. The Four Tops had the smooth sound they were trying to push and Jack was still doing his blues stuff."

In the early 1950s Mario Lanza, an Italian-American, was amazing audiences worldwide with his extraordinary tenor voice. Lanza wasn't singing opera, he was singing American romantic ballads in pseudo-operatic style. Jackie, too, was impressed and, what's more, he was able to sing with the same operatic quality, but with an even broader vocal range. It's not that one or other was the better singer, Jackie just sang with more raw soul and passion. Jackie took Freda to see the 1951 movie, *The Great Caruso*, starring Mario Lanza as the Italian opera star, Caruso. Jackie immediately started emulating Lanza: "Mario Lanza played that guy Caruso," remembers Freda. "Lanza was Jack's idol. Jack could almost break glass when he was practising his Mario Lanza stuff; he could make you cry doing that. So he got the music although he couldn't read music, but he'd remember how it sounded and then he'd find anyone who could play piano. He'd go down to Saint Antoine [Street; where Berry Gordy lived and where there was a piano] and have someone play this music.

"His chest really did expand about two inches, you could see it swelling when he was going to let all that power out; and then his voice would come all the way from his stomach. It was really fantastic and personally, at first, I liked those songs better than anything else, because that showed his full potential. But like they say in the business, 'It's not commercial.' He still loved blues, that's why every chance he got they had to put some blues in, or he wasn't going to do nothing. That was his first love – blues, gospel, and then rock 'n' roll. But he really wanted to do Caruso-style songs: his diction was always good and his enunciation…"

Johnny Jones was now out of the army and, as usual, willing to assist his friend who he knew was going to "make it". As Freda puts it, "JJ was always there. He helped Jack get his stuff together. They'd pawn their stuff – everybody pawned their stuff. When Jack got back from The Dominoes, he had a little money coming, but we needed more. He needed some [promotional] pictures of himself. He didn't want to look like he came back from The Dominoes and didn't have nothing. Everybody was helping every way they could, so that he would look good." He mostly needed impressive clothes for both on and off the stage. He had to look the part.

From around the same time Freda recalls a beautiful event which typified Jackie and the esteem in which the people of the neighbourhood regarded him: "One time my mother cooked a whole bunch of food. I said, 'I'll give Jack my share.'" Freda was pregnant at the time and, with Jackie's huge appetite it wasn't enough. "They were all still hungry. He'd just walk in the BBQ place – it was on Oakland, too. He just put his hand up there and takes the BBQ ribs – it was hot too – and brings them home. He took so many ribs." Jackie had not forgotten his theft from the small shop. Freda explained how he attempted to atone: "So when he 'made it' and he came back we went up there to Oakland, he said, 'Miss M, how much do I owe you for when Freda was pregnant? All she wanted was BBQ ribs, and I know I took a lot.' She said, 'Jackie, you don't owe me anything; it's just so sweet that you remembered me and came by.' So he gave her five hundred dollars anyhow. He said, 'You never came to my home and you knew where I lived; you never said nothing.'"

At the time, the Mecca of black night clubs in Detroit was the prestigious Flame Show Bar, located on the corner of John R Avenue and Canfield Street, a block east of Woodward Avenue. The acts were generally black entertainers from Detroit, or elsewhere, such as "Little Miss Sharecropper" (LaVern Baker), Ivory Joe Hunter, Louis Jordan, T-Bone Walker, Dinah Washington, Billie Holiday, John Lee Hooker and popular local, Singin' Sammy Ward.

The Flame was owned by Morris and Sally "Sal" Wasseman and run by Albert "Al" Green. All three were Jewish. Green also managed talented singers; the white crying-crooning specialist Johnnie Ray, LaVern Baker and Della Reese, who were regular and well-loved acts at the club. Green would become instrumental with the advancement of Jackie's career.

The Flame was luxurious, with a sunken entertainment floor, a long bar, with the tables grouped around the stage in semi-circular fashion. The club also had the unique custom of patrons expressing appreciation of the act by banging wooden gavels on the table tops. Patrons generally dressed flamboyantly; this was the place to be seen. In a word; it was *class*. There was a particular Mob feel to the Flame and many believe it to have been owned by the powerful Detroit underworld; certainly it had that association about it.

For more than sixteen years the band leader was the musical genius Maurice King (with his band, The Wolverines). The well liked and highly regarded black arranger would later be instrumental in creating the Motown sound that would bring Detroit's musical talents to the attention of the world. King also provided arrangements for the road shows that were becoming increasingly popular. He admired Jackie and the two got along well.

Working for many years under King was saxophonist Thomas "Beans" Bowles, who was also destined to be a major musical force with Motown. "They didn't let Jackie in the Twenty Grand [Club]; they wanted the Las Vegas, up-scale music style. They wanted to attract the middle-class blacks who had a little more money to spend, rather than the blues people. There were only a few blues people there at that time that made it in that circuit. BB King was on the fringes, but T-Bone Walker and Big Joe Turner were the guys that were drawing people.

"Al Green wasn't what you'd call a likable person himself...a Humphrey Bogart type. He was very direct and didn't give a damn about nobody." Still, Green appears to have been well liked and it required a particular toughness to succeed in the business. "He was a hard, up-front, cookie, but he'd give you the coat off his back. He gave [jazz saxophonist and band leader] Charlie Parker a coat 'cause he was walking around cold in the snow just two weeks before Parker died [in March 1955]. He was a good guy, gangster type; we all got along well with him.

"It was common knowledge in them days that the Jews and Italians were involved – cross relations. Money and contacts were what they had in common. The outlet for entertainment has always been gangster controlled. Night clubs had always been under the auspices of the underworld...still are," reveals Bowles.

To understand Detroit of the period it is necessary to make mention of its Purple Gang who were essentially Jewish and very tough and ruthless. Like Al Capone in Chicago, they rose to wealth and power smuggling Canadian booze across the St Lawrence Waterway during the ill-conceived Prohibition period. When that avenue of funds was closed off they concentrated on vice and the entertainment business, especially night clubs and concert promotion.

William Weatherspoon, who with Alonzo Tucker wrote 'As Long As I Live' and 'Why Can't You Be Mine' for Jackie's very first album plus some tunes with Berry Gordy, relates: "Al Green was like the Mafia; big cigar and all that. Al was probably fronting at the Flame Show for some other people. Al was very powerful; when he talked to men they acted like children."

Fatefully, through the Flame Show Bar, Jackie reconnected with Roquel Davis, his friend since the early street corner singing days. The meeting would be fortuitous for both men. Davis was raised in the Northend of Detroit by his grandmother. His first cousin Lawrence Payton, of The Four Tops, shared the same house. Jackie lived within two miles of Davis and was treated like one of the family. Davis was therefore familiar with Jackie and his singing talent. Davis puts it this way: "Billy Ward might say Jackie was a 'diamond in the rough', but to his fans and the people he grew up with on the Northend, he was the Hope Diamond. He gave hope to all of us who aspired to become singers. He was a true diamond.

"Jackie came back after leaving Billy Ward and played the Paradise Theatre. The emotion was always there; he could value one word – the word 'so'; and you'd understand exactly, emotionally, where he was coming from. Impeccable phrasing, because he had such control over his voice. He could change octave anywhere in the song; that was total control."

Gwen Gordy, sister of Berry (who later founded the Motown record label), worked at the Flame Show Bar where she had the hat check, photograph and cigarette concession with her sister Anna. Both were young and attractive women who established excellent contacts later to be useful for their now famous brother. Davis had a relationship with Gwen, and Green would let him use his office on Woodward Avenue for songwriting because the office had a piano in it. It was to Davis that Jackie first came when he set off to establish himself as a solo artist, and through Davis and Gwen that he was introduced to Green and granted an audition. "It was my impression that Al Green was the manager of the Flame Show Bar and may have had a controlling interest," says Davis. "Green was quiet, reserved and strong, knowing a lot about a lot of things. He had a lot of connections due to Johnnie Ray and LaVern Baker."

"Jack went to the Twenty Grand Club but they didn't want him without a group," explains Freda. "So he said, 'I'm going to sing by myself.' He went to the Flame and that's when Al Green listened to him by himself. Green had a good eye and ear for talent, and promptly signed Jackie, with himself in the role of manager. He advanced Jackie a little money to get some stuff to get himself together, because all his uniforms belonged to The Dominoes."

Jackie became a regular and popular attraction at another mixed club, Phelp's Lounge, on Oakland Avenue, although it lacked the class of the Flame. He also occasionally performed at Arthur Bragg's Paradise Club at Saginaw, Michigan.

As Davis establishes, Green's major client was Johnnie Ray. Born in Oregon in 1927, Ray sang with the power charged vocal delivery of a black soul artist (quite unimpeded by the hearing aid he wore). He hit the big time in 1951 with 'Cry' which held Number One position for eleven weeks, a song which had an R&B flavour and was a far cry from the big band sounds of a few years previously. A major talent, Ray was also a style pioneer for all who would follow, including Jackie and Elvis Presley. His stage performances were legendary: Ray put every ounce of emotion into his delivery, falling to his knees in expression while women shrieked, screamed, cried and fainted. He went on to worldwide popularity, making numerous overseas tours.

LaVern Baker – who incidentally had taught Johnny Ray how to sing blues – was Green's second major client. Born Delores Baker in Chicago in 1929 she began performing at seventeen as "Little Miss Sharecropper". Baker had two local hits in 1952 before signing to Atlantic Records and achieving numerous R&B and pop hits from 1955 to 1965. In 1955 her hit 'Tweedlee Dee' reached Number Fourteen on the Pop charts. Over the next three years 'Jim Dandy' and 'I Cried A Tear' followed. As a performer Baker was in many ways the female version of Jackie. She could make any song uniquely hers and had a powerful voice. She was also versatile, going from up-tempo R&B to jazz and Latin numbers with ease. Roquel Davis wrote a catchy follow-up song for her entitled 'Jim Dandy Got Married', in 1957.

To help keep his roster of stars Green had a few "assistants"; Harry Balk and Irving "Irve" Maconic, both always looking for an angle – a fast way to make a buck. Money also prevented Jackie appearing live as often as before, as Beans Bowles recalls. "Jackie wasn't a regular at the Flame Bar," reports the former Flame Show musician. "He appeared there very little because, number one, he couldn't get the money he wanted and, as Al Green was his manager, he wouldn't let him on for no money. When Al got him, Jackie'd just left The Dominoes; he had no hits, he wasn't a big star. But they asked a lot of [appearance] money for him because of The Dominoes work. His singing of 'Danny Boy' they still talk about."

Investment in the act was working however. On stage Jackie always looked the part, favouring tight fitting suits and expensive silk shirts. In the fashion of the time he had his hair processed to straighten it and also to have it coiffed in a high style, similar to how Presley had his. "Once his hair was processed it was fixed," remembers Freda." It was done with a chemical [lye]; it would last a long time. He knew how to fix himself. His mother would get him some clothes and she'd make him look good." The use of lye caused a burning sensation to the scalp which was quite painful. With hair cream to keep it in place, Freda said it was "as hard as a rock" to touch.

Having learned footwork in the boxing ring, Jackie always was a natural mover, although not a natural when it came to dancing with a partner. Freda: "He could not dance; we'd go to a dance or a party and do the foxtrot just like they taught you; just straight up and down foxtrot. He didn't add nothing to it. He was glad when you could forget about what the lady was doing." But most who saw Jackie perform on stage would agree that he was unsurpassed; pure grace. He would appear to glide out on stage and perform spins and splits with consummate ease, executed flawlessly after innumerable hours of practice.

In the 1940s and 1950s tap dancing was the rage and one of the best exponents around Detroit was Ziggie Johnson, who also ran a dance school. Indeed he was somewhat of a legend around those parts, just as Bill "Mr Bojangle" Robinson was elsewhere. In later years he MCed at the Twenty Grand Ballroom and the Flame Show Bar. Freda recalls: "Ziggie Johnson was the MC at the Flame Show Bar. He was watching Jackie sing one night; he just came down to our table and he said, 'Look, Jack, you need a little help on your dance routine, so why don't you come to my school?' I'd been over there when I was in high school a few times. I said, 'Ziggie you remember me?' He said, 'Yes, why don't you come too.' I wanted to see what Jack did, but I said 'no', he might be embarrassed for me to see. I didn't go, I waited until he got it together and had his stage routine together. He taught himself that little twirl.

"Ziggie helped him put his little routine together. He told him to do his boxing steps and taught him how to do the splits so it became second nature to him. He could do it without missing a note. He could always throw that mike around; I used to think sometimes, when he was a little high, he was going to miss it or fall off the stage, but he never did. Ziggie taught him to do whatever he felt comfortable with and try little things, and then put 'em all together. That's exactly what he did. First he started with a single spin. Then he did the double spin. Then he did the triple spin, and I don't care how high he was he never failed. I had to go down to every show."

Their daughter Denise agrees. "My father was not your average good-stepping black person," she admits. "He was like, an out of step, out of tune. Nobody knows it." Yet to see Jackie on stage was to see a graceful dancer; pure poetry in motion.

Jackie lacked only one thing at this stage – suitable songs that he could turn into hits, which is where Roquel Davis and Berry Gordy came in. Davis had been given a break in the most amazing way. In 1956 he had sent a tape of some his compositions to Chess Records in Chicago, sung by his Four Aims group. The white Chess brothers, Leonard and Phil, had a tremendous feel for black music, having formed the label in 1950, after noticing a lack of recording opportunities for the talented artists they'd seen around Chicago's many night spots – Muddy Waters, Elmore James,

Howling Wolf and Willie Dixon. Davis explains the response he received: "Phil Chess wrote back in longhand, 'We like your tape of the Aims, we'd like you to come to Chicago and give me a call.'" Davis caught a bus to Chicago, "I called Phil Chess. What they really wanted were the songs, not for the Aims, but for The Flamingos and The Moonglows. The Aims wanted to sing like The Four Freshmen and Hi-Lo's [both white groups] with close harmonies and no outstanding lead. Chess was an R&B company; they thought nothing of us as a group, or Levi Stubbs's marvellous voice."

So Davis began work with Chess while The Four Aims, now without him, became The Four Tops. Together for more than forty years, they had enormous success, starting with 'Kiss Me Baby' which was recorded on Chess. Robert Pruter in his definitive book, *Chicago Soul*, quotes Davis: "So I had a relationship going with them [Chess] over the years, working with their artists, Bo [Diddley], Chuck Berry and Muddy [Waters]. Quite often, whenever I was in town, they would request for me to come over."

Davis's musical career further progressed when he combined his songwriting skills with those of Berry Gordy. Davis: "Al Green, because of Gwen working at the Flame Show bar, told me Berry Gordy was coming to his office and had some songs. One Saturday Berry came to the office with his reel tape. He had six to eight songs. He was heavily influenced by jazz music and had early basic piano lessons. I said to Berry I thought he had some good ideas, but that he'd have to make his material a bit more commercial, melodically and lyrically. It was in the jazzy or blues – down, negative vein, but he didn't want to change anything. So when he left that meeting he was a little upset, but he came back that Saturday, or another Saturday. I remember him coming up. No one there again but myself, but with a slightly different attitude. I said, 'Have you written any songs?' 'Yes, I've written a couple.' But he was always suspicious. I was working on an idea when he came and we ended up working on a tune together. That meeting then led us to eventually writing together.

"There was a piano Al Green's office. Berry said, 'How are we going to do this?' I said, 'Whatever chord changes come into your mind, play them. I'll work on the melody, you play what you want to play and I'll start singing words I think are going to make sense.' We developed that kind of working habit. 'Here's an idea' and 'let's discuss the feeling of it'. We'd hear something we loved and write that down...words, any words. We couldn't write music, so we either recorded it or remembered it. I can remember one hundred and fifty of all my songs; I can sing them all. Being street singers we stored them all."

While working at the Lincoln-Mercury plant and being a talented boxer, Berry Gordy decided he'd prefer to achieve fame and fortune as a songwriter. He was eight years older than Davis and four to five years older than Jackie. As his real musical interest was jazz, he had opened a jazz record store in Detroit in 1955, which had gone broke. So it was back to the Ford plant. His sister Gwen evidently believed in him and there was a strong love between them. "Gwen would give him money when he wasn't working. They looked out for each other," says Davis.

Looking out for each other worked both ways. "We both had a lot of songs, but we decided to become partners in every sense of the word," Davis continues. "We combined all of our efforts – all the current efforts became *our* effort. All songs that we wrote had became *ours*, whether we collaborated on them or not. Every song we wrote from that time became ours and it remained that way. I never tried, and Berry has never tried, to separate who did what. I only get a third on some since we cut Gwen in, but seeing she never wrote a note, we didn't really have to cut her in. It [songwriting re-publishing] only comes up once in twenty-five years, but I continued to cut her in on most of the songs; I have no regrets about that. The publishing rights I do have some feelings about, but I can't change one without the other. It means two thirds of the rights, including two thirds of publishing rights, go to Joebete [Berry Gordy's music publishing company]." Songwriters must share fifty-fifty with the music publishers.

Jackie had the talent, they had the songs, but they all still needed the right connections. Eventually it all came together, as Billy points out. "I introduced him to the Chess brothers. They didn't like him. They naturally regretted it." Even Chess were not infallible when it came to recognising great talent. Davis tried another approach. "I took him to Al Green," he says. "Al signed him up." Green had good connections with the New York recording industry and, equally, with the Mob. Davis and Gordy had the songs. Freda remembers, "When they started off, just Berry and Jack would be rehearsing at Berry's father's little newspaper shop." There was a piano at the print shop on St Antoine Street.

Around Al Green's office at the time was a young man, Nathanial "Nat" Tarnopol, who many thought was Al Green's partner, though subordinate is more accurate. In reality Tarnopol was little more than a "gofer" for Green. He earned a living cleaning a car lot, selling tyres or, at one time, even selling ice popsicles. But he would soon assume a major role in Jackie's career.

Nat was born in January, 1931. In 1957 his mother had died and he was living with his Aunt Lena who still spoke with a thick European accent. Tarnopol's son Paul recalls: "At that time my dad was helping at Mercury [Records, where The Platters recorded]. My dad met Al Green at the Flame Show Bar; he was working for Al. His parents came to the USA from Europe. They were close to orthodox – very conservative – Jewish. Nat sold car tyres, but his love was the music business. He was into black music; he'd listen to R&B in the basement. Nat knew Jackie before he came to Al Green [this may be so, but there is no record of any relationship]. Al was nervous about taking Jackie on. Jackie was a wild card at times, even back then."

Says Beans Bowles, "At the first part of it, Tarnopol was a guy learning the business. He worked for Al Green. They eventually went into business together; I suppose Green must have sponsored him. He evolved out of his relationship with Al Green. Nat was just a fascinating, energetic young man. We kinda all liked him. He wasn't like he ended up being. He started dealing in the big money and it kinda distorted his thinking. People that are very aggressive are generally not liked very much anyway, but he caught on quick. As he got started he knew where to find the money." Finding the money was what it was all about, as producing stars and recording hits was highly speculative. Only people with big money were likely to be prepared to take the risks.

Roquel Davis came to know Tarnopol well. "The Jewish people totally controlled the music industry," he recalls, "especially in those days. I couldn't think Nat would recognise talent if it looked him in the face. But it was Green, who was so well connected."

First it was necessary for Green to arrange for Jackie to have a recording contract. He had signed R&B singer LaVern Baker with the progressive Atlantic label, while Johnnie Ray had been signed to Okeh Records, a subsidiary of Columbia. Despite this, for Jackie, Green first approached Bob Thiele of Decca Records, in New York. Thiele had extensive music production experience having worked with Teresa Brewer (who later became his wife), Pearl Bailey, The McGuire Sisters and Lawrence Welk. In 1957 he had signed Buddy Holly And The Crickets who became a major rock 'n' roll act.

Green previously had taken Thiele to the Apollo Theatre to see Billy Ward and his Dominoes. He vividly remembers seeing Jackie for the first time: "I freaked out, 'This kid is amazing!' Jackie was utterly fantastic. This guy was not only a great singer, almost in the James Brown style, but also a great performer. They are entertainers as well as creators. Jackie could do it all." It's high praise from one who has worked with the best of them. Thiele said to Green, "'I'd love to sign that guy Jackie Wilson.' Green said, 'You've got him.'" There is some ambiguity here: Roquel Davis is adamant that it was he who put Jackie in touch with Green – *after* Jackie had left The Dominoes.

Nevertheless, there is no dispute that it was Thiele who signed Jackie to Decca. He continues: "We prepared an agreement between Decca/Coral and Jackie Wilson through his manager, Al Green. Green was staying at the Taft Hotel. When the contract was ready to be signed, he said he'd meet me there the next day at 9am. Everything was to be signed and Jackie would be on Decca/Coral at that point. So I rang up to his room and Nat Tarnopol answered the phone and said, 'Al Green died last night.' I said, 'Look, I've got his contract.' Nat came down and said, 'I can handle it; I'll take care of things.' Jackie must have signed it and Nat signed it. All of a sudden Jackie Wilson was signed to Decca/Coral." It was a most opportune event for Tarnopol, who at that point had no management experience.

As Davis told Robert Pruter of *Goldmine* magazine, "A lot of people thought Nat was Al's partner, but that was not true. He was around the office a lot and assisted Al, but by Nat having the image of a partner, he stepped in and assumed the management of Wilson."

In a radio interview on New York's WBCS (FM) with DJ "Mr Music", Norman N Nite, Jackie discussed his involvement with both Green and Tarnopol: "Well actually I met Nat through Al Green who was manager of LaVern Baker at the time. We were all from Detroit. Nat was a young hot headed kid who wanted to get ahead, and was doing all the publishing for Al Green. Al Green took me when I left The Dominoes and he started to manage me. And he got me a contract, through LaVern Baker, with Decca, which was for Brunswick. And then, God rest his soul, he died and Nat decided he was going to try his hand. Although there was several other guys around, Nat just took me by the arm one day with his raincoat over his arm and just ran. I never will forget…and we ran."

The "other guys" referred to by Jackie were Tarnopol's business partners, Harry Balk and Irving Maconic. Jackie is indeed making a long story short here, because Balk and Maconic probably felt they were just as entitled to have a piece of Jackie's management after Green died. When Jackie said they "just ran", he probably meant from these two partners.

Balk and Maconic became managers of one of the other Detroit vocal talents, and Jackie's friend, Little Willie John. They were described in an unflattering way by a person who was on the scene at the same time: "They were both big cigar smoking types. One was short and dumpy and one was tall and hefty – they were a strange company. They both went to jail for mail fraud back there. They worked together in an office, separately from Tarnopol. Tarnopol got involved later. You didn't know what the relationship was, but all music related. Harry Balk had no musical talent; he was a manager type."

William Weatherspoon chips in: "Nat Tarnopol and Harry Balk were like Green's laddies in those days. Nat and Harry would help him deal with his artists. When Al died Nat took his artist to Decca and left Harry Balk holding the dog. There was always some strange shady stuff going on in the early days."

Certainly before Green's death Tarnopol, who at the time was still living with his aunt, had few prospects. In Freda's words: "Nat didn't know hardly anything. He was sweeping the used car lot. At the time Jackie was singing mostly at the Flame. Jackie said, 'I don't know if he knows anything about the music business.'

But Jackie wanted to keep everything going." So he entrusted his career to Tarnopol. And having signed with Decca, Jackie and Tarnopol moved to New York. Eddie Pride, recalls the period: "Jack never had any education. When he went to New York, Tarnopol bought him an old raggedy Cadillac and put some money in his pocket. Tarnopol robbed Jack blind. But, hell, that was no more than Billy Ward did." Pride believed his childhood friend deserved better.

Decca management preferred rock 'n' roll singers not to record on the primary Decca label. "The company didn't like the fact that he would be on Decca or Coral," says Thiele. "They probably didn't think a black singer should be on a white label. They felt it could look bad so I remembered we owned the trade name 'Brunswick'. That's what I had to do with Buddy Holly. Decca thought that they were inappropriate to be with mainstream artists. We put The Crickets on Brunswick. Later we put

Buddy on Coral and The Crickets remained on Brunswick."

The original Brunswick-Balke-Collender Company was founded in 1921 and manufactured billiard tables and player-pianos, before becoming involved with music recordings. Earlier artists on the label were Al Jolson, Bing Crosby, Fred Astaire, The Andrews Sisters, Harry James and The Mills Brothers. Due to financial hardships brought on by the Great Depression, the label was sold to the American Record Corporation (ARC) in 1931. One of the directors of Brunswick, Jack Kapp, who had been responsible for much of the earlier success, then left to establish Decca. In 1938 Columbia Broadcasting (CBS) bought ARC, although the Brunswick label was put on hold. CBS sold the label to Decca in 1942.

At that stage Jackie was the only artist on the label; Jackie *was* Brunswick. Freda and others believe the deal was that Jackie and Tarnopol held equal shares of this half share, but no evidence of this could be found.

As Jackie's manager Tarnopol set up an office in the Brill Building on New York's Broadway. "The Brill" is a beautiful, large and impressive building, then totally occupied by songwriters, music publishers and people involved in the music business. It was the era's version of "Tin Pan Alley", which formerly was located nearby. In the office next door were the Goodman brothers, Harry and Gene, who had the musical publishing businesses Regent Publishing and Arc Publishing through which most of Jackie's hits were, and are, published. Another of the brothers was world famous big band leader, Benny Goodman. The Goodman connection with Brunswick is both long and strong; Gene Goodman, especially, was very close to Tarnopol and they were directors on the Brunswick board.

Another who knew Tarnopol was Larry Maxwell. Maxwell, went on to form his own record label, Maxx Records, and manage and record a young Gladys Knight. He also became manager for the Four Tops, remaining in that role for seventeen years, recording them for Maxx prior to their signing with Motown. Widely considered one of the best record promoters of the time, when he first knew Tarnopol he "was working at a garage fixing tyres," Maxwell remembers. "A guy who used to manage a lot of shake dances gave him fifty dollars to go to New York." Tarnopol became involved in concert promotion and through this became a friend and colleague of influential DJ, Alan Freed. Freed became a fan of Jackie's and gave his songs national exposure.

On the surface things were coming together nicely for Jackie, nevertheless Freda wasn't so sure. "Nat had everything all set up just the way he wanted it, that's why Jack came out like he did – *with nothing*. That's why Nat got him away from Detroit as soon as he got a hold of him. He just wanted to sing; he didn't want any responsibility. I told him to get his own lawyer, not one of Nat's friends, but he said, 'No, no, no, I trust Nat.' Jack gave Nat power of attorney, first shot. Brunswick was created just for Jack."

Jackie took his old friend JJ and another, Billy Frazier, along with him. They filled the roles of bodyguards, valets, drivers, procurers and plain "pals". In Freda's words: "His best friend was Johnny Jones till the end. He knew him from childhood. Ralph Peterson was his friend till he couldn't function any more. Jack sent for him to New York and tried to get him ready to sing, but he could no longer sing."

Tarnopol had Alonzo Tucker move across to New York, for his songwriting skills, but he also doubled as a driver for Jackie. Tucker, like Jackie, had a distinct fondness for women and partying and there was always a great respect and friendship between the two, despite the age difference.

In 1957 Dick Jacobs began a nine year working relationship producing and directing for Jackie. At that time Jacobs, who was music director with Decca Records and director of artists and repertoire (A&R) with Coral Records, had an illustrious career in his own right. He'd been staff arranger of the Tommy Dorsey and Jimmy Dorsey Orchestras and producer/arranger for Perry Como, Eddie Fisher, Teresa Brewer, Buddy Holly, Billy Williams, The McGuire sisters, Louis Armstrong, Rosemary Clooney, Steve Lawrence and Eydie Gorme. In a fascinating interview, not long before he died, Jacobs related to Tim Holmes of *Musician* magazine (11 January, 1988) his association with Jackie: "One day Thiele called me in and said Jackie was coming in for his first sessions. We'd have to cut Jackie fast since he didn't have any money to stay in New York for an extended period. Since time was tight, I was concerned about the songs we'd be recording. Jackie was bringing in a couple of tunes penned by one Berry Gordy Jnr [and Roquel "Billy" Davis]. Not only was the singer unknown, but who the hell had ever heard of the songwriter?

"When Jackie arrived, he was ushered into my office for an introduction and goddamn if he didn't look like he had just come in on a freight train. He was wearing jeans and a sweat shirt and seemed bedraggled and exhausted. In retrospect, this first meeting was entirely out of character for Jackie. I remember him being very fussy about his appearance. This was a guy who wouldn't appear on the street, or on a record date for that matter, unless every tonsorial detail was sculpted and perfect. He is the only guy I ever knew who could spend hours in shoe stores. Yet, on this first meeting, he looked like any other kid off the street.

"I asked him if he had the lead sheets of the songs he intended to record. He said, 'No,' I'd have to write them down as he sang them to me. I'd been down this road before with other vocalists, and as I wrote out the music for 'Reet Petite' I began to feel some respect for the unknown tunesmith. 'Reet Petite' had an unusual melody and a strikingly inventive chord construction; even before recording it, it felt like a new kind of hit.

"After I'd written down the music, Jackie and I sat down to figure out what keys to record in. I began playing piano chords in what I considered the usual male keys, but Jackie kept telling me to take it higher. I transposed the keys until they hit the female range, a full octave above where we'd started. Jackie explained that since he had laryngitis he couldn't sing along, but kept saying, 'Take it higher,' in a gravelly, phlegm filled voice. I had no idea what he'd sound like in these upper register helium arrangements he insisted on.

"The whole set-up was making me very nervous. I went into Thiele's office and told him that Jackie's keys seemed all off to me; he hadn't sung a note and I really hoped we hadn't signed a lemon. Thiele – ever the philosopher – just said, 'Oh, what the hell, we only signed him to get LaVern. Do the arrangements in any key he wants.' Bob always had good gambler's instincts. We'd just do the session and see what happened."

The mention here of LaVern Baker, the powerful R&B singer is of interest. She was hot property having already had chart success on the King label and, more recently, on Atlantic and Green had apparently dangled her as bait to get Jackie the Decca contract. However she was still contracted to Atlantic and, most likely due to the untimely death of Green, Decca never did get Baker signed.

Jacobs goes on: "Jackie and I discussed the instrumentation. We hired Panama Francis on drums, Lloyd Trotman on bass, Ernie Hayes on piano, Sam Taylor on saxophone and Eric Gale on guitar. I figured with all these seasoned pros in the tune, the session couldn't be too bad. We held the session at the Pythian Temple on East Seventieth Street in Manhattan. I passed out the arrangement of 'Reet Petite' to the band and ran over it a few times to do the necessary fine tuning. The band gelled and purred like a Mercedes. Jackie commented that he liked the arrangement very much. Now it was his turn. I got him behind the microphone and said a silent prayer that this aerial key he'd picked to sing in would be okay, and that this guy was a reasonable approximation of a singer.

"Jackie Wilson opened his mouth and out poured that sound like honey on moonbeams and it was like the whole room shifted on some weird axis. The musicians, these meat and potatoes pros, stared at each other slack-jawed and goggle-eyed in disbelief; it was as if the purpose of their musical training and woodshedding and lick spitting had been to guide them into this big studio in the Pythian Temple to experience these pure shivering moments of magic. Bob Thiele and I looked at each other and just started laughing, half out of relief and half out of wonder. I never thought crow could taste so sweet. For years afterwards, Jackie and I often joked about my initial underestimation of his range. In fact, his vocal spread encompassed so many octaves that he could sing not only in female keys but an octave higher without a hint of a strained falsetto. 'Reet Petite' came out and did very well, although nothing like the hits that would follow." This took place on 12 July, 1957.

When Roquel Davis turned his efforts to professional songwriting, he found it to be a craft with a formula, as he explains about Jackie's first hit: "'Reet Petite' was a common phrase used in connection with a fine girl. It was about this girl that was small in size and build; she was an actual person. It was also lyrically inspired by her. Musically it was inspired by a riff known to everybody – a boogie woogie riff. This being one of my early compositions; I was around sixteen."

Some of the earliest Jacobs sessions were, for some unknown reason, done at Joe Syracuse's United Sound Studios in Detroit. Says Davis, "I was in on the early United Sound Studio sessions with Jackie. That was the studio Motown used prior to [Tamla/Motown's] Hitsville USA studio being built." The first release, 'Reet Petite', in August 1957, did poorly in the USA, reaching only Number Sixty-Two on the Pop charts and not making the R&B charts. In Britain, however, it held Number One for four weeks.

'Reet Petite' featured a Jackie interpretation; a rolling of the "R" in the word "Reet" throughout. But Freda recalls one occasion when that distinct "R" embarrassed Jackie during a concert performance. "He was appearing with Dinah Washington. Jack blew his two front teeth out singing 'Reet Petite'. It was his denture. He did that thing [with the rolling of the Rs] and his two front teeth came flying out. He stopped singing right there; he wanted somebody to find his teeth. He wasn't going back on stage with no teeth." Jackie's daughter Denise interjects: "He said, 'I'll never sing it again,' and he never did. He probably rolled over in his grave when he learned it was Number One in England and Japan [in 1986-1987]." Jackie rarely performed the song on stage again.

The record's flip side was the well known 'By The Light Of The Silvery Moon', which will never be done quite like that again. Half way through the song Jackie exhibits his vocal skills by singing a skat falsetto that is more like a female yodel. No doubt it was one of his own innovations.

DJ Norman N Nite, in his radio interview, asked Jackie about his first hit on Brunswick. Jackie answered: "That happened through a young man, he's got a small label called Motown; Berry Gordy Jnr. He was doing the writing for us then. That's why I liked it, but I was very hoarse that day in the studio. I couldn't hardly talk because I'd been working that hard in the studio and on the road, and so I couldn't hit, as Nat would say, 'the bird', the high note [high C]."

Jacobs, on all his recordings with Jackie, used full orchestras. He didn't want Jackie to be a two hit rock 'n' roll singer, with guitar and drum backing. Jacobs also used white back-up singers, including the Ray Charles Singers, and received criticism for doing so. As Jacobs explained in *Musician* magazine: "This did not reflect a racial bias, nor was it an attempt to 'clean up' Jackie's sound. The simple fact was in the early-to-middle 1950s it was tremendously difficult to find black vocal groups who could read music, and we simply didn't have the budget for the time to teach them the parts. When we did find black groups who could read charts, we used them on black and white sessions. Besides, Davis, Gordy and Jackie were happy with the orchestral and back-up treatments."

One of the many affairs Jackie had was with a stripper and dancer, Angel Lee. Angel was a gorgeous schoolgirl when wild rock 'n' roller, Little Richard, first spotted her in her home town of Savannah, Georgia. "I was his choice, he was not mine," says Angel. "I was walking down the street and one of the girls said, 'Little Richard wants to meet you.' I said, 'What!? Does he know I'm female?' I was sixteen years old. I used to go and see all the concerts, but this was one I was not going to see; I didn't like his music." Nevertheless she met Little Richard and ended up following him on the road. More than that, she fell madly in love with him.

Angel, who stands five foot two inches and has a large bust, is of white, American Indian and black descent. In 1957 she and Richard had plans to marry, but while on tour in Australia he had a frightening experience in an aircraft when one of the engines gave out. Richard, ever religious, prayed and promised that if he survived he would give up rock 'n' roll and take up Christian ministry. Before doing this, and perhaps to prove a point, he tossed some very expensive jewellery into the Sydney harbour. At the peak of his career, in September 1957, Little Richard retired from showbusiness and entered the Seventh Day Adventist Seminary in Huntsville, Alabama.

Angel was heartbroken; they had even set the wedding date. She became reclusive, living with her godmother on 116th Street in New York. Her godmother advised her, "'Get out of the house...go to the Apollo Theatre.'" Angel says, "So I went to the Apollo and I met LaVern Baker, [comedian] Slappy White [later Baker's husband] and Jimmy Rogers." They all went to see this "new singer" at the Baby Grand Club. The singer was Jackie. "He was staying at the Teresa Hotel and working the Baby Grand when we first met." This was December 1957 when Jackie had his first hit, 'Reet Petite'. Angel and Jackie had an affair that lasted, on and off, for a few years.

One time Angel met with Jackie's wife; a meeting which led her to a deep admiration for Freda. "I went bouncing into Jackie's dressing room in Richmond, Virginia. There was ["Rockin' Robin"] Bobby Day, who I ran around with, his wife Jacqui, Freda and Jackie. I was introduced to Freda and I said right then and there, 'It's nice meeting you. Bye.' Jackie would not let me out of the dressing room; I was trying to think of a million reasons to get out of there 'cause I'd heard about Freda's tough reputation. Jackie was about to go on stage and I said, 'Bye.' He said, 'Don't you walk out of that door.' He turned to Freda and said, 'Now if you don't want to fight tonight, don't let her go. If she disappears you know what's going to happen when we get back to Washington.'

"He left to go on stage. I said, 'Goodbye,' to Freda and she said, 'Stop, I know who you are, I know all about you. But do me a favour, do not leave. I really don't feel like fighting Jackie tonight. Not only that, you tried your best to show me respect and he wouldn't let you. I like you for that.' That's how we became friends. I think it may have been better for Jackie if he stayed married to Freda."

Jackie had a strong romantic interest in Angel. Whenever he was in New York he'd get in touch with her or send JJ and Frazier to call by the Alvin Hotel on Fifty-Second Street, to collect her. Angel claims, "I was from the kind of family that if you belonged to one man, that man is supposed to belong to you." She therefore spurned Jackie's advances. When JJ and Frazier arrived at the Alvin Hotel, the front desk would call to warn her they were on their way up. "I had my room next to the fire exit, and I dressed running down that sparrow cage more times than you can imagine. I found out what type of person he was, and from there it was, 'Leave me alone, Jackie.'" She was referring to Jackie's well known reputation for sleeping with any woman who took his fancy, regardless of their marital status. "I was avoiding him because of the womanising. I'd say Jackie loved every woman on earth. Jackie was one of these 'do as I say, not as I do' people. Jackie wanted to mess with every women on earth but didn't want them screwing around with another man."

Angel recalls him slapping her for no reason, but only once: "JJ and Frazier kidnapped me one time. I was getting on the elevator at the Teresa Hotel in New York. The moment I saw them I knew I was in trouble and they lifted me right up and said, 'Jackie wants to see you.' I said, 'Jackie doesn't even know I'm in town.' They actually have kicked in doors of mine. The time they kidnapped me I ended up in Providence, Rhode Island with him. One time when I complained, he said, 'Why are you complaining, they know you as Mrs Wilson around here and you've got the albums.' I said, 'Yeah, if only I could get the man.'"

Angel, who says she dated Jackie for about a month, also remembers Tarnopol, although not kindly: "Don't you believe that Nat was a nice guy – I was there! Nat did everything he could to get me into bed with him, but I never could get past the personality." She had her own special way of getting back at Tarnopol: "I couldn't stand Tarnopol, I disliked him intensely. Tarnopol used to tell me if I didn't go to bed with him, I couldn't see Jackie any more. I said to him, 'I just won't see Jackie any more.' I used to find out where Jackie was working, get a cab, have the cab parked, and go right up front where Jackie could see me. He'd be on stage singing and I'd leave. I'd tell the cab driver, 'Don't leave yet,' and within five minutes Jackie would be off that stage and in the cab with me. I only did that when Nat Tarnopol made me angry. I used to tell Nat, 'All you've got to do is leave me alone and I'll leave Jackie alone.' Jackie didn't hate Nat in the beginning; he was so strung out on the coke and fame." Jackie was being exploited by Tarnopol, but he just couldn't recognise it.

While reckless in love, Jackie had many years behind him in terms of singing experience. As Jacobs explained in *Musician* magazine: "Jackie was the consummate professional in the studio. He never asked to change anything on an arrangement and could get a track down in two to three takes max. One night, after the band had gone home, Nat Tarnopol in a happy delirium over a playback, sat down on the control board, pressing down the record button and erasing eight bars of a master take. Fortunately, we were able to splice in a section from an out-take and save the recording. I'll leave it to you to figure out which Jackie Wilson tune has the hidden botch.

"When we'd go over songs to select keys, etc, for the sessions, we'd sit around a piano and plan an outline for the arrangement. Jackie loved to hear sustained strings behind him, which meant that the strings just played a pad which gave him room to stroll with the melody. But Jackie would always say, 'Dick, gimme them "substained" strings,' which became a big gag; I could never figure out if Jackie couldn't pronounce 'sustained' or if he simply refused to. Nat, on the other hand, had a big penchant for tympani; I had to wedge a tympani part into songs even when they made no sense in the arrangement. But even a tympani roll at the tail-end of an arrangement made him happy, so it was easy enough to do." Praise from Jacobs is a big compliment; he'd worked with many of the major artists of the time.

Due to Jacobs having other commitments, the second recording session in the final months of 1957 was directed by Milton De Lugg, the big band leader. Only eight tracks came out of the session. One was the beautiful ballad by Davis/Gordy 'To Be Loved' which was given Jackie's silky treatment. Released in February 1958, the song was perfect for Jackie and reached Number Seven on the R&B charts and Number Twenty-Two on the Pop charts. It was Jackie's first Top Forty hit as a solo performer and six years since he recorded 'Danny Boy' on the Dee Gee label. Only rarely did his stage performances not include the song thereafter.

In his radio interview, Norman Nite asked Jackie about 'To Be Loved'. "That was Berry's idea too and his penmanship. He decided I could sing better than I could gimmick. He wanted to prove I could do both." Jackie unfairly neglected to mention his old friend Davis who co-wrote the tune. The likely reason for this is that Berry Gordy was more famous, being the founder of Motown.

Davis says, "'To Be Loved' probably sold more R&B than anything, even though it was a ballad. It had more of that appeal. At that time R&B artists were not getting that much Pop exposure on radio or television." Most likely it was Jackie's most performed stage song.

He continues: "The big sales of R&B artists began to happen more in the mid sixties. As the years went by we [black song writers and artists] got more exposure and sales increased. Sometimes they became 'Pop' first. 'Night' was getting a lot of play on R&B stations. It sold well. Black fans knew he could sing anything. After 'Doggin' Around' came out – that was totally different for Jackie – there was of talk about that. Wow! A lot of the pop jocks [white DJs] didn't think he could sing that bluesy."

In the late 1950s studio technology was still in the electronic stone age. Davis recalls: "Three tracks didn't come along until 1962. At Chess we had one of the first three track Ampex recorders in the mid west. They didn't use it the way you'd think. They said, 'Okay, well, put the voice on one, the band on the other – I don't know what we're going to do with the third track,' that was the attitude for a long while.

"The band would came in and we'd run it down a few times to get the kinks out and then we'd start. The singer would then come in and – a few takes – you'd have it. A small mistake and you started all over again. A mistake was great; that made the producer do his work. They couldn't splice two halves of a song together back then because they didn't have a click track which means the tempo from 'take' to 'take' would be different. The arranger would start, 'One, two, one, two, three, four.' The next track could be, 'Two, one.' There was nothing going click, click. It was all how you felt, so the tempo could vary in the song – the drummer would get the feel of the song. I tried many times to splice only to discover the tempo didn't fit."

Band leader, Henry Jerome, had the responsibility of putting the huge studio bands together for most of the Dick Jacobs recording sessions. Jerome chose well: nothing but the best musicians would suffice. The back-up singers were talents in their own right; cousins Cissy Houston and Dionne Warwick, and Lillian Clarke. Jerome insists Tarnopol was only executive producer; which really means he had minimal involvement with the actual studio sessions, despite numerous record album credits.

Apart from the very early recordings, which were done in Detroit's United Sound Studios, two New York recording studios were used for the Jacob's sessions; Bell Sound Studios and the Pythian Temple, where the large hall sounds resulted. Henry Jerome, not only put the bands together, he also worked in the sound studio adjusting the sound input levels; the mix. Recordings were done live, so a mistake by anyone meant the whole song would have to be re-done from the start. Originally only three and later on four tracks were used to record the huge orchestra, background singers and Jackie. Today, with digital recordings and forty-eight track recording, a single wrong note or an entire piece can be edited out without difficulty. Says Jerome, "They were cut quickly, that was the way it was in those days. The artists had to perform in those days; no patching in."

Incredibly, from where he sat he could see neither Jackie nor the orchestra. When stereo recording started to come in, it was up to Jerome to work the levels in order to get the ultimate finished product. He relied on his musician's ear, because there was no going back later to alter the mix. Sometimes the stereo mix didn't work out well, so the record would be released as mono. Jerome speaks highly of Jackie as a performer and a man. "Jackie was one of the all time great acts, absolutely," he says. "A gentleman, a nice thinking human being, and exceptional talent. I think his weakness was that he wasn't a businessman."

Another black singer with ability from Detroit was Eddie Holland. With a very similar vocal pitch to Jackie, Berry Gordy would have Holland do the demonstration ["demo"] recordings so that Jackie could get a better feel for the song. Holland doesn't recall which songs he demoed, but conceded their vocals were similar. When Gordy founded Motown, one of the first to record for him was Holland. He had four Top Forty hits, the best known being 'Jamie', but he didn't live up to everyone's expectations. Along with his brother Brian and Lamont Dozier, he later went on to form one of the most successful songwriting and production teams of all time – Holland, Dozier and Holland – writing hit after hit for most of Motown's major artists. He recalls: "My first recording session was done on Jackie Wilson's session. It was in New York. Jackie Wilson allowed me to take one of his session songs as a second cut. He allowed me to take some of his session time. The arranger was Don Costa; a great arranger." Costa, although not credited, worked on many of the early recordings, also working with Sinatra, Paul Anka and Sarah Vaughan.

Jackie sometimes did his own "dubs" [demonstration recordings] recorded directly on an acetate disc. In 1957 Jackie and Gordy got together in the basement studio of Detroit DJ, Bristol Bryant, and recorded two songs, 'To Be Loved' and 'Lonely Teardrops', both of which featured a tinkering piano played by Gordy with Jackie's haunting vocal treatment. Luckily quite clear copies of those demos are still around today.

In 1995 Berry Gordy heard them again after thirty-eight years and was moved by the memories they evoked. Listening to a cassette of the songs he says, "That's incredible. That's wonderful. Boy, that guy was incredible. Jackie could do a tune. It was a rehearsal with Jackie. That's the way I felt it at first ['Lonely Teardrops']. You see I'm a blues man at heart." He also reminisces about the writing partnership he and Billy Davis formed: "What we did – before we had a writing partnership – we had already written some songs. He said, 'You'll get a piece of songs I've written with other people.' I said, 'Okay, you'll get what I've written with other people.' Some of the songs I wrote myself like 'Lonely Teardrops' and 'To Be Loved'. There are lots of songs, with different writers, I actually wrote myself."

Gordy's recollection is that he wrote 'To Be Loved' alone, although Davis recalls the writing of the song differently: "Berry tells a story in his book [*To Be Loved*, Gordy's autobiography] of how he came to write 'To Be Loved' and of course he makes no mention of anyone else. He states that he and his wife had a big falling out this night about his kids. He was upset and she put him out of the house and he discovered that she was suing for divorce. He came up to his sister Gwen's apartment. He was sort of lonely and in despair and upset because of what had happened. That's when he decided to write 'To Be Loved'.

"He says, and it's not true, he started to write a song about his kids. As it developed, he discovered it was not just about his kids, but was about being loved by everybody. It went on to be a hit. That's the story he tells in the book. Actually he arrived at his sister's house, where I was staying at the time. Gwen and I were soul mates at that time. I was there and asleep. I heard noise in the living room. There was a Wurlitzer electric piano there and Berry was playing on it. I went out and said, 'What are you doing here this time of the night?' He went on to tell me that he and Thelma had this argument. We sat there talking and I said if we are going to be here we might as well write a song about it. He was doodling with some chords, but it was I who came up with 'To Be Loved'. You know, love is great, the greatest thing in the world and to have someone who really loves you – there's nothing like it. As we usually do – Berry started doodling with some chord changes, without melody – and I began to see what I feel melodically there, what came to mind, and that's how the song came to be written. The song was written and completed, with the exception of the bridge, that night. We had the melody, but not all the words. I finished the words to the bridge the next day." To be fair to Gordy, perhaps he'd just forgotten they had co-written the song – on account of his very busy life.

Freda was friendly with Gordy's first wife, Thelma, who was also anxious for the success they both expected. Said Freda: "Thelma and I used to cry on each other's shoulder. 'My water is cut off; what are we going to do?' Berry was screwing around with this girl [that] Thelma didn't know about. He always appeared very sincere. All the money was going right back in the business. They were both trying to get somewhere. I knew Jack would eventually – even though we stayed in the old raggedly house, with no locks on the doors." Freda recalls that Jackie held Gordy in high regard, but he too was getting impatient for success. Says Freda, "Nothing ever happened. Jack said, 'There ain't nothing happening there.'

"Then at last we did get a little something. I was working at the Harper Hospital – I was pregnant with Tony. Then 'To Be Loved'; Jack called me at work, which he never did. 'We've got a hit!' I ran down the hall screaming, 'We made it, it's a hit.' It sold five hundred thousand." On the very same day Freda took maternity leave from her job at the hospital. She was seven months into the pregnancy. Their second son, Anthony ("Tony") Duane, was born on 21 February, 1958.

Jackie was again suspicious that this child may have had a different father. Tony had very dark skin and when Jackie visited the hospital he began inspecting the infant minutely. "Why you doing that?" asked Freda, "Checking the bone structure," replied Jackie. Denise adds, "He was like some kind of damned doctor. Because Tony is dark skinned like her [Freda's] side of the family, got a keen nose like hers, he had to have blood tests for the child." Freda continues, "He kept getting me pregnant and then he'd come and say, 'Whose is that?' Acting like he was crazy. Fifteen times pregnant! I almost went crazy with the four children."

Jackie's suspicions were, of course, more to do with his own weaknesses than his wife's. His infidelities were many, and various. Freda remembers one unusual situation. "This rich, white girl, Carol, took care of me and my kids," Freda says. "She was nice to [Jackie's half-sister] Joyce, to Mama, nice to me. She bought us things. When I had Tony she sent everything. A bassinet, a baby buggy, stroller. She was so nice I didn't know she liked him like that for a long time. I was really stupid, I thought she was just a nice lady trying to help him out. Whenever I had a baby, something would come for Freda Wilson. I said, 'I didn't order nothing.' They said, 'It's paid for.' Baby things and bassinets; all kinds of baby stuff, expensive stuff.

"Carol bought for Jack for a long time – even when he became famous. She used to come over and help my mother-in-law take care of the kids. She'd stay upstairs. She'd clean the house from top to bottom. She'd comb the kids' hair. Everyone in the house got an allowance. She never acted like she was in love with him. It took me years to finally realise there was more to it. Finally it dawned on me; she don't get no money back. I never did hate her like I did some of the other women."

Possibly Freda really understood better than she let on, being aware Jackie had been a "ladies' man" since he was very young. She knew there were other children he'd fathered, such as Brenda, to Suzie, and Sabrina, to Molly Byndon, in 1954. "Like I say, he was a busy man."

He was just as busy professionally. The first opportunity for Jackie to be seen on coast-to-coast television came with Dick Clark's hugely popular *American Bandstand*. The show was an institution, especially with the young. To perform on it almost assured chart success in the USA, and it was also syndicated to many countries in Europe and to Australia. *Bandstand* began in Philadelphia in 1952, then headed by Bob Howan. Clark started out as DJ on Philadelphia radio station WFIL in 1951, but in 1956 he replaced Howan as *Bandstand* host. It became *American Bandstand* when ABC networked the show in August 1957. The format of the show involved especially selected teenagers dancing while the artists performed their records. They not only had to be excellent dancers, but also would have to look and dress just so. For many years *Bandstand* was strictly white teenager dancers and audiences, although Clark gradually introduced a total racial mix.

He hugely admired Jackie and vividly recalls their long involvement: "The first time I ever heard a Jackie Wilson record was in 1957 and that was 'Reet Petite', and both that and 'To Be Loved' were written by my friend Berry Gordy. We played him on *American Bandstand*. He was an extraordinary performer. I've always said he was the most exhilarating performer I ever saw."

On Jackie's first appearance in 1959 he performed 'Lonely Teardrops'. The unwieldy television cameras didn't allow him to give full rein to his performance, as at his concerts, so it was a watered down version the huge audience witnessed, although his majestic voice was its usual best. Over the years Jackie appeared on the show seven times, doing two songs each time. They are amongst the best visual records remaining of his smooth stage routine.

Roquel Davis recalls how vital the *Bandstand* appearance was to gain exposure to white audiences. "If it was not for Dick Clark, Jackie may not have been played on Detroit radio," he says. In any case, Jackie's next few years were his peak, with non-stop touring and numerous single and album releases. From 1958 through 1961 he had seventeen Top Forty hits, out of the twenty-four for his entire career. The money was pouring in for Jackie, Tarnopol and the others controlling them.

Influential Philadelphia DJ, Jerry Blavat ("The Geator"), while still young, had been road manager for Danny And The Juniors. The group had enjoyed enormous success, culminating with their smash hit, 'At The Hop', which was Number One on the charts for seven weeks in 1957. Blavat was a champion dancer and this led him to a professional role on *American Bandstand*, where he got to see Jackie first hand. In his words, "I was also one of the original dancers of Danny And The Juniors in 1954. I go back from the very beginning of rock 'n' roll. Without a doubt, there are certain performers, that had they been alive today, they'd be gigantic superstars; Bobby Darin, Jackie Wilson, Sam Cooke, Dinah Washington."

Following the show Jackie's first album, *He's So Fine*, comprising eight Milton De Lugg produced tracks and two from the first Jacobs session, was released. Jackie was now hot property and through 1958 there were four single releases including the song that would be his signature tune, 'Lonely Teardrops'. It achieved Number One on the R&B charts for seven weeks, even gaining Number Seven spot on the Pop charts, his first Top Ten hit and yet another Davis/Gordy tune.

Jacobs explained to *Musician* magazine how the session went: "Nat told me that in the future I would be Jackie's sole arranger, and that he and I would co-produce on the sessions. He handed me a lead sheet for another Berry Gordy composition, 'Lonely Teardrops', and asked me to call Gordy in Detroit to discuss the arrangement. This would be the first of many phone calls over the years, but this time I had some questions. The chord progression of 'Lonely Teardrops' struck me as being a little unusual and I asked Gordy if it was correct. He assured me that it was and we went on to discuss the arrangement in highly technical terms. Not only was Gordy a budding populist genius in terms of knowing the teen market, he was a brilliant and knowledgeable music theorist. The phone conversation ended with me inviting Gordy to New York for the 'Lonely Teardrops' session."

Davis and Gordy supervised the session, meaning they did everything from rehearsing Jackie to organising arrangements. They even helped produce. The resulting *Lonely Teardrops* album, Jackie's second, included five Davis/Gordy compositions. This time, probably to ensure a more commercial product, no string backing was used and a reduced brass accompaniment. Jackie's uninhibited shouting style was given full rein.

One highlight of the album is 'Singing A Song', which credits "J Wilson, E Wilson and F Wilson" as the songwriting team. E Wilson is Eliza Mae, Jackie's mother, while F Wilson is Freda, his wife. *Lonely Teardrops* is believed to have sold more than one million copies, but Brunswick, like Motown later on, was not a member of the Record Industry Association of America (RIAA), so sales figures were not audited and they may well have been overstated. The common practice then was for the record company to provide the gold disc representing sales exceeding one million. In other instances record sales were understated in order to defraud the artist.

Jacobs said in *Musician*: "It was the flip side of 'Lonely Teardrops' that really caused problems. Bob Thiele had left the company to become the head of A&R at Dot Records. The new head of A&R at Coral/Brunswick, Paul Cohen, came from the country department at Decca. To put it charitably, Cohen and Tarnopol hated each other with a passion. Cohen always wanted one of his, or one of his friends', songs on every session and Tarnopol objected vehemently. Cohen won the battle, if not the war, by issuing Nat a simple ultimatum: unless the flip of 'Lonely Teardrops' was an old ballad called 'In The Blue Of Evening', there'd be no session. Nat was furious and came up with an ingenious sabotage scheme. He told me to deliberately write the arrangement in the wrong key for Jackie. That way, 'In The Blue Of Evening' would get so screwed up that we could pull one of Jackie's older sides for the flip. The scheme would've worked had it not been for Jackie. I wrote the arrangement in what I thought was an impossible key, Jackie, unaware of the subterfuge, took the arrangement and – without breaking a quaver – turned out such a beautiful performance that we were forced to use 'In The Blue Of Evening'. His rendition of this smouldering chestnut of a tune was the first clue we had to the incredible versatility of his singing."

Tarnopol, too, was generally anxious to have one of his friends' tunes on an album or single B-side, because songwriters' royalties were split evenly between A- and B-sides, or between the tracks on an album.

Davis explained that 'Lonely Teardrops' came out different to how it was envisioned: "It was originally a blues ballad, and because of the cha-cha dance at the time, it inspired the rhythm to be changed. That was the one thing we didn't do."

Jackie's version of the recording of 'Lonely Teardrops' came in his Norman Nite radio interview: "It's an okay story, but a good one. It was supposed to be a ballad – a blues ballad. It was written also by Berry Gordy Jnr, and Nat and I flew in [to Detroit] from New York. We heard the song, liked it, and took it back to New York. And then we did record it as a blues ballad, but we didn't like it. So then we decided to play with the guitar a little bit and we had a great arranger at the time, Dick Jacobs. And we had him finagle with it a little bit and we played and we got a good tempo going and it was like a chalypso [a cross between calypso and cha-cha] which at the time was very popular. And we took it and we liked it. We brought it back and gave it to the disc jockey; it was hot off the press and we told him to play it. So they put the record on and Berry was there waiting patiently and everybody was just waiting. And they put it on and Berry said, 'Oh, my God, you've ruined my song. What have you done to it?' And tears came out of his eyes."

'Lonely Teardrops' became one of Jackie's best sellers. On his *Spotlight On Jackie Wilson* album in 1965, Jackie did sing it the way it was intended. It's glorious, but with not the same chart appeal as the chalypso version.

In February 1959, when *Lonely Teardrops* was released, Jackie sent a touching telegram to Freda in Highland Park from New York. It read, "DEAREST FRIEDA EACH TIME I LOVE YOU MORE AND MORE THAT'S WHY I LOVE YOU SO = SONNY XX". It's partly in code, but easily deciphered by Freda. 'Each Time (I Love You More)' and 'That's Why (I Love You So)' were two of the songs from the LP.

Another song on the second album, 'The Joke', was written by Janie Bradford. In 1959 Janie co-wrote the enormous hit 'Money (That's What I Want)' with Berry Gordy and went on to have a successful songwriting career with Motown. Her involvement with both Jackie and Gordy is a fascinating one. In her words: "My sister, Clea Bradford, is a singer and she and Jackie used to work the local circuit, the Fox Club and the Flame Show Bar in Detroit. Jackie was a neighbour and lived right down the street. He would often come over and fall down on the floor and spend the night there. Naturally, when he got his first hit record, 'Reet Petite' in 1957, he came and told my sister he wanted her to come over and catch his act and hear his new hit. At the time I was only fourteen, but I was five foot eight, so I dressed up in my sister's clothes so that I would look older and I went on down to the club with her. Jackie had told me, 'If you come I want you to meet my songwriter.' You have to understand by Jackie being a family friend he was not a star in my mind, just someone with a hit record. This writer person who wrote the hit record, that was a star. I couldn't wait to meet Berry Gordy, but I didn't know what I was thinking, I didn't see no halo, no angel rings or anything. I was so disappointed and being such a brash kid at fourteen, I said, 'If you can write a hit, I can too.' So he took that to mean I had some songs.

"A few weeks later Berry came by to see some of my songs and listen to them. I didn't have any, but, being a quick thinker, I went out the back and got my book of poems. I had always written poems for the school bulletin board and everything. And I got this big notebook of poems and I said, 'Here are my songs.' And so he looked at some of them and took a couple and, to make a long story short, in a couple of months I had two songs out on the *Lonely Teardrops* album." Apart from 'The Joke', she is too modest to explain which of the other songs she was involved with. But Bradford goes on: "After that he sat me down and taught me how to take the portrait out and put more of the lyrics in, that was my big introduction to Mr Gordy. Mr Gordy was the star and Jackie was just a friend.

"I wasn't old enough to go to the Flame. Gordy would come to my house and get the lyrics and he'd put the melody to it. After that his sister, Loucye Wakefield, joined and we started writing in the basement. I used to go over to Nat Tarnopol's office, where he and Jackie worked. I didn't have any reason to deal with Nat. He seemed okay to me, but I was only fourteen. Jackie and I remained friends. He would always come back and say 'hello', whatever.

"Before Jackie became a star he could have been a comedian or whatever. He was charming, witty...just someone nice to be around all the time. That's if he liked you and if you were a friend of his. He was a charmer with the ladies. Jackie was such a lovable person. He was definitely a character. Yes, I was a big fan. The way he could get down on the floor and do the splits. I still think he's the most amazing performer. I've never seen anyone to compete with him. Even though I love Michael Jackson, he still doesn't quite have the energy that Jackie had. Jackie was on fire, dynamite. Most other singers can only point to the 'bird note.' Jackie could hit the 'bird note' any time he wanted." In Jackie's case the 'bird note' was high C, extremely high note for a male.

In 1959 Berry Gordy's brother-in-law, George Edwards, was standing for re-election in the Michigan State Legislature. He needed a campaign song and so Davis and Gordy wrote 'Let George Do It', which Jackie sang. It was a catchy rock 'n' roll number which became a minor hit in Detroit. Some copies of the disc can still be found today, however they are now worth a few hundred dollars apiece. Unfortunately, it wasn't enough to have Edwards re-elected. Gordy later related the episode: "Jackie thought it was a commercial song. He didn't know, he was just singing it. So they made it and it was on jukeboxes and all over town. People were dancing to it, they liked the beat."

Driving from Detroit to New York for a session one time, Roquel Davis recalls, they all almost lost their lives. It would have been a tragedy for the music industry. Jackie's friend, Johnny Jones, was driving Jackie's bronze El Dorado Cadillac and in the car were Gordy, Davis and Jackie. As usual JJ was driving too fast and the roads were icy. "Johnny loved to speed – we were all sleeping in the back, it was winter, snow and ice everywhere. Jackie would wake up and swear and say Johnny was going to get us all killed. Then we'd doze off again. Johnny lost control of the car and hit the centre guard rail and span out of control into the path of a semi-trailer in the right hand lane. The truck driver barely missed us.

Jackie wanted to kill Johnny, but the car wasn't badly damaged. When we took off the truck driver had stopped and was standing outside his truck...he was angry and frightened."

1959 was an excellent year for Jackie and another Davis/Gordy tune. 'That's Why (I Love You So)', reached Number Two on the R&B chart and Number Thirteen on the Pop. This was followed by 'I'll Be Satisfied' (Number Six R&B, Number Twenty Pop). Jackie's third hit for the year was his own composition and the song he'd sung in Alan Freed's rock movie *Go Johnny Go*, 'You'd Better Know It' (Number One R&B, Number Thirty-Seven Pop).

Unrelated to Jackie writing his own material, there was also growing resentment between Tarnopol and his crack songwriting team of Davis and Gordy. It stemmed from a number of differences, but mainly because they felt Tarnopol was under paying them. Their belief is well borne out, because as well as the initial writing, the duo worked hard on the production side, as Davis explains: "I was very impressed with Dick Jacobs; he wrote out a lead sheet faster than anyone I've ever seen before. We could stand up and sing a melody for him and before we finished the song he had it completely written. Berry and I were flabbergasted with his technical music ability as an arranger.

"Jacobs was the producer, but one might argue who the producer really was. It depends on what you think the role of the producer really was. I could say, Berry could say, Jackie could say, 'We are the producers.' We could say it collectively, we could say it separately. I don't believe Dick Jacobs could say he was the producer. He could say he was the arranger and when it got to the studio the instructions came from other people. What was right, what should be changed, and when the tempo was right. In the background, although we were songwriters, most people took their instructions from Berry and myself. I say to a lot of people, we were the producers in the sense of making sure that the song kept its integrity as it was intended, as deemed by us.

"Most of the time a tape was given to Dick Jacobs of the song already demoed. He would take it from that, score it, just in the same format it was given to him. Just try to capture what was there; what was there was generally what we felt. He would dress it up with horns, brass, strings to his style and try to recapture the rhythm that was given to him. It never came off as funky as it was originally, but it was different and so big that I was flabbergasted. Really the only time I saw Jacobs was during the sessions. Berry and I were not just writers. We wrote, arranged and produced. We did the whole bit; rehearsed Jackie to learn the songs in the first place, we played a major role as producers, and we worked the songs out with Jackie.

"This music was a little different for Dick Jacobs. There were a lot of questions as to whether he should be doing the arrangement at all. The first time I heard 'Reet Petite' I didn't like it at all, because it had more big band and brass horn treatment than I every imagined – or Berry. We viewed it a lot simpler, predominantly rhythm, with Jackie being featured. Dick, of course, did this big horn arrangement, which didn't bother Jackie because there was no way of overpowering him."

Despite all their involvement in Jackie's success, Tarnopol would not consider paying Davis and Gordy for their production contribution. Davis says the other dispute with Tarnopol involved the B-sides. "He wouldn't put our songs on the B-side. Berry and I had separate meetings with Nat and we came away with the same conclusion. We told him, 'Screw you, too.'" Davis says Tarnopol insisted on putting his friends' tracks on the B-side so that they would end up with fifty per cent of the writers' royalties. Tarnopol wasn't alone in this practice.

The second half of 1959 saw the rift between Davis/Gordy and Tarnopol lead to the final separation. As Davis told *Goldmine* magazine writer Robert Pruter: "We rehearsed Jackie and wrote his arrangements. Dick Jacobs did the arrangements on the New York sessions, but they were based on our demos. I was at most of the sessions and Berry was there for some and we had a great deal of input in them."

In any case, Tarnopol didn't think he needed this successful song writing team and they sure enough didn't need him. Davis was disappointed that Jackie didn't exert more influence on their behalf with Tarnopol to help them get a better deal. They were, after all, long time friends. Regardless, Davis and Gordy both went on to very productive and rewarding careers, Davis with Chess Records in Chicago and Gordy to establish his Motown label.

"If not for Nat Tarnopol, Motown would not have been given birth," Davis opines. "If he hadn't treated Berry and I like he did, Motown wouldn't have happened. We were used and misused and did not get paid for our production work. He wanted to put his name on our songs. We said, 'To hell with that.' Nat didn't get away with putting his name on our songs." Other songwriters were not as fortunate and either

Tarnopol's or his friends and relatives names are misleadingly listed as songwriter.

The fact that Jackie was instrumental in the foundation of the Motown recording empire is often overlooked. His hits provided part of the financial capital that such an enterprise required. Gordy's first wife, Thelma ("Peaches"), also contributed along with an eight hundred dollar loan from the Gordy family. But it was Tarnopol's perceived under-payment that finally caused Gordy to take the enormous gamble that was Motown. Motown pioneer singer Gino Parks explained: "It's one of those things. If Berry had not gone to New York to try to get his money from Nat, Motown never would have happened. He never would have formed his own record company. He should thank Jackie for that."

On a happier note, Davis says of Jackie: "He had a gold name bracelet made for me and Berry. A sort of 'thank you'. Jackie spent his money like it was all going to last forever. Of course, he didn't get nearly like he should have gotten over the later years. He had everything he wanted; he just wanted to be performing and singing, fancy clothes, fancy jewellery, a big car."

Jack "The Rapper" Gibson was an influential black DJ who would later take up an offer by Gordy to be the first national promotions manager for Motown. He confirms: "There wouldn't have been no Motown if Nat Tarnopol would have given Berry what he wanted. He went to Nat and said, 'Can I get some points on Jackie?' Nat said, 'Get points? You're just a song-ass writer. Just write the goddamn songs and don't worry about the points.' So Berry said, 'Fuck you,' and he went and started his own recording company."

Many have surmised what would have happened if only Jackie had gone to Motown, but that is pure conjecture and the fact is he was already tightly bound in with Brunswick. Rightly or wrongly Jackie believed he had a half share of the Brunswick label, along with Nat Tarnopol. No documents have ever proven that to be so: once again, Jackie proved financially naive.

One of the clever things the more astute Gordy did when he formed his organisation was to sponsor the annual convention in Detroit of the National Association of Radio Announcers (NARA), which was comprised of black disc jockeys. Mable John, one of the first artists to record for Gordy explains, "At the first black disc jockey convention, the jocks on the east coast decided they'd organise one. Berry Gordy decided he would sponsor it in Detroit, so we were at the Lee's Club Sensation where they held it. I made up the sandwiches and the punch. The disc jockeys got together and decided they were going to break a particular artist. So if a record was breaking in Detroit and a DJ in Cleveland didn't have it, he would get on the phone, talk with each other and decide to break the record." Gordy had quickly realised that to sell records the first thing required, after producing a reasonable recording, was national airplay – exposure.

Early in 1960 Jackie's highest charting record, 'Night', was released. It reached a credible Number Four on the Pop charts and Number Three on the black R&B charts. 'Night' is an almost operatic ballad set to the melody of 'My Heart At Thy Sweet Voice' taken from the Camille Saint-Saens opera *Samson And Delilah*.

The flip side was a bluesy song written by Alonzo Tucker, although not credited to him, called 'Doggin' Around'. The songwriter is listed as Lena Agree, Nat Tarnopol's aunt. It charted very well, also and achieved Number One on the R&B charts and Number Fifteen on the Pop.

Latter day writers, such as black music writer Nelson George, have severely criticised the Dick Jacobs big band accompaniments and white backing singers on Jackie's early recordings. In his book, *The Death Of Rhythm And Blues*, Nelson has this to say:

> Even in the songs that made his legend – 'Reet Petite', 'Lonely Teardrops', 'That Is Why' and 'A Woman, A Lover, A Friend' – the production was laden with white sounding backing voices, too many strings, and a general emptiness at enhancing Wilson's pleading style. His musical masters may have understood 'Night', an over-ripe, completely schlock ballad that received the kind of lumbering production it deserved. But Tarnopol and company could turn the frisky, light hearted shuffles he recorded, like 'Lonely Teardrops', into a white bread sandwich. Anyone making a claim for Wilson's greatness must ignore, or at least explain, production that drags down his hits. The fact is Brunswick only sporadically sought out writers and producers who could truly showcase Wilson's talent. Wilson spent the 1960s wading through crap like 'Danny Boy', and he only rarely ascended to something as

sublime as 'Higher And Higher', always without any coherent direction.

Happily for George, he was able to say this from the safety of thirty years of twenty/twenty hindsight. Both 'Danny Boy' and 'Higher And Higher' *were* "Jackie's style". George is apparently ignorant of the fact that 'Danny Boy' was Jackie's all time favourite song. Jackie wasn't singing only the material that George liked, nor was he recording what may have been the narrow fashion of the moment. Jackie was happy with the material Tarnopol and Jacobs had him sing, and the orchestral backing. Jackie was too talented to be doing James Brown screamers.

Dick Jacobs, again in *Musician* magazine, remarked on the choice of material Tarnopol selected for Jackie: "With 'Lonely Teardrops' demolishing the charts, Jackie became a one man hit factory with 'That's Why (I Love You So)', 'I'll Be Satisfied', 'Talk That Talk', 'A Woman, A Lover, A Friend', and on and on. But somewhere in his heart Jackie Wilson really wanted to be taken seriously as a ballad singer. Like Johnny Ace before him, Jackie wanted to be the Black Sinatra, a Mario Lanza of soul. And he sure had the pipes to deliver any kind of record he wanted to. We got a big orchestra with lots of swelling strings and Hollywood heavenly white voices and I wrote this lush lavish arrangement which critics to this day claim was too powerful for Jackie's voice. What the critics don't realise is that it was impossible to overpower Jackie Wilson's voice; you couldn't do it with a chorus line of Sherman tanks. Besides, that wasn't the point. This was the sound Jackie wanted and this is the sound I gave him. But what the hell, the record went through the roof and into the hearts of Jackie's fans, which is where the sound really mattered."

Tarnopol provided other opera based tunes for Jackie, and although they were rarely commercial enough for the buyers of pop records, they enabled Jackie to fully demonstrate his majestic vocal skills. In September 1960 'Alone At Last', with a melody based on Tchaikovsky's 'Piano Concerto Number One In B Flat', was released. It charted well; Number Eight Pop and Number Twenty R&B. 'My Empty Arms', based on 'On The Motley' from the opera *I Pagliacci* was released in December 1960. In 1962 he recorded 'My Eager Heart', the melody of which was taken from a Wagner opera and in 1966 his version of 'Be My

Love' was released as a single (it was never on an album). Mario Lanza recorded it previously in 1949.

Detroit nurtured many talented songwriters during the 1950s and 1960s. Two close friends, Alonzo Tucker and William Weatherspoon, knew Jackie from the earliest days of his career. Both started out with singing groups, Tucker with The Royals and Weatherspoon with The Tornadoes and together they wrote 'Why Can't You Be Mine' and 'As Long As I Live', both released on Jackie's first album. On the same album 'It's Too Bad We Had To Say Goodbye' is believed to have been written by the pair, although their names don't appear on it.

Charles Sutton previously of The Royals knew Tucker well and, like everyone else, liked him. "Those were lean days for Alonzo, particularly in Detroit. So they sent for him to come to New York and have him fool around with Jackie. He was paid a minimum amount. He was Jackie's chauffeur but also wrote tunes for him." Many of Jackie's recordings that credit the songwriter as J Wilson, J Roberts, N Tarnopol, Lena Agree, were in fact Tucker's compositions.

Tucker didn't fare well at all says Jimmy Smith, who became Jackie's touring drummer for ten years: "Alonzo got messed around. He only got a free place to sleep." Tarnopol supplied him a house, which his family was evicted from when Tucker died in 1977. As one friend of Jackie's, Simon Rutberg, remarked, "Alonzo was given chump change."

Tucker was not the only person to struggle. Although almost without exception women found his mischievous smile irresistible, there was one incident in 1960 that was to temporarily dent Jackie's rather large ego. At the time he was playing at the Capital Theatre in Detroit. Raynoma Liles, who later became Berry Gordy's second wife, had an attractive, white friend named Judy Robinson who was being dated by Al Abrams. Abrams picks up the story: "At the time Berry was driving us there [to see Jackie's performance] and at the time he had a lot of difficulty driving. He'd get us on and off freeway exit ramps without knowing he was in the exit lane. Anyway, we got to the theatre and Jackie was his usual self and walked up to Judy Robinson and gave her a hug and a kiss...not on the lips, but the cheek. She got really angry about it and came over to Berry and demanded, 'Tell him to never do that again and make him say he's sorry.' Jackie was totally taken aback. She was probably the first woman who complained."

Robinson, due to her friendship with Raynoma, ended up working in Motown's office, but not without some drama. "Eventually I hired her to work in the office," says Abrams who went on to head Motown's publicity department. "One time she was going through the drawers and she found a major cheque for ten to fifteen thousand dollars in royalties made out to Billy Davis [not Roquel Davis, but another friend of Gordy's], that Billy had never cashed. She absconded with it. We heard about it when she was trying to cash it at the banks. I had to fire her and put her out of my life as well." Doubtless Jackie had a chuckle about this when he was informed.

Abrams recalls: "Jackie would always pull women out of the audience. I remember he told me he always chose ugly women out of the audience to kiss. He said those were the ones who'd remember it most.

Adams was to work the management team. "At one point, when I came into it," he recalls, "I tried to pattern myself on Tarnopol, which was kind of a disaster. At one point Jackie and Berry said to try to be myself. I used to dress fairly gaudily and then Berry used to give me his clothes so I wouldn't look so darned awful. At that point we used to wear about the same size. I used to wind up with the younger sisters that Nat would date. Nat used to have a pretty heavy line he'd lay on them, too. Album covers. He'd say, 'I'll get your picture on Jackie's next album.'" Abrams went on, "I did like Nat, because at that time he used to go out of his way to be nice to me. At this time I'm eighteen years old and he was somewhat older than me. He was generally not well known for this. He helped ease me into a scene where we were white working with black artists and entertainers."

Given his colleagues, Jackie also began taking on Jewish mannerisms, such as referring to people he met by the term "Booby", which he would use in a fast, clipped manner. It is a shortening of the Yiddish word "boobela", which is a pet name of affection. The expression must have been picked up from Tarnopol. Jackie also took to wearing a mazuza (a small container which contained a Jewish prayer or Ten Commandments) and a gold Star Of David (Seal Of Solomon) given to him by Nat. Jackie claimed to be Jewish and said he was encouraged in this conversion by Sammy Davis Jnr. However there is no doubt he, at that time, greatly admired Tarnopol and was therefore greatly influenced by discussions with him.

Jackie's ability to look out for his friends is demonstrated in a small incident that had a huge bearing on the careers of The Contours. Sylvester Potts and Joe Billingslea, members of the group, describe what happened: "In 1959 we went down for an audition with Berry Gordy. He wasn't very satisfied and advised us to come back in a year's time. Hubert Johnson was one of the original group, he suggested we go and visit his cousin, Jackie. None of us had any idea he was related to Jackie Wilson. He'd never mentioned it. We got in the car and drove over to Jackie's house on Cottage Grove – we had nothing to lose. We met his mother and found out Jackie was Hubert's cousin. Jackie came down and we were formally introduced to him. He asked what was the problem. We explained about the audition and what Berry had said."

Jackie asked them to perform the same three songs, which they did a cappella. "He said, 'Sounds pretty good, man. Go back downstairs and I'll be down in a few minutes.' So we went downstairs. We were glad that he liked it. His mother provided some soft drinks and we was there about an hour. I was getting impatient. I said, 'This cat don't like us; he's just got us sitting around for nothing, let's go.' Hubert said, 'We're not going, he's coming back.' I said, 'If he didn't come in about five minutes, I'm going.' Jackie came down and said, 'Come back upstairs.' We went back upstairs. He was on the phone to Berry, blah, blah, blah, he hung up and said, 'Go back over, Berry wants to see you.' So we drove back over there – right down to Motown. We sang the same three songs for Berry and he said, 'You're great,' and we signed a contract."

The Contours went on to record some big hits for Motown starting with 'Do You Love Me' in 1962, which reached Number Three on the Pop chart, ironically, one spot higher than Jackie ever achieved. A sad footnote to The Contours story is that in 1980 Jackie's cousin, Hubert Johnson, committed suicide. "Singing was all he ever knew, and when we ceased to sing he lost the desire to live. He contemplated it and talked about it many times; he finally succeeded," reports Potts. The group had disbanded and he felt there was nothing left to live for. He left a wife and three children.

While Jackie was charting well around the world, he was travelling all around the country on what was referred to as the "Chitlin' Circuit". This was the term used for the live entertainment venues that served the Afro-American community. Chitterlings is a popular meal of Afro-Americans, particularly in the south, which consists of pigs' intestines. The circuit was gruelling and involved often doing one or two nighters and everyone travelling by either car or bus, loaded down with instruments and sound equipment. Patrons generally paid two or three dollars admittance and generally got to see ten or so major acts.

Freda was annoyed that, being at home she rarely saw her husband. "The first time he took me on the road," Freda recalls, "he said, 'Come on, Mrs Wilson, you've been wanting to go on the road. Get your rags together.' He told me to bring mostly slacks." She was in for a few shocks; it wasn't quite the fun she'd imagined. "He had to haul that little thing up the back [referring to the small box trailer they towed behind the limo which contained all their baggage, instruments and sound equipment]. He told me to stretch my legs. He'd stretch out and lay his head on my lap. You had to be in the next place the next night and they had to get there as fast as possible. He didn't even have a chance to take a shower. If he had time he'd stop at a motel just so he could have a shower and get dressed. He didn't have time to lie down. He was used to travelling. You do adjust to the inconvenience, but it ain't fun and I was ready to come back home."

Freda was fast learning not only that life on the road was tough, but being cooped up with the same people day and night further tested the strongest friendship. Jackie had the added pressure of the adoring fans, fanatical females and sharp talking hucksters who always had an angle. He had a passion for dogs and insisted on travelling with them, despite the inconvenience this must have caused. At that time it was his little Chihuahua, Poochie.

Freda now witnessed Jackie performing, and the hysteria that was created. She says: "They took off their panties and threw them on stage. I thought it was bad enough with 'Mr B' [Billy Eckstine, who also caused the same phenomenon]. 'This Guy's In Love With You' was always one of my favourites.

"Jack'd look at me when he sung it, and he'd look at someone else and they'd feel the same way. He did a lot of stuff that Sinatra did. He would listen to Frank Sinatra and then say, 'I don't like it like that.' He'd get it his way. And when he'd wink and say, 'Come on...'" Freda began to appreciate the demanding life Jackie lived: "All those people, and those lights up there are so hot. People think it's so easy."

She remembers one very embarrassing performance where his pants split right down the back. "Tight! I don't know how he got into them. It's just as well he was wearing those jockey shorts, that's all I can say." The audiences would sometimes try to get their hands on him and take a small souvenir, too. "They'd try to get his ring when he dropped his hand, or his shoes when he laid down. He was the only person I know who wore a suit all the time. That's why, when he got home and changed, he was always wearing jeans and a T-shirt."

Jackie was the consummate performer and, like an athlete prior to an event, he would never eat prior to a performance. He did, however, enjoy his food although witnesses were often appalled at his table manners and "wolfing" of his meals. "He never ate until everything was over, says Freda. "He'd get it all in one sitting. He'd start with something light first. He liked BBQ ribs, black eyed peas, greens, ham hocks and hot water corn. He liked hamburger. He liked gravy."

Throughout his entire career he would run the scales – limbering up – for around one hour prior to a performance. This would take place while taking those long baths he enjoyed so much. Says Freda: "Jackie would sing with a finger in his ear; singers can hear better that way. He would practise the scales. He listened a lot to himself [listening to records at home], listening for mistakes. He played Jackie Wilson music to see if it sounded the same."

Another concert ritual was that he did his own make-up, begun after an unfortunate incident when he allowed someone else to do it and he appeared "looking like a ghost". Freda: "He did his own make-up all the time. He used bronze powder and did his own eyes."

He would also drink a whisky before he went on stage, possibly to calm his nerves. "He had a Scotch on the rocks before he went on, but he never looked like he had a hangover," his wife remembers.

Hangovers would come later on because around Jackie there was always plenty of partying, usually of the sort that went on all night long or sometimes for days. Freda drank but did not experiment with drugs, making her the distinct minority. One such occasion they were partying with The Four Tops and either the pot was laced with something more potent, or they weren't used to indulging. In any case says Freda, "JJ had got some pot and we laughed. They were all high, but then they got deathly ill; they were all sick.

"When they'd go to these entertainment parties – they had cocaine there; marijuana, cocaine piles where you could help yourself. They had this little cigarette machine, an automatic thing, for marijuana. I used to go with Jack. New York was notorious for those parties." Freda just didn't fit in. She says they would ask, "'What does she [Freda] do? What does she want?' I'd say, 'No, I don't want to eat or drink,' – I was scared to drink any pop, because I was scared they might put something in. I'd sit for two or three days."

When Jackie performed in Detroit it provided family members the opportunity to see him and for him to return home after the show. Freda remembers one such show early in his career when he wasn't heading the bill: "We went down to see the show and Dinah Washington was the star. She looked around, like she always does, checking the crowd out. We were sitting right in front. Everyone was looking around thinking what's she looking at, a bird or something? I knew it was Mama's hat, but didn't want to say anything. She [Washington] said, 'Somebody get it out of here. Better yet, kill it!' Then my mother-in-law said, 'Look lady, I did not come here to see you sing. I come to see my son.' Mama loved Jackie. You say something about her, or him, you'd be looking for trouble…I mean, he could do no wrong." It worked both ways, of course. Since Jackie got much of his innate vocal talent from his mother it wasn't unusual for him to call her up on stage with him. Says Freda, "His mother could sing. She sang with him on stage when he was in Detroit. Joyce [his half-sister] can also sing, but she never wanted to sing professionally."

When Jackie returned home to perform at some of the clubs where he started out it could be a boisterous event. "We'd be in the night club in Detroit," Freda explains. "He'd be singing his heart out. [Cousin] Beccy would be with us, and Joyce when she got older. [Step-father] Johnny wouldn't sit with us, he thought we was all crazy. We'd be shaking and shouting and banging the beer bottles hard on the table. Screaming and howling and carrying on. Jack said, 'You all didn't have to go to that extreme.' But it did make him feel better."

There were times, however, when she saw how overwhelmed Jackie became by it all. His lifestyle was physically and mentally draining. "He used to like to go in his room for hours," said Freda. "He liked his silence; or he'd pretend he was asleep. Then he'd tell Frazier to put the people out. And I'd know to sit there and he was on our marriage licence. I always took a back seat, especially in public. If I didn't like something he did, I waited until later. I didn't want him to be embarrassed in public." She knew that, as his wife, it was her duty to remain in the background. Jackie was rather chauvinistic when it came to family matters.

CHAPTER FOUR

You'd Better Know It

Timing is an important element in anyone's career, and it was with Jackie's. Luckily, studio recording and playback technology were improving rapidly. In 1952, when he first recorded, a recording studio was a sound-proofed office or storage area which was cleared while recording was in progress. Enough room for the band and their equipment was all that was needed, with a microphone in the middle to catch the voice of the singer and the band. The recording system was single track: today it's likely to be mixed from a forty-eight track machine, and in all likelihood the orchestra and artist never set eyes on one another.

Columbia Records, in 1948, introduced the long playing record microgroove (LP) which ran at thirty-three-and-a-third rpm instead of seventy-eight rpm. This meant much more music could be packed onto a similar sized product; a major innovation. Sound quality, too, was improved, although initially only classical music was available on the LP. Then in 1951 another major record company, RCA, introduced an equally important product, the small, plastic forty-five rpm single. Naturally, it took a while to supplant the seventy-eight, but it did. Eventually stereophonic recording quickly replaced the old mono recordings.

Of equal importance to Jackie's exposure to the world was "crossover", meaning in the case of R&B music, a black charting song gaining acceptance by the larger and wealthier white audience. The song literally crosses over from the R&B to Pop charts. The R&B charts were no more than a sample survey taken in selected record stores in predominantly black neighbourhoods, while the Pop charts were based on surveys from white neighbourhoods. They were not necessarily accurate as they were often manipulated by record companies trying to gain an edge over their competitors.

Back in the early 1950s, when Jackie started out, the music most people listened to on their radios and record players was sung by Guy Mitchell, Frank Sinatra, Tony Bennett, Perry Como, Vic Damone, Dinah Shore, Jo Stafford, Rosemary Clooney, Kay Starr, Patti Page and Georgia Gibbs. But something big was beginning and all this was about to change. The name coined was rock 'n' roll. It had been there all along, but was only played by blacks and called rhythm and blues, more generally known as "race music". White radio stations wouldn't play it, they believed that to do so was to commit ratings suicide. In 1953 Patti Page's 'How Much Is That Doggie In The Window' stayed at Number One for eight weeks! That's what was considered suitable white fare.

Leaving aside the question of which was the first rock 'n' roll record, it should suffice to say it was a rhythm and blues song which, in turn, evolved from the blues. The Platters, with 'The Great Pretender', are generally considered to have had the first crossover hit in 1955. That year Chuck Berry (a blues artist) and Fats Domino also burst forth. The following year saw Little Richard and the music world was never the same. "The cat was out of the bag" – and the cat was black.

It is now known and accepted that Elvis Presley was totally influenced by R&B and gospel. He took it, mixed it with a few parts country (or hillbilly as it was derogatively referred to) and what he was left with was rock 'n' roll. He first came to the attention of the world early in 1956, at the same time that Jackie, six months his senior, was in his third year with The Dominoes. Coming from racially bigoted Mississippi and Tennessee, it would not have been socially popular for him to sing this "nigger music" in such an overtly black style.

Black artists generally rate Presley very highly. Comments by Sir Mack Rice, of The Falcons, are typical: "Elvis wasn't no pushover. Elvis was good, at the time. The guy had something going. I guess you didn't recognise it then because he was singing other people's stuff that you knew and you can't beat the original. He helped us out, because if they accepted him they had to accept us. He definitely helped out."

Presley led a lot of people to black music, but in the beginning he was seen as rebellious and not a desirable role model. It took squeaky clean Pat Boone to cover songs by Presley and Little Richard to make rock 'n' roll acceptable, if not desirable, to white teenagers' parents. A friend of Jackie's, Simon Rutberg, put it this way: "Elvis really helped popularise the black artist, because before that nobody was listening to them. They say Pat Boone ripped off Little Richard. He didn't. Pat Boone never ripped off Little

Richard. The point is Little Richard sold to the people who were going to buy Little Richard, Pat Boone was going to sell to the people who don't buy Richard."

It took some time, and we are not yet fully there, but music in large part, tore down the Iron Curtain called segregation and, with it, its bastard brother, racial discrimination. If white children were grooving to Chuck Berry and Little Richard, it wasn't easy to maintain the racial divide. Of course Martin Luther King came along in the 1960s and focused world attention on the scourge, but music was a catalyst. The times were indeed a-changing.

Reacting to the shift in opinion, Tarnopol selected material and arrangements for Jackie enabling him to "crossover" to the Pop charts where most of the money was. A close friend of Tarnopol's, Bobby Schiffman, who ran the world renowned Apollo Theatre in Harlem, remembers how unusual this was. "Most black performers at that time did not concentrate on crossover," he says. "They aimed their music at the R&B market and kind of resented the success of white performers doing black music." An example of this was 'Sh-boom' by The Chords which was copied by the white Crew Cuts. The copy sold over one million, compared to one hundred and fifty thousand by The Chords, even though the latter had a four month start and was a better recording. In the opinion of Schiffman, "Sam Cooke's 'You Send Me' crossed. It was one of the first ones. Sam was extremely important, perhaps more than Jackie."

Schiffman came to know both Jackie and Sam Cooke well and says, "Jackie was trouble – he was unpredictable and thus was tough to work with. Sam was clean – a perfect role model – dependable and reliable and a pleasure to work with."

As proved with The Chords' experience, chart success was sometimes a poor measure of how good a song was. But as well as discrimination, the system of payola – whereby the distributors paid money, or in kind, to the major DJs to play particular tunes – was also well entrenched in the 1950s and 1960s. In some instances, DJs were also paid *not* to play tunes.

Effectively the charts could be manipulated, because radio stations were the arbitors of what the public listened to. Quite obviously without radio exposure, the record buying public would not be aware of the tune, so sales would be poor. This was especially the case for black artists. The more white audience would generally have no idea that the song they heard Pat Boone or The Four Lads do was actually a cover version of a probably better black recording.

Credit for enabling black music to be heard by white audiences must be given to Alan Freed. Born in Pennsylvania in 1922, Freed formed a jazz band at high school and became a DJ. At radio station WJW in Cleveland, Ohio he took the name "Moondog" and called his programme "Moondog's Rock 'N' Roll Party". He'd taken the name from a white street musician who used to sit on the street all year round with an old army blanket draped over him. He played little cymbals and things and used the name "Moondog". (Freed was later be sued by this real "Moondog" and had to desist from using the name.)

Freed also played big beat R&B music, but, as he was generally playing to a white audience, he coined the term "rock 'n' roll" to make it more acceptable. Eventually his show became syndicated throughout the USA and to Europe through Radio Luxembourg. He was to expose a huge, young and white audience to black music. He enabled black R&B artists to be heard by white audiences.

In the book *Big Beat* (Alan Freed's biography by John A Jackson), it is claimed Freed's personal relationship with Jackie dates back to his days with The Dominoes. When Jackie went solo, Freed was out there to push his records. He perhaps went a little too far with 'I'll Be Satisfied', which Jackson claims Freed played for forty-five minutes straight! Jackson also explains about the coining of the term rock 'n' roll: "Freed went to PJ Moriarty's, a Broadway restaurant, and sat down with some of the people who had welcomed him to New York; song plugger Juggy Gayles, manager Jack Hooke, Morris Levy. 'Alan was having a few drinks and bemoaning the fact that he had to come up with a new name,' Morris recalled. 'To be honest with you, I couldn't say if Alan said it or somebody else said it. But somebody said "rock and roll". Everybody just went, "Yeah. Rock and Roll." The WINS programme became "Alan Freed's Rock And Roll Show", and a musical form acquired a name. Freed set up shop in the Brill Building on Broadway.'" Better known as Tin Pan Alley, The Brill was also, of course, the office of Nat Tarnopol and his publishing company, Pearl Music.

On the topic of payola it is hard to find a more detailed account than the book *Hit Men* by Fredric Darren. He states:

> "Payola" is a word the record industry has bestowed on the
> English language. The term's familiarity has led to a common
> perception – unfortunately true – that the business is full of

sharpies and opportunists and crooks. But as crimes go, payola is no big deal if the government's enforcement effort is an indication. After Freed's commercial bribery bust in 1960 and congressional hearings on payola the same year, Congress passed a statute making payola a misdemeanour offence punishable by a maximum fine of ten thousand dollars and one year in prison. To date, no one has ever served a day in jail on payola charges. The law is hardly a strong deterrent.

In the early fifties, pop radio was dominated by crooners like Perry Como and Andy Williams. It dawned on Alan Freed that America's youth was disenfranchised by this music because it was hard to dance to. As legend has it, he dropped by a Cleveland record store and became a convert to rhythm and blues. Freed bombarded his growing white audience with the first R&B it had ever heard – LaVern Baker, Red Prysock, Big Al Sears. Freed howled while the records played, beat time on a telephone book, and provided a rapid, raspy commentary: "Anybody who says rock 'n' roll is a passing fad…has rocks in his head, dad!" He was so popular that in 1954, WINS in New York acquired Freed and his programme, *The Moondog Show*.

The Payola scandal of 1960 destroyed Freed's life. He was indicted on May 19, along with seven others, and charged with taking bribes to play records. Freed admitted he accepted a total of twenty-five hundred dollars, but said the money was a token of gratitude and did not affect airplay. He forgot to mention that the Chess brothers of Chicago let him stick his name on Chuck Berry's first hit, 'Maybellene', and that he stood to gain by playing it often. Freed paid a small fine, but his career was over. By 1965 he had drunk himself to death.

Highly influential black DJ, Jack "The Rapper" Gibson, who has enjoyed fifty years on radio, says there were sixteen highly influential black DJs throughout the USA who had a major pioneering role in the early promotion of black popular music. Gibson broadcast out of Cincinatti, while the only other survivor of the sixteen is Hal Jackson in New York.

Says Gibson, "Freed took a composite of about six of us and made it his style. That's how he got his style. I happened to be one of them."

One black promoter of records was Larry Maxwell, who would later become a promoter with Motown. Berry Gordy in his autobiography, *To Be Loved*, said that Maxwell was the best record promoter he'd ever come across. Maxwell's "secret" was that he knew the importance of the DJ in getting a record heard – *airplay!* Says Maxwell, "I crossed records over, 'cause I'd come up with Bobby Darin and had to promote right across the board. That's why I was so successful at Motown; I knew all these white guys [DJs] anyway. I knew the white jocks before I knew the black ones. Because I learned it from shooting pictures of them." Indeed that's where Maxwell got his start in the music business. He started out photographing all the musical sessions at the studios and ran across the DJs during his travels.

Of course Freed wasn't the only DJ to play R&B music to white audiences and credit must also be given to Georgie Woods in Philadelphia, Mickey Shorr ("the Alan Freed of Detroit") and, especially WLAC, broadcast out of Nashville, but with a signal, it is said, that could be heard in thirty-six states. Four DJs there, Horace "Hoss" Allan, Gene Nobels, John Richberg and Herman Grizzard, "were responsible for breaking black music into the white market. That station was more important than any place in the world. They brought black music to the attention of the whole USA," according to Hy Weiss a black music recording pioneer. Weiss claims, "Leonard Chess used to say he'll give you ten Alan Freeds for one Gene Nobel." These DJs made it possible for the world to know the magnificence of Jackie Wilson.

By 1958 Jackie was an established star and was included in the Alan Freed sponsored *Christmas Holiday Show* at Loew's State Theatre in New York. There were some other big names on the bill as well: The Everly Brothers, Chuck Berry, Bo Diddley, Eddie Cochran, Dion And The Belmonts, The Moonglows, Frankie Avalon, Jimmy Clanton, The Cadillacs, The Crests, The Royal Teens, Baby Washington and The New Tornados.

The public was now to get a taste not only of Jackie's tremendous vocal range, but to see his stage performances. He still loved to sing and it didn't matter if there were ten or ten thousand people in the audience, he'd still give a full-on performance. Always impeccably dressed, he would glide out on stage, often with a cigarette which he'd discard, and do twists and spins and the fall back splits, which he perfected, all while holding the microphone and never missing a note. His typical drawn out and impassioned song endings would have him on his knees, by this time his jacket discarded and his tie loosened, sweat pouring from him in a frenzy of emotion. He had the audience in the palm of his hand. At the end of a performance he would often launch himself headlong into the arms of hundreds of frantic fans, or lie on his back on stage, but hanging over the edge, microphone in hand.

Jackie understood that performing was acting, it was the ultimate expression of pure emotion. He gave it his all. At times fans would tear at his clothes and body, much to the consternation of his handlers. It seemed everybody, except Jackie, was in fear of him being torn apart. His loving mother, Eliza Mae, witnessed this on occasions and was heard to gasp in horror, "Oh, my boy, oh, my boy." Typically he would turn on stage and exclaim to his band, "They sure do love me, don't they!" Although Jackie lived for these performances, they were physically very demanding and he would be exhausted afterwards. It was a brave act that would follow him on stage – the audience's expectation would be just too great. The audience, too, would be drained – to see Jackie perform was to have an emotionally uplifting experience.

Jackie joined Freed's "Rock And Roll Caravan" again in 1959, performing to sell-out crowds at venues such as Brooklyn's famous Fox Theatre. Others to share billing with him were his friend Sam Cooke, Buddy Holly, Roy Hamilton, Fats Domino, Bobby Darin, LaVern Baker, Brook Benton, Ruth Brown, Frankie Avalon, Bobbie Rydell, Paul Anka, The Cadillacs and Duane Eddy. Freda vividly recalls this period of Jackie's career. "Bobby Darin would come and sit in Jack's room," she says. "All these young white boys; Bobby Rydell and Frankie Avalon would also come around. Jack went all out to help them; like Fabian, he couldn't really sing. He told them not to be shy. This is Jack, he likes people who don't come on strong. If he liked you, he liked just you; simple person that you were."

Irv Nahan was another who arranged concert tours at the time. Nahan later went on to own the Red Top/Val-ue labels and to manage the Dells, The Spaniels, Little Joe Cook, The Blue Notes and Screamin' Jay Hawkins. He says, "I got to know Jackie pretty well through the business. I go back to when he just left The Dominoes. I took him out as part of a package in the mid fifties; package shows after the various theatres. Irving Feld and I'd put the top ten on the road for thirty days. We were a part of the record deals as well. I was strictly black acts. I had Gladys Knight And The Pips for a while and The Quintones [an all-girl group]. I was part of the corporation that owned The Drifters, also I managed all the groups with Vee Jay records, all the 'bird' groups."

It was in 1957 and 1958 that Jackie was with his tours: "Roosevelt Grier was singer, MC and bouncer. He's a football player; we had no problems when he was around. When we put the shows on down south the whites had to stay in the balcony. It changed during the sixties. We had a special little book that showed the hotels they could stay at. On those top ten shows – ten top artists.

"Jackie was lucky to get three hundred dollars a week. You make money selling the shows for twenty-five hundred a night. But if a group made seven hundred and fifty a week and went to five thousand dollars a week, they still wouldn't have enough to live on. They spent everything. Jackie was one of the best. He did his shows; I can't remember him missing any shows either. He was crazy, but pretty reliable to an extent. He was one of the greats."

Saxophonist and band leader, Paul "Hucklebuck" Williams, had one of the backing bands on these tours. Most famous for writing 'The Hucklebuck', he saw Jackie's performances at close hand. "That's what you call the breeding grounds," he says, meaning that's where an artist learnt to entertain. If the audiences were not satisfied, they would make their displeasure known immediately. "Jackie was tops. Nobody could touch him. He's something else, he was *the* entertainer. Wonderful!"

Jerry Blavat witnessed the early concert performances: "I worked with Jackie as a kid on the road; I managed a group called Danny And The Juniors. I worked with Jackie with a fella by the name of Irving Feld – he was one of the first rock 'n' roll promoters, in the 1950s. It was segregated audiences when we did the road shows. These were one nighters. The black artists would stay in one hotel and we'd stay in another. This was in segregated towns. Music doesn't have a racial barrier. These stars were able to overcome the terrible prejudices that were around at the time."

The Platters were on the Feld tours with Jackie and became his friends. Said Zola Taylor, the only female member of the group, "We did one nighters with Irving Feld's tours with Jackie, twenty to thirty acts on the same show. We travelled in two bus loads. Bo Diddley, The Teen Queens, The Coasters, The Drifters, Bill Haley and The Comets, LaVern Baker – all this on one show. All you did was your hit record. We were blessed, because we had more hits." Typically Jackie would perform only three or four songs. The Platters recorded on Irving Green's Mercury label where Nat Tarnopol briefly worked prior to his taking over management of Jackie. "Irving Green at Mercury was a real sweetheart of a man. Nowadays you don't even see the heads of the record companies. I couldn't stand that man Nat Tarnopol, he was so rude to everyone. He burnt Jackie."

In 1958 Tarnopol arranged with Alan Freed for Jackie to have a one song spot in Freed's ordinary film, *Go, Johnny, Go*. The film plot, such as it is, centres around Jimmy Clanton as "Johnny Melody" a teen idol. However, being a rock 'n' roll centred story, the film did feature some considerable talent of the time; Chuck Berry, Eddie Cochran, Ritchie Valens, The Cadillacs and Harvey (Fuqua) of The Flamingos.

Jackie performs only one song, 'You'd Better Know It', and was sensational, although a tame effort compared to his live performances. The seventy-five minute film was a bomb, but it did enable fans around the world to see Jackie perform live. The movie exposure no doubt also aided his record sales, because 'You'd Better Know It' briefly held Number One spot on the R&B Charts and Number Thirty-Seven on the Pop charts.

Sometimes music writers were critical of the material Jackie performed. An example of this is Don Waller reviewing a compilation of Jackie's recordings in June 1983: "With his glass shattering falsetto, gospel drenched phrasing and his ability to juggle octaves in the space of a single syllable, Jackie Wilson was a singer whose skills bordered on the superhuman. How could such a talent fall into relative obscurity? Wilson's own versatility was partly to blame. He could – and did – sing anything, from scorching rockers ('I'll Be Satisfied') to torchy blues ('Doggin' Around'), from transcriptions of operatic arias ('Night') to supper-club standards ('Danny Boy'). Unfortunately, Wilson's producers saddled him with some of the corniest arrangements in recording history, all powder puff choruses and oceans of soapy strings. As a result, much of his work sounds horribly backdated, even by fifties standards."

Waller's opinion, if widely held, leads one to wonder how huge a star Jackie might have been had he recorded more "commercial" material and been on a bigger label such as RCA or Motown? Looking at the authoritative *Billboard Book of US Top Forty Hits 1955 To Present* by Joel Whitburn we are able to get a reasonable idea of how successful Jackie's career was (see

Appendix). It is quite apparent that Jackie's success was up there with the most popular artists and, indeed, he often achieved much more than better known singers. One can only wonder why this man is so largely forgotten or over-looked and why he was in such poor financial shape?

CHAPTER FIVE

A Woman, A Lover, A Friend

O n a cold evening in January, 1960, twenty-three-year-old Lynn
Ciccone, who lived in the smallish town of Springfield, Illinois, was
feeling miserable. She wasn't interested in rock 'n' roll, being totally into
country music, but that day something happened that altered her life
forever. Jackie Wilson. For Lynn it was "destiny". Jackie had another name
for it – kismet.

"I had two impacted wisdom teeth removed that day," she recalls. "My
mouth was bleeding and swelling so I took some pain pills, laid down and
took a nap. My jaw was out to here. When I got up I was still in pain, so I
laid down on the couch and turned on the TV. Dick Clark came on with Top
Ten of the week. The next song was introduced as 'Mr Excitement' from
Detroit. Well, he comes out. You know that wink, nobody could do it like he
did, twisting out there with one of those tight bolero outfits on. Those huge
dark eyes flashed imperiously. His smile was soul drenching. He did his just
released 'Talk That Talk'. He dashed across the floor, winking, twisting,
jumping, dancing and electrifying the audience. Before it was over I was
sitting on the floor and had forgotten all about the pain. I sank to the floor
in front of the set, hypnotised, a nameless force penetrated my body
unnoticed, changing my life forever. I don't know what happened that
night. It was like I knew this man, he was right here in the room with me.

"When Jackie came back and did 'Lonely Teardrops', it was like, 'I love
this guy, he's great. Who is he, I've got to find out?' I thought he's so
handsome, and he's black; the most beautiful black man I had ever seen.
Jackie appeared to be singing directly to me. I didn't even have any black
acquaintances, except Papa's housekeeper, Essie.

"I woke up the next day and the first thing I think of is Jackie Wilson,
so I went to the record store and bought everything they had. I got up to
the record counter and the lady said, 'You're a fan of Jackie Wilson?"

Lynn hurried home to listen to the voice of her new found idol. "I rushed into the living room and put Jackie's recordings on the turntable. As I listened to his magnificent voice, I read the album covers, over and over, but I was disappointed. There was little of a personal nature.

"I decided to write a fan letter. I told him I thought he was great, could I have an autographed picture? I wrote a very long and personal letter and included my phone number and address. I also enclosed a photo of myself. A week later I got a phone call at work. The caller said, 'Hi there, little lady. My name is Nat Tarnopol and I'm Jackie's Wilson's manager. We got your fan letter and we love it. I called to ask if you're interested in seeing Jackie perform live. He'll be in St Louis February 26 and 27. What do you think?'" Naturally, Lynn was delighted and accepted.

"Tarnopol said, 'Here's our phone number at Pearl Music. Call me back here next Monday.' This was like on a Wednesday. When I called Tarnopol said, 'I've got someone here who wants to talk to you.' It was Jackie, he said, "Hi, doll, this is Jackie Wilson. Nat says you're my biggest fan, but you don't look very big in your picture. You're a very pretty girl, and I love that hair. I won't send my picture, we are going to bring them to St Louis and I'll give them to you there. If you've got any albums, bring them down and I'll sign 'em.' I asked my friend Louise, who thought I was crazy, but, 'yes' she'd go with me.

"I had never been out of Springfield. It was about one hundred miles from St Louis. If I had to divorce my husband, whatever, I was going to go to the show. I just flat out told my husband I was going and he didn't give me any argument. He was too busy working on his car, so it suited him to have me out of the way.

"First thing I had to do was get some clothes to wear for such an important occasion. The dress had to be perfect, extraordinary. I had to dazzle Jackie. The dress I purchased was red, my best colour. It was covered, with lace, the bodice was tightly fitted, clear to the throat. I bought flowing cape and shoes to match and I had a red velvet ribbon for my hair.

"I had to call back later and Johnny Jones would tell me what to do and where to go. They were staying in the Heritage Hotel, which was in a bad part of town." When Louise and Lynn arrived in St Louis they phoned JJ at the hotel. "Oh yeah," he said, "you're the chick that sent the letter. Tell you what, be at Kiel [Auditorium, aka Kiel Opera House] at 7:30. We've got two tickets for you at the box, I'll take care of the rest." JJ informed Lynn months later when he had grown to like her, "Doll, he had already gone through half the white chicks in the country before you discovered him. Boy, you sure are dumb." But she grew to love JJ; he always treated her like a lady.

"We took a cab down to Kiel Auditorium. As we got out of the cab, the driver said, 'Are you going to be all right?' We said, 'Sure.' 'Do you want me to come back after the show?' My friend said, 'Maybe he'd better, there's something wrong. I don't see any white people going in there.' My friend had very poor eye sight and I said, 'You're blind, you can't see anyhow.' She said, 'I might be, but I'm not colour blind!' It didn't bother me, so we went in. JJ came and took us backstage. He also took my albums for Jackie to sign and brought them back out.

"Ike and Tina Turner opened the show. They were unheard of in those parts, back then. The Olympics, with their 'Western Movies' hit, were on and a local, Sugar Pie De Santo, who I'd never heard of. George Logan was the MC at the show that night. JJ took my hand and introduced me to Tina Turner, Sugar Pie De Santo and finally The Coasters.

"I knew before I turned around that Jackie was in the room. He walked up behind me and put a hand on my shoulder as I turned around. With a voice like silken oak, he said, 'Hi doll, you're much prettier than your picture.'" As Lynn rose from her chair, he added, "I didn't know I was gonna meet little Red Riding Hood." Lynn was so excited, words failed her. Jackie said, "Hey, baby, I know you can talk, I spoke to you on the phone." Finally she spoke, "I feel so foolish. I came here to impress you and now I feel so foolish." Jackie wiped the tears from her cheek with his thumb, he said, "Hey, doll, I was impressed the minute you stood up in that red dress. Come with me," he told her as he took off the cape and handed it to JJ.

She followed Jackie to his dressing room. As he changed into another suit, Lynn sat filled with questions that stuck in her throat. With a puzzled look he asked, "Why did you write that letter? How long have you been a fan?" Lynn explained, "January 3, 1960, that's the first time I ever heard of you." "Man," he said, "I've heard a lot of stories from a lot of chicks, but I've never heard anything like that. I thought you were just another chick, playing games with me."

Jackie took her hands in his and kissed her on the lips. Lynn whispered, "I know I'll never be alone with you again, so would you please do that one more time?" Said Jackie, "Yes, ma'am. I guarantee you're gonna be alone with me again. We'll have dinner after the show, okay?" As they left the dressing room Jackie turned and whispered, "I'd like to take off the red dress and see what's underneath. My imagination is going wild. Man, where did you come from?" He whispered in her ear, "I got a feeling you may have a chastity belt under that dress."

Before he left to prepare for the show he said, "Do you have a favourite recording, maybe I can work it into the show for you?" Said Lynn, "I couldn't think of a thing, so I said, 'Raindrops'. He said, 'That's Dee Clark's record, you don't know a damn thing about me.' I said to Jackie, 'I don't really know what songs you have, I'm into country and western, but I've got all your records.' He said, 'You still don't know a damn thing about me. I tell you what, by the time you leave here tonight you will!'

"When Jackie walked out on stage at the Kiel Auditorium and said, 'Hi, ya all, I'm Jackie Wilson,' pandemonium broke out. I'd just met him and I've not ever seen a performance like it! During the performance he just dived off the stage and terrified everybody. You didn't forget a performance by him – not ever.

"After the show, Jackie took me back to the dressing room with him. He rested, then showered and dressed. Now he was a whole lot different – it was like nobody was around him. He began calling me 'Little Red Riding Hood' and asked if we'd like to go to dinner. JJ always referred to me as 'Red' after that.

"After the show we went in his limousine where he held my trembling hand as he talked to the driver about dinner. After we ate we just sat in the car and he was a perfect gentleman. They stayed with us till three o'clock in the morning when the train was due to leave. When I went to get out of the car, he said, 'I'm going to give you a number at Pearl Music, Circle 61990,' and he also gave me his apartment number. He said, 'If you ever want to get hold of me, either Nat can get me or you can call the apartment.' Both were New York City numbers.

"Years later I found out Molly Byndon, the mother of Jackie's illegitimate daughter Sabrina was there, but I didn't know it at the time. Jackie lied to Molly, telling her I had a heart problem and that he was doing me a favour as a final last wish."

After this meeting they spoke on the phone several times and during each conversation Jackie told Lynn he wanted to see her again. Three months after they had first met Jackie arranged for her to fly to Chicago so they could spend a weekend together. Lynn explains, "I was so terrified of flying, I caught the train." At the same time Jackie was extremely reluctant to fly - especially after the plane crash that took Buddy Holly in 1958. Lynn: "Nothing could happen to Jackie, he was 'a big star – I have to be careful,' Jackie would say, jokingly."

Jackie had, in the mean time, been sending roses to her workplace which was causing her some embarrassment. She informed Jackie, "Everyone I work with is making jokes about me. It's very hard for me to go to work every day, but I'm not letting them drive me out. You don't know what it's like."

"Beg your pardon," he said. "You think I don't know what it's like to be ridiculed and put down. Hey baby, I can work in any big hotel in Las Vegas, but I can't eat or sleep there and I can't gamble in the casinos. I have to enter through the back door. Now, come on, I'll make it up to you. This time there won't be fifty other people around. We'll spend Saturday and Sunday together and nobody's gonna put you down, so stop being scared."

Jackie arranged for JJ to pick her up as he had a show to perform. JJ waited for her with Jackie's driver, Clarence "Pop" Watley, who was one of the kindest people Jackie had in his entourage. Watley sensed her scepticism. "Now, I'm gonna be somewhere close all the time," he said, trying to reassure her, "so you tell me if anything is wrong. Don't worry, Jack said you was scared. He'll take good care of you." "Thanks, Mr Watley, I am scared," she said. JJ went inside and came right back with Jackie. Jackie got in beside her, kissing her on the forehead.

"Hey, doll, I can't believe you're really here. You're shaking," he said as he reached to hold her hand. "I promised you a nice dinner, are you starved? Hey, mama, do I have to put a phone in your hand before you can talk? Take us to dinner, Pop, maybe the chick's too weak to talk," he joked.

He ordered dinner and drinks and asked her, "Are there any Indians in your family? Every time I wink at you, you turn all red. Pop was right – Red, that's a good name for you," he said as he bought a red rose from a vendor and handed it to her.

He went on: "I keep a small apartment here. I'm in and out of Chicago a lot. Mama stays here when she visits Aunt Belle Williams." Lynn indicated to Jackie that she'd prefer to stay in a hotel. "Okay," he said, "I don't want to scare you out of town." He got Lynn a room at the Ambassador Hotel then told her to call him if she needed anything. "I don't know what it is, but I don't want you to run away from me. I won't hurt you," he said.

Lynn closed the door behind him and sat down on the bed. It was almost 1.30am when she woke, sat up and looked at the phone. She dialled the number and Jackie answered. "Jackie," she said, "you're handsome and you're devilishly charming, and you tried to be a gentleman. You told me to call you if I needed anything. Will you please come and get me?" "You aren't scared of me any more?" Jackie asked. "No, I'm not afraid of you, but you are overwhelming," she said. "JJ will be there in twenty minutes, be packed, and hey, you won't be sorry."

JJ picked up Lynn from the hotel and drove her to Jackie's apartment. Lynn recalls: "He was not indifferent or insensitive, but we got there, got out of the car. I carried my own suitcase – got to the door—he opened the door and walked in first. My coat was over my arm. I lifted my arm and he threw the coat on the couch. I was standing there with my suitcase. He said, 'Are you hungry? Do you want a drink?' I'm standing there holding my suitcase.

"So it comes time to go to bed that night. He said, 'You can have any bed you want.' I went to bed and there's a knock on the door. I thought, 'Oh, my God!' I was very nervous, partly on account of him being black." But it wasn't too long before she relented and allowed Jackie to make love to her. As he did, he said, "Man, where in the hell did you come from? I can't believe this, I almost feel guilty." Then he said, "Would you do me a favour?" Lynn said, "Okay." He said, "Don't ever tell anybody or tell any of the guys about this – it'll ruin my reputation." He didn't want anyone to know that Lynn had refused him first time round.

Lynn: "Jackie hugged me, kissing my eyes and mouth. He gripped me tightly saying, 'I'm sorry, I'm sorry, baby. Did I hurt you?' he asked. 'How long have you been married?' 'What kind of guy is he? Crazy? You really don't know what happened, do you?' he asked looking puzzled. 'No,' I answered. 'Man, oh, man,' he said, as he propped himself up on one arm and kissed me. 'I've had real young chicks, married chicks, whores and everybody else. This never happened to me before. No wonder you didn't think being married was a big deal.'" Jackie turned off the lamp and pulled Lynn close. "You didn't ruin anything for me, doll. But now I'm gonna tell you about the birds and the bees. No, on second thought, I'm gonna show you and this time you'll know what's happening when it happens."

Says Lynn, "His ego had grown to enormous proportions as he held me, telling me all the erotic things he intended to do. Into the early morning hours, he continued to arouse me with intoxicating pleasure. Jackie said, 'I like the feel of your body close to mine. You feel helpless.'"

They lay quietly for a while. It was daylight. "We gotta get some sleep, doll, but first tell me again about the first time you saw me." Lynn was half way into her story when Jackie began to snore.

She woke to find him smoking a cigarette watching her. "He smiled, put out his cigarette and rested my head on his chest. 'Hey, last night you said we'd never see each other again and that I'd break your heart. I promised, we will be together again. I already got it worked out, and I will never hurt you. Ya know what? I don't think me being an entertainer had anything to do with us. We would'a still met, somewhere, some day, and I would be black and you would be white. It was *kismet*, baby.'" When Lynn arrived home she looked up the word, kismet. It was a Turkish word meaning "fate" or "destiny".

To this day Lynn loves Jackie just as much as when she met him all those years ago: "I can see him like it was today – he had beautiful skin tone, he really did. Photos make him look darker than he was. Those eyes, they'd flash, they'd light, they did everything. He totally mesmerised me."

While Jackie's romantic policy saw no problems with inter-racial relationships, his professional approach was making similar inroads. He was equally at home in the environment of a raucous chitlin' circuit concert or high class supper clubs like the Copacabana or Coconut Grove. As Dick Jacobs recounts in *Musician* magazine, it was at these swish establishments that the kid from Detroit could show his true versatility.

"Jackie always had the ambition to transcend being a rock 'n' roll singer and, as he put it, 'go on to bigger and better things.' So Nat Tarnopol booked him for an engagement at the Fountainbleau Hotel in Miami Beach, opening for the deadpan comedian George Jessel.

"The crowd at the Fountainbleau was mainly your basic Borscht Belt blue-hair-rinse set who didn't know Jackie Wilson from James Brown. However, there was a sprinkling of hardcore Jackie fans at the shows. Jackie knew that the crowd was there mainly for Jessel, so he included an amazing punch-line to his set: a knockdown drag-out version of 'My Yiddishe Momme'. And when this predominantly Jewish crowd got an eyeful of this black sylph gliding across the stage like there's no such thing as gravity and there's no bones in his body at all and he's crooning a mean, mournful and exuberant 'My Yiddishe Momme' that would stop a bar mitzvah cold before sending everybody's heart right through the ceiling, this polite but sceptical crew of Jessel fans went berserk. As a kind of insurance policy, we threw a couple of other standards, like 'California

Here I Come', into the act and restricted the rock 'n' roll numbers to a long medley (to satisfy the real fans in the audience)."

As well as outfoxing the locals, Jackie arranged for Lynn to meet him in Miami, even though Freda was there as well. How he managed to keep the women from running into each other remains a mystery. Says Lynn: "He was the first black entertainer to appear at the Fountainbleau in Miami. That was April 1960, it was my first big concert. One of the poshest hotels, mainly Jewish audience. Even then, although there was no screaming, hotel keys, and notes from waiters were sent to him; 'I'll get rid of my husband and meet you later.' Women adored him."

The next time Lynn saw Jackie was in New York, about ten months after they had first met. "He opened the door, put his hand under my chin and opened my mouth. I said, 'What's wrong?' He said, 'Have you been seeing anyone else?' I said, 'No.' He said, 'I want to see if there's any more teeth missing. Like, Lloyd Price, Sam Cooke, anyone else been seeing you?' Then he laughed. He had this off-the-wall sense of humour."

She says, "I was watching Jackie perform from left stage, with Dee Clark and some of the other performers. 'Man,' one singer said, 'that guy doesn't perform, he entertains. I never saw anybody so agile.' 'Yeah,' Dee said, 'ain't it disgusting. Look at all those chicks goin' wild.' As Jackie neared the end of his song, 'Am I The Man,' the frenzy of the audience reached fever pitch.

"Suddenly Jackie smiled devilishly, then dived into the sea of grasping clutching hands before him. I said, 'Oh, God, Jackie…they'll tear him to pieces. Help him.' 'Help him? Hell, he loves it,' JJ said, as he came running out to see what caused the uproar. I could see Jackie's arms and shoe-less feet thrashing about as the screaming young women tore at his clothes. When security helped him into the dressing room his tie and shoes were missing. All the buttons from his white ruffled shirt were missing and the sleeves were torn. His normally perfectly coiffured hair stood on end. In the dressing room, Jackie sat down at the dressing table laughing as JJ hurried to him with a washcloth and towel."

On one occasion Lynn began to have second thoughts concerning her tenuous relationship following Jackie around: "I started to cry. JJ couldn't handle tears. I sobbed, 'JJ, when Jackie goes to the studio Monday to record, I'm going back to Springfield.' 'Oh hey, mama, don't do that, he does better when you're with us. He's not drinking as much, and I haven't seen him with any pills. Please, at least wait until the tour starts. He knows you're just barely hanging on, he told me that before you got here. You're wrong about him. He won't dump you somewhere. You've got nothing back home, no family, and you said your friends don't like you any more. Nobody here treats you like white trash, Jackie would kill 'em. Come on, mama, don't put him down, please.'"

After a performance at Harlem's Apollo Theatre, the artists and their entourages went to the Four Seasons Club. "As they sat around the table, praising each others performances, the singer Dion Di Mucci came to the table and put a hand on Jackie's shoulder," recalls Lynn. "'Hey Jackie, great show. I see Lynn is wearing out a chair here. Okay if we dance?'" Jackie still didn't dance well as a couple and seemed to indicate it was all right. Sadly for Lynn she'd done the wrong thing. "When I came back he was drinking straight doubles," she says. She knew Jackie's pride had been damaged and she soon found out how annoyed he was.

As Jackie unlocked the door to his apartment, Lynn started to tell him what a lovely evening she'd had. He slammed the door with fury. His eyes were filled with rage as he stood looking at her. "Don't ever do that to me again, white girl," he yelled. "What did I do?" she asked, "You're with me. I don't want anybody else's hands on you, got it?" Her eyes filled with fear as he moved closer, not knowing what he was thinking. Lynn ran into the bedroom, locking the door, crying and praying. She says: "He began to pound and kick the door. Finally the lock broke and burst open, knocking me to the floor. Jackie grabbed my arms and dragged me to the side of the bed. He stood me up and flung me on the bed. 'You hate me, huh, bitch? You are a spoiled, pampered little whore, and I made you that way, didn't I?' he said. Jackie raised himself astride me, placing his fingers around my neck. 'Jackie,' I whispered, 'are you going to kill me?' He removed his hands and sunk down on the bed beside me, sobbing. Slowly I moved to the edge of the bed and dashed into the bathroom, locking the door. I sat in the tub, rocking back and forth. I prayed for him and me.

"After what seemed like hours, Jackie knocked softly on the door. 'I'm sorry, Lynn, please come out, I won't hurt you, baby.' I didn't move. It became quiet; I thought he was asleep. I cautiously opened the door and stepped into the bedroom. I felt his nearness at once. Jackie was sitting on the floor outside the bathroom, with his head resting on his knees." He looked pathetic. He raised his head, peering up at her. His eyes were compelling, magnetic.

"He sat there watching as I put on the pink gown and robe he had bought me. I reached out and took his hand as he stood up, gathering me close to him, 'I'm sorry, I'm sorry, I'm sorry; I'll never do that again, I wouldn't hurt you, you know I'm good to you. But sometimes you make me half crazy.' He went to the kitchen and returned with two glasses of wine. Jackie said, 'I promise I won't hurt you again. I'm sorry.'"

She believed him. In fact, Lynn was so madly in love that she was willing to walk away from her unhappy marriage and just belong to Jackie. "Jackie was a consummate lover, never taking more than he gave," she says. But it wasn't the fairytale ending. "I said, 'I want to stay.' Jackie said, 'You can't stay here. In a week, you know where you'd be?' He said, 'You're not smart. You're naive!' He would look in one ear and say, 'I can see clear through there.' He said, 'You're going home. If you come back, that's not my problem. It's not going to be because of me.'" And he sent Lynn home to Springfield.

No doubt Jackie had Lynn's welfare in mind, but he also had his own. He had begun having a serious affair with Harlean Harris, and was still married to Freda. His career was at its peak and if he wasn't in the recording studio he would be constantly performing and, generally, on the move. Still their relationship continued and over a period Lynn would accrue her work leave entitlements to rendezvous with him around the country. In January 1962 they met in Nebraska. The temperature was ten degrees below zero and Jackie didn't like the cold. Says Lynn: "One night, after a performance, he was very quiet, but restless. He tossed and turned in bed, but never got up. Sometime before daylight he whispered, 'I never wanted you to know what I'm really like.' I sensed his moods and knew he didn't want to talk. I still don't know what was bothering him. I pretended to be asleep."

Jackie had known hundreds of women in his life but the one special woman he "would have killed for" was still his mother, Eliza Mae. Lynn doesn't pretend to have been even the second woman in his life, but there can be no doubt that to Jackie she was "special". Their regular meetings over the years, numerous long distance phone calls and special gifts are proof of this. Possibly one of the reasons that Jackie was happy and content with her is because, unlike many who surrounded him, she made no demands. Her love was of the total giving kind. She was an outsider in every sense of the word, but her devotion to Jackie was unbounded. That love was to cost her and her own mother referred to Jackie as "that nigger you run around with".

Jackie wasn't the best of fathers. He himself had only had a tenuous childhood and in many ways was still a child. From an early age he had lived by his wits – out on the streets. His school attendance was minimal, as he had decided on his chosen career path early. In his most formative years, his father Jack was out on the street with his "wine drinking buddies" and Jackie was singing the churches and street corners for cash at the age most children are still playing with toys. From around the age of nine he openly drank cheap liquor. Then, at fifteen, he was singing in Detroit's night spots.

It was no surprise then, that as an adult he was reading *Captain Marvel* and *Tales From The Crypt* comic books – he had vast collections of them. He also loved old movies, particularly cowboy movies, watching them over and over. He loved his pet dogs, young children and "old folks", who he was totally at ease with. In the body of the man there lurked a child.

Lynn recalls one incident of Jackie's childish simplicity, when she visited him in Denver. "It was very cold," she says, "and I slept with one of Jackie's sweaters on and socks. He had been in a happy mood all day. That evening, after the performance, he even ate cheeseburgers, my favourite food, to appease me. It was my birthday [22 March] and he had given me a beautiful pearl dinner ring, set in a musical bar. He had it made for me. I never cared for diamonds, but I loved pearls. He would laugh and say, 'Not only are you dumb, but you are cheap.'

"I was sleeping peacefully, when he began shaking me. 'Get up! Come on, baby. We're gonna have some fun.' It was snowing heavily and he wanted to have a snowball fight. What he didn't know was that I had been pretty good on the girls' softball team. I really pelted him! We were at a motel and we became so noisy, people got up to see what was happening. When they found out who Jackie was, some got dressed and came out to join in the fun." They also made a snowman and despite Jackie having seen plenty of snow in Detroit, Lynn says, "That time he made the snowman. He'd never made a snowman before! He reverted to a little boy."

Lynn may well have been, as Jackie had said, naive. "At the time I didn't know about Freda. I didn't know until Chicago at the State Theatre when I found out he was married with four kids. I thought it was terrible! He said, 'It's not terrible.' He wasn't ready to be a father and a husband. That was Jackie. He loved women, it was his nature. He wanted them all. There were some that hung around he called 'sluts' and 'bitches'. But he genuinely cared about a lot of these women. He expressed no concern about these children of his all over the country. He didn't write letters; telephones – least line of resistance – fastest and easiest."

Lynn, more than most, got to see the sweeter side of Jackie and many times experienced his well developed sense of humour. "As a compliment, when I was feeling down about myself, he would put his index finger under my chin, raise my head, look in my eyes and say, 'If I could buy you for what you think you're worth and sell you for what you are worth, I'd never have to work again!' Then he would hold me while I cried and felt sorry for myself, because my family didn't want me any more. If not for Jackie, I would never have known or experienced what true love really means. I think it means caring more for someone else than for yourself. Everyone wanted something from him. Most of all they wanted to live well. Did they only want to take and never give?"

As he'd already proved to her, Jackie also experienced childish jealousy. When they went for the first time to the Copacabana in New York, with Nat Tarnopol and road manager August Sims and their wives Lynn saw a side she had tried to forget. The feature act was singer Jerry Vale ('Pretend You Don't See Her'). Lynn recalls: "I was enthralled with his performance. After the show we were having dinner and I was aware Jackie's mood had changed. He put his fork down and said, 'How come when that motherfucker sang you melted and ran all over the table? You don't act like that when I sing!' He shocked me. His ego was dying. I said, 'Jackie, listen to me. He has a beautiful voice and he's a great performer, but what you saw was on the outside of me. When I look at you all my feelings come from within.' He looked at me for a moment and said, 'Damn, I guess I should have stayed in school.' Then he finished his steak."

The envy was misplaced where Lynn was concerned. She saw innumerable performances by Jackie over the years and describes them all as being "awesome". "He was a natural born performer artist. There were two songs he would close with if I was there; 'Little Things Mean A Lot', and Nat 'King' Cole's, 'One Moment With You'. He'd say, 'That's for someone special.' You had to see him. There was a lot of frenzy around."

There could be as much frenzy around off stage. Once, when Jackie was appearing at the Lazy Boy Supper Club in Charleston South Carolina, Lynn had stood with Pop Watley watching Jackie end his performance with her favourite song, 'Little Things Mean A Lot'. After the show they went out to dinner and chose to walk a little, with Pop following behind in the car. "We talked and laughed and held hands – Jackie liked to hold hands," she says.

"Suddenly a voice said, 'Hey, you, nigger-boy, we wanna talk to you.' When we turned around we were facing three huge white men. 'Oh, he's one of those pretty niggers,' one of them said, putting his hands on his hips. 'Look, boy, you don't come down here and mess with our white women.' Turning to me, he said, 'You get yourself on home, white trash.'

"I moved closer to Jackie and said, 'I'm not one of your women, and I'm with him.' 'That's right,' Jackie said as he removed his jacket and handed it to Lynn. 'I own her,' he told them. 'Nobody calls me "nigger" or "boy" and she's not "white trash", she's a lady.' 'Look, boy, we know who you are and we don't care. You take your white whore and get your black ass out of town,' he told Jackie.

"As I started to speak again, Jackie put his hand up and said to me, 'Shut up, mama, and get behind me. They're gonna eat those words.' I dropped Jackie's coat to the sidewalk and took his hand. I told him, 'I'll stand beside you, Jackie, but I won't hide behind you.' At that moment, Pop Watley pulled the limousine over to the kerb. He stepped out with a tyre iron in one hand and a machete in the other. 'Is there a problem here Jack?' he asked. 'Get back in the car, old man,' one of the men said. 'You wanna go?' Pop asked him. 'I'm ready, and when we're done, somebody's gonna be hurt bad, or dead.'"

Unbeknown to Jackie and Lynn, Jimmy Smith, Jackie's drummer, had been sleeping in the back seat of the limousine. Smith opened the door and stepped out. "Put Lynn in the car," Jackie told Jimmy. As he reached for her arm, Lynn said, "I'm not leaving you, Jackie." "Get your ass in the car and shut up," Jackie yelled, but Lynn didn't move.

They were all squared off, outside a tavern, when three black men stepped out onto the sidewalk next to Jackie. "Need some help, buddy?" one of them asked Jackie. "I'd appreciate it, man," Jackie said. "Me and my woman here, were just out takin' a walk before dinner and these bastards don't like it."

"Okay, slick, you win this time, but if you ever come back here, you're dead," one of the white men told Jackie. "Hey, man, you got a deal, but tonight I'm takin' my girl here out to dinner and we're goin' back to the motel and we're goin' to bed," he said, defiantly. He gave the three black men some money and got in the limousine. "Well, now," he said to Lynn. "You were gonna go all fifteen rounds with me, weren't you?" "Yes," she said, as he put his arms around her. "Jackie, I'm sorry about the things they said to you." "You don't have to apologise for white people, baby. Besides,

I know what good white people are like. They're like you, and I love you."
"Are we ever gonna eat?" Pop yelled. "Yeah," Jackie said. "Let's get
Rocky Marciano here a big steak so she'll have the strength for a couple of
wrestling matches when we get back to the motel." Pop said, "Well, man, if
you don't wanna wrestle with her after a big dinner, I will." "When we get
back to New York, Pop, you'd better look for another job," Jackie said, as
he winked at Jimmy.

Lynn says now, "People put black people down. Jackie gave me self
esteem I previously never had, I never knew I was entitled to." But that
journey towards self esteem led to an amusing incident in 1963, which
resulted in Lynn appearing on stage with Jackie, much to her chagrin. She
had become pregnant to Jackie, but was afraid to inform him lest he dump
her. "I began avoiding him," she remembers, "failing to show up when I
said I would. Finally, he told me to be in Houston or he was coming to my
work place." So, Lynn met Jackie in Houston and, as she put it, "It didn't
take long for him to notice the problem." He said we would talk about it
after the show.

There were a group of people backstage just prior to the show. Jackie's
keyboards player, Truman Thomas, had just told a joke and everyone was
laughing. Says Lynn, "Jackie was standing next to me while I sat on a chair.
Then my hair was nearly waist length. I leaned forward against Jackie
laughing. My head was just above his belt-line. Jackie was laughing so hard
he was twisting back and forth. His hands were in my hair. My hair became
tangled around the buttons on his shirt and entwined in his belt buckle.
Then it was time for his performance. Everyone tried frantically to separate
us, to no avail. Finally Jackie said, 'Well, baby, you're about to have your
stage debut.' He pulled me out on stage with him; I was dying of
embarrassment. He was laughing so hard. He said, 'Folks, I know this looks
bad, but it isn't what you think. I'm not even going to try and explain.'
Somebody found scissors and freed me. Later he said the audience
probably thought it was a gimmick, but regardless they laughed as much
as everyone else backstage."

Lynn's pregnancy was not something he found easy to discuss, but he
raised the subject on one occasion. "One afternoon, in Colorado," says
Lynn, "Jackie and I were playing cards – I was four months pregnant. Out
of the blue, he said, 'Didn't you think that this could happen? Weren't you
afraid? If you thought your friends didn't approve of you seeing me, how
do you think they're gonna feel now? You ain't had trouble like you're

gonna have.' I just smiled at him and said, 'I love you, and I need two cards.' He shook his head and said, 'Man, you're some kinda crazy chick.'" Gina was born in April, 1963. Jackie sang to his baby daughter on the phone, over the years, however Gina was thirteen years old before Lynn informed her who her father was.

One of Jackie's entourage once described Lynn as "the best kept secret Jackie ever had". She believes there was another reason so few people remember her being around. "I wasn't a night life person, while Jackie lived it seven days a week." However, he also enjoyed "cutting down" in his terms. It meant totally relaxing at home, not shaving and getting only half dressed. "I loved him that way, it was the real Jackie. He loved neck and back rubs, I liked to have my feet rubbed. He didn't mind because he usually found a way to go beyond my feet and my legs."

Most who knew him describe a cool and confident individual who appeared not to have a care in the world. The real Jackie was a warm, generous, loving person, but below the surface lurked an extremely angry man. This anger was almost always held safe and in check, but an excess of alcohol would often lead to it boiling to the surface. Much of his anger steamed from being treated as a lesser human being purely because of his skin colour. Jackie knew what vocal talent was. He knew who had it and who didn't. Never did he not give credit when it was due and he never hesitated to assist other singers with talent. Jackie knew that he had the voice and he had the performance. If his skin was white he would have been a superstar without peer. Jackie spent his entire career "getting over the hump".

In 1963 the Civil Rights Movement, headed by Martin Luther King, was in full swing. "Jackie was real excited about the civil rights bill, but it hasn't changed anything," says Lynn. In some ways she is wrong. When Jackie got started, he often had to enter by the back door. Many hotels and restaurants were totally off limits. At least with President Johnson's 1965 Civil Rights Bill, there were laws that forbade such practices.

Lynn came from a secluded mid-western background and grew up with all the inherent prejudices. She says, "Once, shortly after we met, we were discussing the racial problems. He said, 'You really are screwed up and prejudiced, but don't worry baby, I think I can straighten you out.'" And he did. Lynn says she learnt more about love from this one black man than she did from all the people she'd been associated with while growing up.

She also learnt of his generosity, especially the time he asked, "Do you want to sing?" Jackie knew Lynn was a country music fan and, so, prior to a regularly scheduled recording session, he got some members of his band together and they – Jackie, drummer Jimmy Smith, and organist Truman Thomas – quickly wrote a tear jerking country song. The recording session, in a room of someone's New York home, was done in a jovial way, although Lynn was all nerves. "They'd call each other 'nigger' in front of me. He went all out to do this for me," she says. "He paid everyone personally. The back-up singers weren't really that at all [it was actually JJ and the band]."

Jackie's drummer, Jimmy Smith, came in dressed in western-styled clothes. "He played with his eyes closed," she remembers. "Fabulous drum work. He was totally strung out, but he so softly brushed the drum heads you can barely hear it. The guitar man was fantastic, his name was Donald Mason. Several months later he died in a car crash. Jackie was standing in front of me not trying to be funny; he almost went down on his knee with his arms up saying, 'Come on, out with it.' He had to be director. When it was over he fell over backwards on the floor. When I got through the song he put his hands in the air and fell back trying to get me to go higher. He kept putting his hand in the air and mouthing, 'Higher.' They were all laughing."

Although it was in 1963, the recording was done on a wire recorder. The result was a formidable first effort and could well have been developed into a commercial recording, with Lynn's well balanced vocal delivery. As for Jackie and the musicians, it is testament to their talents, especially as the musical genre was far removed from their field. More than anything it shows the relationship wasn't all one way between the two.

More fun was had on tour. "They used to play cards between shows," says Lynn, "and I could not play. So while Jackie was on stage, JJ and I worked out this system. While he walked around the game he'd hold up some fingers, or put his hand over his heart for a queen. If it was a king he'd scratch his head." This worked well for a while, until Jackie realised what was going on. "Jackie would say things that were funny, but he didn't realise it. He said, 'I knew you cheated, but JJ I didn't know you were helping her.' He said to me, 'You are so damn crooked if you die, I'll have to screw you in your grave.' JJ answered, 'You'll probably try, Jack!' Everyone laughed so much they nearly fell off their chairs."

JJ and Lynn built up quite a rapport. "He was my buddy. It was his mission to take care of me and he never steered me wrong." Some commented that JJ was one of those who were stealing from Jackie, to which Lynn just says, "JJ was always there, but he knew he wasn't going to get anything out of it, so he took what he could. He wasn't any different from all the others in that regard." Jackie knew he was being financially bled at every turn and would say to Lynn, "I have money, but I don't have money, you know?" Says Lynn, "He told me he was being ripped off. He knew he was, but he really did think he was an owner of Brunswick. Jackie trusted them. He just wanted to sing."

As for investing his money for when his performing days were up, sadly Jackie didn't have much idea, nor did he receive good advice. "The diamond mart was a big thing for Jackie," recalls Lynn, "He spent a lot of money down there. Diamonds were a big thing; they never had 'em before." Jackie had to endure a lot, but he would have been the first to admit that he was living his destiny – and it sure beat working at the car plant! On top of that, he had some fun along the way and provided immeasurable pleasure for his legions of fans.

Sadly, from his earliest years, a lot of Jackie's fun came from alcohol. He drank heavily, and any time of the day was the right time. He had no concept of "enough". Lynn relates one incident: "After a big evening of too much Scotch, Jackie woke up at 1.30pm with a terrible hangover. It was my job to bring tomato juice and coffee. When I sat on the bed and handed him the juice, he said, 'Don't jump on the bed and don't touch me!' I said, 'If you think your nose is bad, you should see your eyes, or *can't* you see?' Jackie sat up and said, 'Don't yell so loud. After I feel better I'm gonna slap the shit out of you. You're always saying I don't look good.'"

His day started at two to three in the afternoon and alcohol was forever present. "Jackie drank Chivas Regal straight or on the rocks; he was hooked on that," says Lynn. "He drank a lot of stuff straight. He could drink and drink and not show it, but when he got drunk he would pass out. As for drugs, the only thing I ever saw Jackie use was these red capsules, uppers. He was also a first rate cusser. At the same time, he had a lot of compassion. I think it was because of the music. You hear it in his music.

"Sometimes when he had a cold, he could be a bear like anyone else. 'Don't touch me,' or 'I can't talk to you because my vocal cords will be swollen.' He had to be taken care of when he was sick. But no sympathy for anyone else when they were sick. Oh, no."

Jackie didn't want to understand death or illness and wouldn't go near a hospital or a funeral. Lynn explains: "He was very complex. He cut himself off from people for fear of being hurt. He loved people – certain people, but was afraid of getting too close to them. He could make you nervous; you would know he was watching you."

As befits a control freak, Jackie liked to be aware of Lynn's impending visits, but on one occasion she decided she'd make an unannounced appearance. "I was going to surprise Jackie once in Las Vegas [he was playing at the Sahara Hotel]," she says. "I thought I'll surprise him, but it was me who got the surprise." The fact was, Jackie was with another woman.

"He didn't know I was coming and they wouldn't let me in," she recalls. "I was sitting in the lobby crying. JJ happened to come by and saw me. He took me back and I had to wait in another room. I got tired of waiting so went to the dressing room and overheard Jackie saying, 'Look, I didn't know she was coming. I've got to spend some time with her in the evening.' He was talking to this other girl. I went in and said, 'You don't have to do me any favours.' Then there was a big fight and JJ came to my rescue. It ended up all right, he went with me. It was funny when it was all over."

Other women troubles were manifold. One of the subjects concerning Jackie few wished to talk about, and still fewer knew about, concerned an affair with Alona, the daughter of a notorious New York mobster. Her father was one of those who had a stake in Jackie's career. Just what problems this caused for Jackie, if any, could not be determined. Then there was one with the unusual name of Fadwah Peace, a Cajun voodoo from New Orleans. Jackie is said to have had two children with her and would often phone her from various parts of the country.

The recipient of many phone calls herself, Lynn had almost been ostracised on account of her relationship with Jackie. Their daughter Gina also had to come to terms with a father she barely knew. By the time they decided to inform her of the actual relationship Jackie had been stricken by the heart attack and would never speak again. Gina says now: "I do not have the fond memories of him that my mother can so ably recall. At best I seem to remember feeling as if I were out of place when we were there with him. At times he had this need to almost hide us from certain of his acquaintances." This observation is more than likely correct, given that he married Harlean in 1967 and was living in a de-facto relationship with Lynn Crochet from late 1970.

The other emotive factor in Gina's formative years was a tyrannical and bigoted maternal grandfather. "My grandfather was undoubtedly the coldest, harshest person I ever encountered, but for some reason he accepted me. Perhaps he only used me to hurt my mother. At any rate I too lost respect for him when at dinner one evening he referred to mother as 'a disgusting, dirty little nigger lover who disgraced him and the whole family'. My mother is a good, decent, gentle and very loving person. She just happened to fall in love with someone who certainly was not deserving of the faithfulness and loyalty to his memory that she has been so steadfast in."

Gina recalls that Jackie did show her affection on a couple of occasions: "Mama and JJ left me with him once. We were playing a children's card game. Suddenly he threw the cards up in the air and they fell to the floor. He told me to pick them up. Then he got on the floor to help me. He laid face down, looking at me. After a moment he squeezed the end of my nose and said, 'Yeah, you're gonna look just like your mama.' Then he pulled one of my long curls and helped me pick up my cards.

"Another time we were sitting eating in the suite. I didn't want to eat. My mother was arguing with me when he picked me up and held me on his lap. He cut up his food and recited the old standard, 'Through the lips and over the gums, look out stomach here it comes.' I recall laughing and after each bite he would kiss me on the cheek.

"My other memories were not unhappy ones, but not necessarily endearing. He did exhibit genuine concern when I broke my leg at the age of seven while trying to imitate his acrobatics. He picked me up and was running down the corridor yelling for someone to help. But I also recall the smell of liquor on his breath when he would kiss me hello or goodbye. He only spanked me once. I suppose I was very spoiled. I kicked Mama on the leg in anger. He jumped off the bed, pulled up my dress and let me have it. Then he pointed at me and said, 'Never again, get it.' I did."

Many years later, Jackie's former road manager August Sims, told Gina about the relationship between her parents: "They had fun; they got sick from eating too much at a carnival and going on rides. Jackie would take her to a Western movie and insist they sneak in the side door without paying... as he did when he was a boy. He told me they could destroy a hotel room with pillows and throwing buckets of ice at each other, and food fights. He said you could hear Jackie's most commonly used phrase from their adjoining rooms. 'Goddamn you, Lynn, I'm gonna knock the hell out of you,' followed by more laughing."

Jackie Wilson had come into Lynn's life and had turned it completely upside down. She says, "I've never found a word that epitomises him. He was unique, he was the ultimate performer; he was a real entertainer. Jackie never was just a singer; he could sing any type of song at any time. On stage he was total control. They never tapped his full potential. He would have been the video king had he been around today."

Most of all she has no regrets, save the wish that Jackie were still alive. She says, "Till the day I die, I will wonder why, of all people in this vast world, I was fortunate enough to have known and loved him. I believe there was no one love of Jackie's life, but perhaps I was there because he needed someone who truly loved him. I feel confident that Jackie knows my love for him grows daily. All the others [the other family members who benefited while he was alive] want him to set them up again and provide them with the good life they once enjoyed. If I could have only one wish, it would be to be with Jackie again and look upon that beautiful face. I once said to him, 'I love your nose and your face.' He laughed, 'Doll, my nose *is* my face.'

"I dried and pressed nearly every pink rose Jackie gave me. Even with his many faults he became my salvation, my reason for being. And then I had Gina. I have told her I want them buried with me as well as most of the pictures."

The love that Lynn felt for Jackie is certainly one of the most unselfish and enduring forms of this human emotion, but she can hardly be faulted for the quality. Jackie, in turn, expressed his love through his voice to millions. It wasn't the financial rewards that caused him to sing so passionately.

Gina believes Jackie should have treated her mother better. "I don't dispute that he is undoubtedly one of the greatest entertainers who ever lived, but I believe that is the sum total of the man. He certainly took mother's heart and soul with him when he went."

Although Gina cannot understand the enormous hold Jackie held over her mother, she is sure her mother would have taken better care of him. "If Jackie was in mother's care he still wouldn't have recovered, but the quality of life would certainly have been maintained. She would never have allowed him to languish as he did."

CHAPTER SIX

I'm Wanderin'

The black youth of Detroit were especially proud of their home grown hero, Jackie Wilson. Contours manager, Jack Ryan, who grew up in Detroit during the 1950s and 1960s, says: "Everyone here knew the reason many kids here wanted to be a singer; Jackie proved he could make it. He was black and from Detroit and he made it. It was like Joe Louis was to the boxers. He was proof positive that anyone could make it. Hank Ballard, same thing. You didn't have to go to a factory to make it. I'm a white kid and I knew what Jackie meant to Detroit."

Detroit group, The Falcons, first formed in 1955, had included such notables as Eddie Floyd, "Sir" Mack Rice and Wilson Pickett amongst its line-up. In 1959 they had their one major hit 'You're So Fine', featuring the lead vocal of Joe Stubbs, brother of The Four Tops' lead singer Levi. Stubbs discussed the tour they'd been on with Jackie on a Savannah, Georgia, radio tribute to Jackie broadcast in 1988. "We were down on the road one time in St Louis – me, The Midnighters, Ruth Brown – whole lot of us were there – Sam Cooke. We did our show and come off. Jackie was last. I heard this guy gesturing to people and different things. Jackie did his show and was coming off and the guy grabbed his coat and tore his pocket. So Jackie hit him and knocked him off the stage. Two or three more came up so Jackie knocked them off. Billy [Davis guitarist with The Midnighters] was playing for Jackie, too…Billy is a 'pug' [boxer]; hell of a guy, knock you out in a minute. So I got beside Billy Davis 'cause they were starting to surround us. People was coming up getting ready to come up on stage. We were backing out to the back entrance, so they came out to the back entrance. So Jackie and Billy started knocking out guys and I got to do a little hitting, too. We got back to the hotel and they started busting windows with bricks and we heard some gunfire. That was scary."

With an obvious respect for Jackie, Stubbs went on: "Jackie was a good guy, he had a heart of gold. I got a good heart myself. Jackie was the star of

137

the show and I told Jackie, 'Hey, Jackie, see these people,' there was about forty of them, 'they ain't got no money to get in.' Jackie said, 'Let 'em all in.'" Summing up what life on the road with Jackie was like, Stubbs says "hectic and chaotic". It's no wonder that the name given him by Alan Freed, and the name that stuck, was "Mr Excitement".

Singer and writer, "Sir" Mack Rice also became one of The Falcons and later went on to write some big hits, the best known of which are 'Mustang Sally' and 'Respect Yourself'. Rice knew Jackie well at the time, having been considered for The Dominoes' replacement position: "He was just a fantastic guy, man. Never saw him mad in my life, always had a smile on his face. He loved everybody, always kissed any woman, fat, greasy, ugly whatever. That would make the women go crazy. He was the hardest working guy I ever met."

Rice recalls a more amusing incident on the same tour: "I was in St Louis Missouri, a big package show – Jackie, Sam Cooke, Midnighters, Baby Washington, Gladys Knight And The Pips – before she had a hit – Johnny 'Guitar' Watson, Jessie Belvin and Bill Olsen's Band, and many other acts. Rodney Jones, a black DJ out of St Louis, had this 'record hop' at a white high school that Jackie was supposed to do. Somehow, Jackie hadn't got into town, so the DJ took our lead singer, Joe Stubbs, and used him as Jackie. It went over swell." Had he seen anyone who could match Jackie on stage? "Heck, no, nobody could move like Jackie; he just had his own movements. Taking that coat off, getting down on his knee, laying on his back; he was a clown on stage. Michael Jackson took a lot of them."

Rice explains the rivalry between the talents of Sam Cooke and Jackie. "That package show we were on, Sam Cooke was the star," he says. "Him and Jackie were star and co-star. They had a little argument about who was going to star and Sam won out in some kind of way, 'cause he had a hit out – all those big records – was smooth and all that. Each night, man, I felt bad for Sam, because Jackie would destroy him. Jackie beat and destroyed him. No one would follow Jackie on stage; Sam wouldn't either any more. By the time Sam came on people [the audience] would start leaving.

"Sam had the clean cut image, good guy like, while Jackie was the nasty – he'd do all kinds of stuff. As an entertainer and a person Jackie was one of the best I've met; best I ever met in my life. Couldn't beat his personality."

Rice spent much time performing in his home town of Detroit where there were loads of singing "greats". "Little Willie John, Levi Stubbs and

Jackie; they were the 'baddest' acts in Detroit. Willie John was the only guy Jackie would back off of. He was a singer and a mover – not like Jackie, though. But his personality would get him over easily. John was great, man. He would have gone a long way."

Over many years Rice met and worked with some of the all-time best singers. He says wistfully: "Sometimes the stars get, like, too heavy. Seems like all the superstars have some kind of hang up, like. I guess that's the way it goes. People catering to them and that don't help much. I've seen it happen to guys I thought I knew well, once they got that one gold record. Some people live off yesterday and still think it is yesterday."

Grady Gaines was for many years part of a band highly regarded as rock 'n' roll pioneers. In the 1950s and 1960s, no band had a hotter reputation than The Upsetters who were comprised of black former classmates from Houston, Texas. They first came to the attention of the world in 1956 when they backed Little Richard. Ben Bart's Universal Attractions booked almost exclusively top black acts, and The Upsetters were the exclusive touring band they used. "Every tour they put together, The Upsetters would have to be on it. We were their number one band," Grady explains. "The master of ceremonies on these tours was the flamboyant Gorgeous George. We'd go out on those shows thirty-five to forty days at a time." The first such tour was in 1957. "Sometimes Jackie and Sam Cooke would headline together. They would get a headliner and The Upsetters would be the band to back all the acts. They'd have eight to ten acts on the show. Jackie would do about three numbers."

As Rice found, with two of the greatest voices in contemporary music, there was bound to be some friction. "We went on this tour with Sam Cooke and Jackie Wilson together," says Grady, "all major cities in the US. The way they had that billing, Sam Cooke would star the show, the next night Jackie would be the star. Sam Cooke had four or five records in the Top Ten and one of them was Number One. Jackie Wilson had some in the Top Fifty. Sam Cooke was just burning Jackie up with those hot records. They would both tear it up. That was one of the greatest tours I was ever on."

At the end of the tour it was all smiles: "In the beginning they were kind of worried, who would star and all that. But when that tour was over they was the best friends you've ever seen," Grady remembers. "I'm going to tell you, Jackie Wilson was one of the baddest cats that ever lived in showbusiness. Sam and Jackie were bad and when I say bad, I mean good. If Jackie was living now he'd be all over the Pop charts."

Grady finds it incredible Jackie didn't achieve greater recognition. "He started everybody that's out there now; they got something from him. Jackie Wilson had a voice...tormenting! That cat could go so high and do it with ease; I'm telling you, he had full control. I got along so good with Jackie. That was the greatest tour," says Grady nostalgically. "He definitely lived hard and fast. I was right there with them, I was riding on their glory." Grady and the musicians helped create that glory. They provided the driving rhythm. It's doubtful anyone ever walked out of one of those concerts feeling they hadn't got their two to three dollars' worth.

In 1959 Jackie, a major headliner, earned only around two to three thousand dollars a night. With the average American man then earning only around one hundred dollars per week, this would seem adequate, but out of that he'd need to pay for food, accommodation, his entourage, travel costs and management. Typically Jackie took three musicians with him and, by pre-arrangement, picked up the rest at the venues along the way.

For a time he travelled with the hard driving, brassy Chris Columbo band, another of the pioneer rock 'n' roll acts. Gil Askey who played trumpet with the band, travelled with Jackie for nearly two years. "I met Jackie when 'Lonely Teardrops' came out in 1958," he recalls. "We did a show in Detroit. I think I was getting thirty dollars a night. We didn't fly in those days, we had a truck we travelled in. The whole band would get two hundred dollars, and Jackie used to pay it out of his pocket."

With Jackie running across the stage, sliding on his knees and diving into the audience, his shows generated tremendous excitement. But his hard driving bands contributed to that. "I remember this one time we did this show," says Askey, "and Lloyd Price had a fifteen piece band, yet there was only five of us. When Jackie showed up on the stage he was magnificent. We just destroyed Lloyd Price's band. Lloyd said, 'Man, you've got some fine music there.' This was at Carr's Beach, Maryland. We'd been swimming and worked in our bathing suits with a towel around our shoulders. Earlier we did a show in Philadelphia and Lionel Hampton's band was there. Lionel Hampton couldn't believe it. He said, 'Where'd you get that sound?' We wiped them off the stage.

"Jackie was so powerful and we had to go to keep up with him. He'd do those splits, twirls, and we'd be romping – all we had to do was drive it home to him. Jackie never rehearsed. I used to write the horn parts out. The first guitar player was Billy Johnson [formerly guitarist with The Moonglows], then Dickie Thompson followed." Earl Van Dyke, another member of the band and extraordinary keyboards player, would later become one of the famous Funk Brothers, the driving force behind the Motown sound.

"The tours were arranged by big time promoters like Henry Wynn in Georgia and Howard Lewis in Texas," says Askey. "They promoted dances and concerts; that's how they made their money. If they had someone of the standing of Jackie Wilson, they might get four to five thousand dollars a night. That's where the real money was. If Jackie earned three thousand a night back then, it was considered big money." Yet, barely a few years later, Welshman Tom Jones came to the USA and demanded seventy-five thousand dollars a night. Indeed, to sign Jones the promoters put up thirty-five thousand just to get the date with the other forty thousand two weeks before the show.

Although The Four Tops did not have their first hit record until 1964, by which time they had signed with Motown, they often were on the same tours. "We went out together with Jackie when he got hot," remembers distant relative Lawrence Payton. "Those were wild times, man. We almost had riots everywhere. We were in southern Illinois one night. Everyone had arrived and we were waiting for Jackie: he'd always show, but he was late as a mother. They had us under siege. We tried to stave them off, but they were ready to kill everybody. 'We want our money back.'

"Trouble followed Jackie, but he was up to it, man. He was one of the gangsters himself, he loved it. That was his life and those were his friends." Payton is correct. Jackie couldn't live life any other way but on the edge. The company he kept led him further down the path to trouble.

Saxophonist and flute player Thomas "Beans" Bowles, during the 1950s, worked behind Maurice King at the Flame Show Bar, as a member of King's band The Wolverines, and so knew Jackie. "I recognised Jackie as a major talent in the early days – absolutely," says Bowles. Afterwards, when Jackie had had some major hits, he and Bowles were often on the same tours, Bowles with Marv Johnson in his early days with [organ player and band leader] Jack McDuff's band and Bill Jennings playing guitar. Bowles witnessed the pressures Jackie endured: "Every time I saw Jackie he was so tired; he was always trying to get into bed, and all these kids and these people idolised him and worried him to death. He was such a genial guy he let them do it. I found him one time in Pittsburgh – I had to use the 'john'. There were two suites and an interconnecting john. I went into the room and tried to get in – it was locked, so I waited a while and tried again.

Finally the door opened and it was Jackie. He'd been in there with his puppy. He had a pretty little dog he carried with him. He was sitting in there trying to rest. I said, 'Why don't you take my room?' He did and slept for about eight hours. Nobody would give him a chance to rest. His room was full of fans loving him to death and it just wore him out. He'd have to chase them out – they'd stretch him to the limit."

The ploy of hiding out in the bathroom was used often to gain a bit of solitude, but also for drug taking. Jackie preferred that only his trusted cronies, such as Billy Frazier and JJ, knew of his indulgence. Certainly, Bowles didn't see any. "I don't think Jackie used too much of anything. He kept a little champagne and stuff around." He adds, "JJ was his right hand man; he protected him and did everything he could."

Jesse Belvin, a young singer from Texas, was becoming increasingly popular. He had written the huge Penguins hit 'Earth Angel', and had a hit of his own in 1958, 'Guess Who'. Described as "somewhere between Nat 'King' Cole and Sam Cooke", he had a bright future and Jackie liked him a great deal. Together with Marv Johnson, Al Hibbler, Della Reese and Arthur Prysock, they were on tour. After the show in Jackson, Mississippi there had been some partying to celebrate Jesse's wedding anniversary to Jo Ann, a co-writer with him on some songs and his manager. Afterwards they drove to their next engagement in Little Rock, Arkansas. Bowles, who was travelling far behind the limousine carrying Belvin, his wife and driver, came across a blazing car wreck. He reached it in time to assist Belvin's wife, but Jesse was already dead with a broken neck. The driver also died; most likely he had fallen asleep, because he had careered into the back of another car heading in the same direction. The date was 6 February, 1960; Belvin was twenty-seven years old. His new album had just been released and the future had looked bright for him and his two young boys. The name of the album was off the mark: *The Best Is Yet To Come*. Gil Askey remembers Belvin: "Lovely singer, lovely guy."

Despite the obvious evidence that the driver had been drinking and was tired, many still believed the crash was no accident, being related to a racial incident in Jackson. The belief was that angry whites had slashed the car's tyres, because Belvin had insisted on performing at the black venue before he sang at the white one. Jackie firmly believed this to be the case and immediately offered a reward of ten thousand dollars leading to the arrest and conviction of the perpetrators. The reward offer was never taken up.

The travel was always a problem as Gil Askey relates: "Jackie would wait until the last minute before leaving for these gigs and then drive 110 miles an hour to get to the gig one hour before the next gig was over. I remember we were going to Savannah, Georgia one night. It was 285 miles. I was in the car with Henry Wynne, the promoter. They left after 8pm, but Jackie still got there on time. JJ and Frazier sat on one hundred plus on the interstate. Cops pulled them over, but they still got there by midnight."

One musician who backed Jackie on these gruelling tours says: "We didn't like to see him surrounded by people who weren't musicians, but he needed them. They are takers and bleeders. They couldn't do nothing but drive a car and they had guns. They had pistols 'cause of some of the promoters. You weren't living in the Hilton and Holiday Inn and you might be carrying three to five thousand dollars. You could be in a violent area. The gun's a deterrent...not that they ever used them."

Jackie occasionally stayed at the Forrest Arms rooming house, in Atlanta. "Jackie went mad once there and he ripped out the toilet seat," says Askey. "He was despondent." It wouldn't be the last time that Jackie vented his long pent up rage in some room. Life on the road was demanding and at times he couldn't cope with the pimps and the pushers and the adulation. At times, he'd call his mother in Highland Park, speaking to her as though he were still a young boy.

"On one occasion Jackie refused to perform," continues Askey. "It was a huge audience and we were afraid there'd be a riot once the audience knew Jackie wasn't going to appear. They wanted me to get up and make an announcement that Jackie wasn't going to appear. I said, 'Man, I can't get up there and tell 'em that. They're going to be throwing shit at me.' People have been waiting for two, two and a half hours. So I got up and announced, 'Mr Jackie Wilson has just arrived, so we're going to get off here to let Jackie's band set up.' The other band was thrilled, because they thought they were going to be backing Jackie Wilson. We packed up the Hammond organ and speakers, drums, guitars and loaded 'em all into the truck and we got out of there and left – in a big hurry! Naturally Jackie got sued for non-appearance at times."

Askey also recalls Jackie's affection for Poochie, his little Chihuahua dog. "Jackie would sit out in the car with the dog for two, three hours. And he'd kiss the dog, he'd tongue it – right in the mouth of the dog! Jackie would say, 'Dogs don't carry germs...people do.'"

While his dog was well cared for, the four Wilson children, like all youngsters, desperately needed a father. But to earn a living Jackie needed to perform, which meant constant touring and he didn't get home to Highland Park often to see them. This form of existence was not exactly normal, but it was the life he had chosen since his earliest years.

It was left to Freda to deal with any problems with the children. One worrying instance was with their first born, Denise. Jackie's father had died in 1953, but Denise was seeing his ghost. Freda explains: "Denise was little, she called to me, 'That man is here again. Go away, go away.' Mr Jack was there. She was afraid. Jackie said, 'They only come because they care or want to show you something. They can't hurt you.' He did stop coming."

In 1960 when Jackie performed at the Allen Theatre in Cleveland, Ohio, Freda and the children travelled to see him. Jackie called the three oldest – Denise then aged nine, Sandra aged seven and Jackie Jnr aged six – on stage to perform with him. Little Willie John performed on the same bill. Motown pioneer Singin' Sammy Ward recalls he and Berry Gordy drove from Detroit just to catch the show.

In the south, audiences were either totally segregated or they performed to blacks one night and whites the other. But Jackie fans crossed the racial divide and he loved them dearly. Askey recalls one such gig in 1960: "I remember how he was when he played for the blacks in Jackson, Mississippi. This place out in the Jackson State College – it could hold around two thousand people, the biggest hall there that was available. The kids were trying to get in the dressing room to see Jackie. The cops were trying to push the crowds. Jackie said, 'No, No, don't push my friends, just let them in here, three at a time.' He'd hug and kiss them like a lover, he'd tongue kiss them all. He had all this sweat on him…he had all this love."

During 1960, at Toledo, Ohio's Civic Centre, Jackie's mother had come to see the show. Things got a little out of control as Askey relates: "During those days you had a dancing show, the band came on from nine till one. Maybe Jackie was due on at ten for about an hour. He would come on again at twelve till one. There was a walkway between the stage and the pit. A cop was walking around there and we warned him, 'You'd better get out of there, because when Jackie reaches the stage…' 'Oh, no,' said the cop, 'I've got it under control.'

"We went on at 9pm, Floyd Smith on guitar, Jimmy on saxophone, Chris Columbo, me on trumpet and guitarist Dickie Thompson [conducting at that period]. There was two and a half to three thousand people, drinking and all. An hour passed and we expected Jackie. We played for two hours. No Jackie! People were throwing bottles at us, so we took a break.

"Jackie was out in the parking lot sitting in his Cadillac with his Chihuahua dog. He hated to be doing this show. What was going on, I don't know. He just wasn't happy, but he came in about twelve and he said, 'I better go on before these people wreck this place.' Man, when Jackie hit that stage, people went over the rail and went straight over that cop. How they got up on that stage I don't know. They were cuddling him... they had him on the floor. They didn't care nothing about him being late. The organ was on top of the organ player. With all the chaos, Jackie was just smiling."

Things again got out of hand in another town, recalls Askey: "In Dayton, Ohio, at the Walpole Theatre which seated about four thousand people. It was summer time – warm – they had this podium in the middle like a boxing ring – sticking up – where Jackie was going to sing from. We, the band, were over the other side entertaining the people and we told the promoter Jackie wasn't going to hear us from over there. They told us, 'We've got it all set up, it'll sound like the band is there.' We kept saying, 'He's not going to be happy. Jackie likes his band right behind him.'

"Jackie was back in the dressing room, late as usual, and he was so close we could hear him talking. He kept stalling and stalling. By this time the crowd was thinking that Jackie was going to be up on stage with us and they massed right in the front of this space where we were. Anyhow, Jackie came out and they had to try to get him through them four thousand people and up to this podium. It took twenty minutes. We were being crushed. It was chaos. Jackie got up there and started, but he got half way through the first piece of music and he called out, 'I can't hear my band.'

"So now they are going to bring him back through the audience. They had pulled off his coat, his silk shirt had been ripped off – never wore any under shirt – and he had nothing on but his pants. Jackie looked at up and laughed and said, 'Boy, they sure do love me, don't they?' He wasn't worried about anything. He loved all of this stuff. He did his show; how he performed.

"These things are easy to remember because of the chaos and for the beauty of what came out of it: through all of this mass hysteria he would get up there and perform for one hour, or an hour and half by himself. He didn't like to do two shows, because when he got off he was soaking wet. Every time we played anywhere there was chaos because the places were not big enough. Ninety per cent of our audiences were black."

Jack "The Rapper" Gibson came to know Jackie well over the years and while a DJ in Cincinatti, in 1960, he also knew Berry Gordy who had just begun his fledgling Motown hit making organisation and he recalls how he joined it. "Berry asked me, 'Jack why don't you get in the record business?' I said, 'I can't sing, I can't dance and can't even hum.' He told me, 'But you know everybody.' You see I had formed the National Association of Radio Announcers – I became the first president – so I knew all the different black disc jockeys in the country. He said, 'Jack, why don't you come over and work for me?' I said, 'What kind of salary will you pay me to work for you? I'm a big star in Cincinatti – I'm making $125 per week and all the payola that can come my way.' He said, 'I can't pay you more than $125, but I'll give you an American Express Card.' I said, 'When do I start work?' So Berry Gordy and I have been close. I have been there to put together The Temptations and The Supremes. I was there when there was no Motown." Gibson became Motown's first national public relations director.

He explains the philosophy that proved so successful for Motown: "Berry decided the music was to be for everybody – not just blacks. Then it became the sound of young America. As public relations director I didn't have no money to pay no disc jockeys, but I knew what it took to get them to play a record. Instead of paying folks, I said, 'Take one of my records and make it a hit and I'll bring you the act in a few weeks.' They'd play the hell out of the record for a few weeks and I'd come to town with the act. That gave the DJs a chance to set up a dance and make their money legitimately."

By most accounts, Nat Tarnopol encouraged Jackie to be constantly out on a financial limb. That way Jackie would need to always sing for his supper. Their friendship became increasingly strained. Freda says, "He never could break with Nat, but he did do a little something about it. He had been trying for years." Freda was referring to 1960 or 1961 when he changed managers from Tarnopol to Johnny Roberts, although still remaining bound to the Brunswick label. From Tarnopol's standpoint, Jackie was increasingly unmanageable. Numerous times he failed to appear for an engagement or recording session, both of which are costly for a manager.

Nobody could recall exactly what contractual arrangements Tarnopol had drawn up with Jackie, indeed all documents pertaining to management fees and royalties appear to have been lost or, more likely, destroyed along the way. Tarnopol kept Jackie either in the recording studio or touring. Either way Jackie was earning large sums of money for Brunswick. His earliest contractual arrangement with Brunswick was said to be only three per cent of retail royalties, with a minimum guaranteed of fifty thousand dollars per year. When Jackie and Tarnopol renegotiated the contract in 1968, the share became five per cent.

Throughout his entire career Jackie engaged Herbert Lippman as his lawyer. Lippman was the nephew of Jackie's original manager, Al Green, but, more ominously, was a crony of Tarnopol. Was this ethical or advantageous to Jackie?

Freda recalls how it was not uncommon for Tarnopol to phone in the middle of the night and Jackie would have to get up and go out to entertain some client. In the beginning, Tarnopol was like Jackie's shadow – never out of his sight. To his credit, Tarnopol was somewhat of a workaholic, being first to arrive at the office and the last to leave. Brunswick was once again becoming a recognised label and he soon required more salubrious surroundings than the Brill Building provided. He moved the operation to the nineteenth floor 888 Seventh Avenue, in mid town New York, while still finding sufficient time to organise concerts with his friend Alan Freed.

Son Paul reckons it wasn't always easy for Tarnopol, either, being manager. "There were major problems all through his career with Jackie," he says. "Jackie would wind up in jail regularly. He would get into trouble with white women. Nat would get calls from all over the country asking to bail Jackie out. He'd be in a hotel with a girl when he should be on stage. My dad had to get a road manager, Augie [August] Sims, just to make sure he was in the right place at the right time because Jackie just couldn't do it by himself. Throughout his whole life he was rebellious.

"At one time my father told him he had to stop doing this; stop getting into trouble and showing up late. Jackie would have cars, rings, furs; spending on people like crazy. One time he got a call from Augie saying, 'You'd better talk to Jackie. He is not going to be up for the show.' My father told him, 'If you miss the show we're going to be up for a lot of money and you could end up in jail,' and he said, 'If I go to jail, I'll just give them an autographed picture and I'll be out.' That same night, at 10pm, dad got a call from a chief of police saying he was in jail. Jackie said, 'You've got to get me out.' Dad said, 'Why are you calling me? Just give them an autographed picture and you'll be out.' Nat finally got him out.

"Nat and Jackie would often fight and Jackie would say, 'I don't need you any more.' One time Nat said, 'Okay, I don't need you,' and tore up the contract. Next day Jackie was back again. There were times when Nat and Jackie nearly got lynched [in the southern states]. Partly because there were white women in the audience. There were shootings, too."

Roquel Davis believes Jackie would have had more success in the charts with better guidance. "All performers were in awe of Jackie back then," he says. "They couldn't do anything else but be in awe. He had a great personality, charisma...unbelievable. You couldn't help but love him. Jackie didn't have anybody musically conscious to guide him. Nat thought he could. Nat didn't know one piece from another; he always pretended he did. He was totally out of step. Prior to Jackie, who was Nat Tarnopol? He was a 'gofer' for Al Green."

American Bandstand's Dick Clark knew Tarnopol. He says: "Nat was a very colourful man – lots of rings and jewellery and loads of cash in his pocket at all times. I got along very well with him. Years ago I went to see Jackie. He appeared in Atlantic City in a roller skating ring – it was an all black audience – with a friend of mine, Al Wild, a little short guy, fat, Jewish man who was a manager. Nat was backstage where Jackie had his hand maidens giving him rub downs, amongst the roller skates, and waiting on him like a king. It was tawdry, squalid, awful atmosphere with the empty gin bottles and broken glasses after the show, but everybody was paying homage and court to him backstage. My friend Al Wild embraced Nat and proceeded to lift several thousand dollars from his pocket. Al said, 'Wait till he finds out I took his wad.' He gave it back to him of course, but the joke was that at the time he was picking his pocket."

Freda rues how Jackie had trusted Nat Tarnopol so much he signed power of attorney over to him: "Even I knew better than that. After Al Green died I knew better. Green would have been fair with him." Freda suggested he should proceed with caution, but Jackie was trusting and naive: "I said, 'Even if you gave me power of attorney I might be tempted to do something.' Especially if I got mad; I might take the money and put it in a bank account in my mother's name. I said, 'Don't do it.' Jack was having problems with Nat...with his money. Nat kept saying to us he was not taking his ten per cent [management fee]. Then, all of a sudden, there was no money that should have been in the bank. Nat had authority to use his money in any way he saw fit. That's why he lived in that hotel...he was making sure he was secure even before he got married."

Paul Tarnopol believes otherwise: "Jackie would demand money and he would get money. Jackie never gave over power of attorney to my father. If that was the case there couldn't be any discussion about money. Legally he couldn't do it; as a record company it would be illegal."

In the beginning Jackie relied totally on Tarnopol to take care of his financial affairs and the power of attorney claim is believed by many to be correct. Davis is one of those who believes it existed. "They [Brunswick] even wanted power of attorney over Berry and I," he reflects. "I think Al Green also had power of attorney over Jackie."

Aware Tarnopol was holding back his royalty earnings, Jackie became increasingly unreliable, either appearing late, or not at all. Many years later, when the legal system finally caught up with Tarnopol, it became known that he was selling Jackie's records "out the back door". It is certain that the Mob also benefited from these illegal sales, all to the detriment of Jackie's financial position.

Gradually Jackie realised he was not getting his just desserts. A classic example of this is a story related by Gil Askey: "Jackie woke up one morning – he's just come off a great three month tour – and he called his bank to find out how much money he had in his account. They told him an amount, say '11-85'. He said, 'You mean $11,085?' They said, 'No, I mean $11.85.' Jackie fell out of bed, fell on the floor, and nearly had a heart attack. So he went down to the bank and opened his safety deposit box. It contained a bunch of IOUs. Tarnopol had power of attorney and the key to his deposit box." Of course the sums quoted may not be accurate but the situation was typical of what was going on. The power of attorney question may be debated, but one thing was clear: Jackie was singing his heart out and seemingly getting deeper in debt.

Part of the reason Jackie was legitimately short of money may have been because the artist had to pay for all the session time and promotional activity, before he saw a penny of his royalties. In Jackie's case this would amount to large amounts. His sixteen piece orchestral backing were top flight musicians. Add to this the studio cost, studio production people and the back-up singers. This would be covered if the session produced a million seller: if not, the amount owed would be debited to the artist's next project. Brunswick was not alone in this practice.

To be fair, for a record company, producing hits is a high risk business. Berry Gordy was fond of saying that only one or two per cent of songs recorded actually became hits and, therefore, presumably the other ninety-eight to ninety-nine per cent of recordings were money losers or, at best, broke even. Obviously, some artists never succeeded and so cost the company money on them.

Royalties based on sales are paid to the artist on the recording. As might be expected, there were some pretty unfair contracts signed. Popular singers generally didn't have high educational levels, whether they be Frank Sinatra, Elvis Presley, or Jackie Wilson. Little Richard is said to have been signed to a one per cent of retail contract with Specialty Records. It is also said early Motown artists were on one or two per cent royalty contracts. Michael Jackson today enjoys over forty per cent, while it is believed Nat Tarnopol originally signed Jackie up for three per cent. This was re-negotiated in 1968 to five per cent. Six to eight per cent royalties were more the norm and considered fair.

Childhood friend Hank Ballard believes Jackie's real problem was desperate loneliness. "I think most of the people surrounding Jackie were hangers-on and users," he says. "He knew why they was there. He had drug addicts, heroin addicts hanging on there. He was giving them…buying drugs. He was just too generous. I think that's why he was so lonely."

Guitarist Dickie Thompson agrees. "The thing I remember was Jackie didn't like to be alone. If he didn't have someone around, he'd go crazy. He would always have someone around in the dressing room and if he didn't, he'd call me or find me. Jackie would pick up almost anyone off the street, get 'em a haircut and a brand new suit of clothes, take 'em on the road with him as a driver. They couldn't drive for shit, but they'd tell him, 'Oh yeah, I can drive, man.' He'd put them behind the wheel and fifty miles out of town they'd get lost.

Thompson travelled at that time with Jackie and The Chris Columbo Band: "Those times, it was strange for me," he says. "I didn't really want the gig. I told them I couldn't read music too well, but I'd been around, played with everybody. So they said, 'What I want you to do is conduct.' So between Gil Askey and Earl Van Dyke [later to become one of Motown's rhythm section] they said, 'All you do is keep time; you start the thing and you end it.' Once you know the tempo, it's easy. He would change his vocals, but the back-up was the same. No rehearsals. Jackie always said, 'Watch me, watch me.' His basic show was the same ten tunes, so after a time I didn't watch him any more. Now and then he'd slip in an extra one or two songs. Jackie said to me one night, 'You don't even look at me any more.' He smoked a lot and drank a lot – he could drink anytime – always had a frog in his throat." But Thomson adds ironically, "If he had so many true friends, how come he was always in trouble?

"There were some scary moments, especially through the south. Once around Jackson, Mississippi we got lost and it was the time the black boy was trying to get into the white college [James Meredith attempted to enter the University of Mississippi in 1962]. They had the National Guard out, and here we are, lost, with two cars with New York plates! They gave us directions – took us to the town limits! Jackie knew what was going to happen and he pushed it to the limit. We got into brawls all the time."

Hank Ballard confirms one of the consequences of Jackie's success. "We [the Midnighters] were the first to come out of Detroit with a hit record, but Jackie was the biggest entertainer to come out of Detroit and elsewhere. He was magic, man. He could go to Las Vegas and play those rooms; he was a class act. Off stage he was different, but on stage he was class. He was a party man. If anyone bruised him or violated him, you'd have to kill him. He would fight."

He would need to. Being black and driving around the southern states in a Cadillac with New York licence plates, could create problems, as band member Askey explains: "The way the times were, there were a lot of prejudices. We couldn't stop on the highway in Georgia or Alabama and go to the toilets in one of the road side parks 'cause they had 'Whites Only' signs. At filling stations in the middle of the night we could buy gas but we couldn't go to the toilet. These things usually ate at the heart of Jackie. He kept a lot of stuff inside him.

"In 1960 we did a concert in Birmingham, Alabama. At that time you did a concert Sunday afternoon for a white audience and Sunday night for the blacks. Jackie refused to do the show for the whites. Arthur Prysock came out with us, and Larry Williams. The next day we went to Florence, Alabama, same situation prevailed, but he went on. These little white girls five, maybe ten of them, moved upstage and Jackie would go into these gyrations, he'd do spins and flips and the girls would scream, then they would stop real sudden because everyone was looking at them." Well behaved southern white girls didn't get excited over black performers, did they?

It was little wonder if Jackie felt anguish or bitterness, when despite being world famous, he wasn't allowed to sit down and eat in a restaurant in a large area of his own country. "Sir" Mack Rice recalls touring at the same time: "When we was travelling Jackie had his big new, shiny Cadillac. Anyhow, we was going down the highway touring down south, and there was Jackie eating watermelon on the side of the road. We all stopped there, just to see! We couldn't get into big restaurants – we'd have baloney and sandwiches and stuff."

He also remembers seeing Jackie and JJ, along with some large amounts of money: "I've seen him and JJ after a gig. They'd have a briefcase full of money and they'd put it into the trunk. A briefcase, just like the gangsters. Jackie was like Isaac Hayes – he cherished his friends." Gil Askey, too, recalls the briefcase full of money that they had. "Jackie never had any money on him, but JJ was there and had his little briefcase full of money. And it better be his money, 'cause he's supposed to send the other money back to the office in New York."

One steamy July night in 1960 at the Municipal Auditorium in New Orleans, a riot broke out at one of Jackie's performances, where up to five thousand people were said to be present. Singer Chuck Jackson, a long time close friend of Jackie's, was with The Dell Vikings at the time. He remembers: "I was there when Larry Williams was performing. The police told us before we got there, 'Don't come off this stage, black boy.'

"They had police lined up all around the stage. And Larry Williams had his foot up on the piano like Little Richard. He was doing 'Dizzy Miss Lizzy' and he ran to the edge of the stage, but didn't jump off. He got down on the edge of the stage and women came forward – white women! Jackie was standing backstage and the cops took Larry and pulled him into the audience and started beating him with their sticks. Jackie came from backstage like he was Johnny Weismuller – he ran like he was Tarzan – and he leapt, like he was leaping into a lake, into the crowd of policemen. When he hit the floor, he was like a little rabbit. He went down on his knees and when he came up, like he does on stage, he hit this cop…big red cop. He messed him up bad. They beat him and nearly killed him.

"We finally pulled him out and had to take him to the hospital. They took him to jail and we got him out. It took us a matter of minutes to get out of town. They had his picture in the paper, where he hit the cop." The riot received coverage in the newspapers, stating police laid charges which "ranged from attempted murder to assaulting police and inciting a riot. Wilson was booked with disturbing the peace, inciting a riot and assaulting an officer."

Also present was Midnighters guitarist and friend, Billy Davis: "Larry would jump off the stage into the audience. The police said, 'Don't you do that no more.' The second the show started and Larry jumped out again.

Jackie jumped up and the big cop pushed him back, then Jackie punched him out cold and Jackie could punch like George Foreman for a little guy. The cop was six foot one, 225 pounds; Jackie was 140 to 145 pounds and five foot nine. We were all locked up, but only for a few hours."

Trumpeter Gil Askey was also with them. "We were told to get out of town 'cause they were putting our guys in jail," he says. "They'd caught Arthur Prysock on the street and a couple of Jackie's people. Jackie got out on bond and we hit out of town at three or four o'clock in the morning. We went up to Atlanta. We played to packed houses in Houston and in Fort Worth, but the IRS came and took all the money, because the promoter owed taxes."

With all the excitement of the riot and his being so keen to rescue Jackie, JJ completely forgot to look after the briefcase full of money, which he left unguarded in the dressing room. Luckily, band leader Chris Columbo closed up the briefcase and took care of it. However, the New York office must have heard about JJ's blunder, because soon after Johnny Roberts joined them on the road. Roberts formerly worked with Queens Booking Agency and had a fearsome reputation as a Mob enforcer. His role was to take care of the money, but also to provide protection for Jackie. Although he was usually the perfect soft spoken gentleman, when he fixed his icy stare on someone, they would become extremely nervous and do exactly what was expected of them. Certainly, with Roberts there, no unscrupulous promoter would consider short changing anybody. After the show, Roberts would take the money over to the Western Union office where it was wired back to New York."

Nobody doubted that Jackie could handle himself in a scrap. What was harder to understand was why, when he was so often a victim, did he have to be the initiator of trouble. Jimmy Smith remembers a social occasion that Jackie nearly turned into a war zone because of his near phobia about eating in public. "A DJ called Buddy Beau had a barbecue going on," he says. "He had two, one for the hoodlums, one for the classy people. He sent the limo to pick us up: me, Jackie, Billy Johnson and Watley. He took us to the hoodlums' place. Jackie was kissing and going on and we were doing our thing.

"They had a great big old hog on the table and they wanted Jackie to eat. Jackie said, 'Just fix the food,' so he can take it with him to eat. They said, 'No.' So Jack told Watley to go and fix him some meat. The guy stopped Watley, so Jack went in there and snatched the whole hog up. And man, we got to it! We were fighting like hell. I jumped up on the bed and was trying to hold on to the briefcase – it had the money in it. We went downstairs and Jackie struck up another fight with those guys. One guy pulled out a pistol and started shooting; that's the only thing that stopped us." Seemingly, things ended amicably, though. "They came to the dance that night and we bought 'em beer and stuff. It was fun."

Johnny Collins, a singer who married Jackie's half-sister Joyce Ann, opened for his brother-in-law for a couple of years, and has vivid memories of the indignities Jackie suffered. Indignities of every form, such as one occasion when a southern sheriff had him beaten to pulp after white women had become interested. Collins recalls: "Anyone who understands the music business has first got to understand what it is to have emotions. That's a roller-coaster ride and not everybody made the ride. Entertainers have to live the lives of a true solo artist; that is the epitome of heaven and hell.

"When Jackie walked out on the stage after having his ribs cracked, he sang as hard as he did when he was fine. He heard things that would destroy you; the public have no idea what made the performance. The better the entertainer, the better the confrontation, the deeper the feeling. Jackie was the most honest. He gave all he could give. That made him special. He was different. Entertainers start out as human beings and then turn into something else. Boxing and music were the two most violent games there were. He wanted to be a pro boxer, so he did it both ways." Jackie never gave a fair performance. He gave body and soul; regardless of the personal pain he may have been feeling.

The Midnighters' Billy Davis recalls a near riot situation which further illustrates Jackie's dedication: "We were in Houston, Texas, at the Houston City Auditorium. Hank Ballard And The Midnighters, Jackie Wilson, Sam Cooke, The Flamingos; about fourteen or fifteen acts. They introduced Jackie, he came up there; the crowd went nuts, went haywire. They had ten to fifteen thousand people; you could feel the building move.

"Jackie was doing his usual opening number, 'I'll Be Satisfied', and they sent for the chief of police, who came on stage and told him, 'You cannot sing, we can't control the people.' The cops told the audience two to three times, 'You've got to sit down, otherwise there's not going to be a show.' The security guards took the mike and stopped the show. This went on for twenty to thirty minutes. They escorted Jackie backstage. He was furious because he could not sing. The promoter told him, 'Jackie, don't worry, you're going to get your money.' Jackie said, 'It's not that, I just want to sing!' He just loved to sing."

Another singer who came out of Detroit, a little later than Jackie, was Barbara Lewis. Famous for her smash hit 'Hello Stranger' in 1963, she remembers her fellow Detroit singer with fondness. "I think Jackie Wilson was one of the finest performers from our era," she says. "Very charismatic on stage and unique the way the audience became enthralled in his performance – and they became a part of his performance. They would tear all his clothes off. That was not a common occurrence – to get an audience in that state of mind. His talent was so powerful…his voice was so powerful. I can't think we've had another male entertainer of his magnitude – I can't think of any.

"Michael Jackson is great, but not in the same category. Jackie was charismatic – you either have that, or you don't – it's not taught or learnt. What other entertainer do you know that had that? They were some of the hardest audiences and he was put to the test. He came out victorious on stage. Many audiences don't show a lot of excitement. Naturally, he would transform them. Not many could do it. Sammy Davis Jnr could bring an audience to his feet. I've seen Wilson Pickett and Joe Tex and they'd get an audience to scream, but they never captivated an audience the way Jackie did. He was an entertainer's entertainer. When you're a singer's singer, you're something. You could hear within a song R&B, pop, opera, and blues. I think if he was doing today what he was doing then, there would be no one in the world who did not know who he was." Lewis regrets never performing duet with Jackie, although they shared the same billing – the last time at Atlanta's Peacock Club.

Friend and vocalist with the successful Dell Vikings, Chuck Jackson, first met Jackie in 1957, the year they had their three Top Forty hits. "He started me as a single act; a solo artist," says Jackson. "That was 1959; I left The Dell Vikings in 1960. I did the theatre chain with him; the Apollo, the Uptown Theatre [in Philadelphia]."

There was rarely a dull moment travelling with Jackie, who mischievously often instigated it. Alcohol likely played a large part. "One time we were in Texas – I was only about twenty," says Jackson. "I'm a mild man, I think. Jackie would always say, 'You never get really upset.' He was already a star but I was trying to be a star and I had to watch my Ps and Qs. So we were in this place, a very small town, and he was drinking and he said, 'Chuck, punch JJ.' I said, 'I'm not going to punch JJ, are you kidding?'

"Don Harris was his bodyguard then; he looked like Jackie. 'Okay', he said, 'I'm going to have Harris whoop you.' I said, 'No, nobody's going to whoop me.' Don jumped up and we went to it. It was just one of those things we did at the time; we'd just try each other to blow off steam. I waxed him and nobody messed with me no more after that. When it had finished there was nobody mad. It was kind of fun."

He recalls another crazy incident: "I was riding in the car with him on the way to a gig on the same tour, and he had a gun. We were in the limousine, driving down the Texas highway shooting signs. We'd come to a sign saying 'Cross Roads Ahead', we'd shoot the sign and it would turn. So if you had to make a left turn and saw that sign, you'd turn right! We were doing it one day and the gun went off. The window was still up and the bullet went through the window and shattered and glass fell all over me. I was sitting facing him. It scared him to death and he never played with guns after that. When he hit the window JJ almost turned the car over.

"One night we were in New Orleans. Jackie and I were there with The Dixie Cups and their manager. We played the job that night and had a lot of fun. Their manager at the time was Jones; he wrote all their stuff. We sat up all night then had to drive all the way to Macon, Georgia – seven hundred miles. The bus left with everyone early. I woke up about ten or eleven o'clock and, as Jackie was next door, I tried to wake him to say we've got to get going. He was still asleep. We travelled together, his car and my car. I was trying to wake him and finally JJ and Sims got him out of bed – one in the afternoon!

"So we finally get in the car at two o'clock and he says he knows a short cut. Jackie Wilson knows a short cut, and he doesn't even drive! He's the worst driver in the world! So we are driving and we are flying, and we got stopped by the cops when we've got about two hundred miles to go and it's, say, six o'clock. Jackie's people gave 'em a story and they let us go. We finally pulled in about quarter to nine, to this job, we were doing 120 [mph] most of the time.

"When we got there, Jerry Butler was on the show and he had sung 'Your Precious Love' thirty times. The people were so sick of it. He was trying to fill in and we kept calling in [by phone] periodically, saying, 'We're on our way, we're nearly there.' So when we pulled at the back of the place, Jerry Butler came running out of the back door. People had started throwing things at him. By this time, the people were in a full state of riot. The police told us to get out of there. We ran and Jackie was trying to get dressed in the car. They were throwing rocks at the bus, it was incredible. We missed the job, and I was mad 'cause I couldn't afford to miss a job."

For all the singer's pranks, Jackson bristles at the suggestion that sometimes Jackie could get out of control. "Who said he trashed rooms? I think every entertainer that came through has done these things, except me 'cause I don't do dope. I was with Jackie Wilson from the later part of 1957 until 1975. I tell you I ate and slept with this man. Never in my life have I seen him put a piece of coke in his nose. I know he did, but he never did it in front of me and there was nobody closer to Jackie than me. We'd sit up and drink a one fifth or a two fifth of J&B [Scotch], but he never ever snorted coke when I saw him. He smoked very heavily, most guys did. I used to then, too."

So what kind of a person did he find Jackie? He answers without hesitation: "He had a definite impact on people. He was completely different than anyone of his period. He was good looking and he catered strictly to women. Guys loved him, but he loved women. He loved everybody. Jackie used to say, 'Every woman is my woman.' I used to say, 'Everyone except mine!' He would steal women from friends. I told my wife, 'I wouldn't leave my woman around Jackie for all the tea in China.' It isn't that I don't trust my woman – I didn't want to have to kill Jackie. I loved him dearly and truly believe he loved me."

Jackson believes that the only thing that prevented Jackie achieving superstar status was his colour. "Then again Jackie Wilson was a pioneer in being the lover black boy, and we don't fare too well in this country when all the women love us; being black. It's a shame, but it's the truth. It seems if you're not a clown you're not accepted. You have to be a clown to be accepted and be around for a long time, 'cause our talents don't do it."

Jackson understood some deep inner pain was eating its way into Jackie's soul. But being so proud and macho made it impossible for Jackie to express in words; even to someone as close as Jackson. "The hate is all over the United States," he says, "and that didn't bother Jackie any more than it bothered Sam Cooke or Jerry Butler. I think what really got to Jackie was that he couldn't get over that hump of acceptance." Jackie knew no one could compete with him as a vocalist or performer, so why did he have to continually be proving himself? Why hadn't he achieved the acclaim Sinatra or Presley had? And why was it that, despite the hits and albums and all the touring, all he had to show for it was a middle class home on LaSalle Boulevard in Highland Park and some jewellery?

Career-wise 1961 was a excellent year for Jackie, in all likelihood his best. The five single releases all made it in the charts. 'My Empty Arms' went to Number Nine, 'Please Tell Me Why' reached Number Twenty, 'Your One And Only Love' Number Forty, 'I'm Comin' On Back To You' Number Nineteen and 'Years From Now' Number Thirty-Seven.

Two albums were also released; the first, *You Ain't Heard Nothing Yet*, in February 1961, was a twelve song tribute to Al Jolson, Jackie's idol. In the New York *Sunday News* interview (October 1961) Jackie stated: "When I was a kid and my friends were either Sinatra or Crosby fans, my idol was always Jolson. I don't know what there was about him, maybe it was because he was such a showman that he got to me. I played his songs over and over. Then I'd sing his songs in my own way, not imitating his voice; but I got a kick out of his gestures, I'd seen them in the movies and watched people who imitated him. I copied his getting down on his knees when he sang – I still do it. I love that flashy kind of stuff and made it a regular part of my act."

Dick Jacobs in the *Musician* article explained the Jolson album: "Jackie Wilson was a super fan of Al Jolson. Jolson had a profound influence on Jackie's singing which I found very apparent on his renditions of pop songs. When Jackie decided to do an album of all Jolson songs, we went ahead and did it. Since Jackie knew and loved the songs so well, we were able to cut the record in two sessions, recording six tunes per studio block. If there's one record in the Jackie Wilson catalogue that demonstrates his amazing versatility, this is it."

The Jolson tribute didn't chart and didn't sell near as well as it deserved. It is clearly Jackie's own style and, as remarkable a talent as Jolson was, Jackie does Jolson far better than Jolson. Jacobs: "The public couldn't accept the benign irony and great tenderness in Jackie's earnest tribute to the white minstrel boy, Al Jolson: it required a stretch of imagination that people weren't prepared to make."

While Jackie's recording career remained to some extent in the hands of the buyers, on stage no one could deny him success. In New York, he performed regularly at the Brooklyn Fox, the Brooklyn Paramount theatres, the swanky Copacabana and the Apollo. Harlem's Apollo Theatre, the black equivalent of Nashville's Grand Old Opry, was started by Frank Schiffman although his son Bobby ran it during Jackie's period and showcased most of the great black performers of the time. For a black artist, if you hadn't "made it" at the Apollo Theatre in Harlem, you were nobody, as Bobby Schiffman explains: "The Apollo was a prestigious date and it was probably only the breakdown of discrimination by the entertainment business that sealed its fate. In its heyday black performers couldn't play the white establishments. They couldn't play the Paramount, downtown smart club or theatre. In the fifties about fifteen to twenty per cent of the Apollo audiences would be white.

"Headliners earned fifty per cent of the gross; fifty per cent, and the performer paid for the show – ie, the band and other acts – and kept the difference. Headliners who didn't get a percentage made about $2,500 a week. Jackie was always on the fifty per cent, and earned much more."

In the 1960s, at their peak, other artists began earning huge sums. Jackie never did earn the truly big money, despite having more talent in his little finger than many had in their entire bodies. Jimi Hendrix was getting fifty thousand dollars a night, The Beatles up to twice as much, compared to Jackie's $2,200 to $2,400 a night, including gate percentages. He and his band worked Las Vegas for around ten thousand dollars a week, unfortunately peaking just before the big money explosion occurred. Putting these payments in perspective, the price of a new prestigious Cadillac was five thousand dollars; seven and a half for a top of the range Fleetwood.

The Apollo audience could be pretty rough if they didn't get the show they expected. Dickie Thompson remembers: "We had just played the Copacabana doing typical Broadway tunes with Sy Oliver conducting a big band full of strings, but they made the mistake of taking the same show to the Apollo where it went over like a lead balloon. Audience hated it. The second Apollo show Jackie did was back to 'soulville' and voilà! He left them screaming for joy."

The Apollo was also hard work: "We worked five shows a day on weekends and holidays," he adds. At the end of the tour Jackie called the band in and handed out six men's diamond and onyx rings. There was a special one for Thompson which Jackie had selected. "I still have it and treasure it highly," he says proudly.

According to Schiffman, "Jackie was for a long time the biggest attraction we ever had. For a long time we would welcome him with open arms. Billy Eckstine was terrific in his time, but never the excitement of a Jackie Wilson on stage. Jackie Wilson was exciting to watch. He hit the stage like a fighter. From an economic stand point he was a big home run for us at the Apollo."

Harvey Fuqua who formed The Moonglows (originally they were known as Harvey And The Moonglows) and later manager to Marvin Gaye, knew Jackie from the 1950s. They'd first met in Detroit at the home of Rev Franklin, father of "the Queen Of Soul", Aretha. Says Fuqua, "He was headlining at the Apollo with King Coleman, Etta James, Frankie Lyman; they used to have ten acts at the Apollo in those days and everyone would perform one or two numbers, five shows a day. One time the crowd applauded so much he was forced to do an encore and he was a little upset with it. He wanted to say, 'Stick to the script. Do your two to three numbers and come off.' So he called everyone in the dressing room and said, 'Don't deviate.' We used to call him 'Mr Do Not Deviate' every time we ran into him."

Tina Johnson, who was part of James Brown's Brownies dance group, well recalls Jackie's sexual attraction and the hysteria his performances evoked: "I performed with James Brown first time at the Apollo. Jackie followed us on. He had that sexual attraction ability better than anybody. In fact girls took off their panties and bras and threw them on stage. Most of Jackie's stage outfits were specifically to take off. He would dress in a tie and suit most times, but his cuff links and ties – he had them by the dozens – just to throw out into the audience. He didn't wear underwear. He did too much moving around."

But, as Schiffman says: "Jackie was trouble. He was unpredictable and thus was tough to work with. Sam Cooke was clean, a perfect role model, dependable and reliable and a pleasure to work with." Cooke, like Jackie, had a fondness for the ladies and probably played around almost as much as Jackie did, but tended to be more discreet. He hid behind those innocent good looks, while Jackie always had that wicked look in his eyes. Jackie definitely had a "bad boy" image. Never known for reliability, punctuality or responsibility, he was a "wild card", but a talented one who was never accused of not giving his best shot.

Schiffman was a close friend of Nat Tarnopol and sees Jackie and his friend through different eyes. He, more than most, credits Tarnopol with much of Jackie's success: "He seemed to have the ability to keep Jackie in line. He made Jackie fulfil his obligations to his fans and to the promoter. Nat made Jackie happen. It is possible that someone else might have done so, but there was Nat doing it everyday. Jackie had his difficult times off the stage: his health was always a question, sometimes we didn't know if he was going to make it to the stage or not. It was a tough period on performers.

"It's also costly when you have musicians sitting around for a session and the product doesn't show up. I know that Nat Tarnopol loaned him a tremendous amounts of money – that's what Nat told me. Every time he dealt with me on Jackie, he was a perfect gentleman and dealt with me in a straightforward and honest way. I had nothing but the greatest respect for him; despite what they were saying out there on the streets about him. I'm not sure about Jackie being ripped off, but I do know that at that time artists were very high livers. Spending money on all sorts of pleasures."

Simon Rutberg, who'd known Jackie for fifteen years, has his own theory as to why Jackie appeared so often at the Apollo and why he was not the enormous superstar he ought to have been: "He was so successful with black audiences they wanted to keep him at the Apollo, rather than capitulate to whites and let him get 'over the hump'. They wanted Jackie to keep that doo rag on his head. Jackie had made it over the hump many times, but he had to keep making it with every record. He made it with 'Night', 'Alone At Last', 'All My Love'; those were the songs, but he'd be thrown back. He did 'For Once In My Life', it was beautiful, yet Stevie Wonder took it and made a hit out of it."

They'd first met while Jackie was touring Los Angeles in 1962, and they struck up a friendship that lasted until the singer's death. The extraordinary story illustrates the humility of the man. The boy, Simon Rutberg, was Jewish, white and fifteen years old. "There were very few people in the world that I really admired; I mean really admired," says Rutberg. "When I saw Jackie I knew I had to meet this guy and become his friend. I walked right up to him and became so tongue tied I could not get one word out, just a few odd sounds. Then he reacted to me and invited me back to the dressing room." Says Rutberg, "I know some heart warming stories; just how nice he could be to people he didn't know and how he could make his fans feel, because he worshipped his fans."

Whenever Jackie performed in Los Angeles, Rutberg was there backstage. He would spend hours in Jackie's dressing room either talking, giving Jackie the rub downs he enjoyed, and fetching him his favourite chicken soup from a Jewish restaurant on Fairfax Avenue. "Sometimes at two or three in the morning he'd send me out for chicken soup from Canters. It was not a glorious life when you're on the road, and in those days you were always on the road. He'd leave the club at 3 or 4am and go back to his hotel room; he'd be tired. In those days if he wasn't working, he wasn't earning."

He confirms the rituals that the singer practised before a performance: "Jackie would be in his hotel room about three hours before show time. He'd be bathing and preening and he would warm up his voice before the show, running up and down the scales and hitting high notes constantly – while getting dressed – slowly, casually.

"Once he was on stage and singing he was it – as confident as could be. Getting up there was hard…always tense, nervous, always scared to go up on stage. He'd come off stage looking like wet rags; his shirts would be soaked. Jackie wore great black silk shirts with his name monogrammed on them. He would often get his clothes torn, if the women got their hands on him."

Rutberg, too, was aware Jackie wasn't a natural dancer either with a partner or on stage. "Jackie couldn't dance; I never told anyone he was a great dancer. He was a great mover. What he does on stage…people who dance on stage, such as Michael Jackson, are performing. People will be applauding the moves and not listening to the music. Jackie, on the other hand, punctuated the music. He lets the moves underline the singing.

"It was so great, so exciting. I wish I could take you back with me, the first few times I ever saw Jackie, because you know how when you're in a race and the guys are in the starting block. 'On your mark, get set, go!' With Jackie it was as if somebody tied a rope around him – he's running, but can't move because of the rope. Then all of a sudden someone cuts the rope and he's gone. The performances are so clear in my mind. What can I say?"

Like all singers, Jackie had those he admired and took qualities from. One of those was a blues singer from the late 1940s and early 1960s, Roy Brown, who had a vocal pitch close to his own. Rutberg again: "Roy Brown; you can see Jackie there. He opens his throat when he sings. That's where Jackie got it. Jackie had phenomenal pronunciation."

Many times the performing and adulation became too much for Jackie. His young friend, Rutberg, was intelligent enough to read that and provide Jackie the space he needed. "I knew Jackie well enough to know if he wanted to be bothered or not bothered. I'd see him be nice to people who didn't deserve it and after they left he'd say, 'That motherfucker.' Would-be stars would come around Jackie's dressing room. Larry Williams was one – he was a pimp. He was shot. There were a lot of hanger's-on. People there who'd come around because they want to use that for something. They were draining him [mentally]. I would go to make myself scarce and he'd say, 'Don't leave. You can't leave yet.' So I had to stay. I'd sit there for four hours and he wouldn't say a word. Then he'd say, 'Well, Sy, bye, I've got to go. I'll see you later.'"

Rutberg would often give Jackie the rub downs he enjoyed so much – rather like a fighter would have before stepping into the ring. "My relationship with Jackie was very special. Like when I showed up in Vegas, I took a bus up there to see him. I wasn't old enough to get into the casinos. He was so glad to see me. It was like him coming to see me – 'the star'. I knocked on the door and he opened it and kissed my face, probably half a dozen times. He was so excited that I was there."

Young as Rutberg was he realised Jackie was deeply troubled: "He'd talk to me and before you know he'd be crying. He wouldn't let the other guys see that, because of the black 'macho' thing. It's an ego thing. Like, if you slap women around and people see you, it's, like 'He must be a big star'. Jackie asked me to work with him and I refused." He told Jackie, "I'd rather be your friend than to work for you," because he'd seen what happened to others who worked with him. Although it wasn't discussed, Rutberg could see the type of people who surrounded Jackie and all the little dramas and knew that by working with Jackie he'd likely lose a friend.

Rutberg also closely observed Jackie's complex personality. "Jackie had many faces. He could look tough or sweet. He had one look in which he looked like a cute little boy...a choir boy. Such an innocent sweet little kid. I have a picture of Jackie where you cover one side of the face and then the other – it looks like two completely different people. He had one of these pictures and he covered one side of the face and he said, 'You see that, Sy? That's my father. You see that, that's my mother.' Two totally different looks.

"The thing is about Jackie, he had a foot in both worlds. He was just a guy from the neighbourhood. He was also taken out of the neighbourhood and placed in high society. He was above the rock 'n' rollers. Take the way Jackie dressed in a suit; he was sharp. You put a suit on him and he looked like he was raised in elegance. Yet at the same time he was a ghetto boy. You have to understand that if you want to know Jackie. He gets up on stage and starts swinging at the cops and also at his audience. It's one thing to fight, but you don't beat up on your fans! A fight would break out in the audience and Jackie would jump off the stage and get right in, because he wanted to fight. In some ways he was like a stupid little kid who never grew up. Literally, a punk." Yet, as macho as Jackie was, or pretended to be, he also had another more endearing trait to his nature. "Jackie had a thing; he loved his mother," says Rutberg. "Whatever she said was law. He'd call her on the phone and say, 'I love you, honey, how are you?'"

The schedules and performances were gruelling, of course. "Nat Tarnopol tried to get Jackie working every night of the year," recalls Rutberg. "That's how they made their money." It would have seemed logical for Jackie to have toured the world; certainly he had an enormous following throughout Europe. "He didn't go on overseas trips because he hated to fly." Travelling constantly throughout the USA, Jackie always went by limo and had a chauffeur. "He was the worst driver in the world. I heard it said that to give Jackie a new car was like giving a child a loaded gun. He cracked up every car he had."

Having observed more than 150 of Jackie's live performances, Rutberg can truly claim to be an expert on him. He rates Jackie the all time greatest contemporary artist and was backstage often enough to also observe Jackie's dedication to his chosen career. "He'd stop eating, say, six hours before the show. A real artist does that. He was like an athlete and to sing at your full potential you don't do it on a full stomach. He was absolutely professional; I have no doubt he got this from Billy Ward. Today they don't know what singing is.

"Jackie could do everything, and I always thought that he figured, 'I'm doing all this and I'm good, but I'm not stretching enough! And the record album sales do not reflect what I want, therefore I'm not doing enough. He always felt, he knew he was good, but there came a point where – whatever! It's good enough, he became lazy. Not to anyone else, but to me it was. Perhaps it was because he was working for Nat Tarnopol, so who gives a shit. That was late 1960s. Jackie knew he was good, but I don't believe he knew how good!"

One of the world's great tap dancers, Cholly Atkins, with his partner Honi Cole, thrilled audiences in America and Europe for decades until the art form became unfashionable. He then enjoyed a remarkable come-back career as choreographer for the Motown stable of artists and is behind the beautiful stage footwork of The Temptations, Supremes or Four Tops. Atkins knew Jackie from often appearing on the same bill at the Apollo

Theatre. He says: "Jackie was a superb performer, a great singer. In my opinion a lot of great singers never had any quality. Elvis Presley, Louis Armstrong, Bobby Darin they had great style – they made you believe what they were singing. Jackie would have made a great politician – he made you believe what he was singing."

An inspiration, Jackie influenced many artists of the time. Philadelphia DJ and former music show host, Jerry "The Geator" Blavat, said: "I interviewed Smokey Robinson. When he first began to sing with that high falsetto sound he was a bit awkward, because he sounded a lot like a girl. He developed his singing style by listening to Sarah Vaughan, but when he heard Jackie Wilson he said he then didn't feel awkward. Dee Clark patterned his style after Jackie – so did Bobby Lewis."

Roquel Davis, knew how Jackie loved to perform: "When he wasn't headlining he still headlined, no matter whether he was opening or closing," he says. "Jackie had a lot of pride. He would have suffered twice as much when he wasn't headlining. The stars of the show would ask, 'Put him as far from me as possible.'

"Jackie loved every minute up on that stage. That's why Nat Tarnopol got away with murder – with his money. Jackie just looked forward to his next performance…seeing his name and his picture, and his fans screaming at him and his continental suits and rings."

Another popular black group of the late 1950s and early 1960s, The Dells were often on the same Apollo billing with Jackie. Chuck Barksdale, who sang bass with the group then and more than forty years later still does, says: "Jackie Wilson, of the artists that came out in the fifties, was the most talented we had. Next to him Sam Cooke, next to him Brook Benton, and then there's a number of others who would take up fourth place. Then we'd come up with an artist who was my best friend – Marvin Gaye. He would rank in that top four."

"Dells lead singer Johnny Carter and Jackie, both being Gemini, admired each other's talents tremendously." Barksdale recalled Jackie's performances: "Having worked with Jackie a hundred times or more, it's like plucking a leaf of a tree; which one's the prettiest? That's how it was with his performances – it all came off the same tree.

"At the Howard Theatre in Washington DC, a theatre very dear to Jackie and The Dells before it closed down, we were on one of many, many shows with Jackie. On this occasion Jackie was a little under the weather for one reason or another. He was hoarse. We finished our bit and got off. Jackie used to stand in the wings and watch, so as we moved into the show he was getting ready. He smoked his cigarette and had a little shot of whatever. He'd knock that whisky down – boom! He'd go out with the cigarette still in his hand. It was part of the act. I thought he ain't going to make it; he could barely speak. I guess it's like Sammy Davis Jnr used to say, 'All I've got to do is open a refrigerator door and I automatically do twenty minutes.' This is what happened with Jackie. He hit the stage – the spotlight grabbed him over by the curtain – by the time he hit the middle of the stage and went through his bit – doing the gyrations and putting the cigarette out, it's like God said, 'Voice, open up.'

"The people had already been informed; it seeped through the audience, 'Jackie Wilson can't sing; he's hoarse. He's not feeling good.' Bullshit: Jackie had them on their feet from the opening. His opening was fantastic enough, without him singing a word – and the women would just get hysterical. He'd shake his head and the hair would fall over his face; it had been wet before he went on stage."

With such a wealth of experience of the great man's performances, Barksdale is well placed to sum up Wilson's position among the all time great live acts. "Jackie was a true, true, true showman – all the way. It's unbelievable. That's Jackie; wonderful man. It was indeed a pleasure and honour to know him and a talent like that we will never see again."

CHAPTER SEVEN

Higher And Higher

The home Jackie's family had resided in since his earliest years, 248 Cottage Grove, Highland Park, was very ordinary. He and Freda shared it with his mother and stepfather and up until around 1960, that's where the extended family still lived. For all its memories, Freda remembers the place as a dump. "We never locked the door," she says. "We used to sleep on the nearby playground when it was hot. I had told Jack there are some rats in there. We were laying down one time and Rebecca [Pitt], his cousin, was sitting on the side of the bed. All of a sudden this big rat comes running in and jumps right across the bed. Jack said, 'What was that?' I said, 'A rat.' He had Johnny [Roberts] come over." Freda didn't say what Roberts did with the rat, but he did have a pistol.

Naturally, she was anxious to have a new home, something more suitable for their social standing. But while Freda was living in such conditions and struggling to get by raising their four children, Jackie was living in his luxury five hundred dollars a month residence at the Dorchester Apartments on West Fifty-Seventh Street, off Broadway, in New York. He kept telling her, "We'll get a house next time, baby." She finally told him if he didn't get her a house very soon she was going to live with him – kids and all. The threat worked and he got her a new and spacious house.

In a New York *Sunday News* (22 October, 1961) interview with Jackie, he talked about his family and the house: "I am also sending my wife to modelling school; I want her to make the most of herself. But I think the thing what gave me the biggest kick was buying a forty-five thousand dollar house for my family in Detroit. My mother and stepfather live in it with Freda and our four children. There's Denise, who's ten, Sandra eight, Jackie Jnr seven, and Tony three. The only fly in the ointment is that I don't get home very much. It's gotten to be a sort of a gag with the kids to rush into the house yelling, 'Ma, here comes Jackie Wilson!' when they see me coming."

The new home was a huge, two storey house on tree lined LaSalle Boulevard in Detroit. The awnings were brazenly painted with the large letters "JLW" (Jack Leroy Wilson) and "F & JW" (Freda and Jackie Wilson). Although faded today, the letters can still be seen at 16522 LaSalle. Inside the home, the shower screen door was also emblazoned with the large letters "JLW". Certainly, it is an upper middle class home, but nothing compared to the stone mansion Berry Gordy Jnr built for himself, only a mile or two away, on prestigious Boston Avenue. Despite being one of the world's greatest contemporary singer/performers, this remained the pinnacle of Jackie's material success.

There may even be some possible exaggeration on his part regarding the price he paid for it. In Freda's words, "I bought the house; Jack gave me the money. I didn't even like the house. I paid thirty thousand dollars first time."

Whatever the amount, Midnighters guitarist Billy Davis recalls getting a call from Jackie telling him he was going to buy the LaSalle home and needed some help to count the money. Davis told him if he put up a bottle of wine, he'd be over. "I helped him get the money together, and count it on his bed, at Cottage Grove," he says.

The new house seemed to satisfy everyone for a time. "We were well supported by Jackie for a while and for a while we thought we were rich," remembers Freda. "Before that we didn't have anything. We stayed in Cottage Grove; they tore that house down. At LaSalle his mother [and stepfather and Joyce Ann] lived downstairs and we lived upstairs."

Although she had a new home, Freda's role never altered. "Jack believed in keeping me barefoot and pregnant," she reflects. "He didn't have to worry about me, I was too busy breeding. Every time he came home it was one of those things. You was married, it was your thing to have babies." Birth control wasn't a priority. Besides, Jackie was firmly against abortion, which was illegal, anyhow.

He had many close relatives living in Detroit and nearby Pontiac. Most had moved from Mississippi over the years. Sadly, there was a degree of dysfunction within the family and Freda was not universally liked. Jealousy was part of the problem, in any case one of the female relatives began acting in a very bizarre way. Freda explains: "She used to tell me to get out of bed. She used to try and get in bed [with Jackie] – she'd be drunk. Some of the family on Jack's side, they were nuts. They hated me, and I was his wife! They'd talk about me." The woman relative was so infatuated with Jackie she seemingly had intentions of usurping Freda's position as Jackie's wife.

When he was away from home, Freda was always being usurped in her husband's bed. It was while living in New York, that Jackie took up residence with Harlean Harris. They'd first met in 1953. According to Harlean, in the 1979 *Sepia* magazine interview, Jackie noticed her photo on the cover of a magazine and got in touch with her. "He got in touch to congratulate me, and that's when our love affair began." At this stage, it was 1958, and Jackie had become a solo act.

At sixteen, Harlean began modelling and became a cover girl on the prestigious *Ebony* magazine. By seventeen she was chosen as "Miss Press Photographer, New York". Some who knew her saw past her beauty and described her as "the most pretentious thing you ever saw" and "a groupie-bitch and a known freak". However, there is little doubt that Jackie was captivated by her.

Although in the interview Harlean doesn't mention it, she had previously been the girlfriend, possibly the fiancée, of Jackie's friend Sam Cooke. Their sharing of girlfriends would not have caused friction between the two stars, nor would it have been the first time. Harlean also fails to make mention of Jackie being married to Freda.

Singer Tommy Hunt was a confidant of Jackie's at the time and recalls, "He'd even think Harlean was doing things behind his back; it was driving him crazy." Harlean rarely went on the road with Jackie and sexual fidelity was not one of Jackie's strong points in any case, so Harlean could hardly be blamed if she too had an occasional fling. And, after all, they weren't married.

Another of Jackie's acquaintances says, "She made him a little miserable." He plied Harlean with jewels and furs while at the same time Freda had difficulty getting payments to support the children. However, at times Jackie could be rough with Harlean, who he referred to as "Harris", so the relationship was tempestuous. The major problem between them was Jackie's numerous affairs, over which Harlean proved she could be rough and vindictive.

In February 1961 Jackie was twenty-six and hot property in the entertainment industry. In the months preceding he had some of the best hit successes of his entire career. 'A Woman, A Lover, A Friend' had reached Number Fifteen, 'Alone At Last' Number Eight, 'Am I The Man'

Number Thirty-Two, and 'My Empty Arms' Number Nine. Life for Jackie couldn't have been better. There was only one way for Jackie's career to go, and it was up.

But his infidelities were also in the ascendancy. Apart from Harlean he had a three year affair with a twenty-eight-year-old woman, Juanita Jones, from Harlem, New York. Quite possibly Juanita had become pregnant to Jackie. Regardless she was insanely jealous and madly in love with him.

Jones was a former WAC – the US Army – so had received weapons training. Around 3 or 4am on the morning of 15 February, 1961 (the day after St Valentine's Day) Jackie and Harlean returned from a late show to their swank Dorchester Apartments in mid town Manhattan. The Dorchester was favoured by entertainers, being home to actors Sidney Poitier and John Payne, and singers Johnny Nash, Demitta Jo and The Four Tops. Juanita was waiting for Jackie, a pistol hidden in her slacks.

Exactly what took place is likely only known to the three people there, but Jones confronted Jackie as he was about to enter his sixth floor apartment and shot him twice – once in the abdomen and once in the upper thigh region. It is quite likely that Jones's intended target was not Jackie, but Harlean. Possibly Jackie lunged at Jones to disarm her and took the bullets intended for the rival. Incredibly, despite severe injuries, Jackie managed to seize the gun from Jones and stagger downstairs to the street.

Freda remembers what happened after Jackie was shot. "That's how they got him. He was running down the street...he had took the gun – with it in his hand. Pretty soon the police saw him." Jackie was fortunate that a passing patrolman, Donald Roberts, noticed his condition and rushed him to the nearby Roosevelt Hospital in a police car. "He was in a critical condition. He was lying down there in emergency for a long time – they didn't understand it was Jackie Wilson the rock 'n' roll singer," says Freda.

Close friend, Linda Hopkins, who had performed with Jackie that night, has a similar account. "JJ told me when Jackie got shot and was taken to Roosevelt Hospital. He laid out in the hallway for ages. They finally got a doctor to come from Long Island to take a look at him. JJ said he had to argue with all the hospital people."

Freda again: "They didn't know until finally Harlean got in touch with Nat. Nat got the Mafia on the case and they were the ones who said, 'Get all your best doctors, for he's a great star – he's Jackie Wilson. Do whatever it takes to save his life; and they did.' They had the chief neurologist, the chief neurosurgeon – the chief everything – in case anything was wrong. They had the neurologist in case of nerve damage because the bullet was right near the spine: if it moved and hit the spine he would be paralysed. They had everybody; man, I never saw so much."

Jackie was operated on, having one bullet removed from his buttocks region. The second bullet was lodged so close to his spine it was deemed too dangerous to remove and was left where it was, to be with him for the rest of his life. Jackie remained on the hospital's critical list for six days and, fortunately, fully recovered, albeit after the removal of one kidney. It was a very close brush with death.

Tarnopol and Jackie's lawyer Herbert Lippman, who also happened to be the nephew of the late Al Green, Jackie's original manager, and a crony of Tarnopol's, concocted a story that would save Jones from being convicted of attempted murder and preserve Jackie's reputation as a devoted husband and father. Legal authorities were persuaded that a demented Jones had come to Jackie's apartment with the intention of committing suicide. Jackie, in trying to wrest the gun from her, had taken the two bullets.

In a subsequent radio interview with New York DJ Norman N Nite he put it this way: "I was shot in the stomach. Actually the bullet is still in there but it's in a safe place. It's in my back, but it hasn't moved. It's not a nice story, but it's not a bad story. The young lady, she wasn't shooting at me, she was shooting at herself. That's why we didn't prosecute her. When a person's a little off at the time they are a little stronger. I grabbed the pistol, but I'm the one who got shot."

The concocted story was apparently believed, as Jones was arraigned in the Felony Court and charged with felonious assault and violation of the Sullivan Law (to do with weapons possession). She was granted $2,500 bail. At the police station a dejected and sobbing Jones was photographed by the newspapers and reported as saying she was "all mixed up and didn't mean to hurt him". She said, "I love him, oh, Jackie!" And so the falsehood was maintained. It was fortunate indeed that the shooting had not left him dead or paralysed.

Dick Jacobs, in *Musician* magazine, vividly recalled the shooting. At this time Jackie was a frequent visitor to his family home. He relates: "Then, one morning at about 6am the phone rang. On the other end was Coral-Brunswick vice-president Marty Salkin soberly informing me that Jackie Wilson had been shot and was in Roosevelt Hospital. That was all he knew. A scalding fear shot through my body and I blasted out of the house and drove like a crazed maniac to Roosevelt Hospital.

"Juanita sure wasn't alone in her ardour for Jackie. Considering the numbers involved, hell hath no fury and all that, the most remarkable thing was that Jackie didn't have a whole lot more slugs in his rump. Jackie had lots of company in the hospital and seemed to take the whole thing in pretty good spirits, cracking jokes about having an extra asshole, etc. I set up a movie projector for him and he whiled away the time as he made a speedy recovery. And then it was back to showbusiness as usual."

Jacobs may well have made light of Jackie's wounds in view of the remarkable recovery he made, but either of the two bullets could have easily taken his life. No doubt Jackie's physical fitness and tenacity helped pull him through.

In the *Sunday News* interview, Jackie said, "I want to forget the incident and get on with my singing. I'll probably carry the bullet for the rest of my days – it's too dangerous to fool with – but I have no malice. I forgave the lady who shot me, right after it happened, and I didn't want to press charges. I want to forget the whole thing and just get on with the show." That's an understatement, as he was reportedly grossing around $350,000 a year at the time.

At the time of the shooting there was another woman with whom Jackie had renewed his association; Angel Lee, international stripper and former girlfriend of Little Richard. Angel now worked for Ben Bart's Universal Attractions Booking which specialised in attracting black acts. She had been on the town that night as she recalls: "I stayed at the Alvin Hotel; we came in around four or five in the morning, and we could barely see straight. There was a message. The desk clerk handed it to me and said it was from Jackie and it said, 'Call your husband.' I remember screwing it up and telling him to file it, and next thing I knew it was Universal Attractions on the phone – Winnie Brown. Winnie wanted to know if I needed an attorney? I said, 'What for?' Anyhow it took ten to fifteen phone calls for it to get through the alcoholic haze – that someone had shot Jackie! They thought I had done it! He had wanted me to come over. That was the note I'd gotten and I didn't go. By the time I got the note he'd already been shot."

Angel remembers the shooting resulted because of Jackie having terminated a three year relationship with Jones. "Juanita Jones had two or three kids with Jackie," Angel says. "She was supposed to have had a miscarriage and Jackie decided she aborted: he accused her of having got rid of his child and got mad. And that's when he stopped seeing her."

Back in Detroit Freda had just returned home that morning, having been to Chicago and New York. Jackie's friend, Freddy Pride, was there. Freda recalls, "My mother-in-law said, 'They say Jack's been shot.' A few minutes later there was a knock on the door; it was the police. They said, 'Freda Wilson and Eliza Lee?' I said, 'Yes, I'm Freda Wilson.' They said, 'We have a telegram here. If you want to see Jackie Wilson alive you better get the next plane out.' They said, 'If you need any help, let us know.'" When Freda read the telegram to Eliza Lee, she was totally stunned by the news and sought some solace: "Frank Gruman had gave us a case of VO [the best brandy]," she says. "That's what Eliza Mae was drinking at the time – she drank almost half a bottle. She said, 'Now, I've never been on a plane but we've got to get on that plane and go and see about him.'"

Freda believes Eliza Mae and Jackie were so close, there existed a transcendental bond between the two. Says Freda, "She knew he was hurt bad. You could tell when something was going wrong. Her heart was hurt. You could see her up that night tapping her feet and humming. Jack was in trouble somewhere. When we were married and he was not in town, she'd come and say, 'He's in trouble again, I hope it's not too bad. The police told us, 'Don't bring nothin'.' We didn't take no clothes."

In New York they went directly to the hospital. "We walked in the hospital and there was so many people. There were people on their knees on the floor – crowding around in the hospital. These were fans. Somebody said, 'That's his wife and his mother.' They were grabbing our clothes, we could hardly get through.

"He had just come out of surgery. His mother was standing on the other side and we was praying. He opened his eyes and said, 'Pee Wee' [his pet name for Freda]. He looked up and said, 'Hi, Mama,' and he took her hand. We were all crying. He held on to our hands."

There was no discussion of circumstances: "Around that time Jackie was shot at a lot. I didn't count the times," Freda says. Lynn Ciccone agrees that there could have been more than one shooting. "At one time, I was already there, before the troops got to town. They were playing cards when JJ came running in and said, 'Jack, we're got a problem, Harlean just arrived in the lobby.' He told her he was going down the hall to play cards all night. She left the next day. He thought it was funny. It was a wonder he didn't get shot more than one time. As one woman was going out the back door, he had one coming in the front."

The first operation had taken two hours, and within twenty-four hours he'd had one bullet removed from his buttock. Being a nurse's aid, Freda was fully aware how serious his injuries were. She continues: "Pretty soon they had taken the X-ray pictures. Three times they took him back for major surgery. The kidney was perfect, but the tube [ureter] that connected the bladder with the kidney was blown apart. They had to re-route it to the other side and they had to go in and get that kidney out. They took that and made an ileostomy tube [this is an opening from the bowel, through the abdominal wall and allows the faeces to drain]. A gun shot is very painful, besides he'd had all these major surgeries and a bullet was floating around. We just sat there all day and all night."

Despite requiring bags taped to his body to take care of his bodily functions and horrendous unhealed body wounds, Freda found Jackie's rampant sex drive undiminished. "Even when he got shot that time we did it," she says. "He told me to go in the bathroom and bend over. I said, 'So you can be all over me and I'll fall in the bathtub and you'll be on me and I'll be dead! I'll hit my head.' I was scared he was going to have a problem or something with the stitches. Then he was hurting."

Until the shooting, Freda seems not to be fully aware of how great a star Jackie was. She says, "You'd be surprised – the letters; Frank Sinatra, Elvis Presley, people he didn't even know well then, and people who just heard of him. Baskets and baskets of flowers, fruits, champagne, cheeses, all that stuff. We really had never seen stuff like this."

A constant stream of visitors arrived to help lift his spirits. One of them was a crony of Tarnopol's from Detroit by the name of Kirschner. Although he was not close to Jackie, he was presented with the 'Lonely Teardrops' gold disc as a token of his gratitude. Kirschner accepted gratefully and it still remains with his family to this day.

Another visitor was Dick Clark. "He caused a phenomenal reaction amongst female fans," says the *American Bandstand* host. "It was good for him and bad for him, and it nearly killed him along the way."

Some visitors reintroduced him to one of his bad habits. "People were bringing him cocaine and stuff in the hospital," says Freda. He'd survived two bullets and now he faced another threat. There was real concern that if Jackie took drugs the result might be that which the bullets failed to achieve. But Jackie was at his peak, with a big future ahead of him: the Mob were going to make sure he remained alive.

"I didn't want him to get addicted like some of these other entertainers had got," she says when asked to fetch more drugs by Jackie. "That's when the Mafia came over to watch him around the clock after he almost ODed – they ended up moving into the hospital. Nobody could come in except me and his mother, and then they suggested that his mother go home because she'd asked the nurses to give him some more pain medication"

A devoted Freda joined Jackie at the hospital, with a roll-away bed in his room. "I'd bring Poochie; I'd put him in my big purse," Freda remembers. He loved the little chihuahua dog and couldn't bear to be parted from it.

Up until then, as Freda left, Harlean would come on in. Now she was refused admittance. Lynn Ciccone remembers the operation to keep the women apart. "They had to do some fast shuffling when he got shot to get Harlean's things out of the apartment before Freda got into town. That was a talent of his. How he juggled all those women without them having confrontation all the time." But things went wrong and whilst Jackie was recuperating, Freda tidied up his apartment which was close by. "I was just cleaning up...The things I learned I learned by accident," she says. "There were bags and bags of pictures and things at the apartment. That's how I got the pictures of him and Harlean in the bathtub." The pictures showed them doing more than bathing. The apartment turned out to be a love nest for him and Harlean.

She was understandably angry, after all, she had made the sacrifices early in his career. Her pay cheques had helped to buy clothes suitable for him to perform in. She had done without so he could be Jackie Wilson. In her anger she hurled a good few of Harlean's fine clothes from the apartment's sixth floor window.

"When I was looking through those things in his apartment," says Freda, "he was already on drugs. I was scared of him about that, because his personality would change. Everything that somebody would do to him, he felt me and his mother and family was doing it to him. He thought we were working, especially me, for the FBI. Out of a clear blue sky he'd be laughing and talking and he'd say it. It would be something real simple I'd say, and he'd say, 'Why'd you ask me that? The FBI want to know that, too?'" The drug taking, together with the gradual realisation that he was being exploited, was causing Jackie to have paranoid delusions.

After five weeks of excellent care Jackie was well enough to be discharged. Newspapers and national TV pictured the beaming smiles of Jackie, his mother Eliza Mae, and Freda as they left the hospital. Freda says, "He was sick when he left the hospital." She had the task of nursing him back to health. However, being only a nursing aid, she wasn't as qualified as she had led Jackie to believe. "I was washing the thermometers in hot water – pop," said Freda, "I didn't want Jack to know I didn't know what to do."

Another revelation to Freda on his release was that despite being at his career peak, Jackie apparently had no money. When Jackie was shot, she suggests, Tarnopol didn't think Jackie was going to pull through and so took the opportunity to clean out Jackie's bank account. Presumably, this also included his safety deposit boxes which the manager had access to.

"When he got out of the hospital he wanted to get a new car," Freda reminisces, "because he didn't want people to think he couldn't sing no more." Rumours were circulating to the effect that because the second bullet could not be removed, Jackie's singing days were over. Jackie thought by buying a new Cadillac it would help dispel those rumours.

Having the patient at home led to other problems for the embattled Freda. Shortly after his release, Jackie went out of the apartment for a period. When he returned, Freda noticed his bandages were wet and set out to renew them. "They had to prepare a tube and make him an ureterostomy, because back then they didn't have the urinary bags they hook on now. They would show me how to do the padding, all the dressing and stuff. Nobody had changed the bandages since he got out and it was soaking wet. Anyway it had ruptured and he didn't want me to see that...I knew he'd been with some woman. He'd been gone too long. He went to see Harlean because she couldn't come to see him. The activity had caused it." It was enough to necessitate a return to hospital for additional treatment: his doctor would not have been impressed.

Fully recovered, late in 1961, Jackie was involved in his second and last movie entitled *Teenage Millionaire*, which again starred the singer Jimmy Clanton. The eighty-four minute long, black and white rock 'n' roll musical was, if anything, worse than the 1958 movie Jackie sang in. The only thing worthwhile about the movie was that he got to perform two songs, 'The Way I Am' and 'Lonely Life'. It was said that Elvis forced his friends to sit through the movie again and again, so impressed was he with Jackie's performance.

By Special Request, an album comprised of love ballads, was released in September 1961. It included some evergreen standards such as 'Stormy Weather', first performed by Lena Horne in the 1934 movie of the same name and two tracks – 'Mood Indigo' and 'I Got It Bad And That Ain't Good' – written by Duke Ellington. Then there's 'You Belong To My Heart', previously performed by Dinah Shore and Eddie Fisher, plus a credible version of the Johnnie Ray 1952 classic hit, 'Cry'. 'Try A Little Tenderness', written in 1932, is best known as a later Otis Redding smash, while 'Tenderly', which Jackie does to perfection, was a song he performed in 1954 as lead singer of The Dominoes and was a Rosemary Clooney number used on the soundtrack of the 1953 movie *Torch Song*. Frankie Lane wrote and recorded 'We'll Be Together Again', but Jackie's version is entirely his own. Another inclusion on the album was well suited to Jackie's style, 'Indian Love Call', which had been a major hit for Slim Whitman in 1952. The song is sung in part in a semi yodelling fashion. Billy Eckstine had a Top Ten hit with 'I Apologise' in 1951, and Jackie's version can be described in a word – *magnificent.*

In the *Sunday News* interview Jackie appeared pleased with his life and career: his latest disc was 'Years From Now' – boosting his earnings in the coming year to a probable $500,000. Jackie stated in the interview, "Well a chunk of the money goes in annuities, but I'm having a ball with the rest. I buy nine or ten suits a month and about as many thirty dollar shirts – they get torn off my back regularly. I've also got a New York apartment, because I love the Big Town. Let's see – what else? I love jewellery."

With so much else happening in 1961, there also came a major turning point in the relationship between Jackie and Tarnopol. Tarnopol's son, Paul, believes the bitterness developed over a dispute concerning the purchase of an apartment or a house. The actual dates are not clear, but he relates it this way: "Around 1960 Jackie was the only artist on Brunswick. At that time Lew Wasserman and Sid Shinberger [the heads of Decca Records] wanted my dad to come over to Brunswick to head it as their R&B label. The deal was that if he developed the label and signed the acts, did the promotion and got the writers, they would give him half the label.

"Lew Wasserman and Sid Shinberger [who were high executives at Decca records] controlled the independents [subsidiary labels with Decca]. Wasserman took a liking to my father in the late 1950s and asked my dad to run the label for him. My dad was the right person, as he knew black music better than black people could. He worked very hard. Lew said, 'I want you to run Brunswick.' Dad said, 'If you want me to run Brunswick and there is nothing [meaning no artists signed to it] in it, I want half.' They agreed.

"About 1961, when Jackie got shot, it came to a head. My father was doing more for Brunswick than he could do for Jackie. I think while he was in hospital he was befriended by Johnny Roberts. Actually Jackie and dad had a dispute about eighty thousand dollars, or thereabouts. It had something to do with a house Jackie bought. While they were working that out, Jackie went to either Johnny Roberts or Tommy Vastola. Vastola had Queens Booking Agency and Johnny was managing artists, that type of thing. They were around. The industry is not like it is today. The industry was almost all in the Brill Building at that time. My dad knew who Vastola and Roberts were, and to that point he had nothing to do with them."

Both Roberts and Vastola were reputed to be Mob figures involved with booking and managing black performers. One well known singer of the time says of them, "The crooked nose guys? That was pretty much the nature of the business back then. ABC [Associated Booking], Queens, whatever…they were involved with those people. You were engulfed. Roberts left a whole lot of hurt knees and legs back there in New York."

Former Flamingos singer and soloist Tommy Hunt began to make a name for himself at that period. "The Mob, as soon as they thought you had the potential to make some big bucks, they were right there," he says. "They'd come out of the woodpile. They tried to get me, but my stepfather knew these guys and kept them away from me. I was scared to death. I'm still chasing money that is owed to me from Sceptor and Wand Records. There was a few million owing to us [The Flamingos]. We were dumb kids… we didn't know the business; we didn't protect ourselves."

In the 1960s two booking agencies booked Jackie throughout the country; Queens Booking Agency and Jack Bart's Universal Booking. Both concentrated on booking black artists; but it was a tough business to be in. Some promoters were unscrupulous. Large sums were involved, most of it in cash. The risks were enormous and so were the potential profits.

The Mob had always been involved in the entertainment business, particularly night clubs, booking agencies, record distribution, promotion and record pressing. The fact that a lot of cash was involved, along with the risk, appealed to them. Another reason was, like the rest of us, they like to be around entertainers…it's a thrill. And, of course, they genuinely like the music.

Tarnopol knew Detroit Mob figures from his earliest days when he was driving a truck. The mixture of black artists, Jewish promoters and managers, and Italian Mob guys seemed to work. The blacks had the marvellous singing and musician skills; the Mob were willing to risk their cash and had the muscle to ensure their artists were treated favourably; and, the Jews had business acumen and an inherent feel for music. Of course, sometimes it all came unstuck and people got hurt. More normally the relationship relied on the reality that they all needed each other.

Tarnopol was a huge fan of the Yankees baseball team and often went to their games. Moreover, he was convinced that some day he would be the owner of the team. As Carl Davis, Chicago record producer and later vice president of Brunswick, explains, it was through baseball that Tarnopol became involved with the New York based Mob: "I think what happened was Nat Tarnopol wanted to be a tough guy, but he wasn't. He was fortunate that one day he and a friend, a doctor, went to a Yankees game and here's a guy possibly having a heart attack. Nat and this doctor friend went over and did whatever they had to do to help the guy. The ambulance came and took the guy to the hospital. He turned out to be the Godfather. He appreciated what had been done and he kind of put his arm around Nat, which gave him the liberty to do things he might not ordinarily do.

"He probably assigned a couple of guys to look out for him. Johnny Roberts happened to be one. Johnny was kind of crazy; he's all right, he just has no concept of finesse. It's either 'right' or 'left'.

"A lot of times you become enthralled with the idea you're dealing with these people. Then, once you get involved, you find them saying, 'We are going to put someone with you – you pay him a salary – he's one of us. If there's ever a problem, then this is the guy you go to and he'll come to me and we'll straighten it out.' They can make things not happen that might be supposed to happen to you.

"You know later Nat Tarnopol abused all of that and it was Nat that went out and got these people to keep Jackie in place. But then there was a guy above Johnny, this Tommy Vastola guy. I think that he may have owned Nat, but not Jackie. Tommy wasn't the kind of guy to screw Jackie around, because he felt like this is your moneymaker. You don't screw your moneymaker. 'Cause he also had Sammy Davis Jnr. He saved Sammy from being killed."

Davis is clear on how an arrangement such as with Sammy Davis Jnr and Jackie might come about. "If you were Sammy Davis and you were out there and you were making money; let's say you were making $200,000 was a lot of money. So I came to you and I said, 'Listen, how much do you think you can earn in a year?' Actually you know you can make a couple of hundred thousand, but you say, 'I can make $500,000.' So he says, 'I tell you what, you sign this little agreement here and I'll give you a million dollars right now – cash, no taxes – this is yours.'

"So when you go to work from this day on, everything you make comes to me, except your expenses. Your hotel and yourself is all going to be taken care of, but your salary comes to me. Sammy jumped at it and what he did somewhere along the line he started spending their money. They sent somebody to blow his brains out, and Sammy found out...somebody told him they were going to do that. He asked around and was told, 'You've got to go ahead and see Tommy Vastola.'

"When he went to see Vastola, Vastola said, 'I'll tell you what. They are going to show up, you know. You just tell them that, "Hey, you got to see Tommy Vastola."' So they did, they showed up. They were going to take him for a ride and Sammy said, 'I'm with Tommy Vastola.' So the guys just stopped, made a phone call, and they clarified that. From that point on, that's who his manager was. I think that also got Nat and Jackie and that whole ball of wax."

Ruth Bowen also had dealings with Vastola. Having formed Queens Booking Agency along with Dinah Washington, she was sole owner when the singer died aged thirty-nine. "After Dinah's death I wanted to go on because she had that much faith in me, and I finally got another partner – he had a percentage of the company – Irv Nahan. The reason I joined forces with Irv is because he had the acts that I needed. We made a good team. We were together many, many years, but I was the major owner of Queen's. Irv had stock, Jerry Butler had stock, Curtis Mayfield and Gene Chandler had stock.

"Tommy Vastola I've known twenty years, but he didn't have a percentage of nothing. He used to own a night club on Cony Island when I first met him. We met him through George Rhodes who had the band at his club out there. That was thirty-five to forty years ago. Tommy asked Dinah to do him a favour and come out and work, because he needed a boost for the club. She did and he paid her. They became friends and I've known him ever since – and his family."

Bowen is a highly regarded woman and a superb booking agent, but the statement that Vastola owned no part of Queens isn't credible. She also omits Carl Davis who owned a share too. Seemingly a lot of stockholders for a small company.

In managing Jackie *and* Brunswick Tarnopol had a conflict of interest that would not be legally tolerated today. Furthermore, having signed over power of attorney to Tarnopol, Freda and Jackie effectively cut themselves off from their proper share holding [the fifty per cent interest in Brunswick]. Jackie, a poorly schooled singer, was far from being an astute businessman and had put his total trust in Tarnopol. But that trust was out grown as Paul Tarnopol remembers: "It was obvious who they [Vastola and Roberts] were involved with. My father pleaded with Jackie not to let them take over his management or get involved, but Jackie took it upon himself to do this. So they decided to end the management with my dad. Dad could look after Brunswick and Jackie could have separate management.

"From that point on Jackie's management was with Johnny Roberts and, I think, Tommy Vastola as well. Tommy was the booking agent. There is obviously conflict of interest with this arrangement [because of their involvement with Queens]. A lot of shows were paid for in cash.

"Till that time everything was fine; they were both earning good money. Jackie had plenty of money, but he didn't invest; he'd fill safety deposit boxes in the diamond district. Harlean didn't know where they were. She had jewels and furs. Jackie would get cash and he'd run down town and nobody knows where it is." In fact, Jackie grossed over three hundred thousand dollars per year in the early 1960s, an enormous income.

Morris Levy may not be a household name, but in the era that Jackie was performing everybody in the contemporary music industry knew him. Levy was feted by the major record corporations. He was from a tough eastside neighbourhood of New York City and was very useful with his fists. Despite being Jewish, most of his childhood and adult friends were Italian. His closest business associates were known figures in organised crime.

Levy also had a record company, Roulette Records, but, of much greater importance, he had excellent record distribution; and he controlled a chain of record stores called Strawberry. The largest distributor of records in New York, he also had a "cutouts" company, whereby he bought bulk unsold records at ridiculously low prices from the major record corporations. These were either unsold warehouse stocks or records that retailers had been unable to sell – "returns". The financial paper work involved with their sale was minimal and although the risks were great, so were the rewards. To have a hit record, more than likely Levy could provide the expertise and contacts. Jackie considered him a friend.

From his childhood years, one of Levy's closest friends was Tommy Vastola. A friend of both men said, "If you grew up on the eastside [of New York], where everyday was a hustle, you had to learn to fight, run and steal. There was a lot of unemployment and prejudice, and not just with blacks."

Nobody who had anything to do with Johnny Roberts (aka Sepio or Robertson) would forget him. He was described by one who knew him, "He had a face like an ice cube; cold as ice. A person not to be messed with." Roberts' real name may have been Probacelli. He didn't need to shout in order to get some co-operation, all he had to do was give you one of his stares. "Johnny wasn't little – about five foot nine or five ten, but 180 to 200 pounds," says one close to Jackie. "JR was a plain guy. He didn't look fancy or nothing; no fancy clothes. When he walked your way you'd move out of his way. But he was polite; he was a nice dude. He was like a bodyguard; solidly build, a light heavyweight. He was changing his shirt one day…he's got all these marks on his body – bullet holes, stab wounds. He might have been a hit man. Whether it was true or not, people believed Roberts to have been related to Albert Anastasia's Murder Incorporated and could possibly have murdered thirty-four people. He was in the work of 'money'.

"If a guy didn't pay his debts," continues the friend, "you'd send someone like JR to collect. He meant business. He didn't fear anything. If you killed him, he expected that. He was immune to fear. They are trained; like a soldier is trained for war. Yet he could walk into the Waldorf Astoria, just like Rockefeller…so long as you have money in your pocket.

"I remember one time Jackie was on stage and there was fighting out there [in the audience]. Jackie did one of his splits and Johnny Roberts picked him up, 'Come on, you son-of-a-bitch, don't you see 'em fighting?' He picked him up one hand. JR was smiling all the time…you never saw weapons or anything. Roberts looked after the money and it wasn't uncommon for him to collect ten thousand dollars for a night's work – in cash. He didn't want cheques."

It is wrong to think that the likes of Levy and Vastola were the parasites of the music industry, reviled by everyone else in the business. These people were the "shakers and movers" who put up large amounts of money to help to produce the hits and promote the artists. Generally, they also had a genuine love of the artists and music they helped produce. One black artist put it this way: "I grew up on all these people; I came up that era. In this business you had to go through and by these people. And I went through and by them and, believe it all not, I never met such wonderful gentlemen. I don't know what they did to other people, but they did nothing wrong to me. It had nothing to do with us, we didn't know nothing about it.

"If you come up with a million dollars you can get a record played – then you *might* have a hit record. The Pop charts were bought space – like buying an ad in the paper. Still is. They go buy what's shipped to get a platinum. To get a future platinum you have to have a good record company – a major."

The music industry was like a magnet to organised crime due to the large amounts of money it generated – much of it in the form of cash – but also because of the glamour. Someone who has spent a lifetime in the industry explained: "During the Vietnam war the Mob were selling albums to the armed forces and the artist never saw any of the money. Everything happened in those days – the record companies, owners and managers were selling records out of the back of their station wagons."

Nevertheless, although Levy, Vastola and Roberts were the people with faces, they would in turn only operate in the business with the express blessing of Frank Costello and Vito Genovese who controlled vice, prostitution, loan sharking *and* the music business. It is beyond the scope of this story to try to explain the complexity of this. It's fair to say the Mob is the lender of last resort – after the banks and the financial institutions have said "No".

The most accepted explanation to the complex question of who actually owned whom, has it that Brunswick Records was controlled by one Mafia family, while Jackie's management and bookings were controlled by another. Undoubtedly there was an amicable working arrangement between both families.

Joel Bonner worked with Jackie as promotions manager for Brunswick Records. He knew all the characters and the complexity of the management of both Jackie and Brunswick. "Johnny Roberts couldn't tell the full story; if he did, he'd be in jail," says Bonner. "I believe Johnny worked for Vastola. They were all 'barracoutas' – Nat, Tommy and Johnny. Nat was the kind of guy enamoured to that kind of life."

Fortunately things have changed in the record industry today, as Bonner explains: "It's not the same today. In the old days they were all around. They were there. The RICCO laws [anti-organised crime Federal laws] have made it so you can't steal records like they used to. They have computers now; you can't do it. Of course they still have bootleg [the practice of reproducing and selling recordings of artists without permission]."

Although always linked to the Mob, it was without doubt the shooting of Jackie and its aftermath that marked the watershed in the relationship between Tarnopol and Jackie. Lynn Ciccone puts the fault at Nat's door: "After Jack got shot in New York, Nat cleaned out all the money and left town. Jackie went to them [the Mob] for money and that's when he really got in." Up until then the Mob had control over Tarnopol and had been involved with Jackie's bookings and promotion. They may well have been earning money from recordings sold out the back door and therefore not accounted for. The move, therefore, must have been one of desperation by Jackie. Nevertheless, it was to Tommy Vastola that Jackie turned.

Vastola and Johnny Roberts, who replaced Tarnopol as Jackie's personal manager, could provide the protection Jackie would need in the rough business he was in and they ensured he would not be ripped off by some of the sharks who booked the acts...but for a price.

In 1961 Nat Tarnopol's son, Paul, wasn't yet born, but his father later related to him his version of events concerning Brunswick Records and Jackie. Paul later got to know Jackie, albeit while a young boy. "Nat agreed to let Jackie go because he had his hands full with the label. But he wanted Jackie to have a professional manager. In 1961 my father was thirty. His partner [in Brunswick Records] – at that time it was Decca – was Lew Wasserman and those guys. At that time, you could not be in the industry without answering to somebody: even Decca Records had to answer to somebody."

Jackie had decided Vastola and Roberts offered him a better option than Tarnopol, so this was arranged. Roberts often accompanied Jackie on his tours, with his primary function being to ensure the promoters paid up promptly and then to send the money, via Western Union, to New

York. Roberts had been out on tours before, the first time in July 1960 when the New Orleans concert had erupted into a riot with Jackie one of the main protagonists. At that time it would have been at the behest of Queens Booking. From now on it was more direct.

It must be said, at the outset, Jackie generally got along very well with Roberts and definitely needed someone with his "skills" to keep him out of trouble. It was Roberts who, in turn, employed the intimidating black individual, August "Augie" Sims. Sims, who weighed around 230 pounds and stood five foot eleven, had formerly been a bodyguard/masseur for world champion and legendary middleweight boxer Sugar Ray Robinson for eleven years.

Sims wore dark glasses year round. His role was as Jackie's road manager and masseur, which he was adept at. Around thirty-eight years of age, he wasn't one to argue with. Sims was under instructions to "keep Jackie in line", admittedly not an easy task. When Roberts wasn't there, Sims was responsible for ensuring *all* the money was sent immediately to New York. Sims first met Roberts and was recruited to work with the Mob in 1963. "I knew Johnny Roberts when I was with Sugar Ray Robinson," he recollects. "He used to come to the Chandu [an after-hours club in Harlem run by Red Randolf]. He wanted to be bad at the Chandu; he hit a nigger there. I told that nigger, 'Why you let that man hit you, man?' He said, 'He's the Mob.' I said, 'I don't give a goddamn if he is the Mob.'

"That's how he got to me. He wanted me and I was *bad*. I was doing all this old crazy stuff and I didn't pay it no mind. I didn't care about nobody; I'll whoop you, shoot you, too. Johnny came to me and said, 'We want you to work for us,' and Jackie said, 'Yes, we do.' I never let Johnny bug me... Johnny was scared of me." With that, Sims became the muscle both to protect Jackie, and to keep him in line.

His first duty was to fire some of Jackie's entourage, including JJ. "I fired every one of those sons-of-bitches. 'Cause all them guys are supposed to be your friend. You were raised with them guys, and those sons-of-bitches are robbin' him more than anybody in the place. That's when they went to work for me." The explanation is ambiguous, but likely means that after they were fired they took their orders from Sims rather than Jackie.

Sims goes on, "I said one time, 'Hey, Jackie, the white folks are stealing from you.' He told me, 'You crazy.' I said, 'You motherfuckers is.'"

There is no doubt, Sims *was* tough and could take care of most problems they were to encounter, touring with Jackie for around a decade. "Nat had to toe the line with the Mob," he reflects. "He couldn't do nothing with me 'cause I was with them. Nat couldn't do nothing but go along with the programme. 'Cause I'd send money and he'd say, 'Did you send Schwartz [at Queens Booking] his money?' I sent them money all the time...made sure I sent the money. I used to keep track of the money, too."

Sims doesn't seem to appreciate that he, as much as the Mob, was fleecing Jackie. Perhaps, in his mind, it is justified by the protection he provided, or that he only followed orders. Today he still has a great love for Jackie, best illustrated by the numerous photos he displays on the basement walls of his home in New York's Bronx.

Freda remembers the new arrangements: "Nat had got out of town. Then they had Sims – he had just got out of prison. When Jackie got hot, Sims knew how to give him a shower and massage and stimulate his nerve endings. He'd do all that stuff. Johnny Roberts was the one who collected the money. The Mafia like family – they are family people. He [Jackie?] was just one of the family."

Another area of controversy is who actually wrote many of the songs that Jackie recorded. A typical example of this is 'Singing A Song', which lists as the songwriters "J Wilson, E Wilson, F Wilson". Quite obviously, Jackie, his mother and his wife had little to do with it. Still, Jackie has his name on more than eighty songs listed with BMI, the organisation which is responsible for the collection of airplay royalties. Many of these songs appear to have never been recorded by anyone and most are co-written with others, in particular, Alonzo Tucker.

A common practice was to buy songs and have them published under the buyer's name. Many of Alonzo Tucker's songs met this fate and many of his bear the name of Jackie, his half-sister Joyce Lee (eg 'Please Tell Me Why' and 'Sazzle Dazzle'), Tarnopol and his aunt Lena Agree (eg 'Doggin' Around' and 'Passing Through'), and even Morris Levy and Johnny Roberts.

Tucker may not have been defrauded, having agreed to sell the song for fifty or seventy-five dollars, but he surely was short changed. 'Doggin' Around' became a Number Fifteen Pop hit and is certainly one of Tucker's, as he was singing it years before Jackie recorded it.

As Jackie became more famous, it was not uncommon for him to demand twenty-five per cent of songwriters' royalties in order to record it. No doubt aspiring songwriters would happily agree so that Jackie used their song. It is true that he often put his own interpretation on a song to the point where he could be considered co-writer. Jackie, though, couldn't read music.

A singer who could read music was R&B singer Roy Brown whose claim to fame is that he wrote and sang 'Good Rockin' Tonight', which Elvis made famous. Considered a blues singer, he sang in a full throated and rocking style which was most certainly the fore-runner of rock 'n' roll. He was generally unknown to white audiences, but incredibly popular with blacks from 1947. Fortunately Elvis knew all about him – and so did Jackie. Born in New Orleans in 1925, Brown co-incidentally had many similarities, in his formative years, with Jackie. At twelve he formed his own spiritual quartet. Like Jackie he was a keen boxer, and performed in amateur singing contests.

Brown relates that the first time he heard Jackie singing 'Lonely Teardrops' on the radio in 1958, he called King Records in Cincinatti and said, "There's a kid singing identical to me. I want to cover the record. I can sound more like me than he can." Incredibly, he also claims that Berry Gordy, the co-writer of the song, offered it first to him at Detroit's Flame Show Bar. "I said, 'Berry, I'm not interested.' I didn't say it that blunt, but I just didn't dig it. When I heard Jackie do it I recognised the song. He got on the Dick Clark show a little later on. Dick asked who his idol was. He said, 'Roy Brown! I can do anything he's ever done and do it better,' and he was laughing." Jackie and Brown are very different singers, but at the same time Jackie would have taken something from Brown's style of delivery. They also share similar higher pitched tenor voices. However, co-writer of 'Lonely Teardrops', Roquel Davis, is adamant that Brown was never offered the song, although he may well have known Berry Gordy.

Shortly after the shooting, when Jackie had recuperated, he was back on the road, touring throughout the country. The first concert he did was at the Uptown Theatre in Philadelphia where an old friend, Gino Parks, was also appearing on the bill. "Jackie's records didn't do him justice," says Parks. "He was a terrific performer, terrific singer. If you could have heard things he did that were not recorded on personal appearances…"

Jackie's keen sense of humour hadn't been dampened by the bullets that had nearly taken his life as Parks explains: "We did the midnight ramble that Saturday night. It was a gas. We hadn't seen each other in some time. I had just come off the stage and I was sweating and tired, and Jackie said, 'When you going on?' And it dawned on me…he used to kid me like that."

Travelling with a star such as Jackie may have been glamorous, but would never make the musicians rich. Always backed by top flight musicians, this tour, with Chocker Campbell's band, was no exception, including talented musicians who became Motown's Funk Brothers. One member of the band was a twenty-one-year-old horn player from Chicago – Mike Terry. "Our rent was fifty dollars a week and we made seventy-five dollars a week," he says. "I don't know how any money got sent back home."

1962 was another good year for Jackie. In April his album *Body And Soul* was released. The orchestra was under the direction of Bob Mersey, with Dick Jacobs supervising. The title song comes from the 1947 John Garfield boxing movie of the same name. It had been written in 1930 and sung at that time by Libby Holman. In 1939 it became a hit for jazz tenor Coleman Hawkins, but here Jackie's version is haunting. Also on the album is the classic standard 'Blue Moon', written in 1934, and a huge hit for Billy Eckstine in 1948. The doo wop group, The Marcels, again turned it into a hit in 1961, then Frank Sinatra and Elvis Presley both recorded it.

1962 also marked another professional achievement. At that time, to be invited to work at the Copacabana meant a singer had really made it. The Copa was white cabaret, yet Jackie proved he could entertain there with ease, as Dick Jacobs described in *Musician* magazine: "Tarnopol managed to book a solid week of Jackie Wilson shows at the Copacabana in New York. It was perfect: the Copa was the hottest club in Manhattan [therefore the world] and Jackie Wilson was headlining. We even planned a live record, *Jackie At the Copa*. I had prior commitments, so Sy Oliver wrote the show and conducted the band. The Copa was packed for every show and Jackie surpassed everyone's expectations. The album came out and, unfortunately, was not one of Jackie's biggest sellers: it has become highly collectible."

To show his complete versatility, Jackie even included 'And This Is My Beloved' which had been sung by Howard Keel in the 1955 film *Kismet*, and by Vic Damone. Jackie's Copacabana debut didn't go unnoticed and a New York newspaper review by Gene Knight, headlined as "New Copa Star Is Born As Jackie Wilson Soars..." is worth retelling in its entirety:

A new sound has been found. Also a new night club star. He is Jackie Wilson, syncopated singer with a seething style.

Practically unknown, he opened last night at Jules Podell's world famous Copacabana. And stirred up such a storm of hand clapping that the rest of this boy's career will be history. Here is the success story: a couple of weeks ago, Mr Podell [owner of the venue] suddenly found himself with an open date in his crowded Copacabana schedule. A night club headliner, set to open at the Copa last evening, got an unexpected Hollywood call to go before the cameras. Always a good sport, Jules told him to go ahead and take advantage of the opportunity. Then the night club impresario began to look around for another star to fill on short notice, his own big theatre restaurant. Mr Podell had heard of Jackie Wilson, the pet of the Apollo Theatre in Harlem. But he had never seen him work. In a tight spot, Jules signed the singer – sight unseen. Or unheard.

Last night, Jackie Wilson came into the Copa with his own conductor, a pianist, two guitarists, three violinists. Plus a vocal trio. This was his crack at the big break. Mr Podell crossed his fingers and hoped for the best. Jackie began to sing. Surprise, surprise! He's got rhythm. He's got style. He's got a new way of singing even old songs. And he's got new songs, too. Here's the punch line…on the dotted line…at midnight last night, Jules Podell, an astute judge of night club talent signed Jackie Wilson to a contract to star at the Copacabana for the next three years. What has Jackie got that other singers haven't got? Well, he is a male coloratura. He can change the pitch of his voice with an inflection that becomes a falsetto. He runs to flexibility and trills that amount to vocal gymnastics.

Good looking Mr Wilson opened with 'Tonight', 'Body And Soul', 'I Apologise.' I loved 'Can't Help Lovin' That Man' and 'My Beloved'. He even put new life in that tired old ballad, 'Love For Sale'. Delivery is dramatic. His songs are sung with the spirit of a spiritual. He has the gusto of a gospel singer, which is the coming thing in night club entertainment. In an eruption of emotion Jackie got down on the floor and sang his heart out. Not since Johnnie Ray first hit New York have I seen such a passion packed performer.

I remember when Billy Daniels, the finger-snapping round-and-round-we go 'OI' Black Magic' man, was first spotted at Dickie Wells' in Harlem. Jackie Wilson, at the Copa is a young Billy Daniels. Wait till the word gets around. He is electric!

In 1962, when Jackie earned this review, he was at his career peak, being known around the world. So Knight's line about Jackie being "practically unknown" makes one wonder what planet Knight had been living on.

At that time it wasn't usual for *Variety* magazine to review R&B singers, however it is worth relating their critique, written by a Mr Gros, concerning the Copacabana debut. It starts by mentioning "six dollars minimum, seven dollars Saturdays" in reference to the minimum charge at the Copa; there was no cover charge. The review reads:

Jackie Wilson has several tricks to give his tune, culled mostly from his disk repertoire, and some okay visual values. He loosens his bow-tie for the casual ballad approach, he takes off his jacket for a spirited rhythm mood and he gets down on his knees for the fervent gospel appeal. It's overly dramatic and somewhat hokey at times but at least he's trying to put on an act and not just duplicate his disk licks sound: the Copa crowd can't help but appreciate that.

There's a lot of trickery in his vocal set-up, too, that seems to put plenty of strain on his pipes. It's not easy to run from a low register to the high notes but he does it often and, most of the time, for good results. It also brings musical shadings to the performance that sustain interest.

He's at his best with the well-established songs. 'Tonight', 'Temptation', 'What Kind Of Fool Am I', 'Love For Sale', the Ray Charles styled 'I Can't Help Loving You' and the fast developing 'I Wanna Be Around'. His turn flows up though when he goes in to an 'and then I sang' routine that recaps his past disk licks on the Brunswick label. They're not too memorable and mean little to anyone but the ardent pop disk fan.

Gros seems to be trying hard to fault the performance. 'Love For Sale' has controversial lyrics concerning prostitution. Jackie sang it with his usual intense emotion. "You could just see this person out there trying to sell their body," when Jackie sang it, says Freda. She also recalls with pride the debut: "Sammy Davis Jnr was sick and Jackie went on for him. A lot of people hadn't heard of him then. When he came out and sang 'Night' he got a standing ovation. They didn't know him by 'Lonely Teardrops' except, amazingly, there were a lot of high school graduates there...they knew. He got another standing ovation. Next thing we knew they wanted him back at the Copa. They loved him." Jackie was also thrilled by the experience, saying, "I thought I was Sinatra Jnr."

By way of contrast, talented Sam Cooke appeared around the same time at the Copa and bombed. Humiliated by the experience, he never forgot it.

By contrast, Freda recalls another time she saw Jackie performing at the Copa: "We didn't have to pay. Denise sang with him at the Copacabana. He didn't know she was there, but when he hit the stage she did too. She ran down there and took the microphone from the piano player. Denise wore a little crinoline dress, and went up there with Jack and tried to sing. She stole the show from him."

Lynn Ciccone also has memories of her time with Jackie in New York where he took her as his guest to the Copa. "Jackie could walk in there like he owned the place," she says. "He could walk into the Copa and there'd be no tables left and they'd find one. He could do it any place he played." Another occasion Jackie and Lynn were there with Tommy Vastola and Johnny Roberts when an altercation occurred. Jackie yelled, "Get her the hell out of here," Lynn recalled. It was Tommy Vastola who escorted her out. "We dined at Sardi's Stagedoor Delicatessen in Greenwich Village," she explains, "and as we walked down Broadway he said, 'This is going to all be mine. Everything here is going to say "Jackie Wilson".'"

The fact that Sammy Davis Jnr had given Jackie his break at the Copa by not appearing didn't stop Jackie from embarrassing him. Jackie's friend, long time drummer Jimmy Smith, recounts the incident: "Jackie embarrassed Sammy Davis Jnr on stage at the Copa; he took the mike out of his hand and finished the song off for him. As a result, Frank Sinatra jacked him up. Sinatra 'put a lock' on every club." Jackie couldn't get into a club in the country. Smith went on, "Not for long. All Jackie had to do was apologise. Johnny Roberts got all that straight."

He may have ruffled a few showbiz feathers, but with the common herd Jackie couldn't put a foot wrong. Johnny Collins, his brother-in-law, says the people in New York adored Jackie. "Let me tell what they did. They said, 'Let me show you where Jack rode down the sidewalk…with his tyre prints in them.' They poured concrete on the sidewalk so he could drive his limo down, just so they could say, 'Jackie drove through it.' In New York [even former mayor] La Guardia never did that! They loved him that much!

"When he went down and sang at the Coconut Grove, they had the largest waiting line in the history of any show in the city of New York." The Coconut Grove was a high class white cabaret club. Jackie had well and truly shown the people of New York he was a major talent to be reckoned with. He had "got over the hump", but would need to do so again and again due entirely to the prevailing racial prejudices.

Another Detroit R&B singer who was achieving success in the early 1960s was Betty Lavette. She grew up in the same northern Detroit neighbourhood as Jackie and often performed on the same bill – especially at Phelps Lounge on Oakland Avenue. Aspiring to perform and to have an a affair with Jackie, Lavette boasted she achieved both. "Jackie acted as if he'd known me for ever," she says. "Jackie was not cocky; his thing was like, he must run the joint. You'd think he *must* run the joint. He's the one in power. Jackie's arrogance went as, 'I know I sing better than anyone else.' But it wasn't a nasty arrogance. You sort of agreed with him too. That made it all right. Jackie tended to speak to everyone that way. He always had someone else to put people out. Someone else always did the dirty work.

"When I came out of my dressing room at Phelps and we first met, I knew we would like each other. I could tell it by his songs. Jackie Wilson wasn't made by this business, that's the way he was even if he'd have stayed on Claremont and Oakland singing. Some other singers were truck drivers or something else. He would have been the same person. That's who he was. His wanting to be in showbusiness takes a completely different kind of person. Some Motown singers didn't really want to dress up, drive around in limousines and sign autographs, to be up all night, to take all kind of drugs and go to bed with all kinds of people. You've got to

The "black Elvis Presley" with the "white Jackie Wilson". Dedicated "Jackie, You got yourself a friend for life, Elvis Presley", this photo was one of Jackie's most cherished possessions

Jackie and Little Richard, Florida 1970

With Judy Garland and Count Basie, 1968

The woman who loved Jackie and Little
Richard – Audrey "Angel Lee"
Sherborne, New York 1971-2

With two backing singers

With The Everly Brothers and Clyde McPhatter

Despite the temptations on the road, Jackie loved his wife enough to send this telegram: "Dearest Frieda, Each time I love you more and more. That's why I love you so, Sonny"

With James Brown

With Sandra Dee

Second on the bill in Alan Freed's *Big Beat Show* at the Fox Theatre

Above and left: Mr Excitement

Showing his boxer's physique, with JJ and friend

Backstage at the Copa Cobana with
guitarist Dickie Thompson and boxer
Floyd Patterson

Hank Ballard, from The Midnighters

Jimmy Smith, circa 1967, walking in the
back door of the Apollo

JJ and friend

In his element with five "Bunny Girls"

Jackie's charisma shone through even in photographs

With Little Dion

In the studio

Although this was a promotional stunt, Jackie did briefly campaign for a presidential candidate

With Gregory Peck, Tony Randall and Alfred Hitchcock

A rare moment of relaxation

The man in the mirror – preparing to go on stage

Collecting a "gold disc" from Dick Clark

Despite his upbringing, Jackie was always well turned out

A promotional shot for Brunswick Records

With Bob Austin of *Cashbox*, 1958

want to do that, and Jackie wanted to. He wanted to go to bed with everybody, to take all kinds of drugs, to sign autographs, he wanted to sing, he wanted to take pictures. He wanted to do all that. That's the kind of person he was. Jackie would do it just as hard for nothing."

The blacks preferred songs with "bop", according to Lavette, and when Jackie had his huge hit 'Higher And Higher' in 1967, she says, "Blacks didn't like it – you couldn't dance to it. But we thought whites would like it and that was great. Blacks like music with lots of 'bop'. We were happy that Jackie was no longer singing R&B; he was going to a better place – like the Copacabana or Coconut Grove. The blacks saw Jackie's doing all the early string backed material as 'right of passage' – getting into white people – when he was no longer singing stuff we liked, he'd gone to a better situation. We in black showbusiness were envious."

Lavette also experienced the women who walked away from their own lives and families so they could follow Jackie, just to be near him. "A friend of mine, her sister was crazy in love with Jackie," she recalls. "Very much from a refined family. They got me interested in Jackie. She was a grade school teacher; she let the job go. She moved to New York and would follow him around. He was living on West Side Drive, New York. She knew all the other women and accepted it. Many of us black women all went with all the same guys – they were pimp types. Tina Turner and Aretha Franklin were in this situation. Many of the women artists. Ike had others; Tina knew and accepted. You were told you are the main woman and these other women will know you are the main thing. We grew to liking crystal rather than glass. We had no education, no money, this business offered us class and money, education – things we otherwise never encountered."

Lavette was no different and, being young and naive, she was captivated by Jackie's charm. Once, when the two worked the same bill together, she had a romantic interlude with Jackie. They did a lot of partying together. "I have seen men look at Jackie; they really admired him. We worked one weekend and we were together *all* weekend. He thought I was a wonderful singer and we liked the same kind of drugs. We both thought it would go on forever. Several people took pictures, but I don't have any of them. I was arrogant, like he was. He was a wonderful, wonderful, wonderful person."

Like many wonderful artists, income tax was one of the furthest things from Jackie's mind. He always left it for others to take care of the details.

Freda recalls: "Our financial problems started because of income tax. See, Nat was supposed to take care of that 'cause he had power of attorney. We'd signed all the papers, me and Jack, and they let us think everything was okay. Any mail [from Internal Revenue Service] that Nat was getting he didn't say nothing about it, so the first we know was when the IRS got in touch with us and the next thing you know it's 'in the name of the United States Government we now seize this property'. They can take everything you've got.

"The tax was way behind and he didn't have the money. He couldn't pay it all at once and had to make a deal. 'How much you can pay quarterly?' Then you're on the road till you pay it."

It was a very shameful moment, as Freda remembers: "I asked the men to please not to put the sign on the front door. They agreed and put a sign on the side door, but told me not to cover it up. It was so much, I can't remember how much. Even when Internal Revenue come they said they believed us that Nat Tarnopol had the money; he'd lied about paying taxes on the house."

So, the family home was put up for auction and they had to buy it all over again for a higher amount. "My house on LaSalle was auctioned off twice," explained Freda. "The second time, when I got it back from the IRS, I paid more, but I can't remember how much."

And at the time Jackie was an international superstar!

In an unusual statement, Freda remarks how "Nat said he was not taking his ten per cent, but he was living good. He had his own apartment. When he started he had nothing. He was taking him some money so he could dress good, he bought him a pinkie ring. He did everything he wanted, but Jack never checked behind him. I told Jack, 'Get your own accountant, your own everything. These are Nat's friends.'

"Lippman was our lawyer at the time. He used to fall in front of cars and get [insurance] money. They would never know [the accidents were staged]. The accountant too; the tricks they used…" Freda was clearly annoyed that Jackie was making so much money for so many people, while he couldn't pay his taxes. "Jackie was the one that was practising all the time; it was hard work. What they did. They gave Jack an office. He was the vice president. The company was Pearl Music – Nat's aunt. All of those records that say Pearl something – she ain't wrote nothing. The lady can barely speak English. Pearl is Nat's aunt. She's very Jewish. She's very nice, but don't know nothing about records. She'd come and get me, we'd go over there she'd make me some bagels and corned beef." Pearl Music was originally the music publishing company set up by Jackie's first manager, Albert Green. Tarnopol most likely purchased it from Green's family after he died. (The name Lena Agree appears as the songwriter of many of Jackie's songs and it is possible Freda is actually referring to her as she was Tarnopol's aunt.)

Jackie's accountant, especially, was widely criticised. "'Issie' Silverman is the reason Jack had tax problems and he was Nat's man. Jack didn't know he had problems," according to a one time lover of Jackie's, Joyce McRae. Jackie's brother-in-law, Johnny Collins, is even more damning, saying, "Isidore Silverman was the best thief in the business. He could plant money anywhere." Collins claims that Jackie's recordings were selling like hot cakes and, therefore, Jackie should have had money to burn. "If a woman liked you [the singer], she'd buy the records. Dish washing liquid – forget it. She'd find the money; the music was in the house."

Generally, there are two sides to everything and so it was with the subject of whose fault it was that Jackie had no money despite earning what was considered huge amounts at the time. Silverman, says it was totally Jackie's fault: "We did his income tax work throughout the 1960s. He was a gifted artist, the man had tremendous talent and phenomenal personality, but he spent money like it was a bottomless well. He had quite a crew, but they were there as much as watchdogs as anything else. They couldn't control him. To Jackie money meant nothing; it was just another day. He loved being with people and entertaining. He was a pleasure to be with; sober and articulate. Out of sight, well..."

Silverman freely admits being a close friend of Tarnopol's. "Many years ago we were in New York and he was appearing at the Roseland Ballroom in Harlem. I'd never been to Harlem. We accompanied his attorney [believed to be Joseph Zynczack], his manager and my partner at that time to that facility that evening. They put us in the wings. I couldn't get over how he had the audience in the palm of his hands. He was great. Nat Tarnopol was there and Irving Grant, my partner [Grant and Sodderman is the name of the accountancy firm]. We parted company [with Jackie] only 'cause we couldn't control him. We told his business manager that as much as we loved Jackie and Nat he wouldn't follow our advice and his record keeping left much to be desired. It was difficult. You can only advise if they follow that advice. If they ignore what you are telling them you can't be by their side twenty-four hours a day. He was earning well over a quarter of a million a year, but it was a wasted talent. He could have been sitting on top of the world."

Those closest to Jackie generally believe that Tarnopol encouraged him to live beyond his means and to borrow against future earnings. Certainly he didn't encourage him to save or invest for the future, as a manager should do. Admittedly, with Jackie, his concept of investment was fur coats and diamond jewellery. But around this time he decided the best way of putting some money aside was to store it, squirrel-like, in safety deposit boxes in the diamond district of New York, an area introduced to them by the Mob – indicative of how charming and generous they could be to someone they valued.

"They took me down to the diamond exchange in New York," recalls Freda. "You have to know somebody to even get in. I came in and sat on the couch with trays and trays...I didn't even know they had yellow diamonds, green diamonds – all kinds! That was fantastic. I said, 'I like green.' And they gave me a charm bracelet with sapphires and rubies on it. Later, getting out the cab, I lost one of the charms with the sapphire in it. I just called them up. They sent me one, *free*, from Johnny Roberts. They gave Denise a black and white pearl ring. They gave Sandy a white pearl and they gave Jackie Jnr a watch and Tony was so little, they gave him one of those magic games." Roberts told Freda, "You will profit by helping me." It was important to have Freda also "on-side" in the hope she would help keep Jackie controllable.

When one considers the 1990s contractual arrangements of singers George Michael (fifty-two million dollars), Madonna, Prince and Michael Jackson (sixty million a piece) and Janet Jackson (eighty million), it's hard not to be incredulous at Jackie's financial predicament. As talented as these artists might be, Jackie was every bit their equal, if not better. Yet he never even dreamed of such sums. Like any pioneer, Jackie paved the way for those who followed.

It wasn't just the main man who was naive, though. Drummer Jimmy Smith remained with Jackie for ten years, despite having no written contract. "During the time I was working with Jackie I didn't know how much I was making," he reflects. "I only knew I could do anything I wanted to do, buy anything I wanted, go anywhere I wanted. He just picked up the tab and kept money in my pocket. He looked after my family."

On the road Jackie had a large travelling family of his own to take care of. As they travelled the long distances between gigs, Jackie and the entourage would try to sleep. Guitarist Billy Davis would at times take over the driving in order to give the driver, Lamar Cochrane, a break. Jackie was not at all pleased with that arrangement, as Davis recalls. "Lamar was from Atlanta, Georgia. He'd always worn a suit and acted like he was the richest guy in town. Sometimes he liked to nod off. We were headed for Florida. Jackie would sleep in the back. Jackie got mad at me because I was driving."

In particular, Smith had a wild crazy streak and was probably the wrong person to be around Jackie. He was easy going and good looking, with great timing; he could "second guess" Jackie's every move on stage. Jackie's daughter, Denise, puts it this way: "They were like lovers; right on the button. Jimmy could hit it; right on time. He [Jackie] owed Jimmy Smith a whole lot of money, but Jimmy loved my father 'cause he took care of his family in Houston." Freda added, "You see that's what kind of person he was, he didn't want nobody's family be wanting." The problem was, Smith drank way too much.

But the substance abuse meant that Jackie and Smith would often perform on stage when they were very much "under the weather". Smith sometimes went off the stage mid performance. "That happened quite a few times. One time I fell off – it was at a theatre – they had a drop curtain and all of a sudden I fell off into the orchestra pit. I couldn't get back up because of the curtains.

"You'd have to push Jackie out when he was drunk," says Smith. "He couldn't stand up in the curtains, but once you put him on the floor, it was just like you'd wind him up. He was like a robot. He'd go through his whole routine."

On the occasions when time and distance didn't allow them to drive between engagements they would fly, but Jackie and Smith preferred to be drunk first. "One time we had a big fight up there on the aeroplane," chuckles Smith. "Jackie and I were flying from Cleveland and we always had to have whisky. We was late, which was all the time. It was on a Sunday and everything was closed. The airline told us they was going to serve liquor on the plane, but they lied to us.

"We got on the plane expecting liquor. The plane took off and we were waiting for them to serve us our drink. Nobody showed up. So Jackie hit the light [for service]. They came and told us they can't serve us no liquor 'cause in the State of Ohio they can't serve liquor on Sundays. At first Jackie sent Sims to get us some liquor. He came back and said, 'They won't serve no liquor.'

"Jackie took the seat and snatched it away from the little old lady sitting in front of us. Her head was going every which way! Jackie just went to the liquor cabinet. He told them, 'I'm going to shoot out every window.' I said, 'The ones he don't shoot, I'm going to kick out, the sons-of-bitches.' The captain said, 'Go and get it out of the cabinet and give it to him.'" Jackie got his way, but could well have been in trouble.

On another occasion he did a stupid thing on board a flight out of Atlanta. "Jackie always carried pistols in shoulder holsters. Well, he took his coat off and the stewardess has seen the pistol. She went and got the captain. The captain said very nice, 'Mr Wilson, I have to have that pistol.' So Jackie said, 'Gladly, but I ain't going to give you but one.' You see, the guy didn't see the other one.

"The captain went right back to his seat, the plane turned and landed back in Atlanta. Shortly we heard over the speakers, 'Mr Wilson, we are the FBI and we're coming aboard.' In court it cost him ten grand for each pistol. You see, the captain knew him. All he had to do was give 'em up."

Late in 1962 Gil Askey got a call from Jackie who he knew from 1959-1960 when he travelled with him as a member of the powerful, brassy Buddy Johnson Band. In Askey's words: "Jackie called me and asked me to meet backstage at the Brooklyn Paramount, where he was working the *Murray 'The K' Show*. He gave me a tape of a rough 'Baby Workout' with, perhaps, a female voice and piano playing. Jackie asked me to score the music for it and take it to Decca Records reception. Jackie said, 'Hey, man, see what you can do with this tape?'"

Askey scored it extremely well, the big band style dance tune was catchy and right on the money and the horn arrangements were superb. Released in March 1963 it zoomed to the Number Five spot, which was second only to 'Night' in terms of Jackie's overall charting success. 'Baby Workout' credits Alonzo Tucker and Jackie as the songwriters. It certainly had Tucker's R&B feel to it and Jackie sure moved well to it when on stage. To this day the song remains a dance classic. Amazingly, although Askey was paid between seventy-five and $150 for a song which made a bundle for someone, he says philosophically, "It was good to have the money and be doing the thing you liked to do." At the time a top musician earned only sixty-five dollars for a studio recording session according to the agreed union scale.

In 1964, after the success of 'Baby Workout', Jackie recorded the wonderful *Somethin' Else* album which comprised great R&B tunes written by Alonzo Tucker and many co-written with Jackie, arranged by Gil Askey. "I went into a studio with just him and Alonzo [Tucker]," Askey says. "It was on Sixth Avenue, perhaps the RCA Building. He just made up these songs. He was constantly watching his watch. He was working at the Copa at that time, and he had a date with one of the dancers. He was trying to get out of there. He was all dressed up and ready for his date. I guess he ran through all of these songs in thirty to forty minutes. They had a beat going, these chords going, they just made up the lyrics as they went along. Most of them. He said, 'You got it, man.'"

When it came to the date for the recording session, Askey says, "Then he comes to the recording session and I've got to have all the lyrics ready for him, 'cause he don't remember nothing." It's an extraordinary story, because there were twelve excellent tunes on the album – all written and arranged in around less than an hour!

Askey continues: "On *Somethin' Else* it was the first time he'd had a Fender [electric] bass behind him as well as an upright bass. The Fender bass player was Bob Bushnell. I was trying to capture that 'Motown sound'. I had heard Marvin Gaye doing 'Can I Get A Witness'; it was a whole new bass sound. At that time you had to sing along live with the orchestra. They were operating on four tracks. Jackie would be in a booth, if he made an error, we had to start at the top. That was at Bell Sound on Fifty-Fourth Street, between Broadway and Eighth Avenue." Although Askey worked on the album only with the assistance of Jackie and his friend, Alonzo Tucker, none of them gets credit on the back of the album. Instead the album states "Produced By Nat Tarnopol And Dick Jacobs". Askey remembers the event this way, "Dick Jacobs didn't have nothing to do with *Somethin' Else*; Jackie produced that on his own."

Sadly this album, which deserved to do well, sold only moderately and Askey believes it was as a result of the ever changing public taste in music. "The 'British Invasion' came in 1964 and changed everything. And Motown came along, as well, with a sound equally palatable to both black and white audiences. When rock 'n' roll, R&B was a having a big crossing over, Jackie was at his low tide. When Motown was at its peak, Jackie was at his low tide in most of those years. If it had happened differently he would have become a lot more popular and successful." Having seen and worked with some of the all time great talents in music, Askey is not easily impressed, but for Jackie he developed a genuine love and respect.

The album deserved to do well if only for Alonzo Tucker's songs. Melvin Moore, who had formerly been a top baritone singer during the big band era of the 1940s, was a long time promotion man with Decca Records and then Brunswick, says: "Tucker was such a wonderful, beautiful man. He knew how to make records. We were together five or six years. We were in the office together. He had a home in the Bronx, but after he passed [in 1977] it went back to Nat Tarnopol's people." Another who knew him equally well was Midnighters guitarist Billy Davis, who says, "Alonzo had so much talent. If he had a voice there would have been no person on earth who could outsing him. He had so much feeling, he just didn't have the voice."

Eddie Singleton, too, became involved with Jackie's recording career in New York and worked with him until Jackie went to record in Chicago in late 1966. Singleton had started out as the first vocalist on Irve Jerome's Pontiac label out of New York, while still a teenager, before pursuing a career as a songwriter and producer. He produced, or co-produced, 'Baby Workout' and went on to produce five of his albums; *Shake A Hand* (with Linda Hopkins, the only duet album Jackie ever did), *Soul Time*, *Somethin' Else*, *Spotlight On Jackie* and *Soul Galore*.

Singleton, who later passed the gauntlet to Carl Davis in Chicago and went on to manage Nina Simone and to produce for her as well, says of Jackie: "I worked with a few evergreen guys, but nobody could stand head and shoulders with Jackie Wilson, the performer. Because he had the instinctive gospel singing relationship with an audience. He knew when to do what with his voice, and not just his voice; he was as tricky with his feet as his voice. He was the whole nine yards. There was no escaping Jackie Wilson. If you sat in the audience he'd find you. He'd find the place you lived, no matter whoever you were. Being a part of that little bit of history is something that's carried me through a lifetime with a lot of pride, because we were also friends and we had a very good relationship." Singleton went on to found his own Shrine Records Washington DC based label and then worked with Motown Records. "I tell you what, it's a matter of place in time. He might have been Michael Jackson, Michael Jackson might have been Jackie. Jackie Wilson and Elvis had a very close relationship. That big diamond encrusted broach Jackie wore around his neck was a gift from Elvis."

Unlike his rapport with the other stars of the era, Jackie's links with the Mob didn't help relations with Nat Tarnopol, as Singleton maintains:

"Around 1965 the relationship was just beginning to go downhill, you know. There were many influences around Jackie at time. Some were friendly to the camp, some were others who were inside the camp, but weren't necessarily there to protect Nat. Nat was a character in his own right. Jackie respected Nat for the history and for what they were able to accomplish together. So there was a lot of camaraderie between them that could not break up. When they fell out it was on their own terms and their own reasons. Nat was very successful in creating a little dynasty around Jackie Wilson, and Jackie always felt he didn't share proportionately in the bounty of all this goodness, 'cause Nat took control and Nat ran the operation, which is how it was set up to be. But it was all done with the innuendo that Jackie had some pure relativity in the big picture. That was a real bone of contention, but it was never discussed openly."

If Singleton is correct, Jackie was also becoming increasingly aware that the money wasn't going to last forever and had begun to seriously hide it from the women in his life. "Like I say Jackie and I were real close, in private and professionally. We were neighbours – off of West End Avenue and Seventy-Second Street [Westside Towers Apartments]. I lived across the street in Presidential Towers. Johnny Nash lived in Jackie's building. He didn't give it all away. He had safety deposit boxes in the diamond centre. They are in the jewellery shops. I went down there many times with Jackie when he'd come off the road. We sat there many times and played with the money. Boxes and boxes – there was over a million in cash. He was saving up for his retirement. Nobody knew about it; Harlean didn't know. Everybody had some inkling that he had something somewhere. I knew where, that's how close I was with Jackie. More than likely they are still there, but the owners would probably wait a period of time after his passing – a respectable period – to wait and see who was going to come along and claim. They probably socked it all away; split it between themselves. There was a considerable amount of cash there they never got a chance to spend. Number one, because he never thought he'd be leaving that soon. Jackie was larger than life; he was a Daymon Runyon character straight out of the book – and he lived it. Live fast, die young – that was Jackie."

Paul Tarnopol confirms Singleton's contention: "Jackie had plenty of money. Jackie didn't invest, he'd fill safety deposit boxes in the diamond district. Harlean didn't know where they were. Harlean had jewels and furs, but Petey [John, the son Jackie had with her in 1964] sold all that stuff when he was on crack. Jackie would get cash and he'd run down town, and nobody knows where it is." Safety deposit boxes and jewellery were Jackie's chief forms of saving or investment. Whether it was a distrust of banks or the stock market, or just plain bad advice, is not known, but more likely it was the desire to keep the money out of the reach of the tax man and Harlean.

His desire to keep things not only from his lover but from his family was made abundantly plain to Singleton one time. "One day, after a session, a broker came in," he remembers. "He was selling blue chip stock; IBM and the like. The guy asked Jackie, 'You've got children?' Jackie said, I never will forget – the epitome of insensitivity – 'Fuck 'em. They have to make theirs like I made mine.' That was his mentality. After we finished work that night we went out and had a few drinks and I got all over his ass. I said, 'Jackie, how the fuck could you sit there and make that statement?' He said, 'I mean it; they're not giving me shit. They wouldn't appreciate it, no how.' But before the night was over he came over to me and said, 'I'm not really that bad!'" In the years to come many would agree; many would not.

CHAPTER EIGHT

A Kiss, A Thrill And Goodbye

In May 1964 Jackie returned to Harlem's Apollo Theatre and to even better reviews. Jose of *Variety* magazine (20 May, 1964) reported glowingly on the performance: "Wilson takes some unusual liberties on stage. It's odd for a performer to place himself in a position which virtually invites femme onlookers in the first pews to participate in the routine. Wilson, during the latter part of the act, works into a horizontal position. The youngsters may or may not be his stooges, but a group of girls approach him to mop his brow and later come to the foots to kiss him violently and with feeling. He made no attempt to move.

"But preceding this display, Wilson proves an excellent singer despite his proclivities for over coloration. He has a vocal spectrum which ranges from a baritone to a falsetto. He works in bold, imaginative tones with warmth and vigour. He's extremely effective here."

He was considerably less effective at home. May 1964 also meant Freda had been married to Jackie for more than thirteen years; and she'd had enough. His philandering had finally become too much to bear so she filed for divorce. Billy Davis wasn't surprised. "Jackie and Freda had a special love," he says, "but there came a time when they had to part. Freda never really stopped loving him; the feeling was always there."

In January 1965, the Circuit Court in Detroit, in a default judgement – Jackie failed to appear or to contest it – granted a divorce. The settlement gave Freda the family home on LaSalle Boulevard, while Jackie was ordered to pay ten thousand dollars plus two hundred a week (fifty dollars per child) to Freda for support of their family.

Considering Jackie grossed $231,862 in 1963, it seems Freda didn't do especially well; in fact, she later recalled that seeking the divorce was the biggest mistake she'd ever made. Quoted in the Detroit *Free Press* (11 January, 1976), she said: "I didn't know what I was doing. I had this dream of his being a knight in shining armour. And when he wasn't, I got all upset and just wanted to get out of it...We had cars and cars and cars. Cadillacs and Broughams and Thunderbirds. We had three cars at a time. I had my own car, and I don't even drive...I used to buy all these clothes, feel comfy. He liked me though. That's why he sent me to modelling school. He wanted me to learn how to sit, how to stand, how to eat cake. He was so proud of me when I learned."

"He told me not to get the divorce in 1964," she claims today. "I just didn't see us doing anything; we weren't going any further. He was on the road, but when I wanted to see him I'd take some or all of the kids. When he came home, he just came home." When it came to divorce or abortion Jackie was "old fashioned". He didn't condone either. In all likelihood he would have preferred to remain married, and to have maintained his liaisons. To have his cake and eat it too!

Fortunately, his beleaguered wife had some welcome assistance. "His mother really liked us and she helped us a lot, and when Jack got a chance he'd get us some money." It wasn't that he was mean spirited, Jackie was just irresponsible. He left most things to someone else. Jackie was too busy giving his all to his adoring fans. Too busy being a superstar.

For Freda it was a difficult time. She faced the daily reality of raising their four children without the help of a father and with the money not coming through. She wasn't coping and turned to the Catholic Church for support. "I had been on the road so much, I felt I needed some help with my kids. Strong help; some male companionship, with the boys especially," she says. "I took them fishing, but I hated to see... you know that poor little fish. The priests helped and played ball with them. They did help me with the kids while I was at work. If they got out of hand they had to go over and clean the convent on Saturdays. Jack'd say, 'I'm a Jew and you're a Baptist, and the kids are Catholic. What a screwed up family.' He wouldn't go to mass. He wanted to be something different. When I enrolled the children in Catholic school, he said, 'How can they be Jewish *and* Catholic?' I said, 'You're only Jewish because you wear a Star of David around your neck.'"

Once children could think, act and talk, they were a threat to Jackie. He couldn't relate to them, although Freda puts a different spin on it. "Jackie loved all children, but he loved to kiss on babies. Especially when they were little and didn't argue. Jackie loved children, but he didn't have a lot of time – he was always thinking about his business, which was singing. But he loved kids. He'd lie down on the floor when he was home and watch the cartoons and eat popcorn and potato chips."

Typical of Jackie's irresponsibility was that he was constantly in arrears with the child support. "Jackie never caught up with child support payments. The Michigan Courts wouldn't get together with the New York courts. Each time I'd go down they'd say, 'Nothing this time.' I had to work two jobs just to exist. The children were used to certain things. Clothes were most important. When you step out that door, try to look good so people didn't know how poor you were."

By March 1966 Freda filed a complaint for non-payment. A non-support warrant was issued reporting Jackie had fallen $7,500 behind in his two hundred dollars a week child support.

Tony, in particular, had almost no relationship with Jackie, being only five when the divorce was granted. He was so timid he'd hide behind Freda's or grandma Eliza Mae's legs. Denise had a much closer relationship, being thirteen when the break-up occurred. She loved him from the bottom of her heart, although her father fixation bordered on the unhealthy. But if the divorce and absence of a father figure helps explain why the children had disjointed lives, the adults involved didn't fare much better. According to Freda the divorce let Jackie fall prey to the machinations of Harlean Harris, while she, Freda, sought solace in alcohol, which only made matters worse.

In December 1964 another another body blow hit Jackie. He was performing in Las Vegas when he got word that Sam Cooke had been shot dead in highly controversial circumstances. Cooke apparently had taken a prostitute to a sleazy Los Angeles motel and, sometime later, had pursued her out of the room while naked. He was confronted by the black female manager and, according to her version of events, she shot him out of fear for her personal safety. Controversy about the real story behind his death abounds, many believing the whole thing to be a set-up, most likely by the Mafia.

Sam Cooke had been one of Jackie's dearest friends in showbusiness. "Jackie Wilson took Sam Cooke on his first tour," singer Linda Hopkins, recalls. "I was on that tour. Jackie was a friend of Sam's and was a big fan as well. Sam could sing nothing wrong."

Hank Ballard blames the lifestyle. "What happens to all these superstars with all this tragedy? There was me, Jackie Wilson, Sam Cooke, Bo Diddley. A big package tour. A week later, after the tour ended, Sam got killed. Seems there's a jinx to be a superstar. Seems like superstars don't have a longevity of living. Something seems to happen to all these superstars."

Lennie "Lynn" Crochet, who would become Jackie's common law wife from 1970 to 1975, reveals that Jackie had his own theory. "He told me that Barbara [Cooke's wife] and [Cooke's guitarist, Bobby] Womack are the reason that Sam is dead," she says. Jackie surmised that if Cooke's wife had been faithful, he wouldn't have gone with a prostitute. Although unsubstantiated, Womack married Barbara within two months of Cooke's death.

In November 1965 Jackie was back to his irresponsible ways, but it was his car that suffered. After he failed to appear at an engagement at the Palladium Night Club in Houston, Texas, the press reported how an angry crowd of two hundred vented their fury on his eight thousand dollar Cadillac. Reportedly Jackie had been taken to hospital with a 105 degrees temperature and required a month's rest, but drummer Jimmy Smith, who was with him, remembers the true explanation for their non-appearance: "We didn't make it – we had a party."

A similar thing occurred in Baltimore, Maryland. "Jackie wouldn't go out," says Smith. "He didn't feel like going out there. They had to escort us out of town." Besides the exhausting routine of his stage act, Jackie was never kind to his own body, being a heavy smoker, morning-to-night drinker, taking innumerable "uppers" and snorting cocaine. It was all taking a toll.

One of the few young women whom Jackie became a close friend of, but not in the physical way, confirms his hedonistic lifestyle. Trina "Cookie" Johnson got to see an intimate side of Jackie that only those very close saw, while working with James Brown as one of his Brownettes. "He had a lot of parties," she says. "He could remember people from a long time. He'd remember what you had on last time. Only people he didn't remember are these young girls he'd take in his room. A lot of the women he was with were pretty. He was a wonderful human being. I was the only female Jackie was around that he didn't sleep with. I was very young…though I know of incidents where age meant nothing. People thought he must have slept with me."

Being so close, Johnson was privy to everything. She observed that

Jackie was over-doing the alcohol and drugs, but he also had moments of calm. "He would do things, like rent a hotel room somewhere and sit in the room and talk with someone. Myself, Lynn [Crochet] and perhaps Harlean he would open up to; if he trusted you. Fadwah [Peace, the voodoo woman Jackie is thought to have had two children with], she was quite close. He'd call her up and confide." But these moments were rare and she puts much of the blame on the company he kept.

Former Shaker Gang member, Harry Respess, was involved with promotion in Chicago when he again reconnected with Jackie in the mid 1960s. "At the Sutherland Hotel Jackie went up to see Little Willie John and they got blasted out of their minds," he remembers. "Little Willie John kept telling me, 'Make me high.' I said, 'You're already high.' He said, 'Make me higher.' They really got bombed. It was all snorting 'coke'." More generally, Jackie was careful not to let people see him taking drugs. Says girlfriend Lynn Ciccone, "I never saw Jackie do cocaine – only pills. They were uppers [amphetamines]. They were red; they were the worst."

Joyce McRae, who these days lives with and manages Sam Moore of Sam And Dave fame, suspects Little Willie John may well have contributed in getting Jackie addicted to drug taking. "If Jackie was true to form it was probably Willie John," she states. "Willie was probably one of the most evil motherfuckers. He turned Sam [Moore] on to heroin. Jackie sounded too much like Willie; he was prettier than Willie, he had more stage presence. He was a threat to Willie. It would not surprise me if Willie did to Jack what he did to Sam. Sam worshipped Jackie and Willie John. These guys were truly the best of the best. It's an era that's going away; culture lost."

Jackie had always flirted with cocaine and now he had a full blown habit. When high, he could be somewhat different. As his friend and confidant, singer Tommy Hunt recalls: "He snorted that stuff and got crazy. He knew he was a star and everybody loved Jackie, but he didn't love himself. Sometimes he'd go off his mind. He'd be so high off of coke. He'd be on the streets cussing and screaming at people. I said, 'You're a star, man, you don't have to act like that. What's wrong with you, man?' But he was so high. When he wasn't high he was the most beautiful person you ever wanted to meet. Nicest guy in the world. When he got high he was a fireball, a thunderstick. He was doing those things because he was lonely. He thought he was strong enough to control those pressures he was under. He couldn't control it. He used to call me, just to talk with me, and cry over the phone. He'd even think Harlean was doing things behind his back, and it was driving the man crazy."

Hunt was saddened, but not surprised, at Jackie's worsening condition. "Jackie did what he wanted to but he just got hooked up in the wrong circles, I think," he reasons. "Like I say, in those days you didn't know who you'd be hooked up with – you just knew you were going to be on stage, doing what you wanted to do, making those girls scream. That's what he wanted. I'm still seeing it, not as much as I did. It's older girls now!"

More often than not Jackie's drug of choice was always alcohol. The problem wasn't helped by his long time habit of never drinking from a pre-opened bottle. "He drank Jack Daniels and vodka," recalls Jimmy Smith. "He wouldn't buy fifths, he'd buy pints. His chauffeur would buy two pints every night, cause he didn't want to drink a big bottle."

In 1965, after their divorce, Freda noticed the changes in Jackie's personality brought about by his excessive drug taking. "The dealer in Detroit had changed...she was not giving him cocaine, Jack could handle that. She was giving him heroin. Jack was snorting the heroin. But he thought it was cocaine. When he went to somebody else he was getting cocaine. All of a sudden it was mixed up. And he was smoking his special blend of marijuana. Then he was drinking."

For Christmas he came home because, even though they were now divorced, Jackie still treated Freda as though they were still married. It was to be the worst Christmas yet. "I was feeling real bad," relates Freda. "I had a virus. I said, 'I don't know if I want to see Jack.' He came in. He seemed okay, but I know his eyes kept shifting away. He could talk about one thing, but you knew he was thinking of something different...in his own world.

"His mother noticed something was wrong 'cause she asked me, 'What was the matter, is he all right?' I said, 'I don't know. I think that 'stuff' has done something to him.' Sure enough they had stopped at this woman's house [to buy drugs] on the way to the house. It was bad. He took me; he said, 'We'll leave the kids here, I don't want to be bothered right now.' That wasn't unusual, the first day." By going to stay at a hotel, rather than the house, Jackie could get some peace and quiet, away from the children and the visitors.

"When we jumped in the limo, Mr Watley asked me, 'Was I sure?', he said, 'Because I'm going back to Philadelphia tonight.' He said, 'There's something wrong with Jackie. I've never seen him like that.' We went to the

Sheridan Cadillac. That's when he blew, really blew! I wasn't saying nothing. He got real agitated. Then he got the magazine *Penthouse*. He ordered some Creme de Cocoa for me, and he ordered Scotch. He had stopped and got my record player and was playing Etta James, the same song over and over – I hate her records."

Then he called JJ and sent Watley in the limo to collect him. "While Jack was talking to JJ he wanted to speak to Pop [Watley]. He asked Pop, 'Where is my limousine?' Pop said, 'Parked in the driveway.' He said, 'You're a liar; shake them keys.' He had Pop shaking the keys on the phone. That's when my mother-in-law said, 'What's wrong with you, Jack? Your car is in the driveway.' He said, 'I know Mama, I was just kidding with him.' I knew he was not right then."

Watley, too, seemed aware JJ was headed for trouble. "Mr Watley, he told JJ not to come down," remembers Freda. "But JJ got in the car and came down." It could easily have cost JJ his life because Jackie's severe paranoia meant he quite possibly planned to kill Freda and JJ, the two people closest to him. "He probably had laid them guns up there on the top of the chest of drawers. Had he not been on the phone, he'd have probably shot me right then."

Freda's misery continued while they waited for the limo to return. "Jack was not saying anything too much at that time," she says. He just told me to keep playing that record. He was standing over there by the window. He said, 'You let the record stop. Put it back on!' I said, 'Oh, God.' He said, 'Here I am, right here.'

"Jack said, 'You take off all your clothes and give them to me.' I did. By then JJ was knocking. Jack opened the door. I pulled the cover up on me. JJ said, 'Hey, my man, where's the party?' I never will forget that smile freezing on his face. Jack looked at him like he looked at me, he jerked him into that room and he said, 'Here's the party, motherfucker!' He was beating JJ and he pulled JJ down a little bit – he was beating the living daylights out of him. He was killing him. JJ never hit him back.

"I didn't say nothing. I was keeping the record going and thinking how I was going to get out of there. He had put the chain on that door. I said, 'Lord, give me strength.' I tried to get that sheet up so I could wrap myself and go, but I didn't have time. When he was really engrossed into beating JJ, I was gone. God gave me strength and I tore that chain off the door and I was gone.

"I couldn't get the elevator, so I started down some steps. I was down the steps and at the mezzanine at the elevator, these guys was cleaning the elevator. I looked around...he was coming down the steps and he had the gun in his hand. They say you look back when you're scared – I never looked back. I didn't care if he got me in the back, but I was movin' real fast.

"Down in that lobby they got some sheets and wrapped me up. JJ had left Nelson Small's brother in the car – the one that was his bodyguard – he was sitting there so long. Small came in as I was going out. I was barefoot; this was winter time. I was going barefoot with the sheets. He said, 'What are you doing like that?' I said, 'Jack is crazy; he's gone completely nuts now. He's killing JJ. You'd better see if you can save his life.'"

Somehow disaster was averted. "They did get Jack together and to the house. Before he came over there, he called my mother and said, 'You'd better save her life.' He was really crazy. He was going, I was going. Nobody could change him. He was scary. My mother got out a gun, and she didn't use guns. The kids was scared to death, they was hiding in the closet. Jackie Jnr was trying to protect me – he was standing in front of me. He had a knife in his hand. I was ready to jump in this closet.

"He wanted to talk to me, he told my mother. I said, 'I can't talk to him.' She said, 'I'll tell him,' 'cause he had broke my mother's front door with his fist. She said, 'Jack, don't hit the door any more or I may shoot you. I don't want to shoot you. If you settle down, you come on up here and talk to us and I'll stay here, too.' He did.

"She put her gun down by her and she sat there. He cried and said he didn't know what was the matter. I didn't either, and I didn't know how to cope with this situation. I said, 'If we can just stay away from each other until you can get this under control.' So that's what we were doing. We were going along like that, just like that because I was scared of him. Scared to be alone with him."

Although exacerbated by drugs, what at least in part lay behind Jackie's out of character behaviour is that someone had stolen his credit cards and run up enormous bills. Jackie was trying to determine who, and thought initially Freda had done it. In calling JJ over, it's likely he had finally figured out, or learned, who the true culprit was.

His entourage were all former street kids who'd got by on their wits. Some habits just didn't die, although they never lost their love for the singer. "They didn't mind dying for him, JJ and those guys," says Freda. "But he paid them more than they could earn. That's why I was surprised when JJ was stealing his credit cards with Cecil." Cecil Franklin was the brother of singer Aretha. His drug taking and womanising, were well known, despite his profession, so the illegal use of Jackie's credit cards wasn't out of character. "Cecil was a minister of religion," sighs Freda. "He was hanging around with entertainers naturally because of his sister. He had just got out of college – they were all doing it…snorting cocaine.

"JJ and Cecil took all these credit cards and they rented a car and they went all around the world. They bought a lot of clothes and stuff. The cocaine was messing up JJ's brain. They used to say he had a big nose, which meant he'd snort a lot. Plus, he could smoke weed at the same time for two hours."

According to Jimmy Smith it was an accident waiting to happen. "JJ used to look after the credit cards and money," he says, "and Jackie wasn't keeping up with what was going on. They just went too far with it. I know Jackie's mother saved JJ. Jackie would have killed him."

In many ways JJ's fate was worse than death. "Jack hated JJ," says Freda. "He got rid of JJ after that beating up in the room. That was really scary." The strong friendship that had existed between Jackie and the ever loyal JJ was severely strained. However, JJ later rejoined him as valet, driver and bodyguard. But the closeness wasn't there.

It was as though Jackie couldn't face losing anyone permanently; not JJ or his wife, although she too would always have an uncomfortable relationship with him. "I never really left him," says Freda of the divorce, "like when he came home, as long as someone was there, I was there. I'd go upstairs and he'd come upstairs and sleep. But I didn't sleep and I had a whole lot of people around all night. They'd just be standing around, like Rever [brother-in-law], my sister. I was scared to go to sleep while he was there. Like, I would be a nervous wreck at the end of ten days. You never could tell though, he had such control. He could control you and you didn't know you were being controlled. You'd think everything was fine and he'd be smiling at you and in his mind all kinds of things would be going on up in there. He'd be planning what he was going to do. He'd be thinking, 'She thinks she's smart – she's got all these people around her. She ain't going to get away with doing me like this. I'm Jackie Wilson.' He got to that point. 'I'm Jackie Wilson, I can do anything I want to do.' 'Cause he was raised like that. Mama will make it all right or someone would make it all right – it's going to come out okay.

"The fact that I was fighting that – he can't handle that. He said, 'I raised you, you don't do this. You don't defy me. I'm Jackie Wilson, your name is Freda Wilson. I made you.' Now I was supposed to be doing like I had all these years. 'Okay, yeah, if you say so.'"

If he didn't listen to Freda's opinions, he certainly couldn't stand interference in what he considered his personal affairs from anyone else. "My doctor said, 'What are you trying to do, kill her? She's been pregnant fifteen times before she's even thirty, yet.'" recalls Freda. "He said, 'That is my wife, I can do what I want to do and you stay out of it or you'll be in trouble. I certainly don't think you'll be her doctor any more.' Things like this. One time the doctor called him long distance saying it's an emergency and he told the doctor off."

Jackie's drug induced paranoia still surfaced, and again he accused Freda of working for the FBI against him. "He thought I was working for the FBI," she says, "so I hated being alone in the room with him. He was trying to make me tell what we did with his credit cards and all this money and stuff. I didn't even know what the man was talking about. He had me in the bedroom, my sister and the kids in their bedroom. JJ and them were standing at the door. Jack was really angry, keeping anyone from going out. His mother tried to get in. He had men downstairs to prevent anyone exiting the house.

"So my sister, Jacqui tied some sheets together and they let her down as far as she could go. Then she jumped. She went and got Rever and he brought Red, the one Jacqui later married, and five brothers and one other guy came to get us out of there. Rever came up to the door. He had a sawed-off shotgun up his arm, which he always carried. They knocked on the door and Rever showed them the sawed-off shotgun. He got everybody out."

But help had arrived too late to prevent Jackie inflicting a severe beating on Freda. "My head was like two heads. Everything was broken in the bedroom. Jack didn't remember doing any of this. They asked him to open the door and he told them to go away he was busy. So Rever and them kicked the bedroom door in. When he saw Rever, Jack said, 'Hey, my man.' He forgot all about me.

"That's when my mother-in-law really knew what was going on. She didn't know this was happening. But she would never have called the police, unless she thought we were really being hurt.

"We got all the kids together and Jack started crying. I went off to my mother's. He wanted me to come back. Nobody told me to come back, I said, 'Let him come over and talk to me. Maybe he's okay now. I'm going to trust him one more time.' So he talked like he was okay, he said he knew what had happened. That this lady had changed it [cocaine for heroin].

"So I went back home and we left the kids with his mother. We went down to the Brass Rail [bar], downtown. That's when he started acting different again."

Freda may have suffered physically, but all the family were scarred by the traumatic incidents, especially the children. "Those kids were really messed up so I had to take them all to a psychiatrist," Freda admits. "They saw me by myself, then they saw each child alone. Then they put the story together. Denise was less affected than the other kids; Sandy wasn't too bad. But Jackie Jnr and Tony were. Jack was their role model. It kind of did it to them."

Jackie's mercurial temperament continued to keep Freda on her toes, long after the divorce. Although she was now living at the home of her boyfriend, Michael, when he returned it was as though nothing had ever happened. "You know when I was staying down in the ghetto with this dude and Gino [the dog], Jack came down there," explains Freda. "Jackie Jnr called me, he said, 'Daddy's at the house.' Jack comes down there, knocks on the door. I said, 'Who is it?' 'Jackie Wilson!' I said 'Little Sonny, don't be fooling around.' He said, 'This is not Little Sonny, this is Big Sonny!' I opened the door and I couldn't believe my eyes. I was still a little scared. Gino didn't like nobody messing with me. Jack kissed and hugged me and Gino just looked. He got down there on the floor with Gino and wrestled. I thought Gino was going to hurt him, but he didn't.

"Jack took me and Gino in town. We went back towards LaSalle and we stopped at every blues bar along the way. He brings Gino in, tells Gino to lie down. 'Nobody messes with Gino, 'cause I'm Jackie Wilson.' Within minutes every little bar was packed; word of mouth. Then everyone wanted him to sing. So he sang in every little bar. By then he's getting 'high', plus he took the bottles with him. Every bar, he took the bottle. JJ was driving, Gino was still in the car. He really tried to get rid of some stress. Gino got to liking him so much, when he started singing Gino went and laid on the stage in front of him.

"We went back to 16522 LaSalle [which now belonged to Freda]. He said, 'My name is Jackie Wilson and your name is Freda Wilson.' It's three o'clock in the morning and he's drinking up some of that Cutty Sark. He said, 'We're going to listen to some Jackie Wilson records,' and he was singing with the records. Everybody was there all the kids and everything. About ten o'clock in the morning he finally got tired and went to bed."

That was not the worst of his arrogance when he returned. Despite the divorce, Jackie still treated her as his wife and their sexual relationship continued as normal. After he awoke, Freda explained, "He came down there and he propped himself up and said, 'Fix me something to eat, woman.' Michael was right there, we was in the bathroom having sex." It is an extraordinary revelation about Jackie's nature, that while he still believed he owned his ex-wife, he tolerated her new relationship.

Although innocuous at the time, another fatalistic meeting in 1965 would cause bitterness and controversy until the day he died – and beyond. According to Joyce McRae, a powder blue 1965 Cadillac convertible pulled over to the kerb next to her and her husband, in New York City, on the corner of Broadway and Forty-Seventh Street. McRae noticed it was Jackie Wilson in the car and told her husband. He replied somewhat too loudly, "If that's Jackie Wilson, then I'm Herbert Hoover." Jackie, with his irrepressible humour, shot back, "Hi there, Mr Hoover, I'm Jackie Wilson." From that a conversation ensued and a friendship developed. Indeed, on Mrs McRae's part, it was much more than a friendship, it was a love that became an all encompassing obsession; even devotion.

Two months after that meeting, McRae – an attractive blonde, born to the wealthy Jewish Chicago Greenburg family – and her husband went to see Jackie perform in Miami. They sent a message backstage, saying, "Mr Hoover and his old lady are here; can we buy you a drink?" Jackie immediately saw the joke and they all got together after the show.

Although there is little doubt that McRae was to get to know Jackie well over the years, nobody indicated that their relationship had any seriousness about it. Remarkably, McRae claims she never met Tarnopol or Jackie's best friend, JJ.

Joyce McRae would remain on the scene for the remainder of Jackie's life, always courting controversy. But one of the unfathomables in his life is her namesake, Jackie's half-sister, Joyce Ann Lee, eleven years his junior. By many estimates, she had a vocal delivery the equal of Jackie, and yet never made a commercial recording. Quite possibly she just was not interested in a stage career.

While Jackie was living the high life in New York, she was keeping herself to herself as usual. Jackie's cousin, Tom Odneal, got her a job as a welder with Chrysler Motors in Pontiac, just north of Detroit, where she has worked for more than thirty years. Today Joyce Lee refuses to speak with anyone on the subject of her brother.

"The relationship between the siblings can best be described as love-hate," says Freda. "Probably, unwittingly, Eliza Mae contributed to this by constantly comparing Joyce unfavourably with her older brother. She used to say to Joyce when Mama'd get mad, 'You're so ugly. Who do you think wants you? You don't know nothing, you don't do nothing.' Things like that she'd say to her. Joyce wrote a story in school about the girl that had the pretty brother and the ugly sister. Parents sometimes don't realise what they're doing."

Husbands don't realise either. "Joyce looks like her dad," recalls her former spouse, Johnny Collins. "She had an accident where her face was dragged – her lips had been pulled. Joyce has an extremely large mouth and displaced teeth. When she hits a note you can look down her throat. She is not the prettiest woman to look at, but she had lungs. When she hit a note you could close your eyes and memorise every single nuance. She could rattle you in a chair with a note."

With such affection for Joyce's looks, it's little wonder that many believe that Collins married Joyce because of her famous brother. Rightly or wrongly, Collins would later tour with Jackie and often opened the show for him. "If you told me I was going to marry her, I'd die," he says. However marry Joyce he did, although it didn't last. They had one daughter, Kelly.

"The only problem I had with my wife was that she was better than her brother," he insists. "Cleverer than her brother. Gave her brother notes to hit. But she would never do it on her own. Joyce was self-conscious. She had a natural talent that was frightening. She had a foundation for music that would scare you. She could go from the lowest of the low – then hit the high note, and come back down – and never miss the fact there was a space in between. That can only be done on certain musical instruments.

"She wanted to be herself and the family wouldn't let her. The kids wouldn't let her be herself. It was like, 'We are the children of Jackie Wilson and you are our aunt.' She said, 'I am my own self person, and because of you I won't sing.'

"Aretha Franklin said she would have stopped singing if Joyce had ever come up on stage with her. Her brother Cecil asked Joyce what would it take to get her to sing. She said, 'Kill everyone in the family.' It wasn't shyness that prevented her from becoming a performer."

Whatever her reasons for not pursuing her talent, on one rare occasion Jackie arranged for recordings of them singing duet. "Jackie and Joyce would go to United Sound Studios and do stuff," recalls Billy Davis. "But, it all got stolen. She was very hurt by it."

Joyce's problems obviously started at home. For her own reasons, Eliza Mae chose to favour her son who was blessed with the good looks and charm as well as the voice, and this affected the children's relationship, according to Collins: "Jackie liked Joyce, but she didn't like him all that much." Eddie Singleton agrees: "They didn't have a good relationship. He was forever trying to win her acceptance, but she had a bridge up. That's something that troubled him all his life, because there's nothing he wouldn't do for her."

Early in the Vietnam conflict, Collins joined the Marines and did tours of duty there. He became part of the family, living for many years in the same house with Jackie and, particularly, his mother. Obviously he got to see the complex relationships played out regularly. "Dysfunction, miss-unction was part of the family," he recalls. "Jack's mother would prepare dinner, make everybody wait; make this big platter and feed him before she'd feed her own husband! It was disrespectful. She adored her son. I wouldn't kiss her ass. When Joyce's mother was mean, vicious and nasty I left the house. She couldn't get over that. As rich and well paid as she is, she's a nasty person.

"But Jackie loved her and that was hard to do. Not many people like Liza, let alone loved her. She was a gangster. She liked to gamble; she liked to play cards. She taught everybody to play stud poker. Liza Lee was a strong woman, she took care of her family. You didn't cross her.

"She would say, 'Bring me some lard.' She put lard on her legs [most likely she actually used Vaseline as a preventative against scaly skin], put on some high heeled shoes, got on a coat, and walked down Lynwood Avenue. Two things about her. She wouldn't put on stockings. You never saw her on a picture with Jack where she had stockings on. And she could walk into the New York mayor's office and not have to wait."

Collins' opinion of Jackie's first wife isn't any higher than his opinion of Eliza Mae. "Freda was nasty; all of them were," he says, free from the family's wrath now. "You have a $150,000 home and rats and roaches everywhere. Was she a good housekeeper? Two and three hundred dollar gowns just stacked on the floor. They would take them off and they'd just lie there. Jack was hard, stomp-down rock 'n' roll star. He kicked ass twenty-four/seven and most of the time when he got home he didn't want to be around her."

Given the motives others have ascribed to his marriage to Joyce, it's not surprising to hear Collins' thoughts dismissed as sour grapes. Guitarist Billy Davis, grew up with Jackie and Joyce and remembers Collins milking his relationship with the singer. "When he married Joyce, we'd be sitting up in the house and he would bring people by, giving them a tour of the house," he says. "He'd take strangers through the house…four or five people walking through the house. Mama was really bothered by it."

In a claim that nobody else seemed aware of, Collins says, "Jackie understood me. The first time he took a swing at me I whipped his ass…and we never had another problem. We only had two fights. One in the hotel, one in the house."

But on one subject Collins is unlikely to be doubted. As an opening act for his former brother-in-law he truly believes he witnessed greatness. "Nobody put their lungs on the line, but him," he recalls. "I watched him sing with the flu, he was sicker than a dog; he sang his ass off. When he sang 'Night', he opened up a whole new world."

It was the hope of everyone involved that new worlds would be opened up by 'A Kiss, A Thrill And Goodbye', from Jackie's 1965 album, *Soul Time*. Written by Rosemary McCoy and Roy Gaines it was, sadly, never released as a single, but its fabulous lyrics and the orchestrations lend themselves to Jackie's powerful vocal delivery, especially an amazing crescendo, where he sucks the air into his powerful lungs and achieves the most incredible range. Credits for the songwriting also list Jackie's name, but as that's a trick already explained. "We just put his name on there because he recorded it," says McCoy. "He really didn't do anything to the song. I was so thrilled to have a record with Jackie." Of the hundred plus songs published listing his name as either writer or, more often co-writer, the suspicion is that very few had Jackie's involvement.

McCoy's successes have been enormous, writing several hits for Nat "King" Cole, including 'If I May' and 'You're My Personal Possession' as well as Tina Turner's huge hit, 'I think It's Going To Work Out Fine'. Like many writers she made most of her money from Elvis – 'Trying To Get To You' and 'I Beg Of You.'

"I can't say I knew Jackie well," she admits, "but he would come in to see Nat Tarnopol at the Brill Building – that was right down the hall from me. I used to talk to Jackie sometimes when we rode up on the elevator together. I went to see him perform. I thought he was like 'tops' – fabulous! He was unreal, and he was so sweet. He used to get down on the floor and kiss the girls. He was so friendly, he was so lovable."

Roy Gaines, her co-writer of 'A Kiss, A Thrill And Goodbye', is an accomplished guitarist and blues singer who used to run the band behind Chuck Willis. Consequently he featured in publicity photographs and people noticed a certain likeness. "Jackie Wilson and I looked a lot alike and people asked if we were brothers," he recalls. "He first saw me when I came in the back of the Apollo Theatre, where the dressing rooms were. He called down, 'Is that Roy Gaines? Tell him to come up. That's my brother.' Jackie was the sweetest man. From that day on we were always in contact with each other. We'd eat together, or bump into each other. There was an eatery next to Birdland on Fifty-Second and Broadway [most likely the Turf Club]. We had breakfast there." Gaines actually tries to give Jackie some credit for helping with the song's composition: "He probably did something, I don't remember. He probably came up with stuff. When we got to Jackie he probably did something from his rendition."

Jackie was personally generous to Gaines, but the guitarist reckons he wasn't the only one to benefit. Jackie's success had a knock on effect in the whole black community. "It was inspirational," he recalls. "In those days we could see the star and be near the star. Blacks lived in black neighbourhoods and they had to stay in black hotels, so they were right near them when they came to town. We could see them in their Cadillacs, new suits and their expensive clothes. We could meet their musicians and learn from them. Money was circulating in the community, so the black community was more successful then."

The Jacobs produced *Soul Time*, released in April 1965, also included another version of Jackie's all time favourite 'Danny Boy' as well as the classic 1929 Hoagy Carmichael evergreen, 'Star Dust', which many consider the greatest of all modern compositions. 'Star Dust' was performed by numerous artists including a non-vocal version by Artie Shaw's band in 1940 as well as Carmichael himself. Ironically, Billy Ward And The Dominoes had a hit with it in 1957; after Jackie had left the group.

September 1965 saw the release of the album *Spotlight On Jackie Wilson*. Containing the usual dozen songs, it is memorable for being comprised of standard evergreens previously made famous by others, with a full orchestra directed by Teacho Wiltshire, a seasoned big band leader. Among them are Judy Garland's 'Over The Rainbow', a Hoagy Carmichael composition of 1930, 'Georgia On My Mind', made famous by Ray Charles and 'You'll Never Walk Alone', written by Rodgers and Hammerstein and made famous, in the 1956 movie *Carousel*, by Gordon MacCrae. Also included was Tony Bennett's 1953 hit 'Rags To Riches', which Jackie had a minor hit with in 1953 while lead singer with Billy Ward And The Dominoes. Another song from Jackie's Dominoes period on the album is 'Until The Real Thing Comes Along', which Ella Fitzgerald had sung previously. 'You Don't Know Me', which country singer Eddie Arnold wrote and made a hit of in 1955, is also included, as is 'What Kind Of Fool Am I?' written by British writer and singer Anthony Newley for the Broadway production *Stop The World – I Want To Get Off*.

In 1965 LaVern Baker ended a long association with Atlantic Records and signed to Brunswick. When at last the two talents of Jackie and LaVern Baker got together in the New York studio, it was Eddie Singleton who was given the honour of producing the session. It was a great success, but also a lot of fun. There was only one single release from the duet, 'Think Twice', backed by a moving 'Please Don't Hurt Me', on which Baker excels. It was released in December 1965 and reached Number Thirty-Seven on the R&B chart and Number Ninety-Three on the Pop. However, the fun part was after the session was completed. "'Think Twice Version X' was at the end of the night," laughs Singleton. "Jackie said, 'I've got some ideas on this thing.' He was joking with me. I said 'Great, let's hear 'em.' LaVern came over to the mike and they started. I fell apart. It was ad lib, Jackie had a couple of drinks and the musicians were on their way out. Matter of fact, I was doing some sweetening [working on the recording mix]. It just was a spontaneous thing. It was my session – both the songs – I produced it and mastered it and everything else. I never kept a copy of it." The "Version X" recording, which was done with the full orchestral backing of the original, was an extremely bawdy exchange of crudities between the two singers, mentioning Tarnopol and others present in the studio. Baker actually makes a better job of it and is very good. Although supposedly only three pressings were ever made – for Tarnopol, Baker and Jackie – excellent copies have reached the public domain.

Baker recorded with Brunswick until 1969 when she did a tour of Vietnam. From there she travelled to the Philippines where she remained for nineteen years. Rumours about her move suggest she was escaping the control of the Mob. Whatever the truth, she too should have been a far bigger star than she was.

Back with Dick Jacobs arranging again – their last collaboration – 1966 saw *Soul Galore* released. Although it featured the raunchy side of Jackie and included lots of hard driving material, such as, 'Brand New Thing' and 'I've Got My Mind Made Up', the album again went nowhere chart-wise. His career needed a new direction and a new location. New York had offered all it could.

CHAPTER NINE

Soul Galore

The career and lifestyle Jackie had chosen wasn't conducive to family stability. Growing children need a father, or a father figure. His children saw him only when he passed through Detroit. Jackie lived in New York and was constantly touring. Not unnaturally, the children began to get into trouble. Some of it was petty, some serious.

An incident in 1966 pretty much set the tone. "Denise and Jackie Jnr went shopping and used some of Jack's travellers' cheques," recalls Freda, sitting alongside the adult Denise, only fifteen when the crime occurred. "Jackie Jnr was only twelve," the daughter reports. "The shops didn't give us no problem – we were throwing hundred dollar bills at them. I had this note I'd written [purporting to be Jackie's authority to cash his cheques]." It was an audacious crime for children, but it worked – for a while. The outcome is unclear, but Freda said to Denise, as she related her story, "When Jack found out he was going to kill you."

There was also the time when Denise showed interest in a young musician, Truman Thomas. Thomas was not any musician – he was Jackie's keyboard player, recruited by Jimmy Smith. "He was from Los Angeles, playing in a house band," says Smith. "I liked him 'cause he was a young kid and he played the hell out of that organ." Thomas was still young when he died of a drug overdose in 1984.

"I'm only sixteen, right," takes up Denise. "I'm still a virgin. Father caught himself being a father, which he had a hard time being 'cause he was too hip, to be that. But, me being a girl, he was looking back every now and then. He said, 'Be careful with all these band members, you might get hot and excited.' He's back in his dressing room and I just graduated from high school and Truman was young and handsome.

"I went to Alexanders [store] and bought this dress that was right down there. It cost me about three hundred dollars and it was all up here. I was only sixteen, but I was trying to excite this man. My father was putting his make-up on. He was checking me out. I was sitting on the dressing table. I went to Truman's dressing room. My father said, 'Come in here!'

"My father did not believe in whooping his kids, he'd just get angry. He could be so cold. He'd look into your eyes – he'd do that to keep you off guard. He won a million fights that way – you'd be off guard. He took his fist and went pow, right on my knee cap and said, 'That's cute, eh?' It hurt so bad, I thought he broke my knee cap. I couldn't even move. I said, 'You're hurting me.' He wouldn't even act like he was angry. He said, 'I'm sorry, baby, I forgot you were a girl. I know it hurt.' I could have killed him."

Freda interjects: "He had a saying, 'As bad as I am, as good as I am.' If he did something that hurt you, he'd try to do something doubly good to make it right." Denise again: "But he immediately checked you if he didn't like something. It didn't matter if he was right or wrong, if that's how he felt emotionally – it could happen in a matter of five minutes, it could happen in a matter of five seconds. He would be on your case."

On occasions even the Mafia were better parents than Jackie, especially the singer's companion, Johnny Roberts. "Jackie Jnr had taken some barbiturates," Freda recalls. "He had bags of 'em, tons of 'em. He'd taken them at school and he passed out. I called Jack and told him. The Mafia, they are family orientated people. I mean, they might have their women on the side, but they keep their family together. Make sure the family is okay, then you mess around. They sent two Mafia lieutenants to my son. One of them I knew; Johnny Roberts. They sent over another one. I said, 'What you want to do with him, kill him?' They said, 'We don't want to kill him, we want to chastise him.'

"They took him somewhere, he didn't know where, but whatever they did they straightened him out, got him together. He couldn't get to nobody and nobody could get in. He could use the pool. He always had nice manners, but he improved that way too! He didn't know where he was. I don't know what they did, but he never did it again. He said they didn't hit him or nothing. He couldn't say what they did. They may have shown him somebody who had messed up on something, or some pictures or something. They have access to all things. So anyway, Jack took care of that; he would take care of things."

All the Wilson children, were growing up and experiencing problems due to, at least in part, not having Jackie around to guide them. "Tony was getting involved with things, so I let him go to Syracuse, New York to stay with my mother," Freda recollects. "She lived on a small farm in the country. I let him go up there to get away from the environment in Detroit. She had him under control 'cause she's very firm. I holler a lot, but it's pitiful. I say, 'Oh, well then.' I had a lot of help with my mother and my grandmother, that's how I could come up pretty good with them.

"Tony went to school for about a month and he met these three white boys who lived out near my mom. They used to drive to school in this little old car. They said, 'We drive right past it, we can take you home, too.' So one night they were coming back and the police saw them. They saw one black dude and three white dudes, so they stopped the car – patted them down – checked the car. They saw a 'roach' [marijuana butt]; they took him to jail. All this for a piece of 'roach'. What that signified, I don't know; New York is very hard about anything. The police said, 'Where's your mama live?' Tony said, 'Michigan.'

"I just called Mr Wilson. Jackie was in New York. I didn't know what to do. They pulled him [Tony] out of there so fast it wasn't funny. I don't know if he'd called the Mafia or not. The Mafia were always telling him, 'If you love your life, take care of the family.'"

After the divorce in 1965, they still kept in contact, although Jackie held back on maintenance. With him in Chicago, Freda had no option: "I said, 'We're going up there to get some of our money.'

"We were signing in and I signed 'Mrs Freda Wilson'. The man behind the counter said, 'Oh, yeah, we've got another Wilson here, Mr Jackie Wilson.' I could have fainted, of all of the motels and hotels; I just knew he'd be downtown some place. Anyway there he was staying at the same one!

"I sent the children over there to see him – to check him out – to see if he's going to do anything. Anyway he took all of Jackie Jnr's clothes off and put his sweat shirt on him, and sent him back and tells me he is coming over. I said, 'Oh, my goodness, what should I do?' There's a question mark there, I'm just sitting up there, I didn't know what to do." Freda need not have worried. "He had this big shopping bag full of BBQ ribs, a big thing of potato salad and all this stuff. He said, 'Hey, baby, we're going to have a party.' That was the last time he ever used a rib to kill me," she jokes.

Jackie also had a saying, when he was trying to control a family situation, according to Freda. "He'd say, 'I'm the bull and you're the ram.' I would say, 'There ain't nothing you can tell me.' See now, with Jack I know I could not control that Gemini. I used to wanna try, because if he didn't want to listen to what I wanted to say, he didn't even hear me. He might turn the radio or record player up to drown me out."

Whenever Jackie arrived in town the children knew what their father expected of them. Denise explains: "When he came home we knew what records to play – Jackie Wilson! I didn't go for that. We kept looking out the window for that limousine. 'Okay, here he comes, hide your records. And don't let us have no James Brown."

Jackie had varying expectations from Freda and his mother. "When Jackie was coming home, that house better be spotless," says Freda. "I mean, there wouldn't want to be a fingerprint on it."

"He wanted her house to be spotless, but at Mama's he wanted to smell food," says Denise. "He didn't bother her [his mother]. Bottom line; two different people, two different loves, two different purposes. He wanted both of them to be fulfilled. His children, we'd better be standing in line, at attention, looking just so cute. 'Hi, Daddy, we've been listening to your records.' You know what I think? It was a form of insecurity. He knew he had us on his side, but he had all these people that loved him, all these women. His records were Number One, but if we didn't act like we liked his music…He knew we were growing kids – especially myself and I'm going to school and have all these friends. My father was a very good friend of mine apart from being my father. I loved him a lot. I truly believe he made music he thought my friends might like – that we could dance to. He didn't want me to feel like an outcast. Even if he'd never done anything you could dance to, he was still 'the man'. It was nice going to basement parties and hearing 'The whispers getting louder...' [from his hit 'Whispers']. I was in the tenth grade [1967]."

"Even my younger sister, Jacqui, and Joyce, they were kind of tight," says Freda. "Jack came home one time – we're divorced now. He gave Joyce fifty dollars and Jacqui fifty dollars, because she lived with me and helped me take care of the kids – 'cause I was busy a lot. They were supposed to go to a dance at the Greystone Ballroom. They went to the dance.

"Now, Joyce liked to hang out. Jacqui said she kept telling her, 'We should go home.' They left the dance and when it was over they went to an all-night movie – stayed there. Jackie was sitting there [at home] drinking and drinking, but he was not high. He said, 'What time do they usually get home?' He looked at me like I'm supposed to know what time...they had never did that before. They had never had fifty dollars before to spend either! They were supposed to have got in a cab.

"Finally he says, 'Get in that car, we're going to find them.' I said, 'Well, where we going to look?' He said, 'We'll find 'em.' We was driving up and down Woodward. Finally we came back past this all-night movie. They played all these old cowboy movies, and there'd be all these winos hanging there. Here they come, strolling out. He backed the car, jumped out of that car. 'Get in there!' They were scared then. At first Joyce was going to try and play it off. She's a Gemini too.

"He takes them back home, brings 'em upstairs, see. Sits 'em down, he says 'Who's the initiator?' Jacqui said, 'I told her, I said we'd better come home.' Joyce said, 'So?' He said, 'What'd you say?' 'So?' He backhanded her. She didn't get smart no more. He said, 'You got any money left?' She said, 'Yeah.' He said, 'All right, keep that money. I'm going to let you go out tomorrow, I want to see what time you're coming home.' They was home at nine o'clock.

"He always liked to protect the girls – that was his thing. Nobody better do nothing to his mama, me or any of those young ladies." Jackie, no doubt, hoped to protect them from predatory males – those like himself!

Due to his life-long habit of not taking care of detail, Jackie fell constantly behind in the reasonable, court ordered, fifty dollars per week child support payments, and after chasing him to other states, Freda was forced to take legal action and had a warrant for his arrest issued. "At first I didn't want to do it, but my lawyer kept saying, if we don't get him now we might never get him 'cause he ain't going to have nothing – or he might die," Freda explains apologetically. "The lawyer said, 'You'd better file a warrant.' So I did. So Jack called me. 'If you'll hold your warrant so I can come there, I will give you some of your money. Just hold it and let me make the gig.'" Jackie had an engagement in his home town, but risked arrest if he didn't reach some agreement. "So I did and my lawyer said, 'I'm not your lawyer any more.' Jack's request made sense to me."

Joyce Lee suggests that, initially, he did send regular payments to Freda, but that "Freda blew it all. Freda went out and ran all the time and never took care of the kids. My ma [Eliza Mae] spoon-fed those children. She always took care of the children." According to Joyce, Jackie chose to send the money to his mother instead, so that the children obtained benefit.

"The fact was," says girlfriend Lynn Ciccone, "he was not the fatherly kind, but he did not deliberately let people starve to death. That was not Jackie's nature."

Denise had a great love and respect for her father, but nevertheless she experienced her fair share of his "unfatherly" behaviour. "I remember humiliations," she grins. "The one I remember most; that great shark skin silk suit – oh, Mr Excitement, you're so tough. My father had this perfectly formed booty [backside] that the girls want. He turned around and showed the girls his booty and he didn't wear underwear; all his ass is hanging out. It was in Atlantic City and his pants split wide open.

"That's where Michael Jackson, Prince and Elvis Presley got the stage moves from. My father loved to sweat, 'cause when he sweat his hair would fall. The girls would go, 'Oh, take my panties off.' His hair was long; he thought he was hip."

While his family fought for money and attention, Jackie – and especially those around him – was still looking out for his career. Berry Gordy's Motown Records in Detroit was having phenomenal success around the world whereas, by comparison, Jackie's New York releases with their big band backing and loads of strings were sounding downright dated. It was Nat Tarnopol who realised that the new soul sound coming out of Chicago was the way for Jackie to go.

At the time Carl Davis was managing Gene Chandler, Major Lance, Walter Jackson and other acts. Davis remembers his first meeting with Nat Tarnopol, who at the time was only vice president, but in effect ran Brunswick on behalf of Decca: "I met Nat Tarnopol at a DJ convention [August 1966] in New York, at a hotel." Both men got along well and Tarnopol appointed him A&R director for Brunswick. "He wanted me to do a production deal on Jackie Wilson; I guess his career had gone down a bit," says Davis. "I told him, 'Okay, but first I'd have to meet Jackie.' I'm the type of guy that, most of the acts I had, I had to have a feeling for. When I met Jackie, we just clicked. It got to the point if I wasn't involved, he wouldn't show up. We worked on some tunes and we finally did a couple of sides and then I had to take it back to New York and sit in meeting with all these so-called heads of Decca, which at that time [still] owned Brunswick."

Record producer Davis was born on Chicago's South Side in 1934. He formerly worked with Vee Jay Records where he produced the massive Gene Chandler hit 'Duke Of Earl', which reached Number One in 1962. With Curtis Mayfield doing the songwriting, they were a winning team, creating hit upon hit. From June 1962, Davis worked as A&R manager for Columbia, which owned OKeh Records, which Mayfield wrote for. The music that came out of this team became known as "Chicago Soul" and Major Lance was their biggest hit maker.

In 1965 Davis was forced out of OKeh Records, however he retained a publishing company jointly with Irv Nahan, a long time promoter and shareholder of Queens Booking Agency. It was through Nahan, in a roundabout way, that Davis became involved with Brunswick; with Jackie; and with the Mob.

Davis explained the complex way he came to be involved with Jackie's career through Tommy Vastola. "Irv and I had a booking agency up in New York called Queens Booking Agency. I had ten per cent, some other people owned ten per cent and Irv owned fifty per cent. Then all of a sudden word got out on the street there was a 'hit' out on Irv Nahan, but nobody could find out about it.

"I didn't know Tommy Vastola at that time, but there was a friend of mine, Larry Maxwell, who knew him. Maxwell called Tommy and arranged for him to meet me. We had to go to the Black Bear, or Bull, or something restaurant on Eighth Avenue in New York City and we sit in their damn restaurant. I see this big black limo pull up, and two guys come in and tell us to get in the car and we drove to Brooklyn somewhere. I was scared shitless.

"We explained what it was all about. Vastola said, 'I tell you what, there is a hit out on Nahan. I don't know what it's about.' So he said what we need to do is get Irv out of town until he can find out.

"I had an apartment in Chicago, down at Marina Towers, so we flew him into Chicago and had him hidden there. I called singers Gene Chandler and Otis Leavil. I said, 'Pick Irv up at the airport.' Otis had a key to my apartment: 'Take him up there and you stay with him.' So we did.

"I was fooling around with singer Mary Wells at that time. I had Irv hidden out at Mary's apartment. Well, about two days later, we got a call from Tommy. We went to some tavern in Brooklyn...pitch dark. They take us through this back door. They had this guy sitting at the table. There are four guys – in each corner, but you couldn't see them...you knew they were there. There was this one table in the middle with a little lamp on it and an old guy sitting there. They said, 'Well here's the deal.'

"Irv Nahan has a group called The Drifters and [his partner at Shaw Booking] Milt Shaw thought Irv was going to take the group out of the booking agency and put them in Queens, which we owned. So Milt Shaw paid ten thousand dollars for a hit on Irv Nahan. We assured this guy at the table it wasn't the case; that we weren't going change agencies.

"After we have got that cleared up, 'Who is going to give us ten thousand dollars?' We were all looking at one another. Tommy said, 'Carl, don't you manage Gene Chandler? This is what I'd like you to do. I want you to sign Gene Chandler up to Brunswick Records. We'll give you fifty thousand dollars to sign Gene Chandler up. You get twenty per cent which means ten thousand dollars, so we keep the ten thousand, and Gene Chandler gets forty thousand dollars for signing with Brunswick to put in his pocket. I said, 'Okay.' I figured somewhere along the line Irv would pay me back.

"At that time Tommy had some part of Nat Tarnopol, or Brunswick, or whatever it was. This is 1966. That was the reason I went to Brunswick."

Davis was treated well by Vastola and remains a loyal friend to this day. "If I went to Las Vegas, someone would meet me at the airport. I had about ten thousand dollars' credit line. I'd get a suite at the Tropicana when I stayed in Vegas; my hotel was free. Tommy used to do that. He was all right with me."

Davis had been introduced to the label but now began his association with Tarnopol: "I went to Brunswick because of Nat Tarnopol, no question about it," he insists. "I liked something about him. At Decca they didn't like him at all because he used to sit there and pick the zits on his face. They couldn't stand him. But he was nice to me and the fact was that after he'd gotten so successful with Jackie he offered me the job of heading up the A&R department and I accepted it. He said, 'I want you to work for me, and I'm going to sweeten the pie and I'm going to give you a share of the company.' So he gave me ten per cent of his fifty per cent. I really liked Nat and I felt he was the kind of person I'd like to do business with."

On top of the ten per cent of the fifty per cent of Brunswick which Tarnopol owned, Davis was later appointed vice president. When Tarnopol acquired hundred per cent control of the company, Davis's share doubled to ten per cent of that. But there was one drawback: "I did eight albums with Jackie. In the beginning I was paid an incentive, then I became a stockholder and got nothing!

"I brought in Gene Chandler, The Artistics, Barbara Acklin and everybody. Every record was go and go, to the point where Columbia had offered, back in those days, twelve million dollars for the company. When [in 1968] he got the other fifty per cent of Brunswick he changed it over to BRC [Brunswick Record Corporation] and BRC Music. Then I had a label called Dacar, which I managed with Brunswick."

Up until the period Davis joined with Brunswick in 1966, Jackie's hit making career was in decline, despite recording some fabulous albums such as *Body And Soul* in 1962 and *Jackie Wilson Sings The World's Greatest Melodies* in 1964. Fine as they were, they were not likely to sell large numbers, and they didn't. And, if Jackie was struggling, so was the Brunswick label.

"When I got on the label he had stopped recording," remembers Davis. "He didn't want to record no more for Dick Jacobs." The early part of this statement is not correct because Jackie recorded with Brunswick for eighteen years, 1957 to 1975, even after his relationship with Tarnopol had turned into deep hatred. However he had not stopped recording; it was just that they were no longer hits.

Davis insisted that he remain in his home city of Chicago, and Tarnopol agreed. He established an office and recording studio on South Michigan Avenue near the famed Chess Records, home of urban blues. "I built that studio, with [sound engineer] Bruce Woodene, from the ground up," he recalls. "We tried all different kinds of sounds. We did reverb with slap-back echo. We'd try to find things within a song and make everyone do it. I used to do the music around the singer. [Berry] Gordy did the opposite [at Motown]."

Woodene is considered to be a recording studio technical genius. He was so highly sought after that he was retained on a percentage basis, working with Quincy Jones on Michael Jackson's *Thriller* album. *Thriller* sold an all time record forty million copies, said to earn Woodene around two million dollars. These days he is employed on all of Jackson's sessions.

Even as late as 1966, Jackie pretty much *was* Brunswick, but with Carl Davis coming on board, the stable would soon include some fine soul singers. Eventually it would be home to The Chi-Lites, The Artistics, The Young-Holt Unlimited, Tyrone Davis, Major Lance, Gene Chandler, Billy Butler, Hamilton Bohanan, Erma Franklin and Barbara Acklin. For a period LaVern Baker and even Little Richard recorded on it.

With Davis's arrival, even the backing artists progressed. The talented studio musicians, despite working for Motown on million seller records, were still poorly paid and Davis regularly called upon them to come over from Detroit to work on Jackie's sessions. They were more than willing to engage in this "moonlighting" arrangement.

"When I was cutting Jackie I had the whole rhythm section from Motown, including the back-up singers," admits Davis. "This was only on the weekend. [Bassist extraordinaire, James] Jamerson was there, Benny Benjamin started coming in. He used to be the drummer, but he'd get drunk all the time. [Arranger] Sonny Sanders used to send them from Detroit. I used to pay them in cash and more than union scale. Motown's Andantes did background vocals. They must have come to Chicago twelve to fifteen times."

The results were incredible, on every level, and all bore Davis's touch somewhere. Even his assistants were getting in on the act. A young Barbara Acklin, secretary in the newly established Brunswick office in Chicago, was to become a successful songwriter, penning Jackie's hit 'Whispers': "I started songwriting when I was in high school," she says. "[Roquel] "Billy" Davis was A&R manager at Chess. I lived across from Chess at the time, in a hotel. I'd run across the street every day with different songs and Billy Davis would grade my homework. He showed me how to write the tune. He only had to show me two to three times.

"'Whispers' wasn't written for Jackie, it was written for The Artistics. Jackie was in Carl's office. Carl kept pushing the tape back and Jackie said, 'What was that?' Carl said, 'You don't want to hear this, it's not for you.' Jackie said, 'Let me hear that one,' and he did. He liked it right away. 'I want that one.'

"Well, he did it and the rest is history. Dave Scott, who co-wrote it, was with a group The South Shore Commission. Scott came over one day and gave me two or three lines and I started working on it. I finished it fast, but didn't have enough verses when it came to the session and I had to finish it in a telephone booth. It got Jackie's career kick started again."

Davis, Jackie and the musicians did the rest, resulting in a hauntingly beautiful love song. Numerous times throughout the song Jackie calls "Peaches", as though she is who the song is being addressed to. "Peaches" was in fact the pet name Acklin's father used for her. "It wasn't in the lyric, Jackie just put it in there," she says. Acklin was there when the session was cut and claims it took only three or four takes. The record buying public liked it, and it reached Number Eleven on the Pop charts. When 'Whispers' was released in September 1966 it steered Jackie's career rapidly back on course. It proved he was far from a spent force.

Acklin fondly remembers Jackie: "He was great. I loved to watch him work. Jackie brought me up in the business. How to look after the money; not borrow and to do my thing; to stay away from the office. He literally raised me. He knew all about the business." She was right about that, but it didn't stop Jackie stumbling into the industry's pitfalls along the way.

Davis, it is fair to say, was enamoured with Jackie and their working relationship developed into a life long friendship. "Jackie is what you'd call a professional, no matter what was required," he says. "You couldn't be around Jackie without being motivated. Whenever he was around me, he wouldn't drink or smoke. I don't know what others say about Jackie, but he was a gentleman. He'd come over to my house and bring the baby and walk around the house like he knew everyone forty years. Everybody loved Jackie. He was a great entertainer. He's the greatest artist who ever lived.

Eddie Singleton, who produced Jackie's last New York album, *Soul Galore*, before handing the reins to Davis considers that half the battle was getting Tarnopol onside. "When Carl came in he was able to get a better relationship with Nat than I," he admits. "But I was the guy who fought all the battles to get Nat to consider being more equitable with the relative people." Tarnopol was gaining quite a reputation as being tight-fisted and seemed reluctant to share the success equitably.

From a hit making point of view, Jackie had needed a change of material and in Carl Davis he found a trusted partner. Without Davis there, he wouldn't even attend sessions. "He had so much confidence in me, that the musical side wasn't his concern. He didn't even feel he had to be there. Either I had Willie Henderson or Sonny Sanders do a song. We would just lay down a demo thing, we'd send it to him and let him get a key. The writer would do the demo." From there Jackie would work out his interpretation and send a tape back to Davis. "He would call me up and say, 'Did I like the song?' He would get this kid who used to travel with him, on the guitar [Billy Johnson, formerly of The Moonglows]. He would work it out on the guitar and find a key. Now the difference was, I would only record two to three tracks at a time."

Pat Lewis, who is also a Detroit native, had the honour of being one of the back-up singers "borrowed" from Motown during some of Jackie's major Chicago sessions. "We did, along with The Andantes, an album with Jackie. We were, like, freelancing. I was seventeen or eighteen. It was really wonderful working with Jackie. It was done at one time, which is called 'from the floor' – orchestra, back-up singers and lead." Lewis was also involved as back-up the next year (1967) when Jackie recorded his great hit 'Higher And Higher'.

Eugene Record, who was born in 1940, did not form the highly successful and innovative Chi-Lites group, but left his job as taxi driver to become their lead singer in the late 1960s. Record was introduced to Carl Davis through another Brunswick artist, Otis Leavil. Davis immediately recognised the group's talent and signed them to the expanding label. Record's incredible falsetto assisted the group with five Top Forty hits from 1971 to 1973; all on Brunswick. Their biggest hit was a beautiful Record composed ballad, 'Oh Girl', which achieved Number One, a feat Jackie never attained. "I was with Brunswick seven years. Wonderful years," recalls Record.

Along with Davis, Record either produced or co-produced three of Jackie's albums: *Do Your Thing* (1969), *It's All A Part Of Love* and *You Got Me Walking* (1970). The Chi-Lites also did a considerable amount of back-up at the sessions. "Jackie recorded two of my tunes: 'You Got Me Walking' and 'Let This Be A Letter (To My Baby)'," says Record – modestly forgetting he also wrote or co-wrote 'To Change My Love', 'Growing Tall' and 'Love Uprising'.

Record, who was physically assaulted by Johnny Roberts over a dispute regarding money he believed Tarnopol owed The Chi-Lites, won't hear of a word against the man: "I loved Nat Tarnopol, we had no problems. He was always warm to me, he always treated me well. Whenever there was a financial thing, he always came through for me. I have no complaints. Whatever he did he did on his own; I don't know what that was. I loved the man. I don't know what he did to Jackie." He was less forthcoming on another matter: "Johnny Roberts is a very unusual man. Wherever his loyalties were, you'll never know."

In the beginning Davis would record the orchestra in Chicago, then fly to New York with the tapes so that they could overdub Jackie. After some problems in New York, Jackie subsequently did all the recording work in Chicago, except for one album done in Detroit.

Davis: "He had a habit – sometimes he would sing it wrong. 'Higher And Higher' – when I gave him the track he would sing it like a ballad. 'You can't sing it like that Jackie.' He would have me sing it. I had the worst voice in the world, but I would know how it should be sung. Then he would take it – one take. We had it to the point that if I pointed up with my finger he knew he was supposed to hit that 'bird note'. I would point and he'd hit the 'bird note' and fly. Not many could go up and down like Jackie. Jackie could go up and down the scale so easily. Jackie could do it great – he could hold it way up here.

"I used to insist two things," Davis continues. "'Don't bring no piece of paper in the studio,' and, 'If you don't know the lyrics then cancel the session.' Jackie was always ready. You'd only have to work on the tempo. The only thing about Jackie is that if a song was too easy, if the song didn't have a challenge, then he wouldn't sing it that well. You had to make sure that lyrically and melody-wise the song challenged him and he'd want to do something special with it. He used to call me and say, 'You wait until you hear what I did with this!' He'd wait for my reaction.

"I'd give him two weeks to learn the lyrics. The best way to learn the lyrics is to write them down while listening to a tape recording. He may have come in with a piece of paper which showed where he wanted to do the kind of singing. It's like telling a story, so you're listening to a guy telling a story and you're quite excited waiting for the end. Then you want to hear the beginning again. That's the way Curtis Mayfield would write a song.

"You know that if somebody understands a story, they sing it better. Jackie was like that, he could sing anything. He could do opera and put some feeling about it. Before I ever met him I used to go to the Regal

Theatre [Chicago] and see him perform. I used to be amazed when he was on stage performing a song to see him skip half way across and half way back. I loved him.

"I never thought I'd get the chance to produce this young man that I was so crazy about. You know, he was great." Apart from the sheer joy of Jackie's performances, he vocalised what most people feel deep inside. Jackie's magic was his ability to touch a person's heart strings.

Shortly after the success of 'Whispers', Jackie had another million seller on his hands with 'Higher And Higher', released in February 1967. It reached Number Six on the Pop charts and was in the Top Hundred for nine weeks. It is also the most often played Jackie record today. There was also a *Higher And Higher* album, again arranged by Sonny Sanders and produced by Carl Davis. Gerald Sims directed it. Once again, says Davis, the Motown musicians, "the Funk Bros, did the backing. There was James Jamerson on electric bass, Eddie Willis and Robert White on guitars, Johnny Griffith on piano and Benny Benjamin on drums."

The origins of 'Higher And Higher' are the cause of some dispute. "There was a young guy that used to write for Chess Records down the street and he had written 'Higher And Higher'," recalls Davis. "One of my writers was Gary Jackson. They all used to write for Chess. Then Billy Davis and everyone jumped in when the record was a hit and claimed writer's royalties. The 'Higher And Higher' tune was huge."

The Billy Davis Carl Davis is referring to is Roquel Davis who had co-written Jackie's early hits with Berry Gordy. At the time he was A&R manager at Chess Records, down the road from Brunswick.

Roquel recalls the 'Higher And Higher' fiasco in rather more detail: "'Higher and Higher' was written by Carl Smith, Reynard Miner and myself, originally. Gary Jackson got on the piece because Reynard and Carl were writers, two of my team at Chess. It was to be recorded by The Dells [who sang 'Oh What A Night'] and Gary came along and he wanted to become a writer. Reynard and Carl liked Gary and were going to make him a partner. I was a publisher, partners with the Chess boys, Chevis Publishing Co., which I own today. So we cut Gary in.

"Gary stole the song and took it to Carl Davis. Carl Smith may have been involved as well. They changed some of the lyrics. The hook was the same, so was the melody. Jackie recorded it…it came out. Somebody said, 'Your Dells song is out.' So I called Carl. 'I've got some bad news for you. This is my song, I recorded it with The Dells.' I took The Dells recording to Carl Davis. 'Well you can tell some hanky-panky went down somewhere,' Carl remarked.

"We got a meeting with Gary Jackson and Carl Smith in Carl Davis's office, and so the truth comes out. So Carl says, 'What do we do about it?' I replied, 'The song was stolen, you produced it, but because of my relationship with Jackie, I'll share it with you fifty/fifty.' Carl said, 'I'll talk it over with Nat.'

"Nat came into the picture. We hug and embrace, the whole thing. Nat says, 'I can't give you half of my song.' The past came back to me. So I say, 'Screw you, I withdraw my offer.' Nat had this attitude. I contacted my attorney. We ended up striking a deal where I retained sixty per cent of the mechanicals, sixty-five per cent of sync and licences, and eighty per cent of everything else. So I ended up with eighty per cent of the song. In return, for the writer's credit, I'm going to leave my name off. Miner was a blind kid. I never spoke to Jackie about it. The original copyright has my name on it."

Fortunately for most concerned, 'Higher And Higher' became a huge seller and has been used on the soundtrack of numerous movies. Roquel Davis's name appeared on the recording when first released, but on later releases he is overlooked.

The interesting interview Jackie had with New York DJ, Norman Nite, revealed how he first heard the song and insisted on recording it. He said: "They threw it in the garbage can, the song itself. The guy that brought it in, brought it in on a tape with a group singing with a little tiny tinkling guitar and nobody could hear it but me. I actually learned the way, I felt it was a church type thing."

Despite the big hit, Roquel "Billy" Davis is mildly critical of the recording career direction that the Chicago period took Jackie. "You listen to Jackie's material after Berry and I left; at least then there was a direction it was being headed and certainly I was 'Pop' conscious. After then the material began to sway all over the place. It wasn't a clear-cut direction for Jackie. He was such a great singer and could sing anything, which I think was particularly the cause of it and unfortunately not all of it had that mass appeal – popular appeal.

"Jackie, of course, burned it at both ends; thought it was going to last forever. Everything he did was to extreme. He didn't look so great in his later years. I was hoping and praying when 'Higher And Higher' became a big hit that was going to do it for him. Then nothing happened after that. But the one thing his life story can't take away from him is his talent."

Horn player, Mike Terry, worked at Motown and was one of the musicians in the Chicago sessions. He confirms how Jackie's role in the recording took place. "The voice was over-dubbed," he remembers. "We'd do the horns and rhythm and add the strings later. Or just the rhythm and then add the horns and strings. Sonny Sanders did most of the arranging. He invited me to go to Chicago and do that with Jackie."

Music arranger, Sonny Sanders, was involved with most of the session work during Jackie's Chicago period. Sanders, also from Detroit, had worked with the famous labels there. Before becoming an arranger, he was a singer, one of the first to record on the new Motown label with The Satintones. It was Sanders who engaged Motown's rhythm section for Jackie's sessions.

"The *Whispers* album, that was many moons," he reminisces. "It was a great session. Jackie was one of the most beautiful people I knew. He was one of the most kind, gentlemanly people you'd ever know. 'Hey Booby' – I can almost hear him now.

"Of course you didn't have to work that hard with Jackie so far as the vocals were concerned, he was a master, man. If there was anything wrong, he was one of the first to spot it and do it over again. I was extremely gratified in being part of that; in bringing him back. I had known Jackie in Detroit, but I had never worked with him. I knew his family and sister, we lived not far away. When the opportunity came to work with him at Brunswick, I was very happy about that. Fortunately we had a couple of strings of hits."

But another lull came when Jackie didn't maintain his chart popularity after 1968. Tarnopol is possibly at the root of it all. "The reasons that hits didn't continue after that were many," Sanders suggests. "I didn't get to know Tarnopol all that well. I feel it could have been the way you dealt with Nat. From what I understand Eugene [Record] had an unusual relationship with him, better than most people in the company. Barbara's [Acklin] relationship was probably pretty good.

"Anytime an artist signs over power of attorney to a record company executive, it has got to be a conflict of interest, as a matter of fact. Any problems that Jackie had, most were probably the result of what happened between him and Nat and a few other people.

"When I was in Detroit I visited Jackie's house a few times. Our relationship was basically business. We got together when we had records to do. When he was in town, in most cases I was writing music. I generally only saw him in the studio."

Horn player, Gene Barge, who did session work on many of the soul recordings done in Chicago and occasionally played for Jackie while touring, is also critical of Jackie's relationship with Nat. "When we were on the show with him Nat would be sitting in the dressing room with him all the time," explains Barge. "If you wanted to talk to Jackie you had to talk to Nat first. He was a rogue. For a while he was good for Jackie; then along down the road something went wrong. Jackie didn't hang out with the musicians. He was surrounded by his people and Nat Tarnopol. He was mostly protected. Jackie was a down-to-earth guy. He was considered a superstar."

Jackie's close friend, Midnighters guitarist Billy Davis, is also mostly critical of the songs chosen for Jackie during the "Chicago period". "For some reason they wouldn't let him record what he wanted to. Carl Davis didn't get it and they didn't let anybody else give it to him. I don't know if it was Carl or what. We took tapes over there. We [Alonzo Tucker and Davis] came up with melody patterns, guitar rhythm patterns. Jackie was crazy about them and they just couldn't hear it. He loved one song so much, he'd sing it all night long.

"Even the stuff that I did, it was totally up to date, we came up with a new sound and everything. Alonzo could write for Jackie better than anyone, but they wouldn't record them. They couldn't produce his stuff. Those guys in Chicago couldn't understand. The 'Chicago sound' didn't fit Jackie. The 'Chicago sound' never mastered Jackie's sound. It's totally different. They tried to mould Jackie into it. It just didn't fit.

"We went through hell to get them to do 'Higher And Higher.' They would come through once in a while with something; every once in a while that he could get it across. But it still didn't fit like the Berry Gordy [composed] stuff. Even though 'Whispers' was great, it was not the typical Jackie Wilson sound. Carl Davis had a certain sound he was dealing with, and most of it just didn't fit Jackie."

Not many would actually agree with Davis's comments, however it is true that Jackie only had limited chart success during the nine year long Chicago period. Indeed, the Top Forty successes were limited to four songs spanning less than a two year period: 'Whispers (Getting Louder)' Number Eleven, '(Your Love Keeps Lifting Me) Higher And Higher' Number Six, 'Since You Showed Me How To Be Happy' Number Thirty-Two, and 'I Get The Sweetest Feeling' Number Thirty-Four. This last song, however, did much better in the United Kingdom, reaching Number Six.

Another who is critical of much of the music that Jackie recorded in Chicago is Jackie's friend Simon Rutberg. Rutberg is also rather critical of the music that Motown produced, so he is in the minority. "The stuff that Jackie did with Eugene Record is boring," he opines. "It has a group sound – Chi-Lites music. 'The Fountain' [a full-on rock 'n' roll single] to me sounds like 'Ball Of Confusion' by The Temptations. It's not Jackie Wilson. His music had guts – sometimes raunchy – he never really played it safe.

"*You've Got Me Walking* album, you'll see there's nothing for him to do vocally. There's too much group in there, singing along with him. Jackie is almost talking words. Too much lyric, too much of a story. There's no melody. He may as well read the damn thing.

"*Higher And Higher* Jackie told me did fifty thousand copies. Most Jackie albums were never released overseas. Now that's out the front door; I don't know what went out the back. Out the back they go for $1.25 a piece." Fifty thousand is not a large number and, if correct, would explain why it was necessary for Jackie to constantly be on tour.

It was while touring in 1967 that he met a young man whom he decided was likely husband material for his sixteen-year-old daughter, Denise. The lucky fellow was Reginald "Reggie" Abrams, an eighteen-year-old singer who met Jackie in Birmingham, Alabama having worked an introduction via some of the other acts. "I knew Gorgeous George, the MC, very well," he says, "but I wanted to meet Jack. I got on their bus with Gorgeous George to the concert. He introduced me to August Sims. I met Jack, showed him my Q-card and everything; 'This is me, my go-go girls and my band.' Jack said, 'Talk to me after the show.' I asked him if I could put on a live audition. He asked if I could catch the bus and audition at the next show. But they wouldn't let me on the bus. So I went back to Jack and he took me in the limo to his bus, and told them I was his people and to let me on the bus. If they won't let me on the bus, then he won't perform – and he's the star of the show! I've been with him ever since. I would open for Jackie."

Abrams was extremely young, slim and good looking. Indeed he looked quite a lot like Jackie and his singing was also similar. While to work with Jackie was the extent of his ambition, Jackie apparently had another plan in mind that would bring them closer.

"The way he introduced me to Denise in Chicago, he said, 'Denise, this is your husband. Reggie, this is your wife Denise. We stared at each other and said, 'Wow, what's he talking about?'

"After the tour, I was going to go back down south, but he asked me, 'Why don't you spend Christmas at my home?' He gave me the plane fare. He told me to stay in New York, for a day or two and fly on and he should be there. I got to Detroit and caught a taxi and got to the house. I told the cabby to wait and went to the side door. I was really skinny and had long hair, I had on make-up. Tony called out to his mother, 'There's a faggot at the door.' Grandma came to the door and said, 'That's no faggot, that's the boy from down south.'"

"Jackie brought Reginald up here to live with us," says Freda. "Reginald thought he was going to be singing with Jack, but Jack left him home and told me to take care of him and raise him, and treat him like the rest of the kids. He brought him up here for Denise, but she was too swift for him. He said she was too fast."

Things didn't go quite according to Jackie's script. Sandra interested him much more, and was quieter than Denise.

"Me and Sandy got together," Abrams explains. "We was running around the house and I thought I was going to get hit because Jack had said, 'Don't mess with my baby daughter. You and Denise can do anything you want, but leave my baby daughter alone!' I tried though. I'm there and two young ladies there."

Sandra was fourteen or fifteen when she became pregnant. The family knew Jackie would be very angry. "I had Freda walking around saying, 'Jack's going to do this to you,'" Abrams relates. "Everybody's worried about Jack...I was worried about Jack! I said, 'How am I going to break this?' So when he called on the phone from New York, I said, 'Might as well get it over with.' I said, 'Jack, I'm going to say it real fast. Sandy is pregnant, and that's the bad news. The good news is I'm going to marry her.' He said, 'Okay.' I gave the phone back to Freda and said, 'You all was worried about Jack, I was worried about Jack, but he ain't going to do nothing.' But Sandy told me later, he ran his fist through the wall when he heard it."

Jackie and Freda's second daughter, Sandra was born in 1953 and was better known as Sandy. Winning such a handsome husband was quite a coup at the time for she suffered from severe visual impairment, having to wear full strength glasses. More often than not, though, she would avoid wearing them due to the cruel jibes of her Catholic school classmates, but that didn't stop her being compared unfavourably with Denise.

Freda regrets it now. "I used to holler, 'Why can't you be like Denise.' I don't know what I was doing," she rues. "The nuns at school gave her an 'A' for nothing. An 'A' for being polite, an 'A' for anything. She'd come home with stars on her forehead." The nuns realised praise worked better than ridicule. "She was slow in reading, because she would not wear her eyeglasses; she had very bad eyes. She was wearing glasses when she was two. She hated them because the kids would tease her; 'four eyes', 'square eyes'. She'd get upset and hide them. I'd say, 'You got the glasses?' She'd say, 'Yes, ma'am.' She was told she had to wear the glasses from the time she got up till the time she went to bed. When she got big she just threw the glasses around, 'cause they were not popular."

But the glasses didn't prevent her marriage to Abrams. They stayed on at LaSalle, Freda's house, and in November 1969 the first of their three children was born. He was named Reginald Jnr and would grow up to become a singer with a similar wicked sense of humour to Jackie's.

Jackie was thirty-five when he had become a grandfather. "When Reggie was born Jack and myself used to play with him like a volley ball," the proud father recalls. "We'd throw him back and forward. Jack says 'Think!' and throws the baby. He was crazy about Reggie. During Christmas he got Reggie Jnr a fur full length coat, a fur hat to match, a diamond ring and a diamond necklace. Gold and diamonds!"

Jackie performed with the young child on stage, as he'd done with Denise. "They took him everywhere they went," says Abrams, "but Reggie wouldn't perform for Jack. I had to be with him. He tried to get Reggie to dance with him, to follow him, but the spotlight hits Reggie and he just stands still. Reggie wouldn't perform with nobody but me.

"When Jack had everyone come up on stage at Phelp's Lounge, he wanted to introduce his family and stuff. Grandma gets up on stage when he starts singing 'Doggin' Around'. Grandma would say, 'You all better stop doggin' my Jack around.' Joyce gets up with him on stage and did 'Danny Boy'. They tore the house down." Freda was left minding the baby: "I took Reggie Jnr up there," she says. "He was on stage with his diaper hanging half on."

For a time Reggie Abrams Snr sometimes travelled with Jackie and would open the show for him. The pair were close and looked alike which led Freda to certain doubts. Despite knowing that Jackie had never been down south as early as 1949, she maintains, "I still think Reggie Abrams could be one of Jackie's children." Abrams even passed for Jackie with others. "We drove through Hollywood, me in the back, Pop driving, and the police pulled us over," he recalls. "They said, 'Who have you got in the back?' Watley said, 'Jackie Wilson.' The cop said, 'I thought I knew that guy. No ticket!'"

Their friendship moved a stage closer when Jackie was asked to Abrams' show in Detroit in the late sixties. "Jack told me to go on as Reggie Wilson, his son," he recalls with pride. "Jack told me he wanted me to change my name from Little Reggie to Reggie Wilson – stage name. It went on air, they said, 'Reggie Wilson, with his father Jackie Wilson.' He would come by and help out when he was in town. I was nervous, and every time I said, 'Please don't let me crack.' There's no telling what he was going to do if I cracked. But I pulled it off and got a standing ovation. The women thought they were grabbin' Jackie Wilson's son."

Jackie's first daughter – and his first choice for Abrams – Denise was much different from her more introverted sister. She was intelligent and hard headed, like her father, and was perhaps a little to fond of him as a family friend reveals: "Denise is an interesting situation. She had a real father fixation and her perception of her dad was not totally normal. It was out of kilter. She loved her daddy, there's no doubt about it – but she was kind of messed up." Because she adored him it was a major disappointment to Denise when, in July 1967, Jackie couldn't find a break in his gruelling schedule to attend her debutante's ball. In June 1968, however, he proudly attended her graduation ceremony at St Gregory's Catholic High School. She was awarded second of her class.

On 3 and 4 January, 1968, there was another high point in Jackie's long career. Nat Tarnopol arranged for him to travel to Los Angeles and record *The Manufacturers Of Soul* album with the world famous Count Basie Orchestra. Unfortunately Jackie made the mistake of announcing on a coast-to-coast TV show, "I'm in Hollywood to record an album with Count Basie." Producer Teddy Reig remembers the effect: "Needless to say, their [Jackie and Basie] friends and fans via the grapevine flocked to the studio en masse. They were all there – finger poppers, head shakers, coffee and soda drinkers, and other kinds of drinkers."

Benny Carter was the arranger and the eleven tracks were laid down in a total of nine-and-a-half hours. The album was only a moderate success, but Jackie's mastery is evident on every track. Most of the songs chosen were other singer's hits, such as Otis Redding's 'Respect', Wilson Pickett's 'Funky Broadway' and Sam Cooke's 'Chain Gang'.

Simon Rutberg, twenty-two at the time, was allowed by Jackie to spend some time in the sound booth while he sang. He remembers the process and the singer's determination for success. "Jackie didn't work with tracks, he recorded live," he recalls. "I was in the booth with him. I couldn't hear the orchestra – only Jackie. A twenty-three piece orchestra, live. That's the way it used to be done. The other way is not warm. Jackie said, 'I want just that one Pop album; one crossover.' But it didn't work." Jackie never did have a major album success.

CHAPTER TEN

I Don't Need You Around

In August 1966 at the Hollywood Trip night club, Jackie was singing and James Brown joined him on stage for a duet. Brown was performing across town, so the next night Jackie showed up and they performed to ten thousand fans.

"James Brown and Jackie were friendly," recalls Simon Rutberg. "Brown loves Jackie Wilson. Whenever he was in town and Jackie was performing, Brown would be there. And Jackie would always say, 'It's a real shame I've never been able to see your show.'"

James Brown also showed up the night in October that year when Elvis Presley saw Jackie performing at The Trip. "Elvis and James Brown were there," Rutberg remembers. "He'd been nervous, but once he was on, man, you'd think he was born to it. You couldn't get him off! He did a show-stopper; it was non-stop and moving. He was cooking.

"The thing Elvis does with his wrist [with arm extended and hanging his hand limply], he took it from Jackie. Elvis was really crazy about Jackie. I saw what I saw. Elvis went nuts. I'm putting it very mildly."

Elvis also did Jackie a good turn as he admitted to Norman N Nite: "Elvis did me a nice favour once. I was in Hollywood, California playing a club called The Trip and we were having a little difficulty getting people to come out, at that particular time. So he came out twice for me and, well, you couldn't get in. They said if Elvis goes, hey, let's go."

Drummer Jimmy Smith recalls: "Elvis came to the club in a white suit and a white Rolls Royce. I said, 'That man's got style, ain't he?' Elvis came into the dressing room after the show. I used to mark [copy] Elvis; the way he did with his legs. Jackie said to Elvis, 'You've got to see a black Elvis.' They had me doing it. Elvis was a nice guy.

To return the compliment Elvis invited Jackie out to the MGM movie set to see him, reveals Sonny West, Elvis's friend and bodyguard. "Elvis didn't go out much, but he went out there to see Jackie because he'd always liked Jackie. They used to compare Jackie to Elvis. They called him the black Elvis. Elvis really liked Jackie and thought he was a terrific showman. He admired Jackie's and Bobby Darin's showmanship. He said, 'Bobby can cut us all when he wanted to.'"

While at MGM they had photos taken, like two old friends. Elvis signed the photo for Jackie, writing, "Jackie, you have a friend forever, Elvis." For Jackie these photos meant everything and they stayed with him wherever he went as Tony Drake, a later collaborator, would discover. "I asked Jackie what he had in the attache case he always had with him," Drake recalls. "I said, 'Let me have a look at some of your pictures?', and the only pictures he had were two eight by ten inch pictures of him and Elvis."

"There are two artists I don't think any two men on this planet ever had the charisma of: Elvis Presley and Jackie Wilson," says Hank Ballard. "The two of them remind me of each other – the charisma. Jackie'd just walk on stage and the house would come down. He would walk out with a cigarette in his hand, do a spin, and the house would come down. Elvis would go out there and shake his ass and legs like he had the rickets. When you've born with that sort of charisma, you're born with success."

But there are degrees of success. During the 1960s Jackie constantly toured throughout the USA; still doing the "Chitlin' Circuit" and, increasingly, to appreciative audiences of every ethnic background. Fortunately, due to the incredible efforts of Martin Luther King and President Johnson, racial barriers that were so pervasive early in Jackie's career were slowly beginning to come down.

But, with the Vietnam War at it's peak in 1967, the States of America were anything but united. Indeed the divisions were tearing the whole country apart. In August 1965, six days of race rioting in the Watts area of Los Angeles had shocked the world. Graphic TV pictures had shown military troops subduing rioters and whole city blocks burnt to the ground. It left thirty-four dead and an estimated two hundred million dollars' worth of property damage.

Then, in July 1967 it was the turn of Newark, New Jersey. Five more days of rioting in the black neighbourhoods left twenty-six dead and more than 1,500 injured.

At the end of the same month it was the turn of Jackie's home town of Detroit. After eight days, 4,700 Federal paratroopers and eight thousand national guardsmen contained the rioters. This time "at least forty" were killed, two thousand injured and five thousand homeless. The irony being most of the injuries and damage had been done by blacks to blacks. "They burned stores, the mama-papa stores, run by blacks at that time. Where you could buy stuff 'on time'," reports Ernestine Smith.

Something was tearing at the heart of the country. After hundreds of years of ill treatment the black populations were finding that they, too, had power. In 1968 James Brown struck an instant chord with his black audience with 'Say It Loud – I'm Black And I'm Proud' song. For others, the song made them a little nervous.

Just before the Detroit riots, in April 1967, trouble again found Jackie. It showed that blacks had still not achieved the liberty they had fought so hard to achieve.

The Detroit *Courier* newspaper reported the story this way: "Caught Nude With White Girl In Columbia, SC. Police in this far south city arrested Jackie Wilson and a member of his band here last week and charged them with having been in the nude at a motel with two white women."

Jackie, who was thirty-two, was touring with BB King. The other person arrested was his drummer and friend, Jimmy Smith, twenty-eight. The two "white women" involved were twenty-four and twenty-five, very much adults. They were charged with "immoral conduct" and "disorderly conduct" and their bonds were set at two hundred dollars each. Jimmy Smith disputes the details: "When the police came in, Jackie was sitting in a chair with his hat and clothes on. He was not nude; he had got up and put his clothes on. It was a messed event. We had to pay our way out of it."

Money doesn't buy peace everywhere, though: "My wife pissed a song," he says. "It took me two years to get her over that."

Sam Moore, of Sam And Dave fame, claims Jackie often found himself in trouble with white women in the southern states. Apparently it wasn't uncommon for sheriffs to send them white women and then break down the door and arrest him. Nat Tarnopol would then get calls from Jackie in the middle of the night asking him to arrange bail.

As ridiculous as these South Carolina "moral conduct" charges may seem today, at the time they were considered dynamite for his revived career. A tarnished reputation could spell disaster, as it had for Chuck

Berry when he was jailed after being convicted of transporting an under-age girl across state lines. Not that Jackie's charge was that serious, but it might mean no radio airplay, or promoters might not book him so readily.

A solution had to be sought and apparently it was Tarnopol who thought it up, according to some who were around at the time. Jackie would marry his long time girlfriend, Harlean Harris. He was, after all, single since his non-contested divorce from Freda in 1965. Harlean, too, was mother of his son, John Dominick ("Petey"), who'd been born in 1963.

With that Jackie and Harlean were married in June 1967, at a private civil ceremony performed by New York Civil Court Judge, Amos Bowman, in his chambers. Present was bridesmaid Mrs Johnny Brantely, August Sims as Jackie's aide, Nat Tarnopol, and drummer Jimmy Smith as best man. The press photo of the wedding shows everyone looking very solemn and Jackie with eyes downcast.

But there was also humour. "I'm holding Jackie's whisky glass and mine," recalls Smith, "and I was holding the ring. I couldn't get the ring 'cause I wasn't going to put my glass down."

Not everyone finds the same joke funny. "Harlean got mad," he says, "because Jackie and I was messing with a couple of lesbians. We always had some lesbian chicks. One time we had a whole party of them. Jack and I used to watch them." Harlean couldn't see the joke and the marriage was off to a very shaky start.

Joyce McRae, who met Jackie in 1965 and became one of his lovers, speaks of the marriage in no uncertain terms. "He had to marry Harlean to save his career," she insists. "I know it for sure. It wasn't that Jackie had any great love for Harlean – it was during that period of time that I was seeing him. He had a lust thing – a freaky thing – between Harlean and him.

"Harlean was a groupie bitch and a known freak. Sam Cooke changed women like he changed underwear. That was the thing in those days with those guys. There was a whole sub-culture; they traded women like people traded underwear." Before Jackie, Harlean had, of course, been going with Cooke.

Another of Jackie's one time girlfriends, Angel Lee, is equally uncomplimentary of Harlean. "I met Harlean when she was engaged to Sam Cooke," she says. "My opinion of Harlean is that she wanted to be 'Mrs Somebody'. She was a Johnson model then, and gorgeous."

Jackie's mother also was unimpressed with Harlean. Says Joyce McRae,

"Mama Wilson never let Harlean in her house. Mama Wilson never acknowledged Petey as a child of Jackie's – never took him as her grandson."

After the wedding, the newlyweds and entourage were feted by the unofficial king of record distribution, Morris Levy, at his mid Manhattan Roundtable Cafe. Press reports say they "were greeted by several hundred showbusiness friends".

In reporting the wedding, the Detroit *Courier* newspaper stated the couple would be living in a $550 a month apartment. Their address was West Side Towers apartments on West Sixty-Eighth Street. The article added that Jackie "commands as much as $2,500 for his one night engagements. Last year his income was reputedly was two hundred thousand dollars gross." It sounded very much like a press release prepared by Tarnopol.

Newspapers also reported that the newlyweds planned an around-the-world honeymoon for August. The honeymoon never happened. In August, a month after the destructive Detroit riots, Jackie performed at the Cobo Arena in Detroit, his first appearance in his home town in two years. Sharing the billing were BB King, The Drifters, Toussaint McCall, Gorgeous George and others.

Soon after their marriage, a serious rift led to Jackie moving out of their luxury Westside Towers penthouse apartment. For Jackie it meant a slide into a dangerously depressive period and serious drug taking stage. He may well have lost the desire to live. Exactly why they separated is a matter of conjecture.

Jackie is believed to have found Harlean in bed with Tarnopol. Although Jackie had untold affairs with women, both married and single, he was devastated that his friend and manager was having an affair with his wife! Joyce McRae says singer Sam Moore was with Jackie when he caught Tarnopol in bed with Harlean. Jackie's daughter, Denise, claims she was the one who caught them out. The truth is not easy to determine.

The effect on Jackie's mental well-being was devastating, due to the initial friendship and respect he had for Nat. Jackie had finally determined Tarnopol was not paying him his due, and, to rub salt into the wound, now found his friend having an affair with his wife. It was the final straw.

Ironically, Sammy Davis Jnr claims in his autobiography that he had a liaison with Harlean, although exactly when is unclear. Probably, to

Harlean, what was good for the goose is good for the gander. After all Jackie was never faithful to any woman. Around the same time Jackie punched Ronald Isley, of The Isley Brothers, down the back stairs of the Apollo Theatre. Whether or not Ronald had been having an affair with Harlean is not known, but Jackie believed it and, when mad, he was not one to trifle with.

Some people deny the affair. Brunswick's promotion manager, of the time, Joel "Joey" Bonner knew Jackie and Harlean well. "I doubt Harlean was screwing Nat," he says. "Harlean didn't like Nat. They were in her way. They kept her on a string. If they fucked with Jackie's money, they fucked with her money. I didn't think Nat was a nice guy. I would have picked up on it if Nat and Harlean had a thing."

However, Jimmy Smith thinks otherwise. "They was," he nods. "Nat swore to God he wasn't doing it, but I always believed he was."

Billy Davis and Pops Watley helped Jackie move from the apartment into the "flop house" Alvin Hotel on Fifty-Second Street, near Broadway. "He took only his clothes, portable stereo, his comic book collection [which was mainly of the *Captain Marvel* series], and his record collection [all his own recordings]," says Davis. "He couldn't live with Harlean, but he always loved her – it was just over."

This was a miserable period for Jackie, although only thirty-four years old, the best of his hit making days were over. The last hit of his career was, 'I Get The Sweetest Feeling', released in August 1968. The album of the same name was released in October, featuring a painting of Jackie with a beautiful woman leaning with her elbows on his back. The woman is Harlean.

The movie *A Lovely Way To Die*, released the same year, starred Kirk Douglas as a New York policeman. Jackie sang the theme song of the same name, yet remarkably it was never released. The film was a flop as well.

Quite likely Jackie had given up the fight. In the 1 November, 1991 issue of *Goldmine* Davis reported: "One night I came back to his apartment in the Alvin Hotel and Jackie was as white as a ghost. At first he wouldn't say anything but after talking till four in the morning Jackie told me what happened. His main concern was with his mother, and he made me swear never to tell anyone lest his mother found out. You know it might have happened more than once.

"Jackie had a number of companies who wanted to record him over the years, but he never went to them because of fear." Jackie had apparently admitted he'd been held out of a high-rise window by Tarnopol's henchmen. Of course no witnesses to this supposed incident ever came forward, but the question remains: how had he remained on the Brunswick label for eighteen years despite the obvious fact that in later years Tarnopol and he hated each other?

The exact year that the incident was said to have occurred varies between 1964 and 1968. According to some close to Jackie at the time, it was done at Tarnopol's behest in order to convince Jackie to marry Harlean, and consequently have more control over him. Others believe that it was to ensure he re-signed to Brunswick. But the one thing that is without doubt, Jackie was controlled; more bluntly, he was owned.

Robert Pruter's thoroughly researched book, *Chicago Soul*, states:

> Joe McEwen, a well respected writer on black music and an A&R man at CBS Records, said of Brunswick that it had a 'dubious reputation'. He was being kind. Brunswick had been the subject of a lot of nasty stories over the years, many of which related to presumed links with the Mob. [Eugene] Record testified at the Brunswick trial that he was roughed up by an associate of Tarnopol when he demanded an advance for re-signing with the label. I asked Record why a company would treat its artists that way, and he replied, 'Hey, it wasn't the company. It was the people who were maybe connected with the company who weren't involved in recording per se. In other words they were outside people that was on the company side.' When I pointedly asked if these 'outside people' were gangsters, Record silently nodded affirmatively, fully cognisant that the tape recorder was on.
>
> Sonny Woods, for many years a member of the Detroit-based Midnighters vocal group, told a tale that at best should be classified as hearsay, but it indicated how artists viewed Brunswick. According to Woods, when in 1964 Jackie Wilson refused to re-sign with Brunswick, Tarnopol and his associates hung the singer by his feet outside the window of a high-rise hotel until he agreed to put his name

on the dotted line.

PR man, Harry Respess, knew Jackie from his teenage years, but was particularly close to JJ. Respess is sure the incident actually happened: "Johnny Jones was there. They called me right after this happened. They wanted him to re-sign with Brunswick, but he didn't want to 'cause Brunswick wasn't putting the money into promotion that he thought was required to get him a hit record. So the big boys just grabbed him and held him out the window. They way I understand it is that if he didn't sign they'd drop him. They let one hand free – so he could sign – while hanging out the window."

Although these accounts are definitely hearsay and don't fit with the other statements that it happened around 1967 or 1968 and concerned Harlean, Lynn Ciccone claims: "Jackie confirmed to me that he was hung out the window because he refused to sign the contact. He was becoming uncontrollable – he wanted out. He wanted something better. He started to wise up. He knew how talented he was."

Joyce McRae says Jackie also confessed the incident to her. "He was told, 'Nigger, you will do what we tell you to do.' I was told by Jackie. It had nothing to do with money."

There was also said to be another episode of intimidation around the same time when apparently Jackie was tied up and kept in a basement. Says Billy Davis, "Jackie told me that. There were rats down there. It was in a dark basement he said, and he shuddered. With him it wasn't really the money. This was because of a contract with Nat. Freda also told me. It would have been mid sixties. It was before the marriage [to Harlean]. He just wanted to sing."

Both August Sims, Jackie's long time road manager, and producer Carl Davis are adamant that the incident did not involve Jackie, but happened to a DJ. There can be little doubt, however, that Jackie was intimidated and found it impossible to break away from the Brunswick label.

While denying any knowledge of the window incident, Carl Davis did say, "At 1650 Broadway a disc jockey was hung out the window. Nat Tarnopol didn't want to pay Jackie for 'Higher And Higher', so Jackie didn't want to record any more. He was pissed that everything he did would go to Nat. But Nat would say, 'He owes me.' It was such a battle going between Jackie and Nat, that I don't think Nat put in any sort of effort on his behalf after that. But that was hard, because Jackie was the best he had. After 'Higher And Higher' Jackie never went to New York. If he called and asked Nat for money, he'd be told, 'No'. It was an uneasy feeling at that time. Nat didn't promote Jackie."

Tarnopol's son, Paul, puts Nat's side. "Jackie had perhaps one complaint with my father regarding money – there was never money being hidden," he says. "Jackie and my father were together over a decade, and there was only one incident – over the eighty thousand dollars for the house. It was regarding money that was advanced for a house or something like that. Nat tore up the contract. Because he decided to tear up the contract, Jackie pleaded with him, 'Don't!'"

Actually, there were two contracts between Jackie and Tarnopol. The first contracted him to record for Decca and Tarnopol's Brunswick label, the second concerned Tarnopol's management of Jackie. These contracts could not be located.

Jackie had hit the low point of his career and seemingly had lost the will to entertain, or possibly even to care about living. "Jackie was disappointed that Nat wasn't pushing more," recalls friend Launa Toledo. "He didn't like to complain. I think he was disappointed. I think he would have liked to have done more serious music than he did. The serious music was never really pushed. The right people never heard it. Nat should have made sure it was heard. He was as good as any tenor...he knew that. He would do it all on his own."

Jackie was always a very proud, macho type individual. He tried to convey the impression that he was in control, totally self-confident. His long time friend Billy Davis knew better, as he related to Robert Pruter in his well researched *Goldmine* article on Jackie. "When I came to live with him [in 1968], he looked terrible. He would lay around the apartment for weeks and weeks, drinking heavily and not doing anything but reading his comic books. He had thousands of comic books stacked in his apartment, mainly Marvel, *Conan The Barbarian*, things like that. I eventually persuaded him to go out on tour again and stop his drinking, but he never complained that he never achieved great success. You could tell, though, it had affected him."

Flamingos star Tommy Hunt loved and admired Jackie, but he could also see that all was not as it should be. "Jackie was scared, he was scared to death and that probably contributed to his drug taking as well," he says.

"He was trying to run away from the reality of it all. I know he was under pressure, he'd always tried to laugh it off. In front of me he was a bigger star than me, so he looked at me as, 'This is my little friend, Tommy,' or 'A little star trying to make it.' He kind of protected me, but I know under all that strength he was trying to show me, there was a little boy trying to get out. He was the macho-type, but I could see through it, because when the guy would call and start crying about his life, and how the people were cutting him to pieces and hurting him, stealing from him, lying behind his back, and trying to be his friend to his face only for the money. I said, 'Listen Jackie, you've got to know how to control that, only you can control it, but taking drugs ain't going to do it, because the more drugs you take you are going to lose yourself further in that hole you're in.' Jackie thought he was God. The fans make you feel that way. Look at Michael Jackson today, he thinks he's God. But you've got to look at reality. There's a 'you' that can do that thing on stage and also a 'you' that needs a real life. That fantasy life is okay, but you need the healthy food and the healthy life.

"I was on drugs, but I knew when to stop. I knew it was destroying me, I was going out of my mind. One day I just packed my bags and left for Europe and I've been here ever since. You never know when your time is up. You have to draw the line somewhere with this singing stuff. It's timing, you have to draw the line, take some time off."

Like others, Hunt, at least in part, blames Tarnopol for Jackie's addiction problem, "If Jackie was high, Nat could control him and Jackie couldn't see which way his money was going."

Jackie developed deep paranoia, as Freda had already experienced. He'd been used and abused by so many, he didn't know who to trust. JJ was his long time friend from Highland Park with the Shaker Gang and Ever Ready Gospel Group, yet Jackie had fired him.

Hunt recalls, "Jackie would have his little tantrums and he'd sack everybody. And then turn around and say, 'I ain't got no friends.' Then he'd want them back again."

One friend was Roquel "Billy" Davis. At the end of the sixties he became the first black executive vice-president of the gigantic New York based McCann Erickson advertising company, becoming especially involved with Coca-Cola. Davis used many of the great black artists to promote the product with his jingles, but sadly couldn't include Jackie, even though he was aware Jackie could do with the cash. "The reason I didn't use Jackie was he was so strung at the time, it scared the hell out of me," he says recalling one 1969 incident, in particular, in Chicago. "I was in contact with him and he couldn't even talk coherently on the phone...scared the hell out of me. So it never happened. He really went off the deep end."

After his separation from Harlean, Jackie became very morose seemingly losing all reason for living. Billy Davis recalls, "All the stars that had looked up to him, they didn't come around. He was stuck up in the Alvin Hotel and he was getting boozed up twenty four hours a day. He just seemed out of it. I could see something bad happening. I lived there more than I did in my own place in the Bronx. I just hang in there, but all these other guys weren't there. The ones that came around later on with something to say, they don't know what he was going through. It was like he didn't have anyone.

"He was coming out of a fairly depressive spell at that particular time. I knew I was responsible for helping to pull him through, 'cause everybody had deserted him. This was a man who had one of the greatest voices in the world and who had been feted by the world and now...he'd just be in moods when he laid around getting high, fucked up for weeks. He would just smoke 'weed' all day long. He would drink and he wouldn't put on clothes for weeks at a time. Just get in the room, get knocked out and lay down. Then he woke up and got enough strength to roll another joint. He kept that up constantly. I never saw him act that way before." Jackie, always a big eater, needed activity to burn off the fat. Laying around he became overweight and this became noticeable as his face fattened.

Davis goes on: "So I started going and taking a guitar. I kind of brought him out of it; I got him interested in singing again. He'd just about lost interest. We'd be up all night, guitar licks and stuff, he loved guitar; he couldn't play it though. Had a couple of fifteen minute lessons, but he didn't have the patience. I had some songs I was working on – I'd get him interested in that. I knew his weakness was singing; he couldn't resist singing. After this, we'd be up for months all night."

The effort to bring Jackie back on track began to have an effect. "We had tapes full of new songs. He started to get back into wanting to tour again."

Davis had another ploy to pick up his spirits: "After the down times in

1968, we'd go and park some place and I'd deliberately get people to ask for autographs. People wouldn't believe Jackie was in that area." Jackie couldn't help but respond when the fans came around and Davis knew it. Gradually, Jackie began to be his old self and the touring began again.

Despite recording around four hundred great tunes during his career, Jackie only ever managed to get one album in the Top Hundred charts, which was *Baby Workout* which achieved only Number Thirty-Six. Quite simply the material he was putting out was not "Pop" enough.

When Billy Davis left Hank Ballard and The Midnighters he eventually joined Jackie as one of his three travelling band members in 1968. "In his whole career, that was probably the most 'down years'; 1968, 1969 and 1970," says Davis. "Some of the dates were the 'Chitterlin' Circuit'. We also did some good sets such as Miami Beach, but we also played some small circuit gigs. Then we'd have some big ones. In Fresno, California, they had to get the Fire Department fire hoses to spray the women to get them off him."

A sure sign that all was not well was when Jackie pulled out of a fight, a challenge he could never resist. "We was on tour and Sims was mad at him for something, so he threatened to hit Jackie," says Davis. "I'd never seen Jackie back-off before like that. I confronted Sims. Jackie stopped me and said 'Billy, stop! You don't understand.' I knew it was something serious and Jackie didn't want me to get involved."

It's true Sims was a big man weighing well over two hundred pounds, but Jackie was a "real scraper", in Davis's words. "He had a punch like a heavyweight." No, it was a lot more than that. Sims was Roberts' and Tarnopol's henchman; put there to keep an eye on Jackie.

On 22 March, 1969, barely one year and nine months after their highly publicised marriage, it was reported that Harlean and Jackie had agreed to separate and had signed an agreement to that effect. Herbert Lippman, Tarnopol's friend and Jackie's lawyer made the announcement. It ended by stating, "She's due to fly to Mexico soon to secure her freedom." Their son "Petey" was five.

Launa Toledo, friend to both Harlean and Jackie, says of the separation: "The reason Harlean and Jackie couldn't live together was partly because of the drinking and womanising, but also because whatever Nat and all them told him to do, he did. Harlean was a beautiful woman; it's hard to know your husband's out and about and this broad is probably going home with him. I'm not saying it was right – it's part of the life."

Freda's explanation is somewhat more blunt. "Harlean was only with him for a year, after she found out she couldn't go shopping when she wanted to she left. She'd rather go back to Jamaica or Long Island and sleep on that day bed. He was married to Harlean, but they only stayed married a few months. He found out all she wanted was his money. After, she found he didn't have the kind of money she thought he had because he owed the income tax so much, then she went to court. He just assumed she was getting a divorce."

Joyce McRae claims a divorce had taken place: "Jackie believed he was divorced from Harlean. He thought he'd signed a divorce. Herb Lippman, who was Jackie's attorney, was on Nat Tarnopol's payroll. It was a conflict of interest. It's called game-set. And remember Nat and Harlean were fucking each other. The reason Jack and Harlean broke up is because Jack caught Nat in his bed with her. He attacked her – he went berserk. It was *their* house and *their* bed. Nat was the person who demanded Jackie marry Harlean."

Jackie's brother-in-law, Johnny Collins, with no obvious axe to grind, says: "Harlean was in love with the word 'love' and the power that went along with it. She had quote, 'him', and she did him, she wiped him. Every chance she got when some attorney came up and said, 'We can get him on this,' she went along with it. She hurt him in every way possible. Yet she couldn't catch him and that's what was destroying her."

Although Paul Tarnopol was born in 1963, and was therefore very young at the time, he recalls, "Harlean loved Jackie, but couldn't be married to him. He would lie a lot and wouldn't take care of his own kids or support them. He'd give money to some women down the street, but he wouldn't support his own kids. He was totally irresponsible, but he still loved his kids. Jackie would bring hookers to the hotel while Petey was there."

It became difficult for Jackie to visit New York, with Harlean pursuing him through the courts for unpaid alimony. "For a time, every time he got to New York they would lock him up," says Carl Davis. "How Harlean would know he was coming in was through Nat, because Nat would know I'd scheduled the session 'over-dub'. Then, all of a sudden, he would get out of the cab on the way to the studio and the police would jump upon him and take him to jail. He would get out on bond. He used to get sick of that and we'd do it all in Chicago after that."

"New York was a bad place for him," Johnny Collins confirms. "He had twelve or thirteen warrants out for his arrest. Harlean had his ass sewn up...his nuts were tied up major big time."

Harlean had her own agenda, always. Simon Rutberg recalls when a fight broke out inside the dressing room. "Jimmy Smith and Sims were trashing Lawrence Welk's dressing room pretty good," he says. "People and chairs flying everywhere. Harlean just sat there putting on make up. The most pretentious thing you ever saw."

Pretentious, but still Jackie's wife, whether he realised or not.

CHAPTER ELEVEN

Those Heartaches

Sadly for his fans worldwide, Jackie seldom travelled to other countries. But he did travel to Mexico City for two weeks at one of the biggest clubs. A problem arose when it came time to leave. "Jackie said he's not going to go in there [Immigration office] and do nothing!" recalls Jimmy Smith. "You've got to go through all the procedures to get out of the country. You know, they locked us up. The folks said, 'You've got to live with our rules.'" The rules won out, as they invariably do. "We went to jail everywhere we went – for a whole lot of different things."

Jail seemed to be a fair risk in the entertainment business, especially if you were on the fringes, and Jackie could have got into more trouble than he did. The "Queen Of Soul", Aretha Franklin, was married to a man with a notorious reputation, Ted White. "Ted White and Aretha, in the later years, wasn't hitting it off at all," recalls a friend of Jackie. "He was beating up on Aretha and Jackie stepped in and Ted pulled a gun on him. He wasn't about to fight Jackie with his fists. Ted wasn't a fighter, anyhow – he was a pimp, a dope dealer."

Considering how open he was about everything, very few people associated with Jackie knew of his involvement with Freemasonry; nobody could say how or when he was introduced to it. "He was in it when I got to him in 1962," says Jimmy Smith. "It was a secret. My brother was in it. Jackie kind of had a little money to push him into a big position there. He approached my brother and approached him wrong [according to Masonic protocol]. My brother, Cheater, had him crying. They'd come into the apartment and talk to him and tried to get him off drugs." They weren't successful. "Ain't nobody going to straighten Jackie out!"

Also less well known was Jackie's involvement with Hubert Humphrey's 1968 campaign for the presidency of the United States. "We did some campaigning for president – for Hubert Humphrey," says Smith.

"We did some commercials. Jackie did some speeches. In New York we went around with Humphrey, campaigning. Jackie got up and made some speeches and stuff, and Nat Tarnopol said, 'My man's going to be in politics one day.'" Unfortunately, as the world knows, Richard Nixon won.

In the late sixties the bond between Jackie and his mother was always strong, but it was when high or ill his need for her was strongest. Billy Davis remembers: "We were at the Saxony Hotel on Miami Beach. We got the doctor. The doctor examined him and told him he needed rest. He'd come off stage and collapsed. We'd be on stage about one to one and a half hours and I'd tell him he ought to slow down. He was fatigued. He called Moma, and said, 'I think I got sugar [diabetes] – it runs in the family.' He was like a child in a sense. Had a lot of little kid ways. Jack's mother and he were extremely close." Eliza Mae was also a chronic diabetic.

Jimmy Smith also got to know Jackie's mother and he recalled one conversation with her. "That lady told me if it ever came to where she had to lay down her life for Jackie, she'd do it. He couldn't have gone on without her. That woman loved Jackie." The conversation was prophetic.

Denise was also privy to Eliza Mae's treatment of her son. "She treated him like two people," she says. "One of them was Sonny and one of them was Jackie. When Jack was in control, cool. But she didn't like Jack messing around with Sonny. He used to call her up on the phone and say, 'Mommy, this is Sonny, you tell Jack to leave me alone. He's making me do this. He's making me act like this.' She would patronise him. She would keep certain things from him and stuff and make him weaker. Weaker to understand certain proofs in life."

On 10 June, 1967, a day after Jackie's thirty-third birthday, his step-father John Lee died. He had been a heavy smoker and had suffered for many years from emphysema. It seems rather pointless, but Eliza Mae initially didn't want Jackie to be told, most likely because she did not want to upset him. "Jack did finally find out and he was angry," says Freda. "He went to see him in the hospital just before he died."

Of course, his mother wasn't the only woman prepared to lay down her life for him. A sad example of Jackie's affect on women occurred in November, 1969 when he was appearing at a club in Cincinnati, Ohio. A white, twenty-one-year-old "ex-bunny", Karen Lynn Calloway, who worked at the club, somehow struck up a friendship with Jackie's entourage. She was married with two children at the time.

Jimmy Smith remembers her. "She wasn't involved with nobody," he insists. "She'd come over to our parties and just sit there on a chair. The girl wasn't in Jackie's room, she was in mine. She was so sweet; I was trying to get to her."

The upshot was that Dennis Calloway shot his wife six times as she ran out of the house a few weeks later. The statement made to the court on behalf of Calloway claimed that his wife had become infatuated with Wilson, and when he confronted her a Wilson bodyguard snapped, "Butt out, man, Jackie doesn't like anyone messing with his women." Calloway is said to have replied, "That's my wife and we have two children. I'm not afraid of being hurt." On another occasion, Calloway's statement to the court said, he came across his wife and one of her woman friends "in a car full of Negro men." The court ordered Jackie to be a material witness at the trial. Jackie explained the true situation to the courts. Incredibly, the husband was not sentenced to a jail term.

By 1970 Carl Davis had Brunswick's Chicago office producing numerous hits, though none with Jackie. Eugene Record and his Chi-Lites were very popular, Barbara Acklin, who'd been his secretary and wrote 'Whispers' was now a singer in her own right. Gene Chandler, Major Lance, Tyrone Davis, The Artistics, Young-Holt Trio, Billy Butler (brother of Jerry), Erma Franklin (sister of Aretha) and Little Richard all recorded on the label. Tarnopol had made a wise decision when he employed Davis, yet despite the success there were tensions between the Chicago office and Tarnopol. Quite likely Davis was being overwhelmed.

By late January, 1970, and with his last hit record behind him, the idea of working with Jackie still thrilled singers. Tony Drake was a young talent who had, in 1969, recorded the ballad 'Let's Play House' on the Musicor label. It did well, according to Drake, selling some 150,000 records. He also did a cover of The Supremes, 'Love Child'. Drake's manager was Leonard ("Lenny") Lewis who introduced him to another no-nonsense manager, Johnny Roberts, who was also Jackie's well connected personal manager. Roberts quickly realised that Drake had the "right stuff" and said, "Well, okay, kid. If you do the right thing you'll make out fine. We're going to send you to Chicago and you're going to record with Jackie Wilson."

He was sent to ask for Carl Davis, but Davis, used to being sent unwanted acts, ignored him, although Eugene Record took to him instantly. Jackie did more than that, and for a fortnight Drake lived like a superstar with Jackie.

He recalls the day Jackie visited the Chicago offices. "I remember everyone lining up to embrace Jackie and he was wonderful to them all," he says. "Jackie became aware of me standing there, and then did what I thought was an eye wink. Later I found out that he had some kind of nervous twitch, but my mind told me, 'See man, Jackie likes you.' So as the people filed out of the office, I stood to the side to let them pass. Then Jackie came over to me and embraced me, as if he had known me all along. I became a little nervous and trembled. Jackie leaned over to me and said in a soft voice, 'Kid, I sure hope you are not a singer.' I said, 'I am, but you have nothing to worry about.' Jackie said that he 'was not too sure about that'. I found it hard to believe that I was actually having a conversation with Jackie Wilson."

After a few words with Carl, Jackie told Drake he was moving him into his hotel. Soon they were both recording their own songs as equals, both produced by Davis. "Jackie would take us out at night. We went to visit [soul singer] Bobby Womack who was staying in a hotel across town, where he was performing at that night. Bobby was also very nice. I remember a heavy set, well dressed man with a Polaroid camera, who took about fifteen pictures of Jackie, Bobby and myself. The man asked me if I wanted any of the pictures. I answered, very modestly, 'No, my friend, you enjoy them.' I felt like I was a star for sure now." Of course Drake now regrets that he didn't obtain copies of those photos.

"The next day, I called my aunt and told her about the picture Bobby and Jackie had taken with me. I thought Jackie and Bobby were laughing at how young and cocky I was, but they did not let on to me, I think they just liked having me around. Bobby played a date that night and the rest went, but I went back to the hotel, because I was flat broke and I didn't want Jackie to know it. I thought to myself, 'How could I hang around Jackie if I was broke.'

"The next day Bobby came to Brunswick looking for Jackie. That day I had gone ahead of Jackie and Bobby directed his attention to me as if we were old friends. I asked him to come into Eugene's office, where I introduced the two. He also asked me why I didn't come to his show last night, but I made up some excuse. Gene Chandler was there waiting for Jackie. By the time he arrived, the room was full of entertainers. They made jokes and everybody treated me nice now, as though I could put in a good word with Jackie."

The close association also meant Drake was in danger of losing his own personality. "On the 23 February [1970], I recorded my two songs for Brunswick," he says. "Jackie and I arrived late in the car with my lady and the others. I mentioned it to Jackie and he said, 'Don't worry, I own the company.' When we arrived, Eugene Record, The Chi-Lites and the musicians were waiting as I walked in the booth to record. Jackie walked right in with me. I closed my eyes and began to sing. As I sang Eugene stopped the track. I asked him what I was doing wrong. He said, 'You're singing like Jackie, sing like yourself.' When the session was over, I asked Jackie, 'How did I sound?' He said, 'A little like Roy Hamilton.' The next day I left Chicago, and I only saw Jackie one more time, which was in New York about two weeks later, but I feel his presence every time I'm singing, or on a stage."

The very same week that Jackie and Drake did their sessions, Jackie returned to Detroit to perform at the Olympia Ballroom in a "Rock Revival Show" with Bill Haley, Bo Diddley, The Drifters, The Shirelles and The Coasters. The all star line-up made Jackie look good to the outside world, but friends like former Detroit Shaker, Harry "Dale" Respess, knew that all was not as it should be. Especially friendly with JJ, Respess remembers how in the late 1960s, Jackie was down on his luck and, through JJ, sometimes sought assistance from him. "Johnny'd come to me and ask for a couple of hundred bucks, from time to time," he recalls. "I'd always help if I could. I got most back…some slipped through the cracks of course. JJ wasn't a quiet guy; he was kind of flamboyant. He played up his association with Jackie. Lots of jewellery and fancy clothes, lots of fancy cars. A 'want-to-be' I'd call him. Want to be something and they're not. But he was Jackie's confidant. He took care of his everything. Jackie relied on him."

JJ made Jackie look and feel a star, both in private and public. "JJ was with him the whole time I was there," says Tony Drake. "When we were sitting in a bar, he would have JJ massage his shoulders while he had a drink. When we saw a beautiful girl he would say to me, 'How do you think she looks? She's fine, huh?' I said, 'Let's call and introduce ourselves.' And he'd say, 'She's never heard of me.' And you'd call the person and say, 'Excuse me, this is Jackie Wilson.' And they'd say, 'Jackie Wilson, the singer?' He was always like, 'You've heard of me?' In the meantime, the whole world had heard of him."

But even JJ couldn't work miracles and as a performer Jackie began slipping. "Toward the end of his career Jackie was losing it," says Respess. "He was out of touch. His clothing was sort of dated, and he couldn't get into the groove of the youngsters. His career went down because he didn't want to change. He really tried to change. He changed his style of dress and started to look a little younger. But after that he did change his style of dress; he was lost in a time warp for a while. Me and Johnny convinced him to change and he did. He was uncomfortable with it at first.

It could be said Respess benefited from Jackie's situation. "I booked him into the Whiskey-A-Go-Go for ten nights and he was overwhelming. I had Stevie Wonder there and only paid Jackie four thousand dollars for ten days. I took him to the Red Lion in Stagger, Illinois, basically an all white community. Jackie was kind of a proud guy. This was 1969 and he was down on his luck and he'd hide out from people. He wasn't gregarious and a show-off like he used to be. He was a little ashamed. I took him there, for $1,500 a night, it was standing room only. He did a full show for $1,500. They loved him. JJ was his driver at the time and had just wrecked the Cadillac. He was rather short of money at the time and he did the show to get money to get his Cadillac out of the work shop."

Until 1964, Nat Tarnopol had simply been Jackie's manager and vice president of Brunswick As a part of the deal with Decca to re-sign Jackie to the label, he was given a fifty per cent share of Brunswick. In 1970, Tarnopol made a major decision that would seem to provide major benefits for himself, but it is entirely possible it also had a nasty downside for Jackie and himself. The whole affair was typically shady. "In 1970 my dad was auditing MCA who owned half of Brunswick," reveals Paul Tarnopol. "Until 1970 my father would make the records, they'd sell the records and report to my father. My father found they were stealing tons of money. He was getting ready to sue MCA and, as they were a public company, they couldn't afford that kind of law suit. So they settled by giving him the other half of Brunswick."

Dick Jacobs recalls another version of events as he explained to *Musician* magazine (11 January, 1988): "Due to the strength of Jackie's records, Nat Tarnopol decided that he wanted to own all or nothing of Brunswick Records. Despite the fact that he did own fifty per cent of the company and was doing quite well financially, his rapport with Marty Salkin was at a low ebb and it was continually one fight after another. So Nat went to Milt Rackmil and Leonard Schneider [Decca top executives] who were both still around and told them in his own words, 'You name a figure and I'll holler buy or sell.' At this time however, neither Rackmil nor Schneider could make a decision and they informed Nat that he would have to go to Los Angeles and broach the matter to none other than Lew Wasserman [Decca's chief executive] himself. Nat thought he would be able to handle Wasserman but little did he know of Wasserman's ability as a businessman. It was like going into a den of wolves with Wasserman the chief wolf. So Nat went and presented his story to the head honcho. Wasserman was so disgusted with Nat's attitude that he took an immediate dislike to him and, after the meeting, he called New York and told them he didn't give a shit how many records Jackie Wilson sold, he wanted Nat and Brunswick out. So a deal was struck and Nat Tarnopol walked away with the Brunswick trademark, all his masters, and the whole thing came to him for nothing more than a handful of beans. Nat, of course wanted me to leave and come with him but my pension was coming up fairly soon and I told him no until I was on the pension. I guess that was the start of the breakdown of the relationship between Nat and myself.

"So Nat left the MCA fold, taking his Brunswick properties with him. Three MCA people went with him. Surprisingly enough, Lee Shep, who was very, very close with Lew Wasserman went with him as a damn good promotion man. Artist wise, Nat took with him Jackie Wilson, The Chi-Lites and Tyrone Davis…he had by this time made a good connection with Carl Davis who had produced Jackie's record *Higher And Higher* and Nat bought into Davis's studio in Chicago and switched his recording activities out there. After some minor successes, and some legal problems, Nat leased all his masters to CBS and for all intents, that was the end of Brunswick. Incidentally, at the time of the break-up, I owned some Brunswick stock which Nat had very graciously given to me. It became necessary for him to retrieve the stock to complete the deal and when he asked me how much I wanted for my stock shares, I told him the figure was one dollar. I guess I could have held him up for a large sum, but Nat had been very good to me and this was one way that I could pay him back. Believe me, doing all those arrangements for Jackie Wilson certainly did a great deal towards building up my reputation in the industry."

Jackie finally decided in 1970 that Nat Tarnopol was not giving him his fair share of his earnings and after a huge falling out, Jackie decided he would be his own manager. Of course he was still bound to the Brunswick label and could do nothing about that.

The break hurt Jackie because he'd always respected Nat. "Jack felt the sun rose and set with Nat," says Jimmy Smith. "He woke up about two years before I left in 1972. He stopped Nat taking bookings for him. He started doing his bookings on his own then."

As with everything, there was a final straw. "What really pissed Jack off," says Smith, "was in 1969 he wanted a new car. All Jack had to do was say he wanted a new car and the car would be at the office. This time, Jackie wanted this limousine and Nat wouldn't get it. Nat was a schemer, man. Jack had to go out on tour and take the money and get him a car. That's when Jackie started waking up on Nat. He ended up with the Sedan de Ville [bottom of the Cadillac range]. He was really upset. Before we had five of them jokers [Cadillacs] out there – everyone had one!"

Launa Toledo also saw the break-up coming. "In the early seventies things started to go sour between Jackie and Nat," she says. "The royalty cheques weren't coming through. Nat was a crook, that's all you can say. Nat looked like an accountant; you'd think he was the nicest guy that ever lived. He'd tell you anything you'd like to hear. He started thinking, 'I've got the goose that laid the golden egg.' Nat would call me up – he would be very charming. And...boom! Behind your back you didn't know what he was doing. I didn't trust him as far as I could throw him."

Carl Davis is sure the falling out began in 1968, which coincides with when Jackie stopped living with Harlean. An interviewer once asked Jackie why he continued to record with Brunswick? He responded, "My mind would say go, but my soul would say stay." The reality was that he was bound to the label out of straight intimidation.

Although the original contracts with Jackie could not be located, it is believed that Jackie re-negotiated a five per cent of retail agreement with Brunswick prior to Tarnopol taking full control. This was up from the initial three per cent arrangement, although it is rather vague if the true sales figures were not known.

One thing is known: Nat Tarnopol would not be losing out. "One time we flew from New York to Little Rock, 'cause we had an engagement," explains Smith. "I said, 'Nat, how rich are you going to get?' He looked up, 'Jimmy Smith, the sky's the limit!'"

CHAPTER TWELVE

This Love Is Real

Jackie Wilson never won "Father Of The Year". With his career keeping him constantly on the move, regardless of how well things were going, it wasn't easy to maintain a strong relationship with his children. This caused him extreme anguish on receiving news that his oldest son, Jack (Jackie Jnr), had been shot to death on the night of Monday 28 September, 1970.

Jack, known to the family as Sonny or Little Sonny, was sixteen years of age. The report in the Michigan *Chronicle* newspaper is worth reporting in full:

> Jackie Wilson Jnr, son of popular rhythm and blues singer Jackie Wilson, was shot and killed by an unknown person, or persons, Monday night as he stood on the porch of a friend's home.
>
> According to a report, the sixteen-year-old youth, who lived at 16522 LaSalle, had rung the door bell at the residence of Richard Holmes, 16625 Prairie and, just as Holmes opened the door, several shots were fired from the street. Wilson suffered a shotgun injury to the upper left back and side, and Holmes was shot in the right forearm.
>
> The shooting occurred at approximately 10.25pm. The two men were rushed to Detroit General Hospital(Central Branch) by police officers who answered a radio run to the scene. Wilson was pronounced dead on arrival at 10.40pm. Holmes, twenty-six, was reported in serious condition.
>
> Wilson, according to a statement from a witness, was concerned about a dispute he had had earlier with a young woman friend who was visiting at Holmes' residence that evening.

He reportedly telephoned Holmes and discussed the argument with him. After affirmation of their friendship, the telephone conversation ended and, a short time later, Holmes answered his door bell and Wilson was on the porch.

Dr Robert Hindman, Wayne county medical examiner, ordered the body removed to the morgue and it was subsequently identified as that of Jackie Wilson Jnr.

Three spent twelve gauge shotgun shells, a twelve gauge Spanish made double barrel shotgun, two twelve gauge unspent rifle slug shells, taken from Holmes' flat, were being held as evidence at the Detroit Police Dept Homicide Bureau. A box with a white plastic bag, taken from Holmes' flat, and Wilson's clothing were also being held by police as evidence. According to police information, an extensive search for the killer or killers is under way.

Only weeks before, Jackie had taken Jack Jnr on tour with him to Mexico, where he worked for two weeks at one of Mexico City's biggest clubs. The shooting started as the result of a dispute between Jack Jnr and a near neighbour, Richard Holmes, ten years his senior. Jack Jnr took another man, Robert Jackson, thirty-four, with him to confront Holmes at his house. Holmes apparently expected trouble and came to the door with a revolver. In the panic that ensued, Jack Jnr backed into the shotgun causing Jackson to fire off three rounds. He wounded Holmes seriously in the forearm, but Jack Jnr was caught in the line of fire and was killed.

One report said the dispute stemmed from a disagreement over a sum of money, but it certainly involved the nineteen-year-old girl, who was with Holmes, as well. Apparently Jackie Jnr considered her his girlfriend. Another suggestion is that Jackie may also have known the girl and this had greatly increased his feeling of guilt. This was not possible to confirm.

At the time of the shooting, Jackie's former wife Freda, lived in Toledo, Ohio. Her ex-husband informed her of their son's shooting. "Jack called me from Chicago," she says. "He was drunk and out of it. He was so hurt when he called me. He said, 'Your son is dead, your son is dead!' I said, 'What you mean "My son is dead"?' 'Jackie Jnr.' I said, 'He is not.' He said, 'Yes, he is.' He was crying. I said, 'You're just drunk. Oh, man, you're out of it,' and hung up the phone.

"He must have called his mother. She called me and said, 'He's at the hospital,' and then I hung up. A few minutes later my mother calls and said, 'I think you'd better get to Detroit.' She said, 'Jackie Jnr...' Then I knew he really was dead, 'cause something hit me. I said, 'Oh, wow.'"

A possible reason Freda didn't catch on to the reality of the situation was, at that time, she too was also a serious drinker. "I didn't have no money. I didn't have no ID, which you were supposed to have to get the money. I went down to the bus station. I said to the manager. He could see by my condition; I must be telling the truth and he gave me a ticket. I was like a piece of ice. They told me to go to Detroit. I didn't, I went straight from Toledo to the morgue. When I got off that bus, I knew he wasn't there.

"My mind said, 'He's dead,' but my heart didn't want to say so. I went to the morgue; that was to prove myself wrong. When I got there they wouldn't let me see him, so I knew he was there. I said, 'I'm part of it.' They wouldn't let me see him, though, until my family got there.

"I called my sisters and they came down. They wheeled him out there and took that sheet off his head. My sister said I pulled the whole railing out. I didn't remember anything. His face was all puffed up. The shotgun blast in the back blew him all up. He had a ring with so many rubies and diamonds; they had trouble getting that ring off. Next thing I remember I was at 16522 LaSalle – that's where we lived."

Eldest daughter, Denise, who was nineteen and five months pregnant, had the grim task of officially identifying the body of her brother. Until then, Denise says, "They had him down as 'John Doe'."

"You could not tell which bullet killed him," continues Freda. 'The man was not shooting at him, he was shooting the doorway. Jackie Jnr went down to the house to get him to open to door, but the guy – with his girlfriend – came down with a hand gun. Police surmised that Jackie Jnr saw the reflection of the gun, which was in the back of him. Jackie Jnr backed into the shotgun. Once you start firing you can't stop [due to shotgun's automatic mechanism] and all the bullets sprayed him from head to toe."

Although sixteen when he died, Jackie Jnr already had fathered a daughter. "Jackie Junior's girlfriend, Ladar, had a baby to him when she was fourteen and he was fifteen," says Freda. "That girl looks just like him, and she wears her hair short – just like his. They named her Sandy. Her attitude is bold."

In an interview with Susan Morse of the Detroit *Free Press* (11 January, 1976) Denise said: "My father wasn't an unhappy man until my brother's death. He blamed himself for that. He admitted to me he didn't consider himself a father to any of us. It was the first time he admitted to any of us that he was wrapped up in what he was doing. The things that Jackie Wilson Jnr did were all for 'noticement'. He was saying: 'Notice me, damn it, I'm your namesake.'"

Denise recalls how her father had taught Jack Jnr to keep two nickels with him at all times, "He had these two nickels stuck together for an emergency call. His daddy taught him that." Freda interjects: "Jack always said, 'Make sure they always have a dime to call me.'"

The tragedy devastated Jackie, but, true to form, he didn't go to the funeral. "Jack was a Gemini, they are all sensitive," offers Freda by way of defence. "His father tried to prevent him from being hurt. When Jackie Jnr was shot, he never went down to see him. He couldn't stand funerals. I directed it. He stayed at the house. He had a photographer take pictures of Jack Snr [his father, who had died in 1953] and a photographer from *Jet* magazine take Jackie Jnr in the casket. He had a bust made from the shoulder up."

"Jackie didn't go to Jackie Jnr's funeral," close friend Launa Toledo recalls. "He said, 'Baby, I brought him into the world...I will not stand by and see them put him into the ground.'" Jackie Jnr rests at Lincoln Memorial Park Cemetery, to the north of Detroit, the same cemetery where his father would later be buried.

Perhaps Jackie didn't attend because he realised it could have been him. Denise remembers vividly how her brother looked: "He had on all daddy's clothes, the white shirt with the pleats in the sleeves, that coat, gaberdine. Jackie Jnr was just like Jackie Wilson."

Without doubt, the killing traumatised Jackie. It caused him to reflect on his lifestyle and, for a time, he completely quit his drinking. But, as Johnny Collins reflects, Jackie's relationship with his children had never been orthodox. "He never had children – he had associates," he says. "It was like, 'Can I have, can I have?'" He was referring to the demands members of the family put on Jackie. Another friend, Simon Rutberg, puts it differently: "He liked really young kids, but if they grew up, they became adults. Jackie wasn't there long enough to be a father. As soon as he had a family he'd start another one."

"When Jackie Jnr was shot that nearly destroyed Jackie," says Lynn Crochet. "Jackie kind of put him on the path he was going on and he regretted it. It changed his whole life. It put him down and I think maybe brought him back up. I really feel he was on the way back when this happened. A grown-up Jackie."

Crochet maintains the loss of Jack Jnr shattered Jackie emotionally. "I saw him cry on numerous occasions," she says. "Usually it was about Jackie Jnr, because the girl that Jackie Jnr got killed over was a girl that Jackie Snr had taken home. Jackie felt responsible for that, and he should have. Jackie was a very emotional person. He had a little boy in him, definitely. He was into the occult also. Jackie told me his son, Jackie Jnr talked to him through me. I don't know, I don't remember it. It happened in Houston, Texas. He believed in the hereafter and being able to communicate back with the living. We never really discussed God, but you could always see that it was there."

The tragedy pushed Freda even more towards solace from alcohol but, naturally, this only made things worse. Eliza Mae Lee, Jackie's mother, looked after Freda and the children. Freda converted from Baptist to Roman Catholic and the children attended good Catholic schools in the Detroit area. She felt the church provided her with support throughout this and the other tragedies that would befall her over the years.

Not long after the shooting, Jackie caught up with an old friend, Eddie Singleton. "I ran into Jackie last time when he was working at the Flamingo in Las Vegas – not in main room," he says. "That's when he told me about the shooting. He shared with me that he had gotten off the booze at that point. He talked about it in great depth that night. Our relationship was such he knew I could relate to it. I knew the child, I knew the history. He described it for me. I hadn't heard about it. He looked well that evening. He must have predetermined their destiny when he hadn't provided for them. They were neglected."

By October 1970 Jackie, at thirty-six years of age, wasn't in good shape. He was once again firmly in the grip of alcohol and cocaine dependence, although he could still knock an audience out with his scintillating performances.

That year Jackie was performing at the Black Knight Club in Metairie, outside New Orleans, where Lennie "Lynn" Crochet was working as head cocktail waitress. Aged twenty-six, this native of Beaumont, Texas was dating the owner of the club, who was also married at the time, and used her influence to book Jackie. "I told him to hire Jackie and I was like Jackie's bodyguard when he got to New Orleans," she recalls. "He was drinking really heavy at the time and doing drugs and shit. Jackie and I became real good friends and Ed [the Black Knight owner] got jealous and fired me because of Jackie. There was nothing going on. Just real good friends, 'cause Jackie Jnr had died. But Ed fired me so that's when Jackie hired me as his road manager. Jackie fired his road manager Sims, and let him go back to New York.

"Ed Delduga was heavyweight...he got very angry, and I wasn't allowed in the club. When Jackie went to New Orleans, the bodyguard stayed with me. There was a contract out on my life and Jackie kept buying it off. It was pretty heavy. I didn't know about it at the time, I found out a year later, then I got kind of scared."

Jimmy Smith had been at home in Texas at the time of the shooting of Jack Jnr. "The first show we did at the Black Knight," he recalls, "he did 'Danny Boy' all night long. It really messed him up."

Lynn Crochet hadn't had an easy time with men in her life. Her stepfather, a deacon in the church, raped her when she was twelve and to this day she doesn't go to church. "It was all hushed up at the time," she says. "When I was younger, I was always an attractive, outgoing person and deep in my mind it was because I'd been raped and wasn't a virgin any more." Her first husband was trouble. "I married an alcoholic, and was married four to five years, and I divorced him."

Perhaps something about her invited men with problems. On 27 March, 1971, Jackie and Lynn (née Belle) Crochet were married in a civil ceremony at the Whiskey-A-Go-Go Night Club in Los Angeles. The marriage was never formally registered, most likely because Jackie realised to do so could have left him open to the criminal charge of bigamy.

Lynn was oblivious of the risk. "She really thought she had married him," says Freda. "Jack did this because he thought if he got caught he would not get in trouble. He had already had that one incident [in South Carolina, 1967] and he didn't want no more trouble with those people down south.

"At first an entertainer went to the bigger towns. But then the other people in the smaller towns started wanting to see them. He didn't want them seeing no riot because of a white lady, unless he could show them papers to show he had got married. But she did talk real southern. He didn't want to marry Lynn, either. This was done for his own protection. I think he knew he wasn't legally divorced from Harlean. He knew what he was doing – I think Lynn knew too."

Jackie's second cousin, Horace Spain, witnessed the wedding. He worked with Jackie for eight or nine months in 1971 as his driver. Years later he made a court deposition stating Jackie told the marriage celebrant not to file the marriage documents. Effectively then it was not a legally constituted marriage. Sonny Forrest, his guitar player, was also present. JJ was no longer part of the road team. Jimmy Smith, August Sims and Johnny Roberts, surprisingly, were also absent.

Lynn realised that Jackie had a major addiction problem: "When Jackie was drinking, he was paranoid, because they had abused him. He'd remember that when he was drunk. He wouldn't have trusted anybody back then. I remember when he would go and buy oil cloth and put it all over the room. It was to protect his stuff, so if it moved, he'd know it. It was bad.

"Jackie was a damn instigator; the old shit head. I've seen him pull a gun on a guy to get on his hands and knees and act like a dog. He slapped me a couple of times, but as far as being real abusive to me, he was not. He would slap me 'cause, as I say, I'm a very forceful woman. I'm three quarters Cherokee and I don't stand any shit when I'm drinking – just like him. I get very arrogant when I'm drunk. I can tell you stories of evil things he did, but at that time he was still on the drink. When the drinking stopped it was another Jackie, and that is the person everyone should remember. He did his dirt, but it was the time; the era he grew up in."

Lynn had to suffer more at Jackie's hands than she lets on. At the time of the divorce from Freda in 1965, when she was granted the house on LaSalle, Jackie purchased another home in Detroit for his mother on Strathmoor. It was here that Jackie and Lynn lived whenever they were in Detroit. "We had lived with Mama, off and on, for five years," said Lynn. "We'd go to Detroit to see her and the grand kids and we moved my mom and two boys [by a previous marriage] up there; they had a separate house."

But although Jackie was long divorced from Freda, he still treated her as if she were still his wife, and often it would be Freda's house, not his mother's, where they'd visit. "One time he brought his girlfriend [Lynn Crochet], left her sitting in the car," remembers Denise. "He went in the house. My mother was living with her boyfriend and my father told him, 'Sit down and shut up!' He takes her in the bathroom. They were in there kissing and slobberin'.

"Then he told Tony, 'Go out the car and tell Lynn what I and your mother are doing. I want to see how she reacts.' Tony's the kind of person if you tell him to say one thing, he's going to add some fool thing – make it really juicy. Lynn came into the house. She got mad. She was saying, 'I don't appreciate that. What the hell's going on? What do you think this is?' She looked at my mother, 'What do you think you are doing? You're not married to him any more.'

"He said to his girlfriend, 'Sit down and talk to my mother or something.' He looked at my mom – especially after he gave her one of those 'old times kisses from way back when'. Anyway, mom gets all 'geeked' up by dad's 'slarms'.

"He didn't say anything. He was going to let my mother control the situation. Of course, he had no idea she was going to control it this way. My dad looked at my mother, 'You hear this? You going to let this woman speak to you in your house, about your husband? I mean, what's wrong with you, oh, God.' Again she [Freda] was high. She had a little fire-water in her – a little Indian-water. Man, she beat that little lady so bad. Tony laughed so loud. He [Jackie] said, 'Get her Pee Wee.' Dad was cracking up.

"My mother even moved to stop him doing things like this. She moved to Toledo. So that when he came home he wouldn't see her."

Freda takes over. "He told me I did a good job. And my [boy] friend was sitting over there. He said later, 'What the hell? I don't really understand this. Tell me what's going on?' After this, Jack said, 'I guess I'll gave to take the poor child to the hospital.' He told me he was not married to Lynn, but she wanted to believe. He said, 'Why do you think I brought her up to see you?' He always said about me, 'That's my wife.' He didn't care what nobody else said."

Lynn is more than tolerant of the other women in his past, having no doubts about his feelings for them. "As he grew older, and matured and sobered up, and looked to life and how it was supposed to be, then I think he really loved...for the first time in his life," she says. "I don't believe Jackie ever loved Harlean. There may have been feelings there, but I don't think Jackie ever loved a woman until he met me. Not any deep love. Maybe puppy love."

As well as his wife, Lynn became involved in Jackie's business, eventually as road manager. And things certainly needed managing. "When I got with Jackie he wasn't making that much money," she says. "He was making $5,500 a week."

Jackie, naturally, had the band's expenses to pay out of the earnings, plus accommodation and travel. The bookings agent's fee of ten per cent was paid by Jackie, as well as the management fee. The usual management fee was fifteen per cent, though some suggest Tarnopol was on twenty-five. Jackie only earned so long as he was performing and this wasn't every day of the week. Still, it was pretty good money, with the average American earning only around $150 a week.

The tax return lodged by Jackie in 1969 provides an interesting insight into his earnings. His gross earnings were reported as $106,696.93, with federal tax of $63,745.37 – leaving net earnings of a reasonable $42,951.56. On the same return he listed three dependants: Eliza Lee, Harlean and their son, John.

In Jackie's 1970 tax return, listed under "other business expenses" are some examples of his professional expenses: outside labour $63,950, hotels $18,732, costumes and clothing $6,518, auto expense $5,206, and travel $3,870. A very expensive business, the entertainment business!

By 1971, Jackie's earnings had crashed. His gross earning was $27,074.41, with a tax bill of $6,642.79, leaving just $20,431.62 net.

By the early seventies Jackie had at last woken up to the fact that Tarnopol didn't have his best interests at heart. "He was never going to record for him again," says Lynn. "Once Jackie sobered up he took care of business and had most of his discussions with Johnny Roberts. Jackie found out there were lean times when he had to live from hand to mouth and it wasn't that easy."

It had taken a long time for Jackie to partially break free from Tarnopol, although he was still bound to him through the Brunswick label. Fortunately he wasn't on his own. "They were all in it together," says Lynn. "Tommy [Vastola] and JR [Johnny Roberts] turned on Nat. That's why Nat went down the tubes. Jackie never did tell me what they did, but he said, 'Nat is out of there.'"

Carl Davis, former Brunswick producer and vice president, remembers Jackie's eventual management move. As usual, it was far from straightforward. "What was happening was, at one point, the booking agency that was booking Jackie would require fifty per cent of the money sent into the agency [Queens]. The agency would pay the management money out of that, and then Jackie would go out and perform and get the other fifty per cent. Then, at the end of the month, the agency was supposed to settle up and give Jackie the difference between what he paid the management and what was left of the fifty per cent. In most managements the fee is twenty per cent. He'd pick up his fee in cash. Then he told the agency, 'Don't book me; I'll book myself.' He was probably getting less than he should, but he was getting it all.

"Then they sent Sims out there to collect their share and Jackie fired Tarnopol. It got to the point that Nat Tarnopol said, 'If you don't pay me management money, I'll not give you record royalties.' And Jackie said, 'Fine, I'm not going to record,' and he stopped recording. Nat Tarnopol really treated Jackie like shit."

In September 1970, Tommy Vastola had run into some trouble of his own and was sentenced to prison. The conviction was for conspiracy to extort twelve thousand dollars from two operators of an illegal dice game. In court Vastola and his accomplice were described as "reputed Mafia soldiers", presumably to co-defendant, Simone "Sam the Plumber" De Cavalcante.

While Vastola was "inside", Johnny Roberts took advantage of his absence and started taking a bigger slice of the pie, which in this case was Jackie. Someone very close to the action, puts it like this: "While Tommy was away they started stealing from each other, and money that was supposed to go to Vastola for his portion, for whatever Jackie was doing; they were spending and saying Jackie was making less.

"It was a big mess and the good thing about Tommy, he will tell you, he don't kill nobody because of money. He kills them for principle. So the fact that they were stealing money from him; that just pissed him off."

But Johnny Roberts now was in deep trouble with people above Vastola. He wasn't safe in New York or New Jersey and ended up moving to Palm Springs, California, where Vastola apparently arranged some kind of truce on his behalf. Says the "informed source", "I think that's what happened and that's who probably saved Johnny from showing up in a barrel."

Lynn Crochet firmly believes there were plans to put Jackie back where he'd been at the height of his career. "Johnny Roberts and them were fixing to put him back on top," she insists. "Nat had lost interest. He wasn't giving him the right kind of music, the right arrangements. They weren't keeping him up-to-date. They were holding him back. It wasn't Carl

[Davis], it was that damn Nat Tarnopol, 'cause I would hear Carl and Nat on the phone during the sessions. And Nat would tell Carl what to do."

Although Jackie was not charting in the Top Hundred during the 1970s, he was still a popular performer. While he was still recording for Brunswick, in 1970, he turned in the excellent *This Love Is Real* album in Chicago. Produced by Carl Davis, with arrangements by William "Sonny" Sanders and directed by Willie Henderson it includes a couple of remarkable tracks written by The Chi-Lite's Eugene Record: 'Let This Be A Letter (To My Baby)' and 'Love Uprising' (which The Chi-Lites had a hit with). Another album released in 1970 was *It's All A Part Of Love*, a compilation of earlier releases, generally love ballads.

In the summer of 1971, Jerry Lee Lewis, the former 'Great Balls Of Fire' singer, invited Jackie to appear on the pilot of his planned TV musical program, entitled *The Jerry Lee Lewis Show*. "Jerry came to see us in Nashville or Memphis," remembers Lynn. "He asked Jackie if he would do it, but I don't think Jackie really believed him, because he was drunk. I remember that Jerry fell off the stage because he was drunk."

The largely country music orientated program never went to air in the USA, although full colour videos of the show managed to show up in England. Rock 'n' roll pioneer Carl Perkins made a guest appearance. Jackie did four songs in a mainly country vein and his voice was majestic, especially during a beautiful duet with Lewis.

Having calmed down initially after his son's death, Jackie's addictions were again dominant. "His drug use was only snorting and he smoked a little weed," Lynn says, trying to play it down. "My thing, when Jackie met me, I was on speed. I'm no saint. I worked so many hours, I had to take speed. Jackie had a lot of pressure. I never saw Jackie do drugs, he would go in the bathroom and do it." At his worst, Jackie would gain weight and, in particular his face would become fat.

But as many had learned before her, Jackie wasn't the instigator in drugs although a welcome participant and so Lynn decided it was time to lose the hangers-on. "Jackie, Jimmy Smith and the bodyguard, Henry, got into it," she says. "They was always getting into it. Jackie let people rob him, but when I was around it didn't happen. I made him get rid of the excess baggage. I didn't want all those hoodlums around our children."

One of those to go was August Sims who'd been with Jackie nine years by 1972. He remembers events differently, claiming after being on the road all those years, he was just tired of it. As well, he was tired of seeing Jackie being ripped off. In 1972 Sims asked to remain in Brunswick Records' New York office.

Says Sims of his role: "I took Jackie off Johnny Roberts' ass up at the Renaissance Theatre, New York one day. Jackie jumped into him. I had to take Jackie off his ass. He didn't give Jackie his money. I said to Roberts, 'He deserves it. He played the gig. Give him all his money.' Johnny said, 'We won't have any.' I said, 'I don't care if we don't have none ourselves, give it to him.' I knew where he was coming from anyway. I said, 'I don't need to be bothered with this garbage.' I'll wind up killing..."

As road manager, Lynn was tough with the roadies and musicians and, consequently, not too popular. "When he was drinking he had cousin Horace driving and brother-in-law Johnny Collins doing back-up singing. I said, 'Why should you pay this man, and then you're paying your mom and they are living in the house for free? You're taking care of them twice.' He got rid of all of 'em. Once he sobered up he saw it himself and it wasn't hard. The band had given me a nick-name 'HNIC' – Head Nigger In Charge – because I took care of all the business."

One who didn't enjoy working under HNIC was his guitarist Billy Johnson. For one thing, she was paying Billy, and he resented waiting for his money. Jackie had always taken care of Johnson, who was stable and reliable. "Johnson smoked a bit of marijuana and drank," claims Simon Rutberg, "but he was the guy that Jackie cried to and would say, 'I'm never going to do this again.'"

It wasn't easy for Lynn on the road, either, sharing her husband with thousands of female fans. "I saw the effect Jackie had on female audiences," she explains. "I used to get so upset. I once sprayed mace in the fans' eyes. I've done some shit. It was because Jackie egged it on. His clothes were designed for tearing off. He wore bikini underwear. He had to; he couldn't let it hang loose. I heard one girl tell him one time his tongue wasn't long enough and I went across the table at that bitch, sure did. He was a stud; he had a perfect body."

After so many years, though, even the fans were losing their appeal. "He got to the point that in the last years he wouldn't be kissing on 'em, and stuff," remembers Lynn. "He didn't want them around him. He wanted to do his gig and go home."

While married to Harlean it was unusual for her to travel with him for any period of time, however with Lynn the converse was the case, especially now she was on the payroll. "Everywhere he went, me and Thor went," she says. "All the other of Jackie's kids were jealous of Thor, because they never had that with their dad. He never went anywhere without us."

Thor Lathan Kenneth was the son Lynn gave birth to in March, 1972, taking his name from Jackie's favourite comic book hero. At the time, Jackie was working in Los Angeles and was as nervous as expectant fathers usually are. When the phone call came through from the Detroit hospital announcing the good news, Jackie was with platonic friend, Trina "Cookie" Johnson. "He was doing a show in Los Angeles, on Western Avenue," she remembers. "I had to knock some vodka out of his hands. I had to knock several things out of his hand that night. I was one of the few persons who could do that. He was nervous 'cause he was waiting for the baby to be born. Lynn called him and he was quite excited. The baby was born and he was happy."

Johnson has no doubt that Jackie had found contentment with Lynn. "I'll tell you about how much he loved Lynn," she says. "How he finally... out of all the women he ever knew – Lynn was the true love of his life."

Thor became the apple of Jackie's eye. Quite likely, at the age of thirty-seven, he was at last mature enough to appreciate the simple pleasure of being a father. "Jackie came back to Detroit when Thor was eleven days old and took us to Boston," says Lynn. "We flew from Detroit to Boston and he performed on stage with him in his arms; and introduced him to the world. That's when Thor made his first personal appearance."

It was different to when he performed on the *Midnight Special* concert in California before the birth. "He went out there and got on drugs real heavy," Lynn recalls. "I had to stay home the last six weeks I was pregnant with Thor. He spent all the damn money he made.

"On the other hand when he went to New Orleans he came back with a bed for me, with a red crushed velvet headboard. He treated me like a queen. To show how much in tune we was, and weren't even aware of it, for Christmas he went out and bought me a black and white mink walking coat. For him, I got a black leather suit with black and white yoke in the front. It was strange, we were always doing these things for each other and yet we didn't know what the other was doing. But we always seem to match."

In September 1972, Jackie and Lynn travelled together on his first visit to the United Kingdom, where he was hugely popular, playing to ballrooms and clubs. Jackie was thirty-nine years old and hadn't had a hit since 'I Get The Sweetest Feeling' in August 1968. The song had charted very well in the United Kingdom, not that long before Jackie's arrival. British audiences are very loyal to the rock 'n' roll pioneers, so Jackie had no difficulty packing them in.

Although content with his career, Lynn began to get fed up with Jackie's addictions. "I cared about Jackie," she explains. "My thing was he was killing himself with the booze and all the bullshit, and I wanted it stopped." She decided to leave him after one angry incident. "The reason I left him was he pulled a gun on me and shot it out the back door. You don't do that kind of shit to me. He'd came back from California after doing *Midnight Special*, and he was all messed up. I rang Eliza from Atlanta and told her, 'Tell him my mother had a heart attack and I have to get up there.' That's how I got out of the house. The next day he was on a flight to Detroit to get me. And I wasn't going back. I said, 'Either me, or the booze.' So he dried out for six weeks in my Mama's house. He got me off the speed and I got him off the booze."

Also in 1972 Jimmy Smith, Jackie's friend and drummer of ten years, decided he'd had enough and left. He felt that had he stayed on another six months he'd have been dead from alcohol abuse. He admitted himself for alcohol rehabilitation and claims never to have taken a drink to this day.

Smith maintains Jackie owed him tens of thousands of dollars, but has no hard feelings, being proud to have been part of it. The problem is he wasn't paid a set wage during his time with the band, and even the question of who paid him has a complex answer. "Most times Sims would have money for me," he says, "or I would just go up to Jackie and get it. Sometimes I went to Nat Tarnopol. I didn't have a certain one. Sometimes I went to Johnny Roberts, whatever. Even Tommy."

Smith was replaced by a seventeen-year-old named Johnny Fox, better known by the unlikely nick-name of "Peanuts". Fox was soon into drug taking and the party life and, as such, wasn't much help in getting Jackie straight. But he remembers Jackie not being the only one with a problem. In fact, his memories of the third Mrs Wilson perhaps shed new light on events. "Lynn was as fucked up as he was," he says. "It was crazy, she had just had Thor and she was so screwed up. We were screwed up, too. We were doing everything in the world and she gives us the baby thirty minutes before the show! What am I going to do with a baby? Our problem started with her in New Orleans and went all the way to Los Angeles. She's a real big bitch. She sacked a lot of the guys."

Fox wasn't the only critic of Lynn. While living at the house Jackie had purchased for his mother, Lynn and the family shared the home with Jackie's half-sister, Joyce. The relationship between Lynn and Joyce was strained to say the least. "Joyce hated her brother," says Lynn. "She'll give you a front that she loved him to death, but it's wrong. She was jealous of him, because his mother loved him more than she loved her. He had all the popularity and he was beautiful and she was ugly." But Jackie believed in her abilities, even managing to have her record a song, 'Love Changes Face'. Nobody interviewed had a copy of it, nor was it released commercially.

Because of Joyce, Lynn also ran afoul of Jackie. "She had gotten pregnant and she needed an abortion, but she wouldn't ask Jackie for the money," Lynn remembers. "She came to me for it and I gave her the money. Jackie wouldn't have approved. He was very old fashioned. It was amazing. He fumed at me for it. I said it was her choice, her body. She already had Kelly."

Joyce's husband Johnny Collins was present when the ill will between Lynn and Joyce came to a head. "Lynn confronted Joyce about something stupid and drew her hand back," says Collins. "Joyce hit her so fast her eye was closed before she could get her hand forward. Joyce said, 'Don't you ever do that; don't you ever come at me that way.'

"Lynn ran up the stairs holding her crotch. Everyone said, 'She hit you in the eye, why are you holding your crotch?' She answered, 'I'm trying not to pee.' That's how hard she hit her! The first time she ever got her ass whipped. The biggest black eye you ever saw in your life."

Lynn encountered antagonism within the family, possibly because of jealousy. Perhaps the family members preferred to keep Jackie all for themselves. "Lynn was a liar and a cheat, a thief and a manipulator," according to Collins. "Lynn allowed anybody who had money, and would slip it under the back door, to manipulate the family. Lynn never cared about the family."

But she cared about Jackie and he cared about Elvis, enough to have gone out of his way to see Elvis perform when they travelled to Las Vegas. After the show Elvis invited Jackie and Lynn up to his penthouse.

Lynn says, probably unfairly, "Jackie was the only black man Elvis liked.

It seemed to me Elvis tried to copy Jackie. We went over to see Elvis at his penthouse. Jackie, Elvis and I spent a whole night together. They sat there and sang gospel songs all night. Elvis's back-up singers were there."

Johnny Collins, remembers the evening well. "They sang gospel and talked crazy to each other all night long. Then Jack ordered a breakfast like no two horses have ever seen. He could wreck a table."

Jackie and Lynn developed a personal relationship with Sonny West who, along with his cousin Red West, worked for many years with Elvis as part of the so-called Memphis Mafia. Sonny West was one of Elvis's bodyguards, but also a close friend, and spoke fondly of his association with Jackie. "He told me when I met him, 'You know what? That's my name, Sonny.' I said, 'Really?' That's what his mom and family called him. He told me, 'You'd better be cool because you've my namesake.' Sonny West was there when Jackie went to visit Elvis at the penthouse. "I was there at the Penthouse in Las Vegas when Jackie visited. Elvis did impromptu gospel songs all the time with entertainers that came up there."

Elvis saw Jackie perform again later that month at the Flamingo Hotel in Las Vegas. West then arranged complimentary tickets for Lynn and Jackie to see Elvis perform in Memphis, even though Colonel Parker had a strict policy of not making such tickets available.

While Elvis was making his enormous comeback in Las Vegas to sell out audiences, Jackie was playing the Flamingo Hotel lounge, which seated only around five hundred people, but both camps still looked out for each other. "We were appearing in Las Vegas and came back stage to see Jackie," says West. "A few days later his manager Johnny Roberts said he'd like to speak with me privately, but didn't want to talk on the phone. I went down there and met him at the lounge at the Flamingo during the day. He told me about someone putting down Elvis; being high on drugs and being like a pincushion.

"Elvis, when he was getting that inhalation therapy, he would have the masseur massage him and also break up that stuff loose in his lungs – so he could excrete it. I think the massage was fifty dollars and Elvis would tip another fifty. It was a few months later that Bill was saying these bad things about Elvis. Roberts said, 'Do you want me to do anything about this guy?' I had all kind of visions in my mind about what might happen. So I said, 'No, let me try something first.'

"I called this guy Bill [the masseur] where he was working and said,

'I've just got one thing to say to you. You run your mouth any more about Elvis Presley – you know what you've been saying – do it any more...you're not going to be able to talk to anybody.' He said, 'Who is it, who is it?' I hung up.

"I told Jackie's manager what I had done. He said, 'You son of a gun.' I said, 'Could you have your guy put an ear to it and see if anything's happening?' And he said, 'I sure could.' The guy went over three or four times a week. A few days later he called me and said everything seems to be fine. 'Yeah,' he said, 'My guy tried to strike up a conversation about Elvis...he had nothing to say.'"

The Mob could be useful, but dealing with them was scary. "When those guys tell you something, you have to do what they say. There's no stopping them. Even when they can say they are businessmen, they are very vicious and vindictive. You can be tough and still be afraid of them. I was in a situation like that and told to keep my mouth shut; I did 'cause I had a family.

"They still do today; just more subtle. It's ironic, but that's the way the USA was founded, to be free and all that. Do what you want to do. These sons of guns took it serious and kill people. It's not right."

While in Las Vegas, Jackie took Lynn to see a show, but it was more of a show than he had anticipated. Says Lynn, "We went out with Johnny Roberts in Las Vegas to see Rossi and Steve Martin. Steve was working at a strip joint. Before he came out they had these strippers. Jackie said, 'I wouldn't have brought you here if I'd known.' We were sitting there as red as hell. We thought it'd only be dancers. Jackie was so embarrassed. So was Johnny. I said, 'This is Vegas.'"

Throughout much of Jackie's career, fans had little difficulty getting to him backstage where he'd hug and kiss them and show none of his Vegas prudishness. This changed in the 1970s when Lynn became his road manager. "After Jackie and I got married they weren't allowed to hang around, so much. It got to the point where Jackie didn't even want the people back in his dressing room. Because he quit drinking after we got together."

Lynn credits herself with getting Jackie to quit alcohol. After a lifetime of indulgence, this would not have been easy. "I got him off the booze. I gave him the choice. Either it was me and his son or it was nothing; his choice. He dried himself out. I want him remembered as the good person he was, not the bad stuff that everyone saw him as."

In time Lynn saw her husband over his addictions. Not surprisingly, the effect on his home life was considerable. "We were the perfect family," Lynn says. "Three years without arguing. If we disagreed about something, we'd sit down and discuss it. It was perfect. I wish more people in this world had the relationship that I had with Jackie. He didn't have anything to drink except Diet Pepsi and Viceroy cigarettes, for over three years. He'd have a pack, pack-and-a-half a day."

CHAPTER THIRTEEN

Beautiful Day

For a few years, in the late 1960s and early 1970s, Jackie's brother-in-law, Johnny Collins, travelled with Jackie. Their relationship was often turbulent and occasionally led to blows, but he has admiration for Jackie and, as an in-law, was privy to the family machinations. He also saw, on the road, both sides of being an international star.

"There were so many people who loved him and so many people who hated him at the same time, who wanted to control him," Collins remembers. "Like this cop in Texas, he hated him 'cause his wife was in love with him. And he beat his wife to death and got away with it.

"Jack and I would switch rooms; he would get a suite and I would get a suite. I would wake up and there'd be women coming in my room. They would pay like twenty, fifty, a hundred dollars to come into the room. I was dead asleep and all of a sudden there's these boobs coming at me in the night! 'Who is this, who are you?' They would say, 'You ain't him.' I would say, 'No kidding! No shit!'

"This woman said, 'What did you do to him?' and emptied her gun; I had a pillow with four shots in it. My head was on that pillow only seconds before. When I told her I was his brother, all of a sudden her drawers are gone. It was like, 'If he's not here, you'll do.'

"He took shit from everybody and survived it over and over again. He got stomped down and he came back up singing. He got beat up and he came back singing. He got whipped and he came back singing. He got sued and he came back singing. He never quit singing. He was true to his profession. I watched them beat his ass and they told him, 'You have to go out there and, if you don't, I'll kill you.'

"They had me outside in handcuffs. They'd kicked my face in. He sang like an angel...bloody as hell. He cracked notes. It was as clear as a bell, with no anger, no hurt and no pain. He did it. He said to me, 'You must separate yourself from your job.'

"I watched him sing with cracked ribs, a cracked jaw, with a gun to the back of his head, 'cause he was supposed to sing at a party for this little girl whose daddy was the law. There was two ways they did it. There were band members and Jack with guns to their heads. Jack said, 'Shoot me.' They answered, 'What about these kids, we'll shoot them too.' Jack said, 'That ain't fair.' They said, 'We ain't about fair.'

"One time they busted his ribs and he went out and did two shows. He left Louisiana and went into Texas and he was with a woman who was not of colour. The local police beat him up. He got stomped. He went on stage bloody. The police chief wanted to degrade Jack because there were two women in the audience who adored him. Do you know what it was like for a white man to find out his daughter, wife, sister was totally in awe of a black man in the south? They were still lynching then. You have to sing to these bitches, they are sluts and whores. The Klan will 'take care' of them. The chief of police said, 'I don't care what else you do, make sure he walks out on stage and shows those other niggers who are upstairs.' They were separated. He had to walk out on stage with the blood on his shirt. They said, 'I don't care what else he does but he does the full show.' And he did.

"Jack said, 'I want to thank the assholes that kissed me tonight,' and they were out in the audience. He said 'thank you' after they beat him up. He said, 'You made me know I could do it – even though I was tired.' He went right down stairs where the paramedics were waiting and they took him to the hospital, 'cause he was bleeding internally. The Texans said, 'Well, the nigger deserved it.'"

It wasn't only Jackie who was victimised. "We went to a club where they had cut off the electricity," says Collins, "because they were trying to harass the black club owner. They put candles on the top floor. We sang in darkness with only a drummer. We did two shows. Sold out! They brought corn whisky. These people had no money. They just wanted to see him. He sang for the lowest of the low and the highest of the high; and just as hard. He was down to earth. Everybody loved him."

Some loved to control him. Collins, who was a martial arts exponent, had difficulty with Johnny Roberts. "I used to open for Jack, and then I sang [duet] afterwards with him. Johnny Roberts was a Mafia bastard, a Mafia chieftain. Jack was supposed to go on stage, but he got sick. I said, 'Jack, take a few minutes and drink some water.' Johnny Roberts said, 'Who the fuck do you think you are to tell him anything?' He said, 'Who are you to walk up to me and say anything?' He hit Jack in front of me. And he took a swing at me; I body slammed him and snatched the gun from his belt and threw him in the trunk of the car. I cracked two of his ribs, and I slammed the trunk on him. When I jumped on Johnny Roberts, you know I knew who he was – I didn't give a shit. Jack said, 'You are out of your mind. Nobody ever challenged him.' Jackie'd been ripped off, raped, beaten and the first time he ever saw anyone stand up to Roberts was me. Roberts said, 'I want him dead by tomorrow morning.'"

Collins was now in serious trouble: "They tied me up and took me out of town. They told me, 'How far can you run in two days?' I had two days. I said, 'Guess what? I'm going to Detroit.' When his friends got back there I had one thumb – and haven't had another one since. They set fire to my car; they thought I was in it. I was stabbed in the stomach and the back." He returned to his home in Detroit, rather than try to hide.

"Johnny Roberts was Mafioso, straight up. Everybody knew that. He said, 'No nigger ever put his hands on me that I didn't kill.' I said, 'Guess what? I don't give a fuck about you, and if you come after my family I'll tear your head off and your family, too. There won't be a member of your family left to fight over.' I don't back off and don't quit."

Remarkably, Collins claims there was another time he challenged Roberts and lived to talk about it. The incident revolved around Launa Toledo, whose house Jackie often visited whilst in California. Says Collins: "Launa told Johnny Roberts: 'Kiss my ass.' He drew his hand back and I put a gun to his head. He said, 'You got away with it twice.'"

"Launa once asked Roberts how many bodies he'd put in the river this week. He answered, 'The barge hasn't come in yet, so I don't know.'"

Collins knew the Mob owned Jackie, just as they owned Sammy Davis Jnr and other entertainers. "Jackie was on three percentages," says Collins, "on the table, above the table and below the table. There were gigs we did he was paid cash. He immediately sent Nat his money, or handed it to Johnny Roberts...always in cash. You booked to do two shows, you did five. They [the Mob] would take a big percentage. They didn't give a shit about talent. They use calculators that never stop counting. They will not allow you to threaten. They will pull up the root. If you weren't protected, you were used. There was no in-the-middle."

Collins' stories about Jackie could not always be verified and seem nothing short of extraordinary. He says: "I had $63,000, carried it all over the country in my clothes, for him. He told me, take it here, take it there. I didn't do anything wrong. We were in Metairie, Louisiana – in the head of Klan country. We were in the Hilton; he hid the money in the curtains. We went on to Atlanta and I had to go back to Louisiana and undo the seams to carry the money back myself." Large sums of money being transported around with Jackie wasn't usual, and why he entrusted Collins with it wasn't explained."

Collins also reckons he knows the root of Jackie's great fear of flying. "He had just talked to Buddy Holly [in 1958] – Holly had asked him if he'd do the short tour with him. That would have been super-major money. He'd said, 'Yes.' The next call he got was that Buddy Holly was dead."

Lynn sums up what a lot of others think of Collins: "He's nothing but mouth. He was on the road with us in 1972. He has a vivid imagination. I can see Jackie slapping the shit out of Johnny Collins, because he didn't respect him at all. Jackie was paying Collins for back-up singing and still supporting his fucking wife. Collins wasn't giving Joyce Ann nothing. I said to Jackie, 'This really sucks, you're supporting him and his family.' I said, 'It's time that he went,' and he fired him."

Collins indicates he left of his own volition, after being offered a recording contract: "In 1971, when they said they were going to offer me a contract and undercut Jack I left. I left her and left him. That was 1972. That's when the 'hit' was on me and I got stabbed. They wanted to put him under control again. That was the year he got the new Ford T-Bird. Jack was just taking off again. That was in Nevada.

"Jack said, 'You're a traitor.' I said, 'But I didn't take the offer.' He said, 'But you talked to them.' Twenty minutes after I spoke to him he came down the stairs and said, 'Stay away from me, keep away from me, they are going to kill me because of you.' The majority of my money I never got."

Collins still harbours resentment towards Jackie and, especially Lynn, for dumping him in 1972. "You know what Jack liked to do? Fuck; that's it. If it was a pretty girl. He thought he's above everybody. He was a country boy who liked to do two things; sing and fuck!" Perhaps Collins should have said "three things", because he adds, "I'm telling you. He could out-drink the average two or three sons of bitches that called themselves drinkers.

"It was never about drugs. He wasn't into that scene. The first time they hooked him up with cocaine it was a trick. They hooked him up with these chicks and it was like his dick wouldn't go down. He said, 'Wow, you mean I can fuck *forever?*' He said, 'I can handle this.' It was not true. Jack had several massive nose-bleeds behind Nat. He beat it for years and years, and then he got it pushed to him through the company. He didn't do it on his own 'cause he wasn't into it."

Collins claims that during this period Jackie was earning $1,700 a day, but that it was costing that much for the cocaine he was supposedly getting from "the company". "You know what made me walk away from it? Their price? Two hundred dollars a day worth of shit. So where did the $1,500 mark-up come from? It wasn't from the quality, because they had the purest quality. They got it straight from Central America." He claims "the company" was supplying the cocaine to Jackie, thus keeping him reliant and broke.

"Peanuts" Fox shares a similar opinion of Collins to Lynn. "There was a lot of bad blood when 'brother John' came along," he says. "I'm talking about kick your ass, 'Get out of there. Don't get on the stage, don't sing.' For a while there John 'the Pelvis' Collins would get on the stage there and tried to outshine Jackie with his little dance routine. Jackie didn't like that, but Collins would always ride on Jackie's coat tails. Collins could hold a note at times, but he wasn't the originator of nothing.

"Jackie would hate the fact Collins left his sister. He never forgave him for that. There was a lot of bad blood there. He never liked him. Can you imagine Jackie having him stay on after Collins kicked him?"

Fox found ways to niggle him on stage. "Collins was very hot headed on stage. He'd say, 'Hit me two times,'" meaning two drum beats whilst he was performing, "and I would only hit him *one* time and *forget* the other one. Naturally that made him look real stupid. Guitarist Larry Blassengame would always say, 'What's going on here?' I said, 'You know what's going on here.' It was crazy man.

"Me and Collins got into it a few times, too. Karate? I do nine millimetre! Jackie said if I killed him, I'd be in a lot of shit. I said, 'Oh, what the hell?'"

Fox wouldn't confirm Collins' assertion that Jackie had hit Blassengame in the head, perhaps causing him a permanent injury. "Jackie hit a lot of people around the head for a lot of reasons." One of these victims was a hotel manager. "We took it over," he remembers. "Jackie pulled the manager of the hotel over the counter and kicked his butt for turning the phones off. That's the first time I ever saw him really box. You couldn't knock him down. So he was a little hot headed, but who isn't? But if things were that bad, he didn't need no help from people who were supposedly taking care of business."

For Jackie, the show had to go on, regardless of what mayhem may be going on around him. "Jackie was shot at a few times," Peanuts recalls. "I remember one time in the south, something broke out. Guns were fired, tables turned over. There was Jackie, still singing. When it all cleared off, Jackie got on the stage and said, 'Well, ladies and gentlemen, there's always a little difference of opinion around here. As the song goes, Baby Workout...' and he'd go on singing as though everything was quite normal. I thought, 'Shit, let's get the fuck out of here and before we get killed.'

"We got into a big gangster thing with [jazz saxophonist] Grover T Washington. That was up in San Francisco. We didn't want to play a third set and they threatened Jackie. It was in-fucking-credible."

In the 1970s Brunswick had moved from the Brill Building on Broadway to 888 Seventh Avenue, nearby. Tarnopol employed Joel "Joey" Bonner as Brunswick's promotions man. His arranged to take Jackie around the country, doing personal appearances; particularly on TV and radio. However, Jackie had a "bad boy" reputation, often not showing for interviews. Bonner needed to improve Jackie's image with a view to getting more radio airplay.

Bonner explained: "When I went over there to work with Jackie he wasn't radio friendly. He was notorious...he wouldn't do [media] spots. Nat was also afraid if he made appointments, Jackie wouldn't show up. When I first started, that was one of the first things I had to do; to mend the fences. A lot of radio stations wouldn't play him. I said, 'Listen, Jackie, first of all your image sucks out there. It's terrible. We've got to go on the road two weeks and say 'hello' to radio. Now if you don't like to do it, just tell me and I can get out of it. But if you commit to me to do something and you don't do it I will leave you out to hang to dry.' He said, 'Joey, if I give my word to do something, I'll do it.'

"The people around him, didn't understand the importance of radio – they weren't record people. They weren't in tune to PR. We went on the road, the first month I was there, for two weeks. Went all through the Carolinas, Chicago, St Louis, Detroit, Cleveland, Pittsburgh, and we stopped and talked to radio stations. He did interviews and he cut what they call radio ID spots, things like that – and he was beautiful. Didn't miss one thing. I was lucky, no question about that. In those days the jocks would talk to one another and the word got around. Radio was really friendly to him again that was in the 1970s, sometime. He did everything I asked of him. He would also call the DJs on the phone.

"I remember one time in Atlanta, he was so drunk, we had to put him in the tub...bathed him and he was still drunk. We put the clothes on him and got him to the gig and we just threw him on stage. For about a minute and an a half it took him that long to realise where he was, then the instincts took over and he put on a hell of a show.

"He knew how to work the audience. He wore great suits and silk shirts, and when they got wet they'd cling to his body. The sweat would roll off him. He was exhausted when he got off. He was the 'baddest' son-of-a-bitch on stage. Basically not even Sam Cooke could hold a candle to Jackie, performance-wise."

Off stage Jackie was far from in control as Bonner, like most other witnesses, points out. "Jackie had all vultures around him; he was surrounded by vultures. That was his big problem in life. Those that he didn't hand out to stole from him. They weren't friends they were all vultures. His valet, Frazier, he was basking in his glory. They would order suits and Jackie was paying for them. They all looked dynamite and they were all blowing his money. But Jackie was that kind of guy. Jackie was in the pitfall of all entertainers. They all think it's never going to end. The problem is, *it ends*; it ends for all of them."

Because of his cavalier approach, even Bonner found Jackie wasn't easy to manage. "I've seen Jackie blow many a date," he says, "and, if he did show up, he'd show up late. Frazier and JJ they couldn't do anything to control him; they couldn't make him get up. Jackie was that kind of person. Bad luck...he self-destructed by himself. And bad luck about those around him – it was like – everybody was going to get what they were going to get.

"Jackie was just irresponsible. He had no conception of the rent's due, telephone bills due, this or that is due...and the people around him made sure he didn't know. I blame them more than him, because he wasn't bright so far as money goes or any thing like that. It was just a sad, sad situation. The wrong people behind him. The managers around him wouldn't let him have financial advisers, because if he got someone who was truly interested in him they would have been knocked out themselves."

Regardless of what might have been, the truth is that the power Jackie exerted over his fans amazed Bonner. "Jackie had a way with women, and with people. I remember one night at the Regal Theatre in Chicago. After he did the show there was a line of people there for autographs. There must have been a hundred or two hundred people. He signed those autographs and kissed every girl. I mean *kissed*.

"Sometimes I've seen JJ and Frazier get nasty to his fans; and he'd get angry with them. 'They're my fans, don't fuck with 'em.' He was a strange dude. There's no question; he had a magnetism.

Despite Bonner's best efforts, in the 1970s Jackie was not selling many records. It may well have been that the fickle record buying public had moved on to a new sound because, listening to the recordings Jackie made after 1970, vocally he was still as good as ever.

Larry Maxwell, formerly a record promoter with Atlantic and Motown, thinks the problem was Brunswick didn't successfully promote Jackie to the lucrative Pop market. He says: "The last time I saw Joey Bonner he said, 'I'm going to tell you, Larry, I'm a good promotion man, I make a lot of money promoting records. But I'm going to tell you the truth, I have never promoted a Pop record.' I was surprised. People always hired him to promote black, so he never had to do good. Brunswick never promoted their records. They never paid anyone to cross their records over."

Regardless of promotion, many of Jackie's records did cross over. An appearance on live television certainly would have helped. In Oakland California, Jay Payton is best known for his role as host to the annual "Entertainers' Awards", which has been going for around thirty years, but for over four years, between 1972 and 1976, he hosted *The Jay Payton Show* and Jackie was his very first guest. "He sang on the show," Payton recalls proudly. "My show was eleven o'clock in the morning. He said, 'Jay, you'd be one of the few people I'd get up in the morning for. I didn't know people got up this early in the morning.' He put on some kind of show. He was one of the all time best; he was superman. He was always the same and he never forgot...if he knew you from somewhere he always knew you. He was one of my favourite people; straight down the middle."

He was many people's favourite. On and off since 1960, when they first met, Lynn Ciccone had kept in contact with Jackie. She'd often flown out to wherever he happened to be, and would spend two to four days with him. In the 1970s her husband was dying of cancer and Lynn was in need of money. During that period, Jackie wasn't well off, but despite that she says: "Jackie gave me $2,800. He continually kept in touch with me, he knew where I worked that's how we kept in touch. He'd call me at work or at my mother's."

To this day, Lynn treasures her time with Jackie and thinks of him daily. Apart from the memories she treasures the gifts he gave to her – a pearl ring, two diamond rings and a pair of diamond earrings.

Launa Toledo also began as a dedicated fan in 1965 who became a close friend of Jackie's. She also became a friend and confidant of Harlean's. "Jack was one of the warmest people to me. He was like a big brother. If I had a problem I could tell Jack. Even if I had marital problems, I'd tell him and he'd go talk to Rudy. He settled many fights between us.

"The first time he ever brought Lynn [Crochet] over he said, 'I'm coming over and bringing somebody with me.' I said, 'What's she like?' He said, 'Well, like you. She looks enough like you to be your sister.' She is the same size as me. I've known Harlean for years, I said 'Don't ask me to pick between 'em, it's not fair. I'm not going to get in the middle. I love you, Jackie, no matter what happens I'm not going to get in between your women.' He respected that and said, 'Well, fine.'

"One night I had just come in and I looked out the window and saw some limousines drive by the house. Jackie always got lost coming to the house. He'd usually go into another house and use the phone. I'd have to go and find him. Anyhow, it was Jack.

"As he was running up the grass slope, he got grass stains all over his white pants...and he had a show to do that night. So he comes in the kitchen. Rudy comes in just behind him. Jackie takes off the pants and hands them to me. They were woollen bell bottoms. He says, 'Throw 'em in the washer.' I said, 'They are going to be able to fit Thor, for Christ-sakes.' He took off his shirt and said, 'Throw this in, too.'

"My neighbour could look right in the window, and so she called me. She's a Mormon lady, Leila. I said, 'Yes, Leila.' She said, 'Do you know there's a man standing in your kitchen?' I said, 'Yeah, and if you are looking real good you can see he hasn't got any clothes on.' She hung up on me! Within the month she put the house up for sale. I swear that was the reason."

One summer's evening, Jackie decided to hold an impromptu party at Launa's house. "I remember coming home one day and seeing a big truck in front of the house," Launa recalls in disbelief. "I walked in, there was Jack and the entire band including instruments. I said, 'What are you doing?' Jackie said, 'We are going to have a party.' He gave me five hundred dollars and said, 'Go and get some stuff, and make a pile of spaghetti, too.' I went and bought everything. He opened up all the windows, then went to all the neighbours and invited them on to the front lawn. He was unbelievable. The mayor even came. At the party, Jackie performed for everyone."

Jackie did other crazy things, says Launa. "He'd lay out on the patio in the back. I said, 'What the hell are you doing?' He said, 'Getting some sun.' 'Why?' He said, 'You know, right now black is beautiful, and I'm beige.' I said, 'You're weird.'

"To drive in the car with him was the most frightening thing in the world. Oh, my God. He would go up the wrong side of the street. If they weren't going fast enough for him he'd go over to the next lane, straight into on-coming traffic. If he wanted to drive on the side-walk, he would. He was the world's worst driver. I'd say, 'You're not driving my car.' He said, 'I'll buy you a new one if I wreck it.'

"Then he'd get on the bikes with my the girls to go to the store. Jackie would sit for hours and play with my daughter. She'd had five major eye surgeries; a birth defect. She couldn't play outside."

Whenever Jackie performed in California, Launa would catch the show. She says something that nobody else has mentioned. "When it came to lyrics and he'd forget and get a stupid look on his face and look down in front to me," she says. "I'd usually be front centre and I'd mouth the words.

"He did the same on the *Midnight Special*. He got on there and forgot the name of his next song. Lynn [Crochet] was sitting in my living room. She said, 'I don't believe he's doing this.' They asked him, 'You have a new record out don't you?' He said, 'Yes.' They said, 'Well, what is it?' He said, 'I can't remember.' Lynn goes, 'You idiot!'"

For Jackie to forget suggests him being under the influence of drugs. Lynn claims he definitely was high while performing on *Midnight Special*.

When in California, Jackie preferred to stay at Launa's house rather than a hotel, because nobody knew where he was and he wasn't. But most of all he would be amongst close friends and he enjoyed Launa's home cooking. "He would still check into a hotel," explains Launa. "His name would be there, but he'd be with us. He said they can call there all day long, for all I care, they're never going to get me."

Unlike many others, Launa seems to remember a high number of "fun" incidents involving Jackie. Most of the time he was enjoying himself, but occasionally he was motivated by others. "He came out one night, he had on a black pants and a black shirt, and my daughter had on all black. I said,

'What are you doing?' He said, 'We are going out to steal a dog.' I said, 'What are you talking about?' He said, 'The guy down the street beats on the German Shepherd all the time. I tried to buy the dog from him. He wouldn't sell it, so we're going to steal it.' I said, 'Jack, you can't do it.' I said, 'If you get caught, Jack, it's going to make every headline in the business.' He said, 'I can,' and he did.

"Jackie called [promoter and artists' manager] Walt Cohen and told him, 'Get a kennel cage and get it over to Launa's. I want you to ship this dog to Detroit to my mother.' And that's what he did. He stole the dog! They got over a six foot fence to get the dog.

"That's Jackie for you. Couldn't stand for something to get hurt. He never forgot where he came from. He was good to everybody, that's unless you crossed him! If so, he usually called up JR [Johnny Roberts] and had him handle it."

Jackie loved dogs. Launa recalls receiving one as a gift from Jackie. "I had one of his puppies. He bought a Cocker Spaniel show dog, Sorry. He called me from Tahoe. He said, 'Would you do me a favour? Could you pick up this six to eight weeks old puppy? Two weeks later I got a phone call from New Orleans. He said, 'I bought the puppy for the girls and paid for a handler to train it.' He called it Sorry because it had lonely teardrops. He'd take the dog on the road when he was in California. He'd sit it on a table while he was singing."

Launa's memories of Jackie include a few demonstrations of his wit. "He used to say, 'There's only one thing faster than a nigger.' I said, 'What's that?' He said, 'A scared nigger!' It was all right for him to say it, nobody else could. He was a crack-up. He liked to tell jokes, but he couldn't. He would start to tell you a joke and he'd think about it and start laughing. He laughed so hard that when he told you the punch line you couldn't understand it. He was a funny man."

Sometimes Jackie and Launa went to the market or store which brought him into contact with the public. "It drove him up the wall if people walked up to him and said, 'Aren't you, er, Johnny Mathis?'" says Launa. "He'd say, 'No, Jackie Wilson!'"

Occasionally, though, recognition would be just what the singer needed, although he didn't realise it at the time. "One time I went to the flea market. He didn't want to go. He said, 'People will jump all over me.' I said, 'It's so busy, nobody will notice.' So we went and got all the way through. A guy spotted him and people started walking over to him. He was his usual amiable self. He said later, 'I'm kinda glad it happened, for a while I thought nobody recognised me.'"

Even Launa, like everyone else who loved him, became exasperated with Jackie. "He and my husband would go out and I told them they had to get in by a certain time," she says. "This one night I locked them out. They came home and went into the patio around the back. I could hear they were both drunk, trying to get in. There was a doggie door. Jackie was trying to get in the doggie door, to get in the house! They were singing, 'Don't you step on my blue suede shoes.' I thought the neighbours might call the cops. Jackie said, 'I've got a key here, it might work.' That's how drunk he was. I jerked the door open and they both fell into the hallway.

"I was mad and went to bed. Rudy went to sleep on the couch. Later, I heard a bunch of noise, so I went down to the kitchen. There was Jackie with a fry-pan and flour from asshole to breakfast time. Oh my God! He was wearing a shocking iridescent blue outfit, and he had flour in his hair and his face and he was flouring pork chops trying to fry them. He looked like a ghost. He said, 'I'm starving, nobody feeds me.' He would do things like that; he was a crazy person."

Launa also confirms what others indicated: that Jackie didn't like to be seen eating in public, or even with anyone he wasn't intimate with. "He didn't like to eat in restaurants. We'd go out and he wouldn't order anything. He would order just before we were leaving and he'd take it 'to go'. I said, 'Why do you do that?' He said, 'Haven't you noticed? Look at people when they eat, it's so ugly! People putting stuff in their mouth and chomping on it; it's an ugly thing.' He said, 'Invariably someone will come in and stare at you and it turns my stomach. I'll just take it home and eat it."

Home cooking was special to him, whatever the time. "Another thing he'd do is call me, say from Chicago, and it would be three in the morning, my time, six where he was and he'd say I'll be there at such and such a time. 'Can you have some Yankee pot roast ready for me, with potatoes and carrots or ham hock, Lima beans and corn bread ready? And potato salad.' I'd go out and get it. I'd say, 'Okay, Jack.'

"I called him Jackie, Jack, depending on the mood. He'd call me Inch High Private Eye. I'm not short. He used to say, 'If I'm on this planet, this one can find me.' I could put myself in his mode of thinking and I'd find him, if I knew he was in a particular region."

Jackie's past influenced his dietary habits to varying extents. The 1961 shooting had left him with one kidney – "I always had to have Bran Flakes for him, because of that" – and after he gave up alcohol, Pepsi was de rigueur, but only if it was unopened – just how he'd been with booze.

"He would never drink anything that someone else opened," says Launa. "If he said, 'Bring me a Pepsi,' and you got it and opened it, he'd look at you and get up and pour it down the sink. He'd say, 'I asked you to get it, not open it!' It came from one time someone had put something into his drink in Texas. When he drank Scotch, he drank Chevis Regal and he'd keep that bottle with him, even as he walked around the hotel room. If it was out of his sight, he wouldn't touch it. If he went to the bathroom, it went with him! He'd get a fresh bottle if it was out of his sight."

In other areas Jackie was as open as a child. Once he took a fancy to one of Rudy's expensive Di Chichi green and gold shirts. What he fancied, he had to have. "Jackie would always try to steal my husband's shirt," Launa laughs. "When we knew Jackie was going to come, Rudy would go to great length to hide it; it was a game. Jackie would come in and say, 'By the time he comes home from work, I'm going to have that thing on.' Jackie would go through that house and when Rudy got home Jackie would have that shirt on. When Jackie would get ready to leave, Rudy would go, 'Ah, ah, open those suitcases, right now!' Invariably that shirt would be in there. I have pictures of him with the kids and wearing that shirt. It might end up in the Rock 'N' Roll Hall Of Fame."

Clothes were often the source of amusement between the three friends. "The funniest time was when the chauffeur forgot to put his wardrobe bag in," recounts Launa. "We got to the club and he didn't have pants to put on. Jackie had a muscular chest and so took the same size shirt as my husband. He turned to Rudy. He said, 'Rudy, take off your pants.' He said, 'I won't.' Jackie said, 'Take off your pants, damn it! I have to go on in five minutes.' He puts Rudy's pants on and they fell off of him. He had a tiny waist and absolutely no rear end. He turned to me and said, 'Take off your pants.' I said, 'Jackie!' He said, 'You've got black pants on...take 'em off.' He wore my black pants on stage. I was about a size seven then. I stayed backstage."

Launa became aware of a little cues trick that Jackie's drummer, Jimmy Smith, had in order to know exactly when to coincide with Jackie hitting his high notes. "When he did 'Danny Boy' he'd do the 'Ave' two, three, or maybe, four times. He'd work up to that last high C. Each time Jimmy would give a roll on the drums. One time I said, 'Jimmy how do you know when he's going to bring it home?' He said, 'You don't really want to know.' I said, 'Yes, I do.' He said, 'I watch and watch his ass. It's the way he moves his rear end. I can tell when he's going to do the final one.'"

Launa clearly got more of the best of Jackie than many others did. He obviously felt comfortable with her. "Jackie was an amazing person," she concludes. "He made life great for everybody...except himself. There wasn't a mean or unkind bone in his body. At least not to me; I never saw one. You'd have to do an awful lot to be his enemy."

In 1973 Lynn Crochet and Jackie co-wrote a very personal song concerning Jackie's addictions. It was recorded and released in November 1973, with the beautiful 'It's All Over' as the B-side. Lynn claims she wasn't aware that it ever was released. "I know where Jackie did some recordings in United Sound Studios, Detroit that I don't think Brunswick has their hands on yet," she says. "We co-wrote a song 'Your Jones Is Too Much For Me'. I know he recorded that song. He never got paid for it." The song Lynn claims to have co-written was actually the last single release before his heart attack, and has to be one of the few bad songs Jackie ever recorded. Entitled 'Shake A Leg', it credits Jackie and Sonny Sanders as co-writers.

More fruitfully, in 1973 a young songwriter and singer called Jeffree Perry wrote an entire album on his own for his long time idol. Even though Jackie was years beyond his gigantic hit making days, the resulting *Beautiful Day* album truly is beautiful.

Like many things in the singer's life, it came about through a chance encounter. "I was in Detroit at the time working with Invictus Records with my brother Greg," recalls Perry. "That time Greg had hits with The Honeycombs group. I was assisting him in that regard. I was also working with the soul group Chairman Of The Board. My uncle, Robert Bateman's group, The Satintones, was the first group to ever record on Motown. My uncle used to do a thing with Sonny Sanders. Sonny was doing the charts for Motown and Jackie. He did 'Whispers' and 'Higher And Higher'.

"Sonny ran into my Uncle Robert and said, 'Have you got anything for Jackie Wilson?' I was in the studio cutting some things myself. Originally some of those songs Jackie did on *Beautiful Day* I was going to record myself. I had just got out of the group Hundred Proof Aged In Soul. We had just cut this song 'It's All Over, Because Now I'm Back'. Sonny took the demo tape to Chicago. Brunswick producer Carl Davis and Sonny got a hold of it and I think the next day they cut it, because they were crazy about it." (It appeared on the *Beautiful Day* album in March 1973 entitled 'It's All Over'.)

Perry continues: "About a month later, I decided to check out what was going on in Brunswick. Carl Davis wanted me to do a whole album with Jackie, which was a first, it had never happened, and we did it. Jackie was trying to break away from Nat Tarnopol and this album was going to be the album to do it."

With magnificent arrangements by Sonny Sanders, Jackie performed Perry's gorgeous songs to absolute perfection, but the album had minimal sales. "Then 'Beautiful Day' came about," says Perry. "We used Sonny Sanders, got all the Motown musicians; James Jamerson, Eddie Bongo, Joe Hunter, Earl Van Dyke – all those cats flew to Chicago. In my opinion, the best musicians that were ever assembled in the world were the Motown musicians."

Perry was extremely disappointed at the album's absolute lack of sales success: "After that I don't know what happened. I just know it was sad. I thought it was a great album. It just wasn't promoted properly. I think it was Nat. He didn't want Jackie to have success at that time, because Jackie was making arrangements to leave Nat. He wanted to break out on his own and try some new things." Of course, at the time, Jackie had managed to wrest management away from Tarnopol, but he was still tightly bound to the Brunswick label and it would seem Tarnopol had totally lost interest in furthering Jackie's career.

Regardless of sales, Perry is unstinting in his praise for Jackie: "In terms of what I thought of Jackie Wilson; there were two people who revolutionised R&B, pop, soul, like no other performers and, in my opinion, they were Jackie Wilson and Sam Cooke. I thought in terms of performer on the stage...Jackie Wilson. I've never seen a performer ever, to this day. Michael Jackson is fine, but his is choreographed. He doesn't compare to what Jackie Wilson did. Jackie was a natural. He just could make up a step and entertain on the spot.

"In my opinion, Jackie was the greatest performer ever...that I've seen on stage. I also think that in terms of singing voice, Jackie was one of the greatest singers. He was somewhat mis-cast though, because he had an operatic voice; he could sing opera. Jackie didn't have to have a microphone.

The wonderful thing about Jackie – he was a high tenor – he never had a bad performance; he never sang off key. Out of all the times I saw Jackie, I never heard him flat or miss a note when he went after it. That's unique!

"Jackie epitomised what it meant to be a recording artist. Jackie was entertainment, twenty-four hours a day. Even when he wasn't on the stage, he was on the stage. And he was a regular person. That's the truth. He was an artist's artist."

Perry also credits Jackie with advances in black rights and Berry Gordy's record empire. "Jackie was a civil rights leader," he claims. "He did a lot to make the conditions better for black recording artists. They had a tough time, especially down south, getting accommodations, the whole bit. Jackie and Sam Cooke helped, but especially Jackie. He was quite outspoken and had a very fiery personality. He was a star and knew he was a star, and wanted to be treated as such. He fought about it. In my opinion, it's by design that Jackie has not received the type of popularity he should have.

"If it hadn't been for Jackie Wilson there wouldn't be a Motown. Jackie was a star in Detroit before he knew Berry Gordy. Jackie was the first major star from Detroit. Jackie was the hero to Smokey Robinson, David Ruffin, all those people.

"I listened to Jackie today. I think it's a shame a lot of people do not know his contribution to the record world. That's what's missing today, everything sounds alike, especially in black music."

Beautiful Day was to be the second last album that Jackie recorded. In 1974 he recorded his twenty-eighth and – he didn't know it – his last. *Nobody But You* again was a beautiful and unique, contemporary recording. So poorly distributed was it, that the people closely involved in its making believed it was never released. It was in fact released in early 1976.

By 1974, at forty years of age, Jackie had lived a fast life and smoked a million cigarettes. Nevertheless, as Lynn Crochet says, "His voice was in perfect shape on *Nobody But You*." The studio recording Jackie did for the album was done by the method known as "tracking", which means his voice was laid down over a previously done music backing.

But Lynn is one of those who believes the album wasn't released. "I was at the last two recording sessions," she says. "They would lay the tracks and we would go to Chicago and he would do the vocals. It didn't matter to him whether it was live or not at that point in his life. To me, the last album was the best thing he ever did." Lynn may be a little biased with her final comment, but it is a fine album.

By this time Jackie and Tarnopol were not on talking terms and it's amazing that it was ever recorded at all. Says Lynn, "Everyone hated Nat – it amazes me he got so far. It got so bad there in the end that he wouldn't even take Jackie's calls. Jackie had to talk to him through Johnny Roberts."

John Trudell, a Motown trumpet player on *Nobody But You*, also denies the album's existence in record shops. "The album wasn't released to the best of my knowledge," he states. "It was done at United Sound Studios in Detroit. Jackie wasn't at the session; I believe he was ill. He put his voice on top of it later. I may have been there two sessions; six hours in total."

The record sleeve credits list that the album was produced by Carl Davis and Sonny Sanders, and directed by Sanders. Sonny remembers the project. "Carl Davis arranged to do *Nobody But You* in Detroit," he says. "I don't know why. It may have been because of the Motown rhythm section. Promotion is probably the reason some of the albums have not been heard."

Davis agrees. "*Nobody But You* was recorded in Detroit. Jackie and Nat had fallen out. It wasn't properly promoted."

The arranger for the album, Motown arranger David Van de Pitt, was also a talented bass and trombone player. "This was the first and last time I ever ran into Jackie at all. We had never crossed paths. We were led to believe the album never saw the light of day. Certainly everyone I know never knew it was released. I think the reason it was recorded in Detroit had something to do with Don Davis [the owner of United Sound Studios]. Or maybe it was because it was to use the rhythm section guys from Motown."

Around late 1974, Jackie, Lynn and the family moved to 2116 Hidden Glenn Drive in Marietta, Georgia where they bought a new home. Apart from two-year-old Thor, Lynn's two adolescent boys, Arty and Randy, lived with them, each with as much of Jackie's love as his blood son. "I've even got a piece of paper where Jackie said 'change their name to Wilson'," says Lynn. "Jackie loved them as much as his own." In fact the inspiration for the move was to protect all three kids. "The reason we moved to Marietta in the first place was to get Thor and my boys away from that environment."

Once Jackie was clean himself, his old lifestyle seemed unattractive to him. This new outlook even extended to his own family, in particular to his doting mother. "Once Jackie sobered up the closeness wasn't there," Lynn recalls. "He would be laying there right beside me and tell me, 'Tell her I'm not here.' Usually she called when she wanted money. She liked to play her numbers. Him and his mom were super-close; until he sobered up. There were times he'd say, 'Tell her I went to the store.' And he'd be right there with me. I felt bad about that. That was my husband, so I had to respect his wishes. Eliza Mae took care of Freda's children and the grandchildren. When I knew him, he was always sending her money every week."

The sober Jackie was even beginning to plan sensibly for the future, something he'd never done before. "Jackie bought several acres of land in the country for when he retired," explains Lynn. "He planned some dog kennels up there and to build a house. We were going to start a kennel and raise Maleneoas. We had Miss Spicy and Loci, and the people we were going into business with, their dog was named Thor. We bought the property. I lost it when Jackie got sick; I had to use the money."

Their home life was the usual domestic scene revolving around the children and, for relaxation, Jackie liked to take Thor to the zoo or picnics, or to watch movie re-runs, especially Westerns. He loved some sports, particularly boxing and football.

Of course there were his comics, especially the *Captain Marvel* superhero kind, which Lynn, too, had grown very fond of. Says Lynn, "We both liked our comics; *Thor, Tales Of The Crypt.* We liked the stories. He didn't have all the record albums he'd made." Apart from that, he talked to lots of people on the phone.

Lynn jokingly called Jackie "Leroy" or "Nigger". He hated his middle name Leroy, but took her jibe with good grace.

Meanwhile, Jackie still had financial problems. The Internal Revenue Service had a lien over his earnings from Brunswick for unpaid taxes. "Jackie still had IRS problems in the 1970s," says Lynn. "He would go to his accountant [Isidore Silverman] in Detroit who took care of it. He was a pal of Nat's. Everyone on the payroll was a friend of Nat's."

As if that weren't enough, Freda took her own legal action for unpaid maintenance payments. "All that time I filed he was supposed to be paying me all the money," Freda remembers. "At the time Tony was going to Chrysler mechanics' school. I got a judgement; he owed me fifty thousand dollars. I gave them Jack's entire itinerary...Tony knew it. My lawyer says they won't put him in jail.

"Tony told us his daddy's address in Atlanta, because he'd been down there. Lynn cursed him out because he was going to wear his daddy's ring and one of his chains and go out somewhere. Lynn called him 'a bastard'. She said, 'You put them back here, now!' She hit him. He said, 'I'm going to tell my daddy.'

"When Jack came back to the house, he said, 'Lynn, did you slap him?' And she knew he was mad. She's in there crying. He said, 'I don't care about no chain!' Tony was mad when he came back and told us.

"Jack had been sick and then he never sent the money. That's why he was so far behind. He was supposed to give me ten thousand dollars, because I didn't want no support, because I could work. But I needed the money to pay for uniforms and the kids' tuition...it kept going up. Jack kept telling me he didn't have any. I kept hearing about Lynn buying houses and this and that. Jackie Jnr had set our house [on LaSalle] on fire; in the attic, everything burnt real bad. I didn't have that kind of money. So the court sent some detectives down. When they went down there, Jack jumped out the window."

Freda was down to such an extent, she couldn't make mortgage payments on the LaSalle home and it was re-possessed. She moved into the YWCA, while Jackie's mother took care of the children at the home Jackie had purchased at 16886 Strathmoor, north of Detroit.

"Lynn called me at the 'Y'," continues Freda. "She said, 'Honey, I don't appreciate you sending the police to my house.' I said, 'Who's this. She said, 'Lynn Wilson.' I said, 'This is Freda Wilson you're talking to, and as long as my husband owes me money, I can send them anywhere.'"

At the time Tony stayed with Jackie and Lynn he was seventeen years old. Lynn had difficulty getting along with him: "We had Tony living with us in Atlanta. He's such a pig...he's sitting back. The only thing he wanted is money."

Jackie's family wasn't the only one to stay with them. Lynn's sister, Linda Cannon, shared the Marietta home with Jackie and Lynn. She says: "I always thought the world of Jackie. When I was growing up in Texas you talked to black folks, but you never had nothing to do with 'em. I think this way: God made everybody.

"I said to Jackie one time, at least one wish has come true; I always wanted to see you sing. He said, 'You always knew a good singer when you heard one.' I said, 'Oh yeah, is that it?'

"Jackie would go out and say he's 'the black Elvis'. Elvis came out and said he was the 'white Jackie Wilson'. Jackie's voice had such a range; operatic. I never heard anyone could sing like him before. Elvis sings good, but I think Jackie was the greatest singer in the world. When you went to concerts, he made you feel like you knew him for years and years and you only just met him."

According to Linda, Jackie of the 1970s was the perfect family man. "If more men in this world were like that man, this world would be a better place."

As Launa has already testified, Jackie's appetite was enormous – "Lynn cooked for that man all the time. She'd cook five, six, seven, eight things at a time – and he still didn't like eating out. "Jack was a pig when he ate," says Lynn. "He enjoyed his food, he savoured it, but he didn't make no noise. He ate like a horse. If he did a one night stand, he'd call me and give me what he'd like by the time he got home. We'd have three or four different meats, three or four vegetables, plus dessert and that still wouldn't be enough. He'd bring home something else."

When Thor was only three-and-a-half years old, Jackie and Lynn took him on tour to Pueuto Rico. "Thor performed with his dad. A born ham. He was stealing the show from his dad," says Lynn. "One time in Florida I had him in a short white suit and red socks. He told his dad, 'I'm not getting down on my knees so my mama will whip my butt.' They had a role where they'd go down on their knees. I had people call me and say, 'What night is Thor coming down to perform?'"

Thor was on tour with Jackie while Lynn was well into the term of pregnancy with their second child. In August, 1975, the last of Jackie's children was born. "I called to tell Jackie about the birth of Li-nie, but the doctor had called before me and he knew what he had," says Lynn.

Lynn and Jackie named her Li-nie Shawn. The name Li-nie is Cherokee for "little one", while Shawn is Irish for Jack; Little One Jack. They received cards of congratulations from Stevie Wonder, Gladys Knight and Red Foxx. Singer, Wayne Newton sent a big potted plant from Las Vegas.

At the time Jackie was busy once again performing with Dick Clark and his *Good Ol' Rock 'N' Roll Revue* revival show. But this was one child he wasn't going to forget. "Jackie used to call her and sing to her three times a day, and then when he got in from Vegas he spoke and she turned her head. She knew that voice," reports Lynn. "I caught him in the bedroom with Li-nie on his chest and telling her she was his second life. He would lay her on his chest and talk to her and he'd have her for hours and say, 'Well, you're my second chance, baby. You and Thor are my second chance.' The night she was born he went on stage and announced, 'I'm a new father.' He was never close to his other children like he was with Thor and Li-nie."

While Jackie enjoyed performing with Dick Clark, to the outside world he was accepting his age; why else would he be relegated to the "oldies circuit" in the mid seventies. He still had all the talent, but the fickle record buying public was looking for something new: this included "the sound of Motown", ironically comprised of artists who had grown up listening to Jackie! Simon Rutberg, who had been a friend and dedicated fan of Jackie's since 1962, witnessed the cabaret tour. "The last time I saw Jackie mid September 1975, in Las Vegas, he was sitting with Johnny Roberts," he remembers. "It was really sad, he was completely dejected. A man so lost. He was on Dick Clark's show. But he was great. I said to him, 'Why don't you go to another label? Go to Motown.' He said, 'We are shopping labels.' If he'd lived something would have happened.

"Jackie was an extraordinary artist, that's why he had flop records, not because songs were necessarily bad. He needed a more powerful vehicle. When it was man to man, as opposed to on stage, Jackie Wilson was the greatest and the big shots in the business knew it and had to admit it. Because if they didn't, their buddies would say, 'You ain't shit compared to Jackie!' Elvis knew he wasn't shit compared to Jackie. James Brown never wanted to admit it and probably still won't."

Others remember Jackie's slide into relative obscurity. "The last time I came into contact with Jackie he was working for twenty-five cents on the dollar," says Thomas "Beans" Bowles the Motown arranger. "The last time I saw Jackie [around August or September 1975], he was in his decline. I think it was at Maurie Becker's Bar, here in Detroit, on Gratiot Road. I think Mary Wells came in to see him. He wasn't doing too good. I did a performance with him at Phelps. In fact he came to my house, we fed him and he rested. We talked about the good old days and he worked. He was still trying to recreate his dream. Then he went to the east coast."

Another horn player who had worked with Jackie throughout the years was Motown musician, Mike Terry. "I saw him in Atlanta in 1974 or 1975. He recognised me right off the bat. He was really down. My wife said, 'Who was that you were talking to?' I said, 'Jackie Wilson.' She said, 'Who? Looking like that!'" Jackie not only knew he was unbelievably talented, but also needed the world to acknowledge it. But in 1975 the world was beginning to forget that Jackie Wilson had ever even existed.

But even in 1975 he was still on the road exciting his audiences and making enough to feed his family, with a little besides for the Internal Revenue Service.

Guitarist and friend Billy Davis had left Jackie's band and been replaced by Ricky Starn. The last time Davis saw Jackie was early in July 1975 when Jackie performed at Detroit's Masonic Temple, just before he left to tour in England and Germany. Davis, who had put on a fair bit of weight over the years, remarked to Jackie how well he looked: "He told me he was strictly clean, that he was totally off [drugs]. Didn't drink or anything. It was amazing how good he looked. Hadn't looked that good in fifteen years."

Freda, too, went to see Jackie perform at the Masonic Temple. "I said, 'Come on Sandy. We are going down there to see your father.' He owed us all a fortune. He owed each one of them fifty thousand dollars.

"He was singing 'Higher And Higher' and he saw us coming. He smiled and reached down and pulled Sandy on the stage. He was reaching for me, so I went to the back and sat on the table back there. He kept singing on the stage with her. He said, 'Ladies and gentlemen, this is my daughter, Miss Sandra Wilson.'"

While Lynn was expecting Li-nie, Jackie and wife made their second visit to the United Kingdom. "We went to Germany first," says Lynn. "He performed the US air bases there. You should have seen the way they reacted towards him over there. They were tearing his clothes off and everything. I said, 'They aren't suppose to act like this, that was twenty years ago that they acted like this.' It was a trip."

A few weeks later Jackie was in Philadelphia and went on Jerry Blavat's TV show. Says Blavat, "When he come into town that last time, I went to see him. He had a son named Thor. He didn't perform, but he spoke with me live for half an hour. It wasn't taped. Jackie said to me what he was looking to do was produce more and develop talent. He wanted to start his own label. He said there were not too many people who had the feel for the music of the 1950s and 1960s. At that point it was psychedelic and protest music."

In the last part of September 1975, Jackie was special guest on the coast-to-coast *Merv Griffin Show*. Nobody, least of all Jackie, knew this would be the last TV appearance the great performer would ever make.

CHAPTER FOURTEEN

It's All Over

D ick Clark, through his influential *American Bandstand*, assisted Jackie in achieving fame by inviting him to perform on his nationwide – even worldwide – TV programme. When Clark put together a nostalgic rock 'n' roll revival tour, Jackie was the obvious choice to head the bill.

"The *Good Ol' Rock 'N' Roll Revue* tours were a series of engagements," Clark recalls. "We started off with them in 1973 in Las Vegas, and took the concept to the Latin Casino at Cherry Hill [New Jersey]. Jackie was a huge star with the black audience and a moderate star amongst the white audience, who were into rock 'n' roll at the time. He hadn't reached the gigantic levels of being an idol that he should have – I can't imagine why.

"When we did those shows at the Hilton and the Thunderbird in Las Vegas, Elvis Presley came in again to see him, because I guess he'd seen him before. Jackie was an influential man; people copied his every move. Later on Prince and Michael Jackson admitted they'd studied Jackie. Anybody that wanted to put on a show looked at him; he was the consummate performer.

"In the seventies, we were both a lot older. He'd been through a lot of personal torment in his life, but he was on his way back. We were just a couple of reasonably mature guys making a living. We didn't rehash the old days. I didn't talk about girlfriends or children or anything; we were just doing our job."

In 1975 it was seven years since Jackie's last hit, however he could still hold a note as well as ever and audiences loved him. Prior to the New Jersey engagement Jackie had headed the bill for six weeks doing the same show at the Thunderbird in Las Vegas. His contract for his one week engagement at Cherry Hill was "c/o Queens Booking Corp", with him earning $7,500 for the week, for two performances a day. Quite a reasonable living.

And Jackie was living reasonably at last, having seemed to have shaken off his bad habits. "I had no difficulty getting Jackie up on time," Clark admits. "By then he was completely straightened out; clean of any addictions he'd been into. He still smoked like a fiend, however. Always on time, two or three standing ovations a night and we used to grind those shows out two or three a night in Las Vegas, like clockwork.

"Jackie's act was four to five numbers. The show had to run to one hour seventeen minutes, or so. We had to turn them in, turn them out, and get them back into the casino. There was no fan hysteria or lots of noise screaming and yelling; this was a casino audience."

Co-incidentally, Terry Gray, who produced for The Coasters, was flying from Florida to New Jersey for the show's opening there the next day. The plane went via Atlanta, where Jackie boarded the flight. Lynn Crochet had to stay in Atlanta because daughter Li-nie had been born the month earlier, on 10 August.

Gray had known Jackie since 1965 when they first met in Las Vegas, so he asked the stewardess could they sit together. Jackie conversed happily along the way and Gray recalls, "He was very up. He talked of his wife and kids. We got in late at night." Jackie's driver, Billy Wilson, collected them at the airport.

The next evening was opening night of the show, featuring Freddie Cannon, Cornell Gunter and The Coasters and Dion Di Mucci, and after rehearsals Gray and Jackie met for dinner. Jackie, Gray noted, was a different man from years before, he wasn't drinking any more and seemed normal in every way. However, all was not well. "The night of the show he ate a steak and it didn't settle well. He also had vegetables. He wasn't feeling too well; he talked about eating and going on stage."

Jackie had developed a headache and said he was going to lie down for a while, prior to the show. Eating prior to a performance was not his normal regime. Although Gray didn't say so, the dinner guests also included manager and promoter Walt Cohen, and Tommy Vastola who lived in New Jersey.

Jackie almost made it through his act. On the night of 29 September, 1975, opening night, he was well into his last routine, which was his signature tune, 'Lonely Teardrops'.

But, as Dick Clark remembers: "As soon as I saw him fall I knew that I'd never seen him before do that. He fell backwards, hit his head on the stage and was in the throws of going into the coma. It looked like part of the act, but he never got up. The irony of it was that Jackie was singing 'My heart is crying, crying,' and did the splits and so forth. It was probably the worst memory of my experience in the entertainment business.

"Cornell Gunter of the Coasters tried to give him mouth to mouth, but it didn't help. None of us knew CPR [cardiac, pulmonary resuscitation]; it's probably some of my guilt coming forward."

Promoter Walt Cohen was in the audience. He said, "I heard his head crack on that floor."

Clark called for the curtains to be drawn.

The most detailed report on the tragedy was carried in the 6 November, 1975 issue of *Rolling Stone*, by Lou Gaul. In it he reported:

> Jackie Wilson was performing an energetic version of his biggest hit, 'Lonely Teardrops', when he grasped his chest, sunk to his knee and fell to the floor. The audience clapped and the orchestra continued playing for about thirty seconds, thinking the fall, which occurred as Wilson sang the words "my heart" was part of the act. Horribly, it was an all-too-real heart attack that has left him in a coma...and in 'very critical' condition.

It's highly exceptional for an athletic, forty-one-year-old man to have a heart attack, particularly mid performance, on stage. More extraordinary that he was doing 'Lonely Teardrops' and singing the lyric, "My heart is crying, crying", so reminiscent of a Greek tragedy.

The *Rolling Stone* article went on:

> Thinking that the singer had fainted, Clark rushed to his side. Unable to revive him Clark called into the audience for a doctor. He then began sobbing and asked the audience to "offer prayers" for Wilson.
>
> As others tore at Wilson's leather jumpsuit and began to massage his heart, Cornell Gunter, flamboyant lead singer for The Coasters, administered mouth to mouth resuscitation. "I looked down at Jackie and said, 'If you're okay, blink.' He blinked twice, and then his eyes rolled up in his head and all I saw was white."

"I remember that terrible night in Jersey we removed all of his jewellery because they thought they'd never see it again," said Clark. "I've got no idea where it ended up." It is indeed a mystery. Jackie had a twenty dollar gold piece around his neck, a gold bar, a watch, a gold bracelet and a diamond ring. Lynn Crochet should have been given the jewellery, but wasn't. It is said Johnny Roberts was the last to be seen with it. He is supposed to have given it to Harlean, although she claims not to have received it.

The ambulance medic, Bud Lauer, who attended Jackie recalls seeing some of it, although he had bigger things on his mind: "He had a twenty-four carat gold bar on a chain around his neck: I remember seeing that. I don't recall any other jewellery. When we got to the hospital, I didn't see it. We never found it."

Jackie, the superb vocalist and performer in the prime of his life, was struck down. The question now: would he survive, or was it the end?

In such a medical trauma the crucial thing, when the patient's heart stops beating, or breathing stops, is the amount of time taken to restore those functions. After only a few minutes oxygen starvation will lead to permanent brain damage.

In an exceptional stroke of good fortune, the ambulance quickly arrived, as *Rolling Stone* magazine reported:

> An ambulance that had stopped at a nearby hotel for an unrelated illness rushed Wilson two miles to Cherry Hill Medical Centre, where a team of six doctors worked on him for twenty-five minutes before obtaining any vital signs. "He came in here with no pulse, heartbeat or breathing," an emergency room doctor said. Although a team of three doctors stayed with him throughout the night, he lapsed into a coma.

This is where events become clouded. One strongly held theory is that Jackie's head had struck the stage and he had suffered severe concussion. Possibly he had fainted or had a minor heart attack, which caused him to collapse. Bud Lauer, in ambulance number 131, was highly trained and very familiar with heart attack victims; he is certain Jackie wasn't one. His belief is that Jackie was a head trauma patient. In other words, Jackie's unconscious state was due to a head concussion. Lauer maintains that Jackie was breathing and doing well enough, but, to his amazement, when they arrived at the hospital he was immediately given de-fibrillation (electric shock heart therapy), which encourages the heart to regain normal rhythm. Indeed, the hospital records show Jackie was given de-fibrillation nine times that night.

The report in *Rolling Stone* magazine quotes "an emergency-room doctor" as saying: "He came in here with no pulse, heartbeat or breathing." Unless Jackie's prognosis changed within a minute or two, the statement was in sharp conflict with that of the ambulance medic.

Lauer's recollections of that fateful night are very clear and troubling: "The call was for a heart attack. I don't know how long it took to respond to the Latin Casino. There was no traffic going on the route to it; I do not recollect any traffic. I don't think the race track had racing in the evening [it was 10.30 to 11.00pm]. I was in the back of the ambulance. I don't recall delays.

"When we arrived at the Latin Casino, there was a nurse on stage. She was doing CPR; she was doing compressions and providing ventilation – mouth to mouth. I don't recall a [oxygen] tank being there when I arrived. Everyone was excited and emotional." There was no medical person on duty at the concert, but it was fortunate that the nurse was in the audience.

"Our response time was two to three minutes. Dick Clark was on stage most of the time. But no evidence of anything [having caused the collapse]. I checked to make sure the tongue wasn't dropped back. Someone advised her [the nurse] to step aside, that the emergency squad is here. You can't [shouldn't] transfer or do a two-man rescue. When you start [CPR] you are not supposed to stop; you should not stop [chest] compressions.

"Right at that time I checked his pulse; *I had a strong pulse*. She [the nurse] was away from him. *He was not breathing*; I did mouth to mouth. He continued to not breathe on his own. The pulse became weaker.

"He was on his back. I don't know if he'd been on his back. I didn't notice any blood, but in checking the victim – his eyes, etcetera – I was told he had a heart attack. In doing that you don't check for broken bones. We had no idea whether he collapsed, or fell forwards or backwards.

"He had a pulse, which is important; so there's no need to do CPR. In fact you should not do CPR, if someone has a pulse; you go against the heart. You could damage the heart. We did not do compressions on Jackie. He was getting blood; he was not blue around the mouth. All I know he was not breathing. He was unconscious. He was not blue; he did not have loss of oxygen, because I was breathing for him. I was doing mouth to mouth on him on the stage, on the way to the ambulance, inside the ambulance – until I got the demand flow, which is an oxygen forced unit in the ambulance [a respirator].

"When you do mouth he only gets about sixteen per cent oxygen. With demand flow he gets full oxygen. He did moan; he moaned, and moaned again. He breathed twice or three times. We had to help him breathe. He wasn't able to speak or open his eyes. His chest cavity was expanding and contracting. He was getting oxygen; he was not at all blue.

"We were moving quite well; it was hard to stand up. At the time we did not have facilities for blood pressure. If that had happened now, it would have been a lot easier. They are quite well equipped. They have medications that medics can administer. Back then, no.

"He had a pulse all the way to the hospital, but he wasn't breathing on his own. We had to ventilate him all the way to the hospital."

So far things would seem to have been going well for Jackie, although at the hospital situation was soon to change dramatically.

Says Lauer, "Cherry Hill was the closest." Being only minutes away, that's where Jackie was taken. "I am not a doctor; there is a lot of things that could cause a person to stop breathing. It could be an aneurysm in the brain that causes that particular motor skill to stop. But in heart attack, stopping breathing is common; your heart stops. The heart could stop beating, slow down, or fibrillate [quiver; causing irregular contractions of the ventricles in both rhythm and force]. Medical experts suggest that with fibrillation the heart will continue to pump blood, though not effectively around the body. This would lead to reduced oxygen to the brain and, if this was to occur for a sufficient period of time, brain damage would result.

"I lost [responsibility for] him at the time we opened the back door of the ambulance. He was not blue. It wouldn't be my position to claim that he was, or not, DOA [dead on arrival]. He was not in cardiac arrest. Even in fibrillation the blood is still moving. I checked his eyes; they were equal and re-active, they were not constrictive [indication of no stroke]."

As to the possibility that Jackie could have been poisoned or drugged, Lauer had no way of ascertaining: "It was not possible to know. At the time there was no paramedics; EMT [emergency medical treatment] was just coming in. All we did was ventilate him. His colour was good; his fingernails were fine. He was getting the blood when he should get it; he just wasn't breathing. In my opinion it would not indicate a heart attack. I don't know why you would not breathe, but the heart would pump. At that time and today I believe he did not have a heart attack. He had respiratory failure, caused by whatever. Could be a head injury, a drug."

Lauer is equally certain that Jackie's condition was not as a result of a stroke, as some have surmised. "It's very strange the whole thing. His eyes were fine, even; which would indicate no brain aneurysm or stroke, anything like that. His pupils were equal, okay. They weren't constricted. They weren't big. The stroke comes up with the eyes. One responds, the other doesn't.

"The man, in my opinion, did not have a coronary or a stroke; he did not. Something happened to cause him to stop breathing, period. He had stopped breathing. He had a pulse...the blood was flowing. His nails were fine.

"What happened inside the hospital I can't say."

In fact, what happened at the hospital was that Jackie was given an electro-cardiac thump immediately he was admitted. This treatment calls for an electric shock to be administered to the patient's chest to enable the heart to beat in a normal rhythm. If Lauer is correct, that he had a strong pulse from Jackie, then this would be entirely an inappropriate course of action. The likely result would be to cause the beating heart to fibrillate.

The likely cause of Jackie's collapse may have been an embolus, a substance in the blood stream which causes a blockage in a blood vessel. This would generally cause temporary loss of consciousness due to either heart or brain malfunction. In the case of an embolism (obstruction of a blood vessel) being so critical as to lead to the bursting of a blood vessel in the brain, this condition is referred to most commonly as a stroke.

Lauer was surprised that the first thing that was done was a electric pre-cardiac thump, even though he had not been de-briefed as to Jackie's symptoms. "Normally they would ask what was wrong, or else an examination would be made prior to the electric pre-cardiac thump being administered. At that time they would ask what happened."

According to Lauer the correct time when a pre-cardiac thump is administered is "normally at the first instance of arrest. I saw them administering a lot of medication – injections into the rib cage." As medical emergency staff attest, a lot can happen to a critical patient between the ambulance and the emergency room, so to be fair to the medical staff it must be said that Jackie could well have suffered a further cardiac arrest on admittance to the hospital.

Although no longer responsible for Jackie, Lauer did stay around for a while in the emergency room. "There were twenty to twenty-five people in there. I remember them cutting his leather suit and fringe. Dick Clark was in the hospital emergency room – he was very concerned – he was standing there at the foot of the bed in the examination room. Cornell Gunter was out in the hall."

The official Cherry Hill Medical Centre report, dated 15 December, 1975, says the following:

> Jackie Wilson was admitted to Cherry Hills Hospital on 9/29/75 in a comatose state. He presented with ventricular fibrillation. Immediate cardiopulmonary resuscitation was started with external ventilation, with the insertion of an endotracheal [by way of the throat or the mouth] tube. He was defibrillated six times in the Emergency Room and three times in the Coronary Care Unit. His status was so critical that he required intracardiac [heart injections] Epinephrine as well as Vaspressors [to counter his shock state and to control blood pressure] for support of a shock state.
>
> Subsequent EKGs [most likely ECGs; electrocardiograph – a machine for recording the potential of electrical currents that traverse the heart muscle and initiate contraction] showed evidence of acute myocardial infarction. It was my feeling that an acute myocardial infarction precipitated ventricular fibrillation, causing the cardiopulmonary arrest leading to a shock state with reduced cerebral profusion [perfusion? – the passage of liquid through a tissue or organ], followed by cerebral oedema [swelling] and compression of vital centres leading to an initial comatose state.
>
> Neurological consultation by Dr Leonberg's group, first seen by Dr Vanna: his feeling was brainstem damage and he made the comment that in view of the history of cerebral anoxia with the resultant edemas [oedemas] and brainstem damage is likely.

Jackie Wilson also developed an initial shock lung state requiring a volume respirator and intensive pulmonary therapy.

While in the hospital, he required a tracheostomy and developed pulmonary infection as well, treated with antibiotics.

I was able to wean Jackie Wilson off the respirator. At this time I am having difficulty closing off his tracheostomy because of a great deal of retained secretions. Except for his initial frequent episodes of ventricular fibrillation, his rhythm remained stable with anarrythmic medication.

As I mentioned earlier, he was initially in a deep coma. Now he does blink and moves his eyes spontaneously but no response to visual or auditory stimuli is present. He does tend to withdraw in response to noxious stimuli. There is no sign of the presence of higher neurological functions. He seems to be functioning at a brainstem level. The patient is not capable of talking or understanding verbal or written language. Therefore he is not competent to run his own affairs and a legal guardian could be necessary.

The authors of the report were Allan Fischer, DO, Stanley Leonberg, MD, and Donald Auerbach, MD. They were saying, in effect, that Jackie's brain had swelled to the point of inducing coma.

Not long after Lauer and his colleague had delivered their important patient to the hospital, he received a call from there asking him to drop by and speak to one of the doctors. This was highly unusual, but he went. "One of the doctors did call us," he says. "I don't recollect his name. We were asked to come up to the intensive care unit and we did. He asked a few questions. I thought it was strange that the doctor should be asking me what happened to him. I don't know why he was asking me – after it's happened. We make out a report on every call we make. They are only required to keep these for seven years."

Lauer also had enough concern to drop by the hospital and inquire about Jackie's progress: "I didn't go in to visit him one to one. I went to inquire how he was...on my own. I was given a very cold reaction, 'We can't give any information.' I left." When he finally heard of Jackie's sad condition, he says only, "I was disgusted."

Personal manager, Johnny Roberts, quickly arrived at the hospital and took charge. Launa Toledo says, "The doctor said to Roberts, 'I'm afraid he's gone.' JR held a gun to his head and said, 'You'd better hope he isn't, or you're going with him.'" It was not possible to confirm this story, or otherwise, though those who knew Roberts say it is true to form.

Toledo also recalls discussing death with Jackie on one of the many occasions he visited her California home: "Jackie used to say, 'Baby, you can't kill a nigger unless he wants to die.' And he said, 'There's only one of two ways I'm going to go; either on the stage, or in bed having a good time.'"

August Sims, although not present at Cherry Hill the night of the collapse, is highly suspicious about Jackie's heart attack, firmly believing it was induced. "Johnny and Tommy Vastola," he says, "you could count on them two doing something for money, 'cause them motherfuckers are hungry. 'Cause they wanted Jackie to sign with Dick Clark. Jackie wasn't going to sign with Dick Clark. Dick Clark is a lousy son of a bitch, he should have been in jail, instead of what's-his-name [he may be referring to DJ Alan Freed]."

It is not clear what Sims may be alluding to here. Jackie was already signed to Dick Clark, and there's no indication of his being unhappy with this. More likely he wanted off the Brunswick label. Clark did have his own record labels in the 1960s, but probably did not by 1975.

Tarnopol and six other Brunswick executives had been indicted only three months earlier on charges that included taking kick-backs from record retailers, wire fraud and cheating the Internal Revenue Service. Jackie would have been called to testify against Tarnopol, whom he loathed.

Brunswick faced a torrid time. "Yeah," agrees Sims, "with the Mob, Brunswick had a lot of shit in there and they [the federal authorities] were looking down on [interested in] his [Tarnopol's] ass, too. Nathan didn't do much because he's scared to go across the street. 'Cause Tommy – he's in jail, you know – 'cause they were looking down on him and he's part of the Mob."

Asked whether Jackie had been victim of a murder attempt, Sims was more circumspect: "I think so; I figure he might have been, unless they gave him too much cocaine." Sims thinks it more likely that Jackie had been drugged in order to give him a fright; to bring him back under control. "I think so and it back-fired on their ass – it killed the kid."

Sims was quick to visit Jackie in the hospital. "He was in coma and he knew me," he recalls fondly. "We always squeezed hands to see who could squeeze harder. We did that; when he squeezed my hand, I said, 'That son of a bitch knows who I am. I felt sorry for him, boy. I said, 'August, you should have stayed out there.' If I'd have stayed a couple of years, he'd still be living. 'Cause I wouldn't let that son of a bitch [Roberts] do nothing to him."

As Sims suggests, friend Joyce McRae, suspects the collapse was the result of a scheme organised by Tarnopol. "Tommy Vastola begged and pleaded to take the contract on Nat," she says. "They wouldn't let him do it. They said, 'Leave him alone.' He wanted to take Nat out himself, personally. Corky [Vastola] loved himself and Jackie Wilson."

Some time after the heart attack, Carl Davis had occasion to phone Tarnopol. The conversation shocked him: "The thing I remember is Tarnopol," Davis says. "I called him one time; I was trying to get twenty thousand dollars for something, and he said, 'Listen, Jackie's in the hospital, I've got this one million dollar policy. Don't worry about it, because as soon as he dies our pockets will have the mumps.' I said 'What? I don't want it that bad.' I went to Brunswick because of Tarnopol, no question about it; I liked something about him." By this time, though, Davis had changed his opinion.

There was indeed an insurance policy held by Tarnopol, supposedly for one million dollars, payable on the death of Jackie. However, this is entirely appropriate for a label to hold such cover. In any case, Tarnopol never collected as the policy lapsed prior to Jackie's death.

Regarding insurance, Dick Clark was more fortunate. "The terribly irony is that, of all the thousand shows I'd put on, this was the first that I took out Workmen's Compensation," he admits. "We used to do upwards of 150 concerts a year and I don't know why. And that was the only funds there was to pay for his hospitalisation. I can't imagine what they were, but it wasn't nearly enough."

Lynn Crochet was at home in Atlanta with their seven-week-old daughter Li-nie. On receiving the news of Jackie's collapse she was obviously shocked, and all the more so because of a recent medical report. "Jackie had a physical here in Atlanta three months before Li-nie was born [or approximately five months before the heart attack] and the doctor that did the physical was a gynaecologist, who was a personal friend; my doctor," recalls Lynn. "He had saved Jackie's life when he was an intern in New

Orleans, because Jackie had walking pneumonia, and he did the physical and said he hadn't seen him in better shape in ten years. That was in Atlanta. Jackie was in perfect health. He looked tired before he went, that was all."

Lynn is very suspicious about Jackie's collapse. "He was supposed to testify before the Grand Jury ten days after he got sick...against Nat Tarnopol," she points out. "That's why he got sick. To the day I die I will always say that Nat Tarnopol gave him something to make him sick so that Jackie couldn't testify. And when I got there to Cherry Hill, I asked them had they run any tests for drugs and they told me, 'No, and it was too late.'

"I have since found out it could have been done and it would have told. You stop and you look at it. Cornell Gunter was there the night he died. Why did Cornell suddenly get killed? We had just talked to Cornell and he thought there was something wrong 'cause he'd given Jackie CPR. All of a sudden he gets killed." Gunter was murdered in an apparent mugging on a Las Vegas street.

News of Jackie's collapse reached former wife Freda at the YWCA in Detroit at four o'clock in the morning. "They said, 'It's your mother-in-law,'" Freda recalls. "I answered the phone and she was crying; and she didn't cry. She said, 'Our Jack is nearly dead.' I said, 'Who, Tony?' She said, 'No, Big Sonny.' I said, 'How did you know?' She said she got this telegram; she didn't have the phone. It probably was Nat or the Mafia; it could have been anyone. It said, 'If you want to see your son alive, be on the next plane out of Detroit.' She had only been on the plane with me when he got shot, prior to that.

"She went to New Jersey alone. I hated to see her go by herself. She didn't wear nothing that much, but when she'd go to see Jack she'd dress up. I didn't want to get Harlean mad by going too. I cried after she left; I was trying stay brave for her. She was staying brave for everyone. Joyce [Jackie's half-sister] went up there later."

Billy Davis drove Eliza Mae out to the Detroit airport for her flight to New York, both of them not expecting the worst. "I took her to the airport and she expected [Jackie to be in] for a few days," he remembers. "He'd just been overworking. We didn't know...I told her to tell him hurry up and get up so I can go back out on the road with him. So we had the attitude he just needs some rest and he'd be up again. Then she got there and saw how he was."

Davis remembers she'd been in a rush to catch the flight and hadn't taken the medication for her diabetes. One morning, staying with Lynn at the home of Jackie's then driver, Billy Wilson (no relation) in nearby Philadelphia, she became gravely ill. Wilson and Lynn rushed her to the hospital. Says Lynn: "They brought her there with no medication and I had Dr Fisher, Jackie's doctor, refill the prescription for her and she was taking the medication, but she still went into a diabetic coma and she died." Lynn believes the trauma of seeing her "baby" in a critical condition had killed her. She died aged seventy-one on 16 October, 1975. She had visited her beloved son only once or twice.

"I tried to call Joyce to tell her Mama was dead," recalls Lynn. "I had to get the police to go there and get her to put the phone back on the hook."

Billy Davis then received a phone call from Jackie's half-sister. He recalls: "Joyce called me, I knew something was wrong. She said, 'Billy, guess what?' My heart started pumping I thought she was going to say Jackie had died. She said, 'Mama is dead.' I dropped the phone, never will forget it. When we was on the road and he'd get sick or anything, and he didn't know what was wrong with him, he'd be on the phone to Mama; just like a little kid."

"Eliza Mae died all of a sudden. She was in great health it seemed, but when she went up there and saw him...Jackie was her life; he could do no wrong."

She lived for Jackie as his daughter Denise explains: "My grandmother loved my father. He was her heart, her soul, her life. That's why she's not here; she gave him her last ounce of everything, so he could survive as long as he did. I'm not saying my grandmother was prejudiced, but no woman was really good enough for him. And then she finally accepted my mother."

Within weeks of the shock of hearing of Jackie's collapse, Freda got another shock. "I went back to the 'Y'. When Joyce called me, she was crying, 'Mama's gone.' She went into a diabetic coma; she could not talk or tell them anything. She knew she was going to die. She knew it, she knew she was not coming back. That's probably why she raised Joyce to be strong and independent. But Jack was dependent – dependent on me and her – we handled everything."

Much to her eternal regret, Freda never went to New Jersey to visit Jackie. She recalls, "Sandy wanted me to take her; I wish I had. She wanted to go so bad. Maybe in her mind she knew something was going to happen to her." Sandy would die before her father.

The mutual love Jackie and his mother had for one another transcended normal family love. They were both dependent on one another. "If she had went before he did he wouldn't have been able to make it," says Billy Davis. "It was such a close thing between them, like when she went to see him in that condition and knowing he wasn't going to get up; she couldn't take it."

Davis makes a very strong point here. Jackie and his mother were so close, needed each other so much, that had their positions been reversed and she was the one in the coma, Jackie wouldn't have been able to go on. Joyce Ann Lee knew this bond existed and was envious of it. Indeed she was always extremely envious of her famous brother. Nevertheless, after the funeral, Joyce did travel across to New Jersey to visit Jackie in July 1976.

Joyce lived in the house Jackie had bought for his mother on Strathmoor in Detroit. "When Mama died they never litigated her estate," complains Lynn. "Joyce Ann just took over the house and kicked out the three grandkids [the children of Sandra and Reggie Abrams] and had them put in an orphanage. She didn't have that right because that house was in Mama's name and the grandchildren lived there. It was Jackie's house and he was still alive. Jackie's children and the grandchildren should get the benefit from it."

Even Freda, who doesn't usually criticise, says, "Joyce Ann had all that money; that money from my mother-in-law was supposed to be divided."

Simon Rutberg recalls the intense love Jackie had for Eliza Mae: "Jackie loved his mother. He was unbelievably sickeningly in love with his mother. He would kill, if somebody would have said, 'Your mother's ugly,' I guarantee he would have killed the guy...just that bad."

Gil Askey, who worked with Jackie early in his career, saw it as well. "No wonder she died after her first visit," he says. "You should have seen her the night at Toledo when all these people ran up on stage, 'Oh, my baby'. She was in hysterics. She loved him, he was her heart."

Lynn Ciccone puts it this way: "Mama Liza loved Jackie. I met her one time. She knew she had brought forth on this earth one of the greatest entertainers who ever lived; and it wasn't about money or being with him. She never usurped him...never. But she was always there when times were bad. He could always come back to Mama. She liked Freda and she wanted Jackie to stay married to her and take care of the children. She has never really gotten her credit."

There was a further twist when the arrangements to transport Eliza Mae's body back to Detroit for burial went awry. Somehow her body was wrongly transported to a medical facility, being lost for a time. "Lynn called me up, crying," says Launa Toledo. "She said, 'She couldn't find her way when she was alive. What chance has she got now?' They'd put her on a milk run; to a medical university or something. They finally found her."

Lynn didn't attending Eliza Mae's funeral, which lead to conflict with the family. She said, "I had just had Li-nie, and was haemorrhaging and had an abscessed tooth and I had to go back to Atlanta. I could not go and watch them put my mother-in-law in the grave, because that would have been like watching them put Jackie in the grave. That's when Joyce Ann and all of them turned on me." Whatever the reason, she soon became enemy to most of them.

Before Lynn returned to Atlanta she'd contacted one time girlfriend of Jackie's, Joyce McRae, asking if she would come across to New Jersey and see Jackie. It may have been that Lynn spoke to McRae and she offered to come over. McRae came and, in no time, through her dominant personality, took over Jackie's affairs. Harlean, in particular, and other family members saw her involvement strictly as a desire to take control of Jackie's meagre estate.

On Clark's *Good Ol' Rock 'N' Roll Revue* revival tour Jackie earned $7,500 per week, but from now on, for Lynn and the children, there'd be nothing. Jackie had left a legal nightmare that raged for twenty years. The biggest problem Jackie's heart attack caused for those around him was, who was to be his legal guardian? Who would take care of the finances, and who would pay the medical expenses? Sure, he'd married Lynn Crochet in 1971, but by not divorcing Harlean, it left a large question mark. It would soon be put to a legal test.

For a short time Lynn visited Jackie in Cherry Hill. "In the first instance there was no way I wouldn't believe he recognised me," she insists. "He would blink 'yes' and 'no' to me. We had it documented, but the doctors wouldn't believe me. They wouldn't come in at night when he wasn't awake and aware.

"The first year I worked very hard to get him transferred to Rio Rancho in California; to get rehabilitated. I felt even if he never sang again, he could get rehabilitated. Dick Clark's insurance was paying for everything. They were even willing to buy a house and put him in it and a van to transfer him back and forth. INA [insurance] was going to do all this and Harlean stopped it. He could have been transferred to California, but Harlean wouldn't let him. And the State of New Jersey courts I fault for what happened."

After almost four months on life support and totally comatose, in January 1976, Jackie emerged from the coma and was taken off life support. However, he still remained semi-comatose, being totally immobile and unable to communicate.

Despite him having lived with Lynn as husband and wife for close on five years, Harlean, Jackie's second wife, came forward saying that she was still the legal wife and would take care of his welfare. Cherry Hill Medical Centre were anxious to know precisely who the legal guardian was with a view to having Jackie's medical bills paid.

A well researched article by Bill Pollak in New York's *Village Voice* (14 August, 1978) explains the increasing dilemma that was developing:

> In order to settle the dispute and get its bills paid, Cherry Hill Medical Centre asked the court to intervene. In March 1976, a month and a half after Jackie came out of his coma, Judge Vincent DiMartino of Camden County Court placed his affairs in the hands of an impartial third party. He named Edward N Adourian Jnr, a Camden lawyer, as Jackie's legal guardian.

Incredibly, lawyer Edward Adourian hadn't heard of Jackie Wilson until that day. It seems he just happened to be in the court building and Judge DiMartino chose him as being a good neutral party. He admits, "To tell the truth, I'd never heard of Jackie Wilson – I'm into classical music – until the judge called me." The choice proved fortunate as Adourian was thorough and dedicated.

The *Village Voice* article continues:

> A month before Adourian was named guardian in February 1976, a jury in Newark had convicted Tarnopol of one count of conspiracy and twenty-two counts of mail fraud. Three other Brunswick executives were also convicted. In April, Judge Frederick Lacey sentenced Tarnopol to three years in prison and ordered him to pay a fine of ten thousand dollars. Tarnopol immediately announced that he would appeal the conviction.
>
> Adourian knew what the Brunswick convictions meant

A Brunswick promotional shot in
leather and make-up

On stage

With Nat Tarnopol

Jackie loved to perform, whether in the
roughest barn, the biggest arena or the
plushest night club

Even after The Crickets joined the label, Jackie was Brunswick's best-selling artist

Losing the cigarette as he appeared on stage became a nightly ritual

The lounge performer

Carl Davis with David Yellen, Chicago 1994

Songwriter Roquel "Billy" Davis, New York 1994

Guitarist Billy Davis with the author, June 1994

David Yellen, Esther Edwards (sister of) Berry Gordy, Detroit 1994

Content with family life in the early
seventies with Lynn Crochet and son
Thor

A break in touring

Jackie was devoted to his pet dogs,
often kissing them. "Dogs don't carry
germs, people do"

The smart suits of the sixties gave way
to more glamorous seventies fashions,
but the cigarette remained

With his Hot Smokin' Brass band and son Thor, 1974

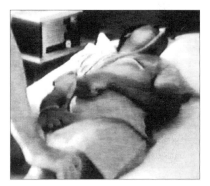

The Las Vegas showman of the seventies

Undergoing therapy during his stay at Medford Leas Medical Centre

Harlean (Harris) Wilson with their son John Dominick ("Petey") at Jackie's funeral, 1984

Freda Wilson's first visit to Jackie's grave, July 1987. "No more lonely teardrops"

Jackie's death certificate

Russell Street Baptist Church, Detroit, where Jackie was baptised and had his funeral

Simon Rutberg, Jackie's friend

Denise Wilson – Jackie's daughter with Freda – at a restaurant in Detroit, 1987. She was shot dead the following year

Thor Wilson – Jackie's son with Lynn Crochet – and Jackie Jnr III, 10 June 1995

Brenda Wilson – Jackie's daughter – with her boyfriend Terry and the author, 1994

Jackie's half-sister Joyce Ann Lee, Harlean Wilson, John Dominick Wilson and Jack "The Rapper" Gibson at the dedication ceremony, 1987

Harlean Wilson and DJ Jack "The Rapper" Gibson at the mausoleum dedication, 1987

The dedication ceremony for Jackie's mausoleum, in full glare of the media

Jackie's grave, which he shares with his mother, complete with memorial bench

to Wilson's financial problems. After Brunswick refused to allow Adourian to see the company books, he filed a suit in Camden federal court asking for a full accounting of Wilson's earnings at Brunswick. The suit charged breach of contract and claimed that Brunswick had failed to pay and account for over one million dollars in royalties due to Wilson.

Somewhere between this one million dollars and the $150,000 that Brunswick claims Jackie owes them lies the true figure of how much is owed to whom.

Adourian, in his attorney's thoroughness, recounted the events as he saw them. "I am told Jackie was in terminal fibrillation – in ventricular fibrillation – I guess they [Cherry Hills] stabilised him. They put the [electric] paddles on him and got a rhythm back.

"At that time, because of lack of oxygen, while he was fibrillating he suffered damage to the brain. He was in the Cherry Hill Medical Centre and, my recollection is, sometime in February...nobody was paying his bills.

"There was a petition by two women [Harlean Harris and Lynn Crochet]. I'm walking down the court hallway one day and the judge didn't know what to do. He sees me and says, 'Well, make him guardian.' I was appointed guardian of his person and property. The first thing I had to do was get some financial backing for him.

"So me and my partner David Schicobie – he was working in workers' compensation at that time – we conceived the idea that when Jackie had his heart attack he was in his employment. He was working for Dick Clark, who had a revival of rock 'n' roll; something like that. And Jackie was singing for this Dick Clark group at the time he had his heart attack. Dave and I went up to see Dick Clark and we convinced him that Jackie was not an independent contractor, but an employee. In other words he had direction over what he sang and what he did. We established an employee status for Jackie.

"The insurance company which was, I think, Pacific Insurance Company, which was owned by the Insurance Company of North America [now Sigma]. They assumed responsibility, so all his medical bills were paid – he would get temporary disability. We could pay his medical bills and maintenance and also we could get monthly temporary disability payments; not very much.

"We were lucky that Clark had taken out insurance there; it paid his medical bills. His hospital bill was $100,000, and various medical bills. They were all paid off. The insurance company paid for him at Morris Hall – even though they didn't have to."

Nevertheless, on 11 March, 1976, barely six months since Jackie's collapse, the Cherry Hill Medical Centre took civil action in the Court of New Jersey against "Jackie Wilson, Lennie Belle Wilson [Lynne Crochet] and Harlean Wilson" over non-payment of medical bills amounting to $83,327.25.

Back in 1976, these medical expenses represented an enormous amount for a single individual. The *Village Voice* article further discloses:

> Adourian also went to court and won an insurance settlement from the Insurance Company of North America [INA]. The company was ordered to pay $120,000 in hospital bills, provide $119 a week in disability allowance and continue to cover Wilson under workman's compensation. But since workman's compensation limits coverage to therapy that will return the insured to his former occupation and on the strength of doctors' opinions that Wilson would never sing again, INA has been reluctant to authorise therapy for him.

Since it is not unknown for similarly brain damaged people to emerge from such an unconscious condition, every opportunity should have been made available to Jackie. There was a further disappointment, as the *Village Voice* article explains:

> Adourian later found out that Wilson should have been covered by Blue Cross/Blue Shield through his union's pension and welfare plan from the beginning. Under Section Thirty-Four of the AFTRA (American Federation of Television and Radio Artists) Pension and Welfare Clause, which also includes all recording contracts, an artist is eligible for Blue Cross/Blue Shield if he earns one thousand dollars a year or more. Wilson had been working on an album, *Nobody But You*, for three months before his collapse, and had put in over twenty-four hours in the studio. Since the rate for

studio time is $81.50 an hour, Wilson should have easily met AFTRA's requirement.

But instead of reporting Wilson's 1975 studio earnings, Brunswick reported to AFTRA that, since Wilson owed them $150,000 against advances on royalties, they did not pay Wilson in 1975. As a result, when Cherry Hill Medical Centre contracted AFTRA, it was told that Wilson was ineligible for Blue Cross/Blue Shield. But, according to Adourian, the point was that Jackie recorded and performed, and regardless of his purported indebtedness to Brunswick, the record company should have contributed to Wilson's pension and welfare fund for time spent in the studio.

Unfortunately, Adourian did not discover this scam until after he had already won the settlement from INA. And once a workman's compensation case has been established, Blue Cross/Blue Shield is not required to undertake insurance payments. However, if Blue Cross/Blue Shield had been paying Wilson's bills from the beginning, Adourian and other friends of Wilson's would not have had to fight to get therapy authorised.

All in all, it amounted to tragic misfortune for Jackie and the rest of his family. Once the insurance was established, Adourian says, "The next thing we had to do was determine what his medical status was, and whether he was capable of rehabilitation. We had to have the neurologist that treated him at Cherry Hill Hospital and his electro-encephalograms and everything else. We were told by the medical people he was not a candidate for rehabilitation but was in, what they call, 'a chronic vegetative state'.

"We also had a computer activated sensor test. In other words they would bombard him with visual and auditory sensation and they would record that and it would go through a computer. What they were trying to find is whether there was any neurological integration between the visual stimulation. They put light in his eyes and sound in his ears; whether there was any integrated response from that. The conclusion was that there wasn't. In any case, just to be on the safe side, we did and the insurance company agree to this – they really didn't have to – they agree to it, even though the information we had said he wasn't a candidate for rehabilitation.

He was sent for several months to a special rehabilitation hospital, near Princeton, at Lawrenceville. He was there for several months and received various kinds of rehabilitation therapy. We also paid extra for speech therapy.

"The doctors told me, when I had to make the decision whether he was a candidate for rehabilitation, that he had a life expectancy of about ten years. A person in that condition is very, very susceptible to respiratory infection, things like that. He was getting physical therapy and we got him a private room.

"We also had him evaluated at the Hahnemann University Medical Centre in Philadelphia, which is a first class medical centre, by a Dr Bill Oakes. They gave him a CT [brain] scan and I remember the CT scan showed dilated cerebral ventricles. All the ventricles in the brain were dilated, which they concluded was atrophy of the cortex [brain's outer layer].

"Their conclusion was he was in a chronic vegetative state.

"I think we were guardian for about a year and ask to be relieved. Another lawyer took it up. His name was Wayne Bryant. He was his guardian for a year. We had him while he was in convalescent home in Camden County and then we had him in Morris Hall – that's a rehabilitation hospital. Wayne had him placed in a very fine facility, Medford Leas.

"First he was in Cherry Hill Medical Centre, then he was in Cooper River Convalescent Home, then he was in Morris Hall; which is the rehabilitation hospital. Then he went to Medford Leas, which is a Quaker institution.

"Then I think Harlean made a petition and she was appointed his guardian. I think she might have been guardian of his person and her lawyer guardian of his property.

"Joyce McRae, she was a third factor that came in. I used her as a para-legal for a period. She occupied a room in our office when we were in Camden. She made a petition. She wanted the guardianship. She had no standing.

"McRae was a very persistent individual and very difficult to deal with. But she was very concerned with his well being. She believed he was not in a vegetative state. She believed he was in a conversion hysteria; for some physiological reason he was withdrawing to escape. The neurological evidence – all the clinical findings – all said he was in a chronic vegetative state. That's what I had to go on at the time.

"The rehabilitation didn't do him any good. He did have a swallow response. I would stand there and she would say, 'He's responding; look at that.' She wasn't seeing what I was seeing.

"We gave her the benefit of the doubt and gave him four months of rehabilitation. He had a flat-out encephalogram. It wasn't registering anything. There was no response; no conception between the sensory impulses and being cognisant of the impulses. They would try to treat him. Put him up on a chair and the nurses would talk to him. He would look back and forth; his eyes were open during the day time.

"The brain needs oxygen and sugar. The only thing he had was the NG tube [for supply of sustenance], no other life supports. They took the NG tube away because he had a swallow reflex. That's one thing Joyce did; she insisted they feed him with a spoon.

"She could be a real pest to the nursing homes. But I'm convinced she had his best interest at heart. Joyce would go in and tell the staff what to do. I tell you, if I were ever in that state, I would want Joyce around; keep everybody doing their thing. Her theory was to treat him as much like a human being; as if he had cognition.

"Wayne Bryant had to go to court to bar her from visiting him. I think that was done in-camera because there were some accusations made against her in an affidavit.

"Another problem – which is a can of worms – is to what extent he was bilked by his agents and people who took advantage of him. We couldn't get involved in that type of litigation, as it is immensely expensive. You really had to know that trade and where to turn the rocks and look for that stuff. We didn't have any expertise. We had limited funds and felt we'd best use the funds for Jackie's physical well being rather than go on a wild goose chase to try to nail Nat Tarnopol."

Within months of Jackie's collapse, Joyce McRae had moved from her home in Chicago to Cherry Hill, along with her nine-year-old daughter. She was prepared to sacrifice much of her life to be by Jackie's bedside and endeavour to help with his rehabilitation. Despite being reviled by the entire Wilson family, McRae's behaviour appears totally unselfish at that time. There's not much joy in sitting by the bedside, day in and day out, of someone who cannot talk or respond; all the more so if that person is not related.

The *Village Voice* article again:

> Through Edward Adourian, who had just been appointed Wilson's legal guardian, McRae arranged for a consultation

with Dr James Richardson, a physical therapist and former president of the New Jersey State Physical Therapy Society. Richardson gave Wilson propio-ceptive neuromuscular therapy (PNT) to develop new pathways to the brain and revitalise old ones. He also prescribed a therapy known as 'patterning' often used by the Boy Scouts and community groups to treat brain damaged people. Patterning, which has been successful in many cases similar to Wilson's, simulates the act of crawling by moving the arms and legs until the brain takes over the newly redeveloped coordination function of the muscles. But, possibly because patterning can be performed by anyone who knows how, it is scorned by some members of the medical profession. Dr William J Erdman of the University of Pennsylvania was called in by INA to evaluate Wilson in June 1976, and he reported to INA that Wilson had no rehabilitation potential, and that Richardson's therapy was useless. On the basis of Erdman's report, INA terminated Richardson's therapy. The only therapy Wilson continued to receive was for a range of motion, which keeps the limbs flexible, but does not attempt to restore function.

McRae became Jackie's constant bedside companion and did her utmost to have him achieve some semblance of normality. McRae says: "I wound up having to go to New Jersey and wound up having to pull faeces out of Jackie's ass, because they didn't know how to do a suppository without hurting him. At that point it was Jack and me trying to deal with it with no help. In fact, a lot of hindrance, a lot of jealousy, a lot of bullshit."

McRae tried all forms of stimuli: "I used to play all kinds of music. I knew Jack would not be at peace until the truth was out about what happened subsequent to his collapse. It didn't matter if he never sang again. As long as he could appreciate the sky or a bird and his songs, and watch his children grow.

"He understood and comprehended, it was stolen from him. Otherwise I couldn't have taught him to eat again. He must have had a certain amount of control, I even had him standing, but they found out and stopped his therapy. Harlean Harris and Nat Tarnopol participated and had it stopped."

McRae became animated when she talked of the man she had loved so much: "I judge friends by whether or not they stood, stayed or did anything to save Jackie's life. I picked up and moved from Chicago with a nine-year-old daughter to try and save the man's life. I was his friend.

"Each person in their own way did things to put nails in Mr Wilson's coffin. I was there in the trenches; getting my house broken into, guns shoved in my ribs, being accused of everything under the sun, having my daughter taken away from me. All the rest of them attempted to make a name for themselves or some kind of profits, or get a corner for themselves of Jackie Wilson's immortality or spotlight. That's not a friend.

"The other women were not the ones who Jackie responded to. They had their own reasons and my motive was simple; I saw my friend being characterised by what I called a murder. Because when he can't fend for himself and his rights are vested in third parties, and they do not give him adequate care, treatment, rehabilitation and they do it deliberately to fill a self fulfilling prophecy; that he will never recover.

"Who stood to gain? Nat Tarnopol, you'd have to have heard that. Harlean Harris stood to gain; she has gained from Jackie's death. Harlean and Nat together. Jackie's half-sister Joyce, she has gained from Jackie's death. They gained from Jackie's collects [royalties]. There were no regular visitors. I taught him how to eat again from a spoon, how to drink again from a cup; I got in the trenches. I wiped his ass, I had to pull faeces out of his ass when it got impacted, because the nurses got so goddamned abusive to him they didn't think he felt. They would injure him and he would moan and he would dam-up and tie-up and it was the most horrendous, the most violative crap I have ever seen. I found him with black eyes, with urine burns."

On one occasion an electric lamp had been set up by nursing staff and focused on Jackie's backside, with the object of drying out bedsores. Somehow the lamp tipped over, with nobody in attendance, causing Jackie very severe burns. The staff were alerted to the problem by the smell of burning flesh.

Relatives of Jackie blamed McRae even though she wasn't present. They accused her of paying a staff member to do it, to prove Jackie was not properly being taken care of. Harlean, particularly, has no doubt. "We know she participated in it and engineered it, so to speak," she says. "Usually someone black and someone in the lower echelons of the staff. She wanted to show me up as a guardian, but I was at work. It was Miss McRae who made the complaint to the Board of Health."

McRae says indignantly: "He was burnt on the ass with a lamp. I was in Chicago. What idiot blames me? That was done at a nursing facility, on a night shift which was understaffed. They allowed him to get bed sores. They treated the bed sores by leaving Jackie – who could not ring a bell or call out, who had muscle spasms – with a light bulb aimed at his ass to try to dry out the bed sores he never should have had. How the fuck did I do that?

"Jackie Wilson should be alive today if he had the benefit of rehabilitation therapy in massive amounts, which is exactly what his condition required. Jackie should be alive today and nobody had a right to deny him his right to treatment. He was violated by Nat Tarnopol, both directly and indirectly from the moment he collapsed till the moment he died. He is still being violated; because they are lying, and his memory is still not proper."

It has to be said the relationship Joyce McRae formed with Jackie was very one sided. He may have known her for years but, by many accounts, he'd tried hard to avoid her. Jackie's daughter Denise claims Jackie had many times told her, "Get her away from me. Get her off my back!", and had given her money so they could go shopping together. Yet, when he was at his lowest ebb, along came McRae to care for and watch out for him. When funds were in short supply for his well being, McRae was on the phone, calling all over the country and the world, and knocking on the doors, to get the donations coming in.

Nevertheless, McRae became close to Freda and Eliza Mae. Freda's grandmother trusted her to such an extent she gave her almost the entire collection of Jackie's family photos, believing they'd be in safer hands, because of Freda's drinking problem.

Says McRae: "Mama Freda, Freda's grandmother, gave them to me for safe keeping. Freda's mother was Mother Leathia; she knew Freda was fucked up, Denise was fucked up, Tony was fucked up, and she knew they were going to rob her of this stuff, and she was ninety years old. I have an autographed photo from Paul Robeson to Jackie. I have photos of Jackie boxing when he was fifteen. I have a picture of Jackie with LaVern Baker and Sam Cooke, with Judy Garland and Count Basie. His personal photos; Jackie and Freda."

The unfortunate personality traits that McRae has are her arrogance and dominance. There is only one truth, which is her truth. She had no difficulty in making enemies wherever she went.

As time went on and it became clear to almost everyone that Jackie was never going to regain much facility for living a normal life, the focus turned more and more to who should be the rightful heirs to his estate. Since attorney Bryant had taken over, McRae's involvement rapidly began to irritate him, as it did with the staff of the facilities that Jackie was moved to. The *Village Voice* article best explains it:

> It's possible that Bryant thought from the beginning that it would be unethical for him to allow McRae to be involved with Wilson as she had been under Adourian's guardianship. According to McRae, Bryant even threatened to have her arrested when she tried to accompany Wilson to a nursing home. McRae continued to visit Wilson regularly, but since she was not Wilson's legal guardian, doctors and nurses were less willing to tolerate her criticisms. When contacted Bryant declined to comment.

But there were strange things happening whilst McRae was around, according to testimony given by some of the medical staff. One staffer, Debra Denyer, claimed in her court affidavit that McRae, "...has called Mr Wilson a 'jungle bunny'. During those periods I observed her hands moving over his genital area. She laid on the bed with the patient kissing and hugging him while her daughter was in the room."

Another affidavit by medical staff member, Elke Persons, says: "On numerous occasions I have observed Ms McRae speak to Mr Wilson in a loud and abusive manner. Specifically, she called him a 'motherfucker'." Persons also claimed: "On one occasion I observed Ms McRae in bed with Mr Wilson. She was trying to put her bare breast in his mouth...I observed her licking excess food off his face...She would lie on his bed and fondle his genital area while pulling the skin on his penis." One other staffer, Kathleen Gentleman, claimed, "Ms McRae would spend an inordinate amount of time inspecting Mr Wilson's genitals." One hospital complained McRae was photographing his genitals. Had these bizarre claims been made by a single witness, perhaps they could be more easily dismissed.

Lynn Ciccone says simply that McRae would never have dared call him by such demeaning names. "Jackie would have killed her. I said to Joyce how he suffered and she said, 'He was only a fucking nigger from Detroit who wanted to sing.' I was so shocked, I couldn't talk.

"She beat him on the back and called him a 'jungle bunny' and a 'nigger'. She said that's how he's used to being talked to. I tell you, not Jackie, you wouldn't say that to his face."

Nevertheless, McRae deserves credit for taking the role she did. Although the Wilson relatives suspect her motives were more to do with gaining control of Jackie's estate, this doesn't stand up to fair scrutiny.

There was another incident which Harlean suspects McRae had involvement with. It involved one of the nursing staff who was on her way to the court to make the damaging accusations against McRae concerning her abuse of Jackie in the nursing home.

The staff member was apparently forced off the road by another vehicle. Says Harlean, "Whether she [McRae] was behind the kidnapping incident? Both incidents [referring, as well, to the lamp story] were around the same time, within a year of him being in Medford Leas. One of the girls who worked at Medford Leas was forced off the road by black men. It was black men who were driving the cars as they came in to testify against her [McRae]. I received so many phone calls from former friends of my husband in the industry...and several threatening things were said in regard to the girl [McRae]. Jackie was loved by millions of people and I got that type of talk from people who were in his fan club. They are not Mafia people. They know Joyce is not what she claims to be."

Jimmy Maslan, who'd known Jackie, defended McRae's treatment: "I saw Joyce when I went to Medford Leas to see Jackie. She was taking care of him a lot. He definitely responded to Joyce. He didn't want to take food from the nurse, but with Joyce he would open his mouth. So he was aware of what's happening. I brought him some albums and stuff."

McRae is adamant that Jackie was a candidate for at least partial recovery: "Jackie got to the point where he was pushing himself around on his wheelchair [hospital staff say McRae would sit Jackie in the wheelchair and wait for a reflex action whereby his leg would jerk and propel the chair]. Where he was standing [others say only after being strapped to a board]. Eating food.

"The insurance company was willing to buy a house in Cherry Hill that was all equipped for a paraplegic and do the therapy." McRae contends that Harlean didn't want Jackie to recover and was against all efforts to improve his quality of life. Harlean's visits were, at best, spasmodic...sometimes only monthly. She lived in New York which is close. Worse still, she ended up restricting visitors to only those who had first obtained her permission.

Producer Carl Davis often spoke with McRae at the time, and has mixed views about her: "Joyce McRae used to take care of Jackie...play his music to him. She'd go once a week to take care of him, or as often as she could. But she was an asshole and may have stolen some tapes of Jackie's live performances to sell them.

"She got him into the swimming pool. She had video tapes of her with Jackie in the pool making him move, rubbing him and all that. Just trying to stop him being a vegetable."

McRae is critical of everyone's role in the sad episode. She says: "Lynn Crochet visited Jackie in September 1975 and I went with her in March 1976. The only other time was for the fund raiser, 'cause she thought she'd get some money. She virtually left Jackie on my doorstep and never came back.

"I have an eight mm film of it; Jackie responded for her. His eyes were opened most the time, except when Harlean would come around and he'd play comatose; a gawk. That's documented; reporters saw it. Jackie was in a deep coma for three months, semi comatose for three months, then he was conscious. He would respond to stimuli, such as a prick in the arm [medical tests do not agree with this contention].

"Consider this: if Jackie allegedly had such a massive heart attack – that he wound up oxygen starved – how come he never needed by-pass surgery? How come he had low blood pressure? How come he never needed a heart transplant? How come he never had another heart attack? How is it possible? I know the answer.

"They never did a brain scan although they had that equipment in those days. When he became comatose he actually became a neurological patient, but he wasn't seen daily by a neurological doctor.

"He was making productive and useful sounds and the guardian [Wayne Bryant] stopped therapy. Some day the truth will come out and this man will be set free. I was chosen to be a vehicle; by Jack Leroy Wilson.

"I found out about Dr Richardson. They allowed Dr Richardson in for a while and they forced him to withdraw after he made progress.

"I was the one person that when I walked by his bed, he knew. I wasn't going to let him down and he responded accordingly. I can show the conspiracy. It was a frame up. Jack knew I would not let him down. Jackie wasn't an angel; he was an enigma. He was his own worst enemy. I once said to him after he was sick, and he just looked at me, 'You did a better job picking your nose than your bitches.'

"I spent two and a half years of my life hands on, the past twenty years of my life, thousands and thousands of dollars plus thousands and thousands of hours. If I got half a million dollars it wouldn't make a dent. Truly, wouldn't make a dent.

"On one occasion a guy showed up and put a gun to my ribs. It was a two bit hood out of north Jersey. When my life was threatened, I took it very seriously."

The first court appointed guardian Ted Adourian tried his hardest to get the best advice and treatment that funds would allow. The *Village Voice*:

Between 30 March and 6 May, 1977, Jackie was tested at Hahnemann Hospital in Philadelphia to find out whether surgery might help his condition and to again evaluate his chances for rehabilitation. The hospital performed a brain scan on Wilson, and concluded that surgery would not be of value. Dr Wilbur W Oakes's discharge summary said that Wilson's potential for rehabilitation was limited but it did recommend that Wilson be given "the opportunity to avail himself of some rehab program on a continuing basis . . . We made every effort to do more than just a passive range of motion here." The summary said, "We had him on the tilt table and (gave him) physiotherapy trying to get him to stand. It was difficult to have him standing at this time but perhaps a more aggressive physical therapy approach with some braces might be able to accomplish this goal."

Dr Oakes's recommendation was never followed. In February 1977, Adourian asked the court to relieve him as guardian because the case was taking too much of his time. At the same time, McRae filed an application for guardianship, asking that she be allowed to care for Jackie at her home. But on 1 April, 1977, a month before Wilson was discharged from Hahnemann, Judge DiMartino turned down her application on the grounds that she was not a lawyer, and that a lawyer, as an officer of the court, could be held more directly accountable for carrying out the court's wishes. The judge named Wayne R Bryant, a Camden, New Jersey lawyer, as

Wilson's new legal guardian.

Some suggest Wayne R Bryant was appointed partly as a result of lobbying by Tarnopol's own attorney. This is not easy to verify or otherwise, but the general consensus was that Jackie's best interests were served while Adourian was guardian.

The *Village Voice* article states:

> Relationships between McRae and Bryant quickly deteriorated. Since INA was only paying for half of the ninety dollars a day room and board fee at Medford Leas, the other half came from Wilson's estate. When the estate was down to ten thousand dollars, Bryant discontinued Wilson's speech therapy. According to McRae, he took this action before he saw an encouraging therapist's report on Jackie's chances of recovering his receptive and expressive language skills.
>
> Infuriated, McRae said that she would pay for continued therapy. "This has been a consistent pattern in Jackie's health care," she says, "and I don't know how to explain it. But as soon as Jackie makes any kind of progress, something always seems to happen to cut off his therapy and allow him to regress."
>
> After a few more clashes between Bryant and McRae, and after several articles airing McRae's criticisms appeared in Philadelphia and South Jersey newspapers, Bryant banned her from visiting Wilson at Medford Leas and again cancelled the speech therapy. Bryant took this action despite the testimony of several doctors and nurses that McRae's presence had a calming effect on Wilson, and that he had developed a definite emotional attachment to her. McRae quickly obtained a court order that allowed her to visit Wilson for two hours a day, but she wasn't able to get the speech therapy reinstated until three months after it was cancelled. (When Jackie's speech therapist finally saw him again in March 1978 he did not respond to her cues as he had previously. This caused her to revise her prognosis and recommend therapy be terminated. A two thousand dollar contribution from a major record company,

which McRae had solicited to pay for Jackie's continued speech therapy, was never used.)

Bryant's actions prompted McRae to file a suit in Camden County Court asking that he be removed as guardian for allegedly failing to carry out the court's directive to "do all things reasonable, necessary, and proper to attempt the rehabilitation of Jackie Wilson to whatever degree or extent possible". She contended that Jackie had regressed badly since Bryant took over as guardian. In addition, McRae again asked the court to name her Wilson's guardian, so that she could care for him in her home. But as the court hearing dragged on and her legal expenses multiplied, McRae ran out of money. Unable to defend herself against charges of interference from Bryant and the doctors at Medford Leas, she had to accept defeat and returned home to Chicago.

To this day McRae maintains Jackie was murdered. There is no doubt she spent far more time at the bedside than Harlean ever did.

There are no shortage of critics of McRae and, in part, her abrasive, dominating manner may be her worst enemy. Says Harry Respess: "She begged everyone; she had a regular fund raiser. She had a number for everyone to send in donations. She was a strange one. She came from a very wealthy family. She was married to another black guy who really raked her over the coals. Bad act. He beat her and the whole bit. She wasn't a very nice person. She got a lot of money. George Kirby, the comedian, she took him for a lot. Most of the people in showbusiness contributed."

The battle for guardianship raged on. Initially Lynn was declared legal heir by the state court of Georgia and yet Harlean later won the same judgement in Camden Court, New Jersey. The Camden County Surrogate Court obviously faced a difficult decision. In April 1978 the Philadelphia *Tribune*, in an article written by Jovida Joylette, announced: "Jackie Wilson's Wife Named His Guardian." The balance of the story read as follows:

> After numerous guardianship hearings and legal entanglements it appears that the fate and future of rock 'n' roll singer Jackie Wilson has finally been determined. On Friday, 14 April, Camden County Judge Mary Ellen Talbot

awarded guardianship of singer Jackie to Harlean Harris Wilson of New York. Judge Talbot's decision to award guardianship to Mrs Wilson has thwarted any chances Joyce McRae, an avowed friend of the singer, may have had in her own attempts to receive guardianship for Jackie Wilson.

Wilson's problems began two and a half years ago when he suffered an apparent heart attack while performing on the stage of the Latin Casino in Cherry Hill, NJ. Since then Wilson has remained in a comatose state residing in various medical institutions and for the past months in a nursing home in South Jersey. Ordinarily, guardianship would have been awarded to next of kin, however, during the first guardianship hearing, more than a year ago there was no ruling as to the legal status of the two women.

Mrs Wilson was unavailable for comment at press time, and has yet to state her plans for the future arrangements she will make for her husband now that he is legally in her care.

The decision to appoint Harlean the legal guardian and, effectively, heir, is curious. The facts were Harlean had married Jackie in a civil ceremony 20 May, 1967, while Lynn claimed to have married Jackie on 27 March, 1971 by the little known Universal Life Church at Modesto, California. Despite Lynn having spent years living with Jackie, Jackie hadn't gotten a legal divorce from Harlean, although after only eighteen months of marriage, both had signed a legal separation agreement in 1969 and Harlean, through the courts, had him arrested on every occasion he set foot in New York state. Assuming the story of Nat Tarnopol and Harlean having an affair is correct, it's highly likely Jackie actually hated her.

Harlean's own attorney claims, "Harlean visited him two or three times a month since he was sick." This seems highly exaggerated, except for the earliest period.

Lynn has had more than her share of heartache since Jackie's collapse. The reality was she had four children to raise with no income. Earlier she said, "I don't want a confrontation with Harlean, 'cause I've beaten her in court already. She doesn't have any right to inherit because of the separation agreement they [Jackie and Harlean in 1969] signed. That's already been decided in the Georgia Court. What is a guardian? She was not a guardian. She did not take care of him.

"I tried to get him moved out to California. I tried to get him moved to Atlanta where I could have been with him more often. I had a baby [Li-nie] I'd just had. I couldn't fight Harlean any more. I didn't work for an attorney like her. And my money ran out. The children and the grandchildren should get the benefit.

"I don't know how aware Jackie was because I couldn't go back up there. I couldn't face it. I had nothing else to fight with and by this time, I had started drinking, and I had the kids to support. I went on with my life, but it was always there.

"I would call and say I was a fan...just to check on him. I would call Launa Toledo, 'cause I knew she was in touch with Harlean, and I'd say, 'What's going on?' and 'Don't tell Harlean I called.'

"I got out of it with Joyce McRae, because of all the bad press she was getting. I didn't know who to believe. The pictures she took of Jackie and released to *Jet*. I knew why she did it, but he would not have wanted it. I got upset with Joyce; she was going about it the wrong way. I had to step out of it, because I was close to having a nervous breakdown. I could not deal with it and raise my kids. I had to step away from it, no matter how much it hurt me. I've had to live with it all these years. I had to step back, I had to raise the kids. Because that was his future. That's what he would have wanted me to do.

"Jackie would have been better off if he'd got the help I tried to get for him. If they'd got him to El Rancho in California, and gotten him away from Harlean and the bullshit in New Jersey. It's where Patricia Neal [a celebrated long term coma victim] went. She'd had a stroke and they brought her all the way back. They could have helped Jackie if they'd have done just what I asked them. Harlean fought me all the way. I don't have anything good to say about Wayne Bryant, but Ted Adourian was in our corner."

Referring to the period April 1978, the *Village Voice* article continues:

> Bryant resigned his guardianship in April. On Bryant's recommendation, Judge Ellen Talbot named Harlean Wilson, Jackie's estranged second wife as his guardian, and her lawyer, John T Mulkerin, Jackie's legal representative. Mulkerin and Mrs Wilson are now faced with the same obstacle that made their predecessors' jobs so difficult: a shortage of funds. "We would never attempt massive rehabilitation even if the

chances for success were only nominal," says Mulkerin. "But one of the things that has to be assessed is what monies are available at the present time to accomplish that. If we had a million dollars, there's nothing we wouldn't do."

In the mean time Joyce McRae kept knocking on doors and accepting contributions. Many claimed she pocketed the money and there's no way of really knowing, but doubtless she had expenses of her own. Clearly funds to rehabilitate and to simply take care of Jackie were not going to be sufficient. His medical care would be required for many years, for as long as he remained alive.

It was arranged for a benefit concert to be held for him at the Latin Casino, where Jackie had been stricken, on 3 October, 1976, just a year after the tragedy. The Spinners, who were huge at the time, were the prime movers. They hosted the concert, paid for all expenses and contributed an additional five thousand dollars. The show lasted three-and-a-quarter hours and featured Al Green, Harold Melvin And The Blue Notes, BT Express, Stephanie Mills, Sister Sledge, Don Cornelius and comic Irwin C Watson. The ticket prices ranged from thirty to one hundred dollars ringside.

The singer Al Green donated ten thousand dollars while the Latin Casino and Gladys Knight And The Pips gave $2,500 each. Dick Clark also attended and showed a film clip from one of Jackie's TV performances. An amazing sixty thousand dollars was collected and donated.

Adourian had other problems: "We had to do something to prevent the IRS getting money from the benefit. We got some money there and we were able to supplement some of these things that the insurance company wouldn't pay for. Joyce McRae did not get the money from the benefits – it went for extras. The insurance company gave him only a minimum."

In the meantime, Bobby Womack, the popular soul singer who claimed to be a friend, established the Salute Foundation which contributors believed was for Jackie's benefit. The foundation seemed to be formed quite legitimately with a board of directors, including Womack's wife Regina, and Eddie Singleton who had produced for Jackie in the early 1960s. Womack claims to have sought contributions from such notables as "Dionne Warwick, Isaac Hayes, Marvin Gaye, Natalie Cole, Aretha Franklin and others".

Singer Barry White donated ten thousand dollars, but was "sickened and saddened" after he learned that his money had not reached Jackie. After correspondence from attorney Ted Adourian, Womack finally turned White's donation over to the trust. It seemed Jackie's dislike for Womack was well founded.

Variety magazine (1 December, 1976) ran the headline, "Ailing Jackie Wilson Has Not Got A Cent From Benefit Fund".

Jackie's wife Lynn reported that the black actor Ben Vereen was behind the concert. The plan was to set up a trust fund for Jackie, whose medical bills were said to be now costing "three thousand dollars a month", while Jackie had a tax lien of approximately $500,000 against him. The trust would supposedly keep the benefits out of the hands of the tax man.

"I heard Michael Jackson sent ten thousand dollars," says Lynn. "Richard Pryor sent me $1,200 for the kids. James Brown sent a thousand dollar cheque, but it bounced. I had to threaten to call *Jet* magazine before he would pick up the cheque. He was broke.

"Stevie Wonder sent five thousand dollars to help me pay for going back and forth. Stevie sent the money to the kids. All the other money went to the guardians Ted Adourian and Wayne Bryant. Ted was an up-front guy. I have no trouble with him, but all the trouble started with Bryant. He and Harlean were in cahoots.

"I met U2 on my flight to New York. I asked them if they'd sent money. They said they sent ten thousand dollars, but it never showed up in any accounts. I never heard from Gladys Knight; she was in awe of Jackie.

"Ben Vereen was going to give a concert. Harlean messed it up. The only ones that followed through were The Spinners. I got the message Elvis called and he sent a telegram. So far as money I never heard."

A telegram from the black comedian Red Foxx was worded, "Get up nigger, we need and love you." It was exactly the way thousands of Jackie's friends and fans felt.

Remarkably, Lynn came to New Jersey for the benefit concert, but didn't take the children in to see Jackie. She says simply, "I wasn't going to beg Harlean."

McRae is cynical about the benefit of the concert for Jackie's welfare: "The benefit concerts didn't benefit Jackie. They benefited Harlean, Wayne Bryant and Ted Adourian, and benefited the guardians and John Mulkerin. They actually went for fees for the guardians."

Sonny West, a close friend of Elvis Presley, could not confirm whether he contributed. Says West, "I don't know whether Elvis helped Jackie. I would like to think he might have done that. Some people made Elvis aware of the situation that Jackie was in and he almost cried. He said, 'Oh no, man.' I don't know if Elvis was ever made aware of any financial condition where he could help Jackie. I will tell you this if he did, he would have...if he'd known.

"Elvis related other entertainers to himself. He just made money and other people took care of it. Elvis didn't do anything else but sign expense forms and tax forms, anything else the money went through other hands. He wasn't even aware of the cost of living going up every month or every year."

Quite a few visited Jackie while he convalesced. In July 1977, his mentor, Billy Ward, visited and claimed that although Jackie didn't speak he was certain, perhaps by the way Jackie gripped his arm, that he was recognised. There was love between the two men. Ward knew Jackie's character flaws, but says simply, "Jackie didn't have the advantages I had as a human being."

Jackie's half-sister Joyce Ann Lee visited him in July 1976. His daughter Jacqueline (Denise) did also and announced to the press that the prognosis was not good.

McRae says: "Al Green, Phillipe Wynn [lead singer of The Spinners] and Bobby Smith came late at night. Lou Rawls came; I quietly snuck Lou in. Harlean became so embarrassed and flustered, she introduced herself as Mrs Rawls. Lou says Jackie turned around and acted totally different.

"Harlean showed up when she thought it was appropriate. Months and months went by and you wouldn't see her. Then if there was a court hearing or something was going on, or if she got mind that Jackie was making progress. Because, in my opinion, it was worrying her. In my theory it was really concerning Nat." Remarkably, McRae has never met Nat Tarnopol, and there's no recollection by anyone that he visited or had concern for Jackie's condition.

Gil Askey, once music arranger for Jackie, commented about the dearth of visitors: "A lot of people told you he will not know who you are anyway. Some people just don't have that warmth in heart. They wouldn't visit if you are in jail, say. When you're hot you're hot, when you're not you're not. Because people can't talk, you don't know whether they can hear or not. I gather there would be tears flowing. Jackie's nerves were reacting. In other words, they're saying it doesn't matter because Jackie was unaware. Everybody figures when you go to see someone it's got to be, 'Hey baby what's happening. Oh man, everything is great.' But you go there to pay homage. It's like you go to your mother's grave; when you go there you say,

'Hi, Ma, how are you doing? I kinda miss you,' and you leave flowers there. Remembering, paying your respects to someone who was very close to you." *That's* the reason people should have visited more.

It wasn't as if nobody was trying to help Jackie. Over the years he was moved around from Cherry Hill Medical Centre to the Cooper River Convalescent Centre in Pennsauken, New Jersey, the Morris Hall Rehabilitation Centre, New Jersey, Hahnemann Hospital in nearby Philadelphia, and to Medford Leas Retirement Centre at Mt Holly, New Jersey, where he spent the longest period.

In 1976 he was also admitted to St Francis Medical Centre in Trenton, New Jersey, "with a possible case of pneumonia". His temperature was 103. In June 1977, when Jackie turned forty-three, he received only six birthday cards, according to McRae. One newspaper reporter commented, "There is life. There is death. There is something in between. Jackie Wilson had inhabited that chasm."

McRae speaks bitterly about those who claimed to be Jackie's friends: "Sure, all these people talk lovingly of Jackie. They loved him in the context of being what he was; *an entertainer*. They didn't love him enough to just do the one thing he needed; to get in there and see him and save his life.

"But in fairness to some of these people, they were threatened, they were warned off. They were bullshitted around. Then there were idiots like Bobby Womack saying, 'I saw him; he was up and walking around,' when Jackie was semi-comatose! It started to look like a family dispute and, in the black culture, if it looks like a family dispute, people run...like from the plague.

"They loved him so much he died. The Jacksons...Michael Jackson came. T Mac went to see Jackie. Levi Stubbs; why did he never visit? I begged Levi to come and see Jackie. Mama Stubbs and Eliza Mae were good friends. They bought the bullshit that he was a vegetable – best to remember him the way he was. They live the lie.

"Denise came, Tony came. Sandy was too sick to come. They came, they spent the time. He and Sandy were kind of close because she had that kind of personality. His true friends were myself, Carl Davis, and Billy Davis in his own way. Tony had almost no relationship with Jackie. He was so timid he used to hide behind Freda's and Eliza's legs. Jackie never had a real relationship with Tony.

"Molly [who had an affair with Jackie, and a daughter, Sabrina], to the best of my knowledge, never visited Jackie. Molly has her own axe to grind.

Molly claims Jackie was preparing to leave Lynn for her. Spare me. Give me a break. They all put forward the myth that they had twenty-four carat gold pussies and that's all Jackie ever wanted in life. All these women have this desperation to be 'somebody'. They feel if a famous entertainer rides them, that makes them somebody special. They have low self-esteem. It's pathetic.

"Where the fuck was Sabrina? I told her, if you loved your daddy that much why didn't you visit him? Her answer was, 'Well my father never would have wanted to see me in that position.' That says to me that the only thing she ever saw in Jackie Wilson was that he was an entertainer. If he couldn't perform, and if he couldn't do something for you; there was nothing for him. It was all about, 'What could you do for me?' 'What have you done for me lately?'"

In a decision that she regrets, Freda never did visit Jackie, possibly because she was fighting her own battle at the time; with the demon alcohol. Most likely in atonement, the former nurse today takes care of a severely brain damaged man in her own home. Leonard, who is roughly Jackie's age, had been viciously beaten and prospects for his recovery were minimal. Freda, with the help of "Doctor God", has done the impossible and greatly improved Leonard's quality of life. Regrettably, she didn't make the attempt with Jackie.

"I didn't go and see Jack, but my mother went up there and she said he didn't look like he was going to come out of it," she says, "but they were surprised he came out of the coma. Jack was a very strong person. He used to will himself to do things."

Sandra loved her father, but Freda wouldn't take her to visit. Says Freda, "She had glaucoma in one eye. It was so bad, they were going to take that one eye out. They were going to put an artificial eye in. I talked to the doctor and she said, 'You don't know how much pain the child is in. The eye needs to come out of there. It's not doing anything. She can see a little bit, but it's killing her.' So that was worrying Sandy and her daddy's condition was worrying her. She said, 'I have to go and see about dad.'"

In January 1976, not long after Jackie's collapse, the Detroit *Free Press* wrote an article entitled, "The Last Song For Detroit's First Black Rock Star, Jackie Wilson" (by Susan Morse, 11 January, 1976). Joyce Ann and Denise were interviewed and made interesting comments:

"We'd see more of him on TV than in the house," said Denise. "When any of us first realised he was a star I was eight years old. He had a record out called 'The Greatest Hurt'. My teachers and friends kept telling me it was Number One..." Denise asked her father if it were so, and was amazed at his response. "He was really hurt. My father sat me down and said: 'Don't you ever forget. Your father is a star and always will be so.'" Actually, 'The Greatest Hurt' was released in 1962 when Denise was eleven, not eight as she recalled.

"My father loves excitement," Denise continued. "As long as my father had his jewellery, fantastic clothes, a big car, and the women...he liked the idea of being able to throw his weight around. When he was in that position, he could go out and say: 'I ain't going to sing,' and the people would tear the theatre up."

In the same article Denise also recalled the absence of her father from her coming out reception in 1967, when she was sixteen. "Who's supposed to bring me out in society but my father? Instead, I got a telegram and a dozen roses...I guess I didn't know how much we needed him around until it was too late."

She finished by saying, "I guess other people must dream of what an entertainer's private life is like, but God all the glory ends when you walk off that stage."

From May 1977, Jackie was confined at a Quaker establishment, the geriatric facility of Medford Leas. Joyce McRae had been barred by the court from even visiting him, since 14 April, 1976. Besides, she exhausted all her legal options and her money. However, always the fighter, she had one more card up her sleeve. She knew Jackie and Elvis were friendly and respected each other. Perhaps he would help financially?

In 1976 she waited for Elvis as he exited from the rear concert door of a performance. In McRae's words: "I tried to get to Elvis to get him to help Jackie. Elvis came out of the service elevator and I called out, 'Elvis, I've got to talk to you about Jackie Wilson. I need your help.' And he literally stopped dead in his tracks.

"Lamar [Fike, one of Elvis's entourage] and some fat old goon stopped him as he walked towards me. They literally picked him up by the armpits and wouldn't let me get to him. They stuffed him into the limo. I threw a picture into the limo, he got it and called, 'Come back!' I showed him Jackie was no vegetable."

Elvis isn't easy to reach on the phone and, at that time, he probably had his own problems, because in August 1977 he was dead at the age of forty-two; he was only six months Jackie's junior.

With genuine concern for Jackie, Dick Clark and his wife, Kari, visited Jackie in the nursing home. Says Clark: "I used to visit him on occasions at the rest home, and they told me that if I sat and talked to him he could hear me. So I used to sit and for a half hour or an hour regale him with stories of the old days. I would study his eyes to see if there was any flicker, but there never was."

McRae dismisses this idea. "Dick Clark is a liar if he says Jackie didn't recognise him during that visit," she fumes. "The night that he visited Harlean had assaulted me, in the hospital. The IV tube had come out of Jack's arm. He had been transferred from Morris Hall to St Francis Hospital in Trenton, New Jersey, because he'd spiked a fever. In fact, Al Green had just been up there. I went with Jack in the ambulance and Al went back to Cherry Hill. It was right before The Spinners' October 1976 benefit. Dick stopped in on his way to New York; he called in on Jackie just after they changed his IV.

"There was a nurse, Teresa, there that told him, 'All he needs is massive therapy, sir,' 'cause Dick was confused – he was astonished. Dick was there with Kari...he looked at Jackie. Dick was astonished that Jackie was as good as he was, it freaked him out. Jackie looked him dead in the face; I got Jackie to make a sound for Dick. He acknowledged that Jackie was responding, and the nurse said absolutely he was. She told him, 'He can come around. This man is no vegetable.' I truly believed that Dick was going to turn around to help."

McRae is bitter that, in her opinion, Dick Clark didn't do more to ensure Jackie was given more rehabilitative treatment. She was angry, too, that Dick Clark had publicly wished that Jackie's life would end. He believed there was no chance of recovery and that death was preferable to the limbo he was in.

McRae saw her opportunity to tackle Clark at an appearance he made on *The Phil Donahue Show*. "Dick was on live from Chicago," she relates. "He sat up and advocated euthanasia for Jackie. At this stage Harlean had ousted me from the hospital. I disguised myself and sat in the audience. I planted someone in the audience to ask Dick Clark the question, 'How's Jackie Wilson doing?' Dick responded, 'It's a terrible situation. He looked so pitiful. I wish the good Lord would take him away. It's a tragic situation.' He was really sorry that they came and helped him. I kept my hand up and finally got my chance. I was the last person to speak. I said, 'I don't know how you can say that when you were at St Francis Hospital.' He turned green and was flop sweating and said, 'Whether he could or could not have survived is a whole 'nother show.' Clark said, 'This woman has done an amazing job and we know how dedicated she was.'

"I said, 'Dick, that is not the issue. You were at the hospital you saw Jackie respond and were told that Jackie needed massive amounts of therapy. You turned your back.' He said, 'It was really tragic and there was no hope' and all that. Phil Donahue was picking up on it. "

Dick Clark liked and respected Jackie. He'd helped Jackie gain nationwide exposure early in his solo career and visited him when he was shot in 1961. When Jackie had the heart attack he was there right along with Jackie after being rushed to Cherry Hill Medical Centre. But in his view Jackie had no prospect of a life other than as a vegetable. By disagreeing with McRae he became her enemy, like everybody she had contact with.

From 1978 to 1984, Jackie ceased to be news. He remained at Medford Leas with very few visitors bothering to pay their respects. Not that it was an easy matter now to gain entry, as Harlean had to approve every request personally.

It's likely Jackie wouldn't have borne the non-visitors any malice because he always avoided illness, hospitals and funerals himself. Nevertheless, it is sad to reflect that this dynamic performer wasted away, almost forgotten by the world.

One relative who made the journey from Michigan to visit her cousin, was Josie Wynn. "We went to New Jersey to visit Jackie in the nursing home, but security was so tight," she reports. "A lot of rhetoric. Harlean cleared us to get in. I talked to her by phone. When I talked to the nurse she said he didn't get many visitors because of the high security. If Harlean didn't know the people they weren't allowed to go in. Maybe people became discouraged and didn't visit. Jack looked real good; I was really surprised. There were pictures that his son had scrawled, on the wall. He responded very well to the nurse. This was a year or two before he died. She told me how to get him to respond and he responded to me. I took his hand. He could grip your hand and his eyes were open, and he could blink his eyes."

The sad but true likelihood is that Jackie may well have been aware, but he had no way to express it.

CHAPTER FIFTEEN

Your Loss, My Gain

As a professional singer, Jackie earned money from his many live appearances, and from (initially) three per cent of retail record sales, which later, around 1969, became five per cent. He also earned from writer's royalties for radio "spins" and from the sales of records, on those songs which listed him as either writer or co-writer. Recording artists only made money from actual record sales and not from songs used in movies or commercials unless they were the songwriter.

The term "million seller" was a loose one in the 1950s and 1960s. Most claimed million sellers or gold records were nothing of the sort. A quarter of a million records sold may well have been enough to provide a Number One hit. The record companies handed out the gold discs. In all likelihood, Jackie had four genuine million sellers: 'Reet Petite', 'Lonely Teardrops', 'Night' and 'Higher And Higher'.

It is noteworthy that in 1986-1987 'Reet Petite' was re-issued in the UK and topped the charts there. At that time it is said to have sold between 700,000 and 800,000 in the United Kingdom alone – more than the combined sales there during his entire career! Jackie used to tell people that 'Reet Petite' sold four million copies, yet it reached only Number Sixty-Two on the US Pop charts, although it did make Number Six in the United Kingdom first time round.

Although it subsequently turned out that many records the record companies said didn't sell a million actually sold a lot more, the RIAA [Record Industry Association of America] doesn't credit Jackie with any gold records. Simon Rutberg admits there was confusion. "I'm not sure what was ever awarded a certified gold record," he says. "'Lonely Teardrops' they say may have sold one million. 'Higher And Higher' likely did; Carl Davis thinks it sold two million. Yet you won't find it listed as a gold record anywhere. If the record company is not a member of the RIAA, and Brunswick was not, the artist has no idea how many records were sold.

They say 'Whispers' was a gold."

As popular as he was and as incomparable as he was as a vocalist and stage performer, Jackie just was not able to convert that to a single Number One record. He did achieve six hits in the Top Ten Pop Chart – 'Lonely Teardrops', 'Night', 'Alone At Last', 'My Empty Arms', 'Baby Workout' and 'Higher And Higher' – while his friend Sam Cooke managed only five, but Cooke is somehow better remembered today.

Just how many records of Jackie's were sold? One of those who is in the best position to know, at least what the official sales were, was Roquel "Billy" Davis co-writer of most of Jackie's biggest hits. He says: "Originally none of those songs were reported as million sellers, however now 'Reet Petite', 'Lonely Teardrops' and 'Higher And Higher' have sold over a million. 'To Be Loved' has not – based on my royalty receipts. 'Reet Petite' has grossed the most royalties for me, because of the 1987 British hit, 'Higher And Higher' is the next biggest grossing, then 'Lonely Teardrops', 'To Be Loved', in that order."

Another person in an excellent position to know something about Jackie's record sales and "million sellers" is Carl Davis, who produced eight of his albums and was also vice president of Brunswick Records. "Back then a record company wanted to boast 'the record sold a million'," admits Davis, "but they didn't want to pay those royalties to an artist or writer, so they were in a dilemma. I even had them call me aside and say we are going to give you a gold record even though it didn't go that far. Sometimes when I did feel it went 'gold' they never paid you on it. You were at the mercy of those guys back then. Unless a record sold two million you never got a report right to you, anyhow, as a writer."

Once a song is published, it is necessary to renew the publishing rights every twenty-five years or it will become "in the public domain". Radio stations are required to have a log book for airplay royalties, which they must send along with a cheque to BMI on a regular basis. Concerning record sales, the record company pays the publisher writer's royalties whenever they sell records.

For the recording artist to be paid correctly, relied to a large extent on the honesty of the label he recorded for. In Jackie's case it was Brunswick.

On 25 June, 1975, the Detroit *News* reported: "Payola Probe Indicts Nineteen, Six Record Firms." It made fascinating reading:

Nat Tarnopol, president and controlling stockholder of Brunswick Record Corps and sole stockholder of Dakar Records, Inc, both centred in New York and Chicago, was indicted of charges of conspiracy, mail fraud, wire fraud and evasion of more than $103,000 in personal income taxes and more than $184,000 in corporate income taxes. Six of Tarnopol's employees were also indicted and all were accused of selling records to distributors by illegal and surreptitious means.

In March 1976, following the 1975 indictments, Nat Tarnopol faced serious charges in the New Jersey court. If there was one person in a position to give testimony against Tarnopol, assuming that he would, it was Jackie. Fredric Danner, in his well researched book on the American music industry, *Hit Men*, best explains the case against Tarnopol: "The seven senior executives of Brunswick Records, including Nat Tarnopol, were indicted for taking $343,000 in kickbacks from retailers, to whom they allegedly sold records below wholesale price; and for using part of the funds to pay off radio stations. Tarnopol was also indicted for conspiring to cheat the IRS and for wire fraud.

"Also caught up in this net were Carl Davis, Brunswick's vice president, but who had nothing to do with the day-to-day running of the company, and Melvin Moore, formerly of Decca, but now Brunswick's promotions director."

Danner continues:

The Newark grand jury was hearing testimony about R&B label Brunswick Records and its president, Nat Tarnopol. He was a well known industry figure who had produced shows at the Brooklyn Paramount with Alan Freed and managed and recorded soul singer Jackie Wilson. Nat Tarnopol was acquitted of thirty-eight counts of mail and wire fraud, but found guilty of one count of conspiracy, in a 1976 jury trial. He was sentenced to three years in jail. Then his conviction, too, was overturned on a legal technicality. Though he was tried again in 1978, the proceeding ended in a mistrial, and the government ultimately dropped the case.

The loss was a sad blow because Tarnopol was a notorious abuser of artists, on a par with Morris Levy. He had taken ruthless advantage of Jackie Wilson by designing contracts that left the singer perpetually in debt to Brunswick, even as his records made hundreds of thousands for the label. The writer's credit of Wilson's 'Doggin' Around' is listed to Paul Tarnopol, Nat's son, who wasn't born when the song was recorded. Even the appellate judge who overturned Tarnopol's conviction took pains to note in his decision that "there was evidence for which a jury could find that artists were defrauded of royalties".

Robert Pruter's "must read" book, *Chicago Soul*, explains about the Brunswick fraud, but in more detail:

In March 1976...Nat Tarnopol and three other Brunswick officers were convicted of various fraud charges and one conspiracy charge. The government found that the defendants sold nearly 500,000 singles and albums at a discount for $300,000 cash and $50,000 in merchandise. Such transactions according to the government defrauded the company's artists and writers of rightful royalties and the government of tax monies. Carl Davis, as vice president, and Melvin Moore, as national promotion director, were also tried, but were found innocent on the grounds that they were not privy to what was going on in the New York office.

Despite the seeming dishonesty of such practices, the defence contended that selling records at a discount was a common means of doing business and a necessity for an independent company competing against the majors in the 1970s. Furthermore, Nat Tarnopol and the other defendants were not intentionally trying to defraud anybody. In an elaboration to me, Tarnopol asserted that selling records wholesale at discount was a means to get the volume to put a record up the charts, which in the end helps an act rather than hurts it. He suggested all companies at one time or another did this, and said that compared to others,

"Brunswick was a baby".

Tarnopol appealed his conviction, and in December 1977 the conviction was overturned. In June 1978, following a retrial, a judge dismissed the charges and declared a mistrial after the case fell apart. Undoubtedly contributing to the weakness of the government's case was the prosecution's failure to bring any witnesses to the stand to testify that they had been defrauded.

Davis said he was mystified by the events: "Nat was a very good executive and that's one of the reasons why I was confused, that he would do something like that. I really liked him and I considered him a good friend of mine, but then after the trial started, I realised that he wasn't as good a friend as I thought. He destroyed something that I had worked hard for all my life. I had always said that when I got to be around forty-five years old, I would have liked to have been able to, you know, sit back and clip coupons. There I was starting all over again in my forties rather than being able to retire."

During and after the trial Davis and all the key creative persons abandoned the company, and all the important artists left as well.

Even Dick Clark, who considered himself a friend of Tarnopol's, exclaims, "It was a very colourful period of time. I don't think the history books would deny that Nat got away with a lot of Jackie's money." And if Tarnopol was defrauding his artists, what of Tommy Vastola and his lieutenant, Johnny Roberts?

Joyce McRae claims that evidence was tended which incriminated August Sims, as well. "During the trials, August Sims was named by the Federal Government as the bag-man and the guy who was driving the car and trading records for electrical appliances and stuff," she says. Sims worked for Tarnopol in the New York office, presumably doing record promotions.

It was revealed in the court that Sims had assisted Tarnopol to defraud the artists, according to Davis: "Then after that Nat started stealing money from the records, he'd take a guy like Sims and load up a U-hire truck and sell records all over the country for cash. Nat bought an El Dorado [Cadillac] with records. Then he had a thing with Cardinal Red something, import-export company, and my God they exchanged a lot of records for money."

All of the artists felt more loyalty to Davis and generally pursued their careers through him. Brunswick was effectively finished as a recording company, with its top artist, Jackie, lying in a nursing home with the grimmest prognosis. Davis, for one, sees some good in the court's verdict. "It was enough that the judge at the trial gave every artist on the label their release because Brunswick was selling their records and not paying them by not putting it on the books," he insists. "But that was too late for Jackie."

However, to this day, Brunswick still owns the masters for all the numerous artists who recorded with it over the previous eighteen to nineteen years.

"I resigned and started Chi-Sound, and all these artists that were Brunswick came with me," Davis continues. "If Tarnopol hadn't been so greedy. He used to have a saying, that by the time we're forty-five, we're going to be clipping coupons…retired. I believed that and looked forward to that. And here he is stealing and ruining the company.

"Tarnopol tried to get me killed because I said I was leaving. They had three or four different meetings, they had me one time up in his office and they had the little guy who represented the Godfather and some big six foot six, three hundred pound goon who made the suggestion – we were on the twenty-seventh floor – 'Let's throw this cock-sucker out of the fucking window.'

"The only thing that protected me was they knew I was with Tommy. And the little guy – he was a little tiny guy – and he told this big guy, 'Why don't you sit your ass down.' He said, 'Carl, you make sure you tell Tommy, you tell him that I was the one that took up for you and didn't let anybody bother you. I was just trying to find out what the truth is to this and what's going on.'" Another meeting was set up.

"So Tommy said, 'You go to the meeting. You don't have to worry about nothing; just tell them the truth.' It wasn't that I'd done anything wrong, it was that they have got a funny thing among themselves: if I bring you into this business and you do something and I don't like it, I can have you killed. That's just the way it is. But Tarnopol didn't bring me into Brunswick, Tommy brought me in, and that's a whole different story."

Without saying so directly, Davis is clearly implying that Vastola controlled Brunswick. Why else would Vastola arrange for Gene Chandler to sign onto it? Also, Vastola was the person who brought Davis to Brunswick.

"It was proven that Nat didn't bring me in, but it took three weeks to clear that up," says Davis. "There was one meeting at the office and two meetings in Jersey, at the restaurant, and at the airport. There was some guy that had made a threat to Tommy, and Tommy wanted to kill him and they said, 'No, Corky, leave him alone.' I left Brunswick with hat and coat and didn't take even a pencil."

Almost certainly the person who had made the threat to Vastola was Tarnopol. Luckily for him, he, too, had his "protectors".

Lynn Crochet is to this day bitter concerning what happened to the man she loved: "Nat stripped Jackie of the company. Jackie owned the company; he had contracts and all. When Nat lost the case and was convicted, all of that was in the court records." But Nat wasn't on his own. Crochet who liked and respected Johnny Roberts, admits, "JR may have been part of the records being sold out the backdoor."

Tommy Vastola had a particular fondness for the music industry business. This was no doubt due to his long and deep friendship with Morris Levy, his childhood friend. In the mid 1960s, Vastola was arrested by the FBI on charges of record piracy. This concerned the not uncommon, but highly illegal, practice of copying hot selling records and passing them off as the genuine article. This was known in industry parlance as "bootlegging", a term derived from the Prohibition era.

Hit Men devotes most of its pages to the activities of Gaetano "Tommy" Vastola and Morris Levy. In September 1986 the FBI made some important arrests. *Hit Men* reports:

> A force of sixty FBI agents had fanned out across Metropolitan New York and New Jersey and had rounded up and arrested seventeen men allegedly connected with Gaetano Vastola's illegal business empire, including Sonny Brocco, Lew Saka, Dominick Canterino, and Nicky Masaro. Vastola and Rudy Farone were charged in the indictment but managed to elude arrest, authorities believed, because they were tipped off to the government's planned move.

It is believed that Jackie named his son, to Harlean, John Dominick after Dominick Canterino although it's not known how intimate their association was.

The cause of the FBI interest in the first place occurred because Vastola lost his temper and severely assaulted a record wholesaler, John LaMonte. The assault, which involved one punch, fractured bones in LaMonte's head and nearly caused him to lose the sight of one eye – permanently. More seriously for Vastola and the others, it caused LaMonte to co-operate with the FBI and lead to the racketeering charges against Vastola and his colleagues.

Hit Men further states:

> The Vastola Organisation, headed by Gaetano Vastola, had "carried out a pattern of racketeering activity", [the US attorney for the District of New Jersey] Greelish said, "involving heroin and cocaine trafficking, loan-sharking, use of threats and violence in the collection of debts and takeover of businesses indebted to the Organisation". If convicted on all counts, Vastola faced 286 years in prison.

The mention of drug trafficking never led to convictions, but is consistent with Jackie's brother-in-law Johnny Collins's claim that "the company" supplied Jackie's cocaine habit.

August Sims, Jackie's road manager from 1963 to 1972, worked for Vastola through Johnny Roberts. One particular event in his mind is indicative of Vastola's power: "I remember in Lake Tahoe, Tommy Vastola came in. I gave him five thousand dollars [from Jackie's earnings]. Then he said, 'Come with me, I got to get money from Vic Damone.' Poor son of a bitch, I felt sorry for him. But he had his hands in him, too. Vic had to give up $100,000; he was making that kind of money. He worked the big room. See, in the big room you make $200,000 to $300,000. The Mob would tell them, 'We want $200,000 to 300,000 for this act,' and they would give it. The casino paid the act anyway. They didn't have to worry about no money." This first hand account implies the payments were good business for the casino and very good business for the Mob who took the cream off the top of the artists earnings – tax free.

An insider, who must remain nameless, said, "Johnny Roberts wasn't in charge. He comes from 'Corky' Vastola. Corky set policy. Johnny was a flunky in that sense. He was the muscle."

In October 1991, Tommy Vastola was sentenced to a hefty seventeen years after being found guilty of racketeering, extortion and eighteen other charges. Although his conviction had nothing to do with Brunswick records or Jackie, it was to do with the sale of what is referred to in the record industry as "record cutouts". Cutouts are the millions of over-pressed and unsold records which are in turn sold to wholesalers for a fraction of their original retail prices.

Vastola was, by most accounts, a very polite and likable character. He was also a good family man who saw to it that his daughter, Joy, received the best possible education. He sent Joy to school in Oxford, England, after which she came back and he started a law firm in New York. Joy Vastola has worked tirelessly ever since, attempting to have her father's convictions overturned.

Morris Levy, who had been feted by the record industry executives for many years because of his ability to distribute records effectively throughout the country, was, in October 1988, sentenced to ten years in prison and a $200,000 fine on charges of racketeering. Levy never spent a day in jail; he died of liver cancer in May 1991, while on bail of three million dollars, pending appeal. Before he died, it is reported he sold his music industry holdings for seventy million dollars.

It is not at all clear how or if Morris Levy was involved with Jackie's career, apart from his close association with Vastola. Quite likely he was. Levy also owned the New York based Roulette Records, which was one of the hottest independent labels of the 1950s with the likes of Frankie Lyman And The Teenagers and Joey Dee And The Starlighters. He is described variously as "one of the pioneers of the music industry", and "a legendary figure in the recording industry". He had earlier owned the most famous jazz night club, Birdland, on Broadway in New York, which featured the likes of Dizzy Gillespie, Count Basie and Duke Ellington.

But Levy had also once owned the major "cutout" distribution company, along with mobster Thomas "Tommy Ryan" Eboli. Eboli died by gunfire in a Brooklyn street in 1972.

Frank Sinatra, Bob Hope and numerous dignities and politicians Levy counted amongst his close friends. He was a generous donator to charities. Levy, a very charismatic man, also had another famous friend – Jackie

Wilson. Regardless of whether they had professional ties, it was Levy who threw the wedding reception for Jackie and Harlean at his Roundtable Restaurant in 1967.

The trial made Carl Davis aware of the way Tarnopol had been defrauding all the Brunswick artists; Davis himself was also a victim because he was a ten per cent stockholder. "I stuck with Nat because I truly believed Nat," he confesses, "until I got the indictment papers and when we got to court. I learned all the money was going everywhere."

He gives an example of the money not going to the rightful owners: "The Chi-Lites were owed ninety thousand dollars [by Brunswick]. Tommy put us on *The Flip Wilson Show*. 'Oh Girl' became a big hit. The Chi-Lites wanted some money. Nat said, 'No.'

"We had a meeting with Johnny Roberts, Nat Tarnopol and Eugene Record. Gene said, 'Where's that ninety thousand dollars [for session work]?' When he said that, Johnny Roberts reached over and grabbed him by the mouth. Gene was crying. Johnny said, 'I'm going to get my pistol.' Nat was right behind him. I sat there with Eugene and told him he had to be careful.

"Tommy walked in and said, 'What's this nonsense?' He ran them out. In the trial it sounded like I set it up. Before Eugene left town The Chi-Lites got a sixty thousand dollar cheque."

It was probably just as well for Tarnopol that Jackie was laying in bed semi-comatose, because he could presumably have given damaging testimony, had he chosen to do so. Johnny Roberts, surprisingly, was not called on to testify. Nobody would have known more than he.

Bobby Schiffman, who had fully taken over the Apollo Theatre in Harlem from his father Frank in 1961, loyally stands by his close friend and firmly believes Tarnopol was nothing but a scapegoat. "They picked Nat out of a lot of people who were all doing the same thing," he says. "This business of paying disc jockeys to play your record is illegal. It became known as 'the payola scandal' and Nat became the scape goat.

"It cost Nat one thousand dollars a day to stay out of jail. And you know what? There were fifty people or more in the music industry who were more guilty, or as guilty as Nat, who never got hit with that legal action. They picked him out and tried to make him an example. He was found not guilty. He was suing the US Government for ruining his life and career and taking his wealth away.

"When he got into trouble with the law, the expense of defending himself cost him his health and his money. The time came when the affluent Nat Tarnopol needed to borrow money to pay expenses. I was one who loaned him money – a lot – and I couldn't afford to. It took a long time, but he paid back every cent. The last of it from the grave [Tarnopol died in December 1987].

"I am convinced that as lovable as Jackie was, he was just incorrigible. He threw his money away. Without Nat, it would have been worse. Jackie could be very arrogant; he mellowed later on."

Schiffman is not wrong when he says that in the years following Tarnopol's trial, life became very hard for him. Nat's son says his health suffered greatly from the stress of it all. "CBS was licensing from my father and paying him fifty per cent," says Paul. "CBS then licensed to Ace Records in the United Kingdom. So the amount my father received wasn't all that much."

Paul too believes his father was unfairly singled out. "Every ten years payola would become an issue. My dad and Alan Freed were good friends; I am sure favours were exchanged."

Much of the music recorded, as well as written, by Jackie was published by the music publishers Regent and Merrimac Music, both owned by brothers of the famous band leader, Benny Goodman. There was a very close association between the brothers, Harry and Gene, and Tarnopol.

Documents supplied by Tarnopol, under court subpoena, list the following names as directors of Brunswick: Milton R Rackmil, Leonard W Schneider of Novel Productions, Martin P Salkin of Decca Records, Harry Goodman, Gene Goodman and Nat Tarnopol.

It's unlikely Tarnopol was defrauding his artists without Vastola and Brunswick's directors being part of the swindle.

Tarnopol's closest friends were Artie Mogul, Bobby Schiffman, Gene Goodman and Bud Prager, the head of SESAC (society concerned with the performing arts). Prager went on to manage the groups Foreigner, The Chambers Brothers and Cream.

Jackie's management team made Elvis's relationship with Colonel Tom Parker seem perfectly normal by comparison. "That's one thing about the colonel," says Sonny West, Elvis's friend. "He didn't take anything but the fifty/fifty. But the deals he made! He made Elvis more money than anyone else could have. That was the perfect marriage; that time in history. To have a promoter like that to come up with a product like that – Elvis – and be able to exploit it, and promote it the way he did."

By contrast, Jackie had a manager who likely started with the best of intentions, but ended up by offering Jackie the short end of the stick. The pity was Jackie seemingly took so long to realise it.

One industry insider who has worked closely with the best contemporary artists, says simply, "It's not the industry that destroys people, it's the money. The music industry is run by big corporations. The star often doesn't have much education – they didn't go to university. They were just family people. Here they were driving around in a Cadillac car, with beautiful women chasing them around. And when there's money there's crooks dreaming up schemes to take it from you."

CHAPTER SIXTEEN

The Greatest Hurt

Medford Leas Nursing Home decided to move Jackie to Burlington County Memorial Hospital on 8 January, 1984 apparently because "he was having trouble taking nourishment". The great man's will to live had gone. At 11.00am on 21 January, 1984 his heart finally beat no more. Jackie was five months short of his fiftieth birthday. At 11.20am he was pronounced dead by Dr James Atkinson III, MD.

The cause of death was listed as "aspiration pneumonia". The hospital performed no autopsy, but a spokeswoman said, "Wilson's family [ie Harlean] asked that no information about the circumstances of his death be released". It had been eight and a quarter agonising years since he'd suffered the heart attack at the Latin Casino, Cherry Hill.

Jackie climbed from humble origins to become a world recognised recording artist and dynamic performer. His fall cut short a career that still had a long way to go.

Joyce McRae, long since barred from visiting him by Harlean, is critical to the end. "Jackie died the most hideous, tortured death imaginable," she says. "He died from massive amounts of negligence and neglect – much of it deliberate. It is verified in his medical records."

Launa Toledo, Harlean's friend, points out one irony of the circumstances of his death, namely that it happened during his sober years: "He'd been living healthy for the last six years of his life [prior to the collapse]. When he was drinking he was fine. When he quit drinking, it killed him."

"Harlean called me crying within thirty minutes of his dying," she says. "In fact they'd been trying to call her. She was on her way there. Lynn's kids learned about the death on the TV. They thought he was dead. She'd told them he'd died. She wasn't going up there any more."

The singer's indignities continued beyond death. The New Jersey undertaker who shipped the body back to Detroit, found Jackie's legs so constricted he had to break them to get him into the coffin.

At the Russell Street Baptist Church in Detroit, an impressive funeral was conducted. Jackie had been baptised and had sung with his gospel group there as a child. Harlean, being legally considered his wife, arranged proceedings. Many of the women in his life attended along with fans, and relatives from Michigan and Columbus, Mississippi.

Even at such a solemn occasion, Lynn Crochet was shunned by the rest of the family. Dressed in white, she sat alone with her children and Sabrina, Jackie's daughter to Molly. "I showed up at the funeral," says Lynn. "I got the message not to show; just to send my children. I told them, you'd better meet me at the city limits with an injunction to keep out of Detroit.

"Me and the children went; I sat at the back and watched the circus, because that's what it was. Harlean with her fifteen nurses. It was so phoney. When I got there and saw the casket open and where they had him, I went berserk. I called Joyce Ann and said, 'What are you doing to your brother? You don't have him down there in a place like that, and you shouldn't have the coffin open.' He wouldn't want people to see him like that. He was a very vain man. He didn't look good in the casket, not to me he didn't. The clothes didn't fit him and it was not something that he would have worn. I just went whacko. As soon as I called Joyce...it was a big production and the casket was closed."

The open coffin was more probably due to Freda than to Joyce Ann. "He wouldn't have wanted to look like he did," Freda confirms. "He was vain; he liked to look pretty all the time. If he'd seen some of those pictures...He wanted people to remember him, in my opinion, like when he did 'Lonely Teardrops', Mr Excitement! That was his exit.

"Mrs Williams, who fixed his body when he came back from the nursing home, she did a good job. It was the same funeral home, Mason and Williams, that handled his father, Johnny Lee and my kids, Jackie Jnr and Sandra. It wasn't decided to have a closed or open casket, but when Harlean, Jacqui [Freda's sister] and I went over to view the body, the people were lined up to see him. I said, 'We have to leave it open.' Jackie looked so young and his skin so pretty."

Mrs Williams, who had prepared Jackie for burial, confirms this. "Freda personally asked Harlean to let the people view Jackie before his body left for the cemetery; to say goodbye," she says. "It was very cold out there and they had been waiting. They were the ones who truly loved him and she knew that. We didn't straighten his hair like he did it. He'd been sick for so long. "

The harmony between Jackie's first and second wives wasn't always there. "At one point they weren't going to let Freda go to the funeral," claims Joyce McRae. "It got very ugly. Freda knows Mama wouldn't even let Harlean in the house. She never acknowledged Petey as a grandchild. She knows Mama had the papers to show that Jack thought he had a divorce – they substituted pages on those documents. I was the one who hired a PI in New York to find the shit; I found the documents. They had it all suppressed."

Johnny Collins is just as bitter about Harlean's involvement. "Harlean came to the funeral with a mink coat that was horrendous, awful – torn to threads," he says. "I wouldn't have shoved my dog in it. Her tears were real; tears of guilt, that's the reality. When you play with the devil and he burns you, don't be surprised. It's just his nature. She loved him, but she couldn't own him. She's partly responsible for all the shit that's ever happened to him. I can't come to any other conclusion but that."

On 28 January, 1984, the Reverend Anthony C Campbell performed the eulogy to a packed congregation of around 1,500. Campbell said, "It's a glorious day to send Jackie home. We cannot gloss it over; we're here to say goodbye." He commented that there were "four escape routes from the ghetto; crime, politics, sports and entertainment." It may have escaped his notice that the first and the last professions are common to all four.

Amongst the notables in attendance were the Detroit Spinners who had been responsible for the benefit concert in 1976. Uzziel Lee, who formerly owned Lee's Club Sensation where Jackie had sung as a fifteen-year-old, was also there. Masses of floral tributes adorned the back of the church, including an arrangement of white carnations in the shape of a record from "James Brown and Friends". There was an arrangement from Dick Clark, Detroit's Mayor Young, and Phelps Lounge where Jackie's career had commenced.

Possibly nobody at the funeral noticed, but someone missing amongst those who had come to pay homage was Truman Thomas, the talented young organ player who had travelled with Jackie in the 1970s. He was intending to be present, but died of an overdose on the eve of the funeral. Could this be a coincidence?

Lead singer of The Four Tops, Levi Stubbs, addressed the congregation:

"Jackie Wilson was loved. People wouldn't be here for any other reason. Jackie was street people in that he never became bigger than street people."

President of the Highland Park City Council and former classmate, Martha Scott, misses her old friend. "Jackie turned school assemblies, that seemed to be so boring, into a happening," she recalls. "We knew he was a star long before the rest of the world."

"Everyone in the neighbourhood cried when we heard what happened to him," says Loretta DeLoach, another childhood friend. "Tears were just streaming down everyone's eyes. It was beautiful but sad, of course. There is beauty sometimes in death. When you see the love that was there all through those years; to me that's beautiful. All the singers came from all over and honoured him."

Harlean chose the pallbearers. The Four Tops were selected along with Jackie's oldest friend, a greying JJ, and, controversially, his former road manager, August Sims. "Harlean ran everything, so it's no surprise that Sims was there," fumes McRae. "The only person who wasn't there was Nat, and Sims was there in his place. It was disrespectful for Sims to be a pallbearer." Overlooked as a pallbearer was Jackie's loyal friend, Billy Davis.

Jackie's body was then taken to Westlawn Cemetery at Wayne, just outside of Detroit, where he was finally laid to rest. His mother, but not his father, is buried at the same cemetery.

After the funeral, close friends and family went to the home that Jackie had purchased for his mother on Strathmoor Avenue. His sister Joyce Ann now lived there with her family. Lynn Crochet wasn't invited.

Both before and after the funeral Lynn didn't cope well. "I lost contact," she admits. "I went off the deep end and I turned to the booze and basically I should have gone to a psychiatrist when it happened, but I didn't. I would burst out crying just talking about him." Her painful memories are exacerbated by knowing how Jackie – her Jackie – would have wanted things. "I know he didn't want to be buried where he is. He wanted to be buried in Marietta, Georgia – on Highway 41."

After Jackie's burial, few at that ceremony would have dreamed that his burial site would remain entirely unmarked, save for a grave site number; B261. Not even a simple headstone. Responsibility for this gross omission is Harlean's. It was her funeral arrangement. Harlean claims she couldn't afford one, despite apparently collecting $45,000 life insurance when Jackie died.

But Freda blames Joyce Ann, Jackie's half-sister, whose envy seems to have carried on even beyond his death. "Joyce had all that money," says Freda. "I couldn't see why she didn't put a headstone out there. Harlean wouldn't care. Even the people in Pontiac wanted to put a stone out there, but Joyce didn't want to give her money."

Despite not having a large part of Jackie's life in terms of the total time they spent together, nevertheless Lynn Ciccone has never stopped loving him. Lynn travelled from her home in Springfield, Illinois in 1986 with a view to saying a final goodbye. Arriving at the Westlawn Cemetery she had difficulty locating the grave site. "I was horrified when I went to Detroit and I said, 'This man has no monument.'" she remembers. "Al Dobbins, the caretaker at the cemetery, put up the wooden cross." The cross had "Jackie Wilson" written on it with a felt-tipped pen.

Lynn, devastated at the lack of a proper headstone, contacted Harlean: "I said I was appalled there was no stone on Jackie's grave. She said, 'Well, there's no stone for anyone. Jackie's mother didn't have a headstone, either.' It seems like they buried them and never went back."

She also called Joyce McRae. Says McRae, "She contacted me and sent me pictures of the unmarked grave. I hit the roof.

"I hadn't gone to the funeral because I felt there'd already be too much controversy...and it wouldn't bring Jack back. So I got in touch with Dave Marsh [a writer with *Rolling Stone* magazine] who was one of the founding members of the Rhythm And Blues Foundation.

"Dave said, 'I can get a fabulous headstone for wholesale price of two thousand dollars. Why don't we get Le Baron Taylor?' He was a vice president at CBS; does special projects on black music. Le Baron contacted Jack the Rapper thinking he could help.

"Next thing Dave contacted me and said, 'What the fuck is going on? Have you seen Jack the Rapper?'" McRae contacted Jack Gibson and was taken aback by his response. She continued: "He tells me, 'It had all started from us,' and he said, 'We don't want any white-honky, motherfucking money.'

The Rapper wanted to do things his way. "At that point Jack and Harlean got together and raised over twenty thousand dollars," says McRae. Money poured in from sympathetic fans, even from overseas, due to Gibson's radio broadcast requests.

With the approximately eighteen thousand dollars in donations from loyal fans, it was now possible to erect a magnificent tomb and to move both Jackie and his mother into the common grave site. Jackie's body had to be exhumed and moved a short distance to his final resting place. The body of his mother likewise was moved to rest by his side. A special section of the cemetery specifically set aside for dignitaries of the church was given special dispensation for them to be buried together. His father Jack Snr, however, remained buried at the Lincoln Memorial Park Cemetery.

On what would have been Jackie's fifty-third birthday, 9 June, 1987, around 150 people attended a dedication ceremony at Westlawn Cemetery where Jackie and Eliza Mae Lee were interned together in the magnificent marble and granite tomb.

The original plan had been to inscribe the headstone with the epitaph "Your love keeps lifting me higher and higher", however this was changed to a fitting "No more lonely teardrops". Says Gibson, "The family allowed me to write the epitaph. I can go to my maker knowing that I did something for somebody. That was the motivation I had. We had so much fun together." Above his dates of birth and death was inscribed "Mr Excitement Jackie".

In attendance were Jack Gibson, Harlean and her son John, now twenty-four, and other family members including Jackie's sister Joyce Ann. Three years earlier she wasn't prepared to contribute for a simple headstone. August Sims again travelled from New York to pay his respects.

At the moving ceremony, two women sang and Jack Gibson spoke to Jackie: "Thank you for touching the Rapper's life. And thank you for the many entertainers that adopted your style. You're truly a legend we will not forget. Here, your final resting place with your mother, will be a shining beacon for all to see long after we are all gone."

Later he added, "A tribute to Jackie is something that some little black kid one hundred years from now will say, 'What happened with music back in the twentieth century?' and then they'll look it up and say, 'Jackie Wilson, let's hear what he did.'"

A spokesperson from the Highland Park Council announced that a street in the neighbourhood would be renamed "Jackie Wilson Drive". It never was, although the Council saw fit to rename Glendale Street Malcolm X Street after the radical black Muslim leader who was not even from the city.

Ken Settle writing of the ceremony in *Goldmine* (17 July, 1987) says: "But despite the joyous tone of the ceremony, one couldn't help but notice the conspicuous absence of many of Jackie Wilson's peers and pupils. Artists who Wilson helped in his halcyon days. 'I'm happy that you people came out,' August Sims, Wilson's road manager, stated. 'I hope that everybody across the country will see this. All the other entertainers that Jackie had on his shows. I don't see many of them here.'"

Most remarkably few from Motown bothered to show up. Pervis Jackson, bass singer with The Spinners was one of the few entertainers present.

The person who was indeed responsible for instigating the movement to have the tomb erected, Lynn Ciccone, sadly remained in the background once again with her and Jackie's twenty-four-year-old daughter, Gina. "At the dedication Harlean sent someone over to talk to her," she says. "We were told, 'Don't go to the reception tonight, or there will be big trouble. Harlean doesn't want you there.' Harlean put on tears at the dedication."

At the dedication, Lynn was shocked by Jack Gibson. "He spoke of Jackie as being 'a black Tom Jones'," she recalls, outraged by this reversal of history. "I said, 'I beg your pardon?"

Absent was first wife Freda, the person who had sacrificed more than anyone to ensure the man she loved would become a star – as she knew he surely would.

Lynn Crochet, the last woman he had lived with, and mother of two of his children, also chose not to attend. Lynn had done what nobody else was able to do; help Jackie overcome his addictions. She says, "I sent Thor to the memorial. I stayed out of it. I wanted him remembered as a family man, not with the two wives. Me and Harlean would have got into it, because I felt she killed him."

In the evening, Detroit's Latin Quarter Club hosted a celebration which heavyweight boxing champion Muhammed Ali attended. Entertainment was provided by the Dramatics and Floaters groups and others, none of whom were well known outside of Detroit. Motown vice president, Esther Gordy Edwards, showed up for this affair.

More money had been collected than was necessary. On Jackie's birthday, 9 June 1991, Jack Gibson went back to the cemetery, this time to dedicate the "meditation bench" which had been placed in front of the tomb. On this occasion Motown singer Marv Johnson attended. So, too, did the well known black DJ, "The Queen", Martha Jean.

Jackie may have been only forty-nine years old when he died, and forty-one when he collapsed, but he'd lived those years to the fullest and achieved much. There were disappointments in his life, but also great triumphs and the fruits of his life will forever be available for music lovers to listen to, and be thrilled by. At last this troubled man found the peace that had for so long eluded him. Next to him lay the woman who had loved him more than life itself.

CHAPTER SEVENTEEN

Postscript

For Freda the glory days when she lived well as the wife of Jackie Wilson are over; she lives in a humble, cramped apartment in Highland Park. Freda lovingly takes care of Leonard, the severely brain damaged man who relies totally on her. Although she receives some financial compensation from the State, the inescapable conclusion is that she is paying penance for her refusal to nurse Jackie after his collapse.

But she has no bitterness after having had and lost so much; including three of her four children. "Heartbreak?" says Freda. "I've had a lot of love and good things too. Then you look at the death of my children; I just say it's God's will. I have no control after that. I believe in an after-life. I believe that Jackie only ever loved me. This vase that Jackie sent me flowers in is thirty-seven years old; I still have it."

Jackie's long time girlfriend Lynn Ciccone met Freda in 1986. "Freda suffered the most," she says. "She was there when Jackie had nothing; helped him get to the top. She had a little job and made clothes for him so he could perform. She was the backbone. She lost it all and three of her four children. She's the one I have empathy for. Freda's getting by; a good person. She's just glad she was part of it. No animosity, not bitterness; just glad she knew him. If I had to say that Jackie only ever loved one woman, it would be Freda. He never really lost contact with her.

"After I met Freda I liked her immediately and I felt guilty that I took things she should have had. To me, Freda...she is most tragic. She went from nothing, to having everything, back to nothing. She's never said a bad thing about him."

Most of the Jackie memorabilia that Freda once owned, including records and photos, has been stolen by relatives. In 1994 she owned only two of his photos and few recordings. "I have times when I have my Jackie Wilson days. I listen to his music," she says.

Jackie's second daughter with Freda, Sandra, was better known as Sandy. Sandy married Reggie Abrams, who Jackie had sent up to Detroit in the hope he might fall for her sister Jacqueline (Denise). She had three children, but was estranged from Reginald. On Sunday 23 October, 1977, at twenty-four years, Sandy died in her sleep. Her body was found by eight-year-old son, Reggie Jnr.

Although Sandy had suffered throughout her life from chronic eye problems and had lost the sight of one eye due to glaucoma, she was otherwise in good health. It was just over two years since her father's collapse. Happily, Jackie was unaware he had now lost his mother and daughter. Sandra was buried at the Lincoln Memorial Park Cemetery where Jackie's father was buried.

"The reason Sandy wound up screwed up and died," says Joyce McRae firmly, "is because, after Eliza Mae died in October 1975, Joyce Ann threw them out of the house. She threw Reggie, Reno and Regina out and they were in foster homes for years. Sandy was sick – she got a respiratory infection – there may have been drug involvement. Joyce Ann threw them out of the house that Jackie bought for his mother; and Jackie wasn't dead yet!"

"Sandy was worried about her daddy," says Freda. "A year after he had his heart attack she said, 'I've got to see my Daddy pretty soon.' I guess she knew something, but she had glaucoma in one eye and they kept telling me they wanted to take that one eye out and put another one in. They said that's how bad it had got; and she didn't want that done, she was worried about that. She wasn't supposed to drink then." Sandy, a troubled woman, had addiction problems, too.

After the death of their mother, life wasn't easy for the three young children and they ended up being taken care of by Freda's mother, Leathia. After she became too old and sick to look after them, they were scattered out into different foster homes.

One close of the family says: "Sandra stole stuff from Freda and sold it, including an oil painting of Jackie. It was the first publicity painting that he had done. Tony also stole stuff. Tony was hooked very bad last time I saw him. All of them just went down; even the oldest, Jacqueline. Sandra abused herself to death; she was using drugs."

Of Jackie and Freda's four children, only Anthony ("Tony") survives today. He is generally unemployed and has been in trouble with the police. Says Freda: "He is crazy about his father; he thinks his father could do nothing wrong. Everybody else could; not his father. He's still proud of his father. He ain't been here at the house often; he calls 1, 2 or 3am to talk about his Daddy...or he heard a Jackie song on the radio."

After working late at the hospital, Freda was waiting for a bus when she was set upon by a man who dragged her in an alley where she was raped and severely beaten. As she lay in the alley, someone came out of a tavern and arranged to get her to hospital. Of arriving at the hospital, Freda says, "I said, 'Here I is, what's left of me.' My face looked like toothpaste; they couldn't recognise me. I couldn't see." The offender, who'd beaten Freda so severely that her eye was almost knocked out of its socket, was caught and sentenced to prison where he was killed. It is thought that, when other inmates learned who Freda was, he was killed out of respect for Jackie.

In 1977, aged sixty-eight, Alonzo Tucker, the songwriter who had known Jackie for around twenty years died. Alonzo had written more of Jackie's songs than anyone. Nat Tarnopol employed him from around 1960 to write and to drive for Jackie. He taught Jackie a lot about music since they met in the early 1950s when he was guitarist with The Royals.

Tucker had written 'Doggin' Around' and 'Passing Through', though his name doesn't appear on them. In all likelihood he wrote many more hits for Jackie listing others as the songwriter.

BMI lists seventy-four songs that Jackie is said to have had a hand in writing, and forty-eight songs that are supposedly written by Jackie and Tucker and sometimes others; including Leonard Chess and Morris Levy. All the songs are published through the Goodman Brothers' Regent Music, or Tarnopol's TMIB Music now owned by Nat's son Paul.

In October 1984 ERB Productions reached agreement with Harlean to do a movie on Jackie's career. Harlean received an advance of $12,500, with agreement that, if the film went ahead, she would get another $27,500, and $17,500 if the film was released for television. In addition she was to have received two and a half per cent of net profits from any recordings that were released in conjunction with the film. Sadly for Harlean the film withered on the vine.

Lynn Ciccone and others put the dropping of it down to tacky script. Says Lynn, "The script, based on what Harlean told them, put down Jackie, put down Sam Cooke, James Brown...put down all the black performers.

It was a big put down about entertainers of that era."

Lynn Crochet believes Harlean gave five thousand dollars of her advance to Freda, who was greatly in need of it. According to Lynn, the rights to the film were purchased by Warner Bros, who in turn sold it to Berry Gordy's Gordy Corporation, where there was some activity for a while. It appears plans for the movie have permanently been shelved.

For a number of years Harlean worked as a receptionist for a New York law firm. She has spent large sums on legal fees proving that she, as Jackie's legal wife, was entitled to inherit Jackie's estate. No doubt she had the best interests of their son at heart, but the reality is that there is no pot of gold waiting.

Royalties from minor continuing record sales and radio plays are accumulating awaiting a final resolution from the courts. Paul Tarnopol, in charge of Brunswick, is holding back until further notice. "I've been advised not to pay anyone until it's all resolved," he says. "When I got Brunswick, the court told me not to send any money to Willard [the lawyer representing Lynn Crochet]. All accounts go to Jackie's heirs. Whatever is owned will be paid then."

A far better outcome would have been achieved, had Lynn Crochet and Harlean reached an amicable agreement, for the sake of Jackie's children. However, their mutual hatred is too intense.

The IRS claim for outstanding taxes which, along with interest, amounted to over $500,000, was settled years ago. Presumably they settled for a lesser sum.

Tarnopol: "In the last contract with Jackie [in 1969] it didn't mention things other than records. It doesn't mention licensing fees such as use of the recordings in commercials or as movie soundtracks, which nobody ever considered. So we have to sit down and establish a royalty rate. Whoever the estate is settled for will get the whole thing."

Jackie's only child with Harlean, John "Petey" Dominick, has had a problem with "crack" cocaine, has been in and out of jails, and in rehabilitation for his addiction.

Financially the legal wife, Harlean, is struggling like the rest. August Sims claims to know why. "When Jackie was going to buy her the house up in Pigskills [a town in upstate New York]," says Sims, "she wanted fur coats. Some time ago she said, 'I wished I'd listened to you and took the house.' I said, 'You'd be a millionaire. Now you ain't got nothing.'

"She always accused me of stealing from Jackie. I said, 'I never stole nothin' from Jackie.' I said, 'When Jackie ate, I ate.' I said, 'Why don't you accuse whites, they're the sons-of-bitches I gave the money to.'

"She's got old now. I said, 'That's your fault you wanted to be up with the Smiths and have a fur coat.' She could've still had it if she'd been smart, but she thought she knew everything.

"She always hated my guts and I saved her ass, ain't that a bitch? From Jackie whoppin' her. Then she got mad 'cause she lost all her shit."

Harlean has so far turned down at least one offer of security. "Michael Jackson tried to buy Jackie's songs," her friend Launa Toledo reveals. "Harlean had renewed all of the copyrights. Those are hers. He offered Harlean three million dollars and she laughed in his face. 'You've got to be joking!'"

The Rock 'N' Roll Hall Of Fame was established in 1986. In that year the inductees included Chuck Berry, James Brown, Ray Charles, Sam Cooke, Fats Domino, The Everly Brothers, Buddy Holly, Jerry Lee Lewis, Elvis Presley, and Little Richard.

The next year, Jackie's turn, and he was in good company; Aretha Franklin, Marvin Gaye, Bill Haley, BB King, Clyde McPhatter, Roy Orbison, Smokey Robinson, Big Joe Turner, T-Bone Walker and Hank Williams. He had been rightly honoured as one of the giants of contemporary music.

However, the acrimony that had become so pronounced since his collapse in 1975, still managed to carry over to this occasion twelve years later. "Harlean excluded Sabrina," claims Joyce McRae. "I wound up getting Sabrina, and Li-nie, who I helped pay for, to fly to New York, when Jackie was getting inducted. It was three hundred dollars a person at that time. I got someone to pay the six hundred dollars. I paid for Li-nie's dress, I paid for part of the plane ticket and we all piled in a room together within walking distance of the Waldorf Astoria." Harlean seemingly wanted to bask in the glory of the occasion without Jackie's children.

Freda possibly agrees. "I was upset because Denise couldn't go to the Rock 'N' Roll award in New York." It is not clear why she was unable to attend. Perhaps it was simply a matter of not being invited, or able to afford to.

Nat Tarnopol died of a heart attack in Las Vegas on Christmas Day 1987. He'd had moved in 1985 because protection was provided by friends there. He no longer felt secure in New York, but occasionally would slip into the city. "He'd come back from time to time," explains Melvin Moore, a former promotions man with Brunswick. Moore left after Jackie's collapse. "He'd kinda sneak in 'cause he had problems with these people. My friend [almost certainly Sims] is a real big guy, so when Nat would come into town he'd call him to watch him."

Son Paul remembers, "Nat was a workaholic. He'd often be up all night and be at the office before everyone. He had a massive heart attack in 1982. After the trial in the 1970s, my father was all alone. He had no friends, no money. When he was flying high it was different. He was sad in his heart.

"After dad died, Johnny Roberts called and said, 'It's your Uncle Johnny. They think you're brain dead.'" Paul didn't consider Roberts an uncle and certainly not a friend of the family. "My father had a couple of million dollars in assets. We had a nice big house in Purchase, Westchester County [in 1963]. He was young and not particularly careful with money. We lost most of everything including the house."

Launa Toledo, through Jackie, had long known Johnny Roberts. The word was out that Roberts had died, but a phone call was to dispel the rumour. "New Year's Eve I got a call from JR," says Launa, "who I thought was dead. 'Happy New Year, baby.' I went 'Ugh?' Someone's playing a joke. 'Who is this?' 'Come on, baby, you know who this is.' My mother was sitting here at the bar. I guess my face drained. She said, 'What's the matter?' It's scary. I said, 'But you're dead!' He said, 'That's the first I knew about it.' I said, 'I know people who attended your funeral.' He said, 'I called to give you my new phone number.'"

There was another reason Roberts had called. It was to give her the "good news"; Nat Tarnopol had died in Las Vegas five days earlier. Says Launa: "Nat Tarnopol was the biggest crook that lived...Johnny and Nat Tarnopol were getting ready to be called up before the grand jury. The only one who could put JR away was Nat Tarnopol. When he died, all of a sudden JR is alive again. So I want to know *who's* in that grave?"

Joyce McRae never met Tarnopol, but she is typically well informed – and opinionated – about his death. "Nat died an ugly hideous death," she claims. "Lee Iacocca [former head of Chrysler Motors] showed up at the funeral. They became very dear friends when he was at CBS Special Projects."

"When Nat died on Christmas Day, you could hear the whole world rejoicing his death," says Hank Ballard. "I doubt that even his family would have attended his funeral. I believe in fair play; I don't believe in someone gaining by stepping on someone else."

Record promotions man, Larry Maxwell, met Tarnopol in a restaurant only a month before he died. He says: "Nat became greedy, that's why he died of a heart attack. Nat killed himself. He turned out not being a nice guy. Everyone knows that Nat did bad things."

Many called August Sims "Tarnopol's man". Certainly they worked together for many years and were respectful of one another, although he was initially employed by Johnny Roberts. Says Sims: "Jackie had his faults, too, but goddamn this Nat man wouldn't help bury the man...and he made millions from him. See, fate has a way of making up for when you do people wrong. You know how Jews is. They hurt each other, and they hurt Jackie."

Since the 1960s, smaller independent record labels were being taken over by the bigger corporations. Gil Askey, who was an arranger with Motown explains: "Warner Bros started buying up little companies in New York and, before you knew it, they owned Atlantic Records. They were the first I knew doing it. The whole business began to change in the early 1960s; nowadays all the record companies were owned by six or seven majors. Warner [part of Time Warner Inc], EMI, Sony, Bertelsmann Music Group [who own RCA], Polygram [part of Philips Electronics], UNI Distribution [part of the Seagram whisky conglomerate] and MCA, [who own Polydor].

"If they control the music industry, they also have the video market, they also control the tape market, and many are hooked up with the movie industry. Nobody cares who writes the music or songs now. If you try to be too strict in this business you go down."

Indeed six multi-nationals controlled eighty-five per cent of the USA CD market in 1996; estimated to be worth $9.4 billion.

Chuck Jackson, who never fails to mention his old friend Jackie when he performs, says much the same thing: "There's a cartel that are running the whole record industry now and they are not Americans. We don't have much to say about anything any more. The American companies are now extinct. This music today has nothing to say about things except killing you, or making love to her the violent way. It's dealing with people who have nothing to give back. You are dealing with a big vacuum of nothing. So when they try to put a thing of substance back in there, they ignore it immediately, because it means they have *to think* to absorb it.

"You can't turn anything around. We are in a losing situation here and I don't think it's going to recover. And I'm thinking of going into banking!"

He also comments on the seeming black characteristic of always seeking that which is "new", while not recalling the great achievements of earlier black notables; such as Jackie. "Why should black people want to remember the past?" he says. "They had nothing in it. Black people do not want to go back to where they came from, because there's nothing there, really. That's why we don't deal in nostalgia, because it's only pain for us. You see, every other race does, except us, and it just hit me *that's why*."

In his book *Chicago Soul*, Robert Pruter says: "Tarnopol continued the Brunswick operation while attempting to sort out his legal difficulties, but obviously he did not have much of a company to work with. The Chicago office mysteriously was kept open, but the staff's principal function seemed to be to turn the lights on in the morning and turn them off at night. After 1981 Brunswick was moribund at an active label, and existed only to license old masters to other firms for reissue purposes."

Carl Davis left Brunswick in 1979 after being found not guilty of fraud. He later opened a bar, the Palace Bar in Chicago, although it didn't do well. He then joined the Sheriff's Department.

Paul Tarnopol, as the present owner of Brunswick Records, holds the masters to all the 322 songs recorded by Jackie during his eighteen years on the label. However, additionally there are still thirty-six songs that have never been released.

It was in 1995 that Tarnopol regained control of the masters. He says: "I lost the masters when Brunswick ran out of money in 1982. The masters are all downstairs in the basement; a storage room. A lot is on two track, some is three track. It's the whole evolution of recording down there.

"When my father passed away, his cousin Arnie was with Polygram [while also managing singer Cyndi Lauper]. I was young and didn't know what to do about this. So I trusted him. He went to CBS; they were licensing it for him and so they split the money. That was in 1989."

Former Brunswick vice president, Carl Davis, explains how Columbia had gained control of the Jackie masters: "Nat Tarnopol owed Columbia money for record pressing. Some of the product was released for a time on Epic, a subsidiary of Columbia, because Nat owed them a lot of money. But once the money was paid back, the rights went back to Paul."

In 1992 Rhino Records in California acquired the rights to re-release a three CD boxed set of Jackie's best recordings. The seventy-two songs were painstakingly chosen by Jackie's friend Simon Rutberg, and carefully re-mastered by studio engineering whiz Walter Devenne. The result is a masterpiece of Jackie's career, spanning his involvement with The Dominoes, the New York years with Dick Jacobs, to the Chicago period with Carl Davis. The set is estimated to have sold up to twenty thousand copies worldwide.

As part of the release, Rhino included a booklet containing Jackie's discography and a well written biography written by soul music authority Robert Pruter. The biography contained information that Harlean and Paul Tarnopol found deeply offensive concerning his father's management and Jackie's addiction problems.

Even though the set with the offending booklet was in the stores, Tarnopol threatened legal action unless it was immediately withdrawn. Rhino offered a seven thousand dollar settlement, to avoid having to reprint the book, which Tarnopol quickly rejected. Rhino had to do an expensive withdrawal and re-printed the booklet in an edited form.

Since the conversation with Paul Tarnopol, he has had the entire Jackie catalogue re-mastered digitally on multi-track, using fifteen to twenty tracks. Apart from being far superior for the purposes of long term storage, Tarnopol says, "It's got sound solutions to take the hiss off everything. It's clearer than it was the day it was recorded, but it's a colder sound. Not quite as warm as vinyl."

These days Eugene Record, of The Chi-Lites, has his own recording studio. Recently he produced his first gospel album after many months of work. The work fits perfectly with his deeply Christian beliefs and is everything the current vogue for rap isn't. "I really believe these young artists are really lost, man," he says. "It kinda hurts. They missed the boat so far as *real music* is concerned. It's not their fault, they've taken the fascination out of being a star in music.

"I believe that MC Hammer was the only one that maintained that image of being looked up to. He recorded one of my songs, as well. The clothes they wear you could get at the neighbourhood re-sale shops."

Again, speaking of rap music, he says, "The copyright can't be worth much; you don't have to worry about them being covered. I believe the music buying public want real music. It's not the youngsters' fault, it's a shame. They want it too, they just don't get exposed to it. Sign of the times."

By comparison, Record's copyright does handsomely. "The royalties are still coming in very nicely for 'Oh Girl'," he grins. "And I still do song writing with Barbara Acklin."

Since Jackie's collapse Lynn Crochet has struggled to look after her four children. She also had a bad experience with Jackie's oldest daughter: "Denise came down here. She took everything I had; she took the mink collars off my leather coat. She wrecked my car...she did a number on me like you would not believe.

"That's not even one of the bad parts. When Jackie was inducted into the Hall Of Fame, Thor was not allowed to go. Harlean and Petey got the award with a gold record on it. Petey took that and sold it for drugs...and my children were not allowed to see it."

Thor has grown up pretty well, leaving aside the usual troubles most teenage boys encounter. Women find Thor irresistible and he has fathered four children with three different ones. Johnny Collins knows the reason: "Thor is like his father; he shakes hands and a baby pops up."

Of Jackie's possessions? "All Jackie's comics were left up in Detroit at the house on Strathmoor Street," says Lynn. "Jackie didn't have a music collection. I don't have anything. None, hardly, except what has been re-released. I had dubs Jackie had done in the studio; Denise took all of that."

After Lynn had invited Joyce McRae to take care of Jackie, they got to know each other well, although they are not close. Says McRae: "I believe Jackie truly cared about Lynn, cared for Lynn. Jackie was at peace and had finally found contentment and happiness. She met his needs while he was healthy; she doesn't have to prove anything to anyone in that context. But past that, she and I know who she is." McRae believes Lynn should and could have done more to assist Jackie's rehabilitation. "I respect the fact that she was good for Jack, and Jack was good to her. If Jack were alive right now he'd beat the shit out of her for what she's done."

Jackie's sister, Joyce Ann Lee, is still a welder at Chrysler in Pontiac, a position she's worked at for over thirty years. Relatives claim she rarely returns their calls and is rather temperamental. She lives to this day in the house that Jackie purchased for their mother. Twenty years after Eliza Mae's death, it is still in her name and could be considered as now being

Harlean's property.

One relative describes the large two storey house as "that dirty ass house. The outside looks beautiful. It's just nasty. The furniture has plastic covers."

Another says, "It is all messed up; it looks like a big barn. Nobody would want it. It *was* a beautiful home; now it looks like a junk yard." On one wall is a picture done in chalk of Jackie and Harlean. Apparently Joyce, too, has none of her brother's albums.

Once, at the tomb dedication, Lynn Ciccone spoke to Joyce Ann and asked for Freda's phone number. Says Lynn, "She said, 'You don't want to talk to her, she's an old alcoholic.'"

Foolishly, too, Lynn asked Joyce Ann to arrange to put flowers on Jackie's grave and sent her a hundred dollars for the purpose. On checking with the cemetery caretaker, Lynn learned that the flowers were never placed there.

As recently as 1993 Joyce Ann was still displaying the bitterness she'd long harboured. In April of that year the Motor City Music Awards Show Ceremony was held at Detroit's State Theatre. Joyce Ann refused to accept the Lifetime Achievement plaque supposedly because one of Jackie's illegitimate daughters, Brenda Johnson, was there. So it was left to Brenda, Jackie's daughter with Suzie, to do the honours.

The Internal Revenue Service (IRS) had a lien against future earnings by Jackie's estate with a view to recouping outstanding taxes of $243,331.37 covering the years 1963 to 1973. Specifically the lien detailed: $66,000 for the year 1963; $8,247 for 1964; $27,226 for 1966; $44,495 for 1967; $27,737 for 1970; $10,565 for 1971; $22,875 for 1972; and $18,048 for 1973. The total amounting to $192,172.52 plus interest and penalties of $42,258.58. These taxes have now all been repaid.

The hand of fate once again reached out on the night of the 22 August, 1988 and struck another of Jackie's children down. This time it was thirty-seven-year-old Denise.

She had just walked out from a party store on the busy Woodward Avenue in Highland Park and, without a word being spoken to her, was shot to death. Freda lived just over the road at the time in what was described as "a flop-house"; she is said to have cried for days.

It was claimed Denise's death resulted from a drug dispute and that her death was totally accidental. Incredibly, three of Jackie's four children with Freda were now dead. The Detroit *News* quoted Highland Park Detective Hubert Yopp as saying: "She happened to be in the wrong place at the wrong time. The man had taken off with drugs and money. They caught up with him. The dealer fired six shots at him as he fled. The shots were fired just as Jacqueline Wilson was leaving the store...She was hit once in the back."

Denise had an unhappy life, earning her living as a topless dancer in Detroit's lounges. Lynn Ciccone had got to know her over the previous two years and became very fond of her. Lynn learned of the death when she received a call from Freda. "Freda called me when Denise was shot," she recalls. "She needed money for a dress."

Denise was buried at the Westlawn Cemetery where Jackie had been buried four years earlier. Lynn travelled from Springfield, Illinois to attend the funeral. "Denise was so much like Jackie," she says. "Her actions, her voice, her laugh; everything was like him. It was an adventure being with Denise."

Lynn knew about the raid on Lynn Crochet's things while Denise was a guest in her house, but she holds back from blaming her. "I can't blame her for what she did. His children were not treated properly; they didn't have what they should have had from Jackie. He sent her to the very best schools; she graduated second in her class. He was never there as a father, and the children resented that. When I met her she was a topless dancer. 'Okay,' she said, 'he was my father, but he wasn't there for me. Hey, I have to do what I have to do to stay alive.' Denise could sing; she wanted to be an entertainer."

There was a sequel to the story and justice of a sort. The Detroit *Free Press* reported that a twenty-eight-year-old man, Gary Johnson, was charged with Denise's murder. Johnson was released on a bond of fifty thousand dollars, and the following July was himself gunned down as he was about to enter a home. Freda believes that his death was a reprisal because of who Denise's father was. Assuming police had arrested the right man, it was a fitting retribution.

Not a single day has passed that former girlfriend Lynn Ciccone has not thought of Jackie. "Everybody has put Jackie down," she says, "but his greatness has never been revealed. We must keep his memory alive – lovingly. I think he knows I love him; will always love him. I love this man dearly, I've never stopped. I know Jackie had a lot of negatives, but there are a lot of good things. There was so much *good* that people don't know about Jackie."

Despite the racial bigotry he contended with all his life, it was he who taught Lynn the real meaning of the word love: "The man I knew taught me more than I ever knew. He taught me about loving and caring. My mother died in March 1995 without forgiving me for loving Jackie.

"I was mistreated most of my life, but Jackie was the positive thing in my life. The one force that never hurt me. He sent money for me to pay the bills when my husband was dying.

"I've shed millions of tears for Jackie, when I'm alone. Sometimes, in the midst of my sorrows, I look up at Jackie's picture and begin to laugh. It's almost as if he's saying, 'What's wrong with you, woman? You ain't got nothin' to cry about.' He would coin that phrase when I felt sorry for myself. I dream about him, but they are good dreams. Nobody ever loved him more than me. And God bless him."

Today Lynn blames herself in part for the tragedy that took Jackie's life, feeling she should have remained with him and kept him free from life's dangers. "My greatest pain is in the knowledge that I couldn't help him when he needed me most. Even if he never improved, just to hold him close and tell him how much I love him."

Lynn, better than most, accepted that Jackie was never faithful to one woman: "It wasn't the nature of the man. Women would send notes to the dressing room offering anything. He had charisma; Billy Ward gave it to him. He taught him how to be charismatic. Jackie said, 'Everything I know, I learned from him.'

"At times people dare to ask me, 'What was the sex like?' I laugh at how foolish they are; it was never about sex.

"Speaking for myself, Jackie was and is my soul mate. The entertainer was incomparable, but the man was totally unique in every way. Maybe I'm totally wrong about all of my perceptions about my time with Jackie. In the end I can only say: 'We loved, we laughed, we couldn't find any faults in each other.' There were many, but we couldn't see them."

It wasn't until Jackie's collapse that Lynn revealed to her then thirteen-year-old daughter that Jackie was her father. Gina had met with Jackie as a very young girl, but grew up unaware he was her father and believing she was Caucasian. Says Lynn, "She said, 'My God, my God.' We had a problem for a while. She said, 'I don't want to know about it.' But when I told her about him and showed her the video, played the records, she said, 'He's great.'"

After they first met in 1986, Lynn helped Freda in some small ways. "When I met Freda, I felt guilty," she says. "I grew to love her. Why didn't he stay there and take care of his family? I helped Freda, because at the time I met Jackie, I didn't know he had a wife and four children. When I saw her and how she was living, I thought, 'I'm not living on public aid, I'm doing okay.'

"I took Freda shopping with Denise. I had great times with her. She brought out an old crumpled picture from 1959 and said, 'This is not you by any chance?' She gave it back to me and I still have it." It was a photo Lynn had given Jackie when they'd first met. Instead of destroying it, Freda had held on to it.

Lynn is critical of the friends and relatives who Jackie had generously provided for when he was well. "He was not able to help them any more," says Lynn. "He was 'great' when he was up and going. If he had a best friend, and he didn't make a lot of friends of that type, it would be his longest standing friend [guitarist] Billy Davis. Billy was in his house when they were children. They were in contact throughout."

Lynn also makes an interesting observation: "Jackie never looked the same. Lay out fifty pictures of Jackie, and no two are alike. They could never capture the 'true' Jackie. His album covers are the same. You had *to see him* in person. Jackie was in his element in an elite night club or Las Vegas; that was his element. He was incomparable."

Little could be learned of Johnny Jones' final years, but after a severe stroke he died in 1992. At some stage he had finally married in New York and had children, but the years of drugs and alcohol had taken their toll on his mind and body. In his later years, JJ did house painting and interior decorating. After his stroke he became partially paralysed. "He would get to drinking and talking loud and wear out his welcome," says one of Jackie's relatives. "He got into painting people's houses. When he got to painting, he might have a suit on. But JJ didn't really work hard and he lost his little house."

Linda Hopkins, the only singer to have done a duet album with Jackie, still performs despite celebrating her seventieth birthday in 1995. Hopkins is also a friend of another of Jackie's duet partners. "LaVern Baker is my dearest friend in the world," she says. "We both got finished doing a Broadway show together, *Black And Blue*, in 1989. She's had a foot amputated due to diabetes. LaVern lived in the Philippines for twenty-one years. She got sick after returning from the States."

It is believed Baker exiled herself to the Philippines rather than be "controlled", as she knew Jackie was. She died early in 1997.

In the name of "progress" Detroit's Lee's Club Sensation has been torn down to make way for Detroit's Chrysler Freeway, while the Flame Show Bar has been converted into a hospital.

In September 1988, only three weeks after Denise had been killed, it was arranged to do an exposé on Jackie's demise on the popular TV program *Entertainment Tonight*. Lynn Ciccone appeared on the programme, which was taped in Detroit. She convinced Freda to be interviewed, also. Says Lynn, "The mayor of Highland Park, Martha Scott, let us use her office and she even said a few words, but they never showed any of it. It was chopped up so badly. After all that, they didn't even put Freda on."

Freda developed sudden amnesia when the interviewer asked her whether it was correct that Nat Tarnopol was having a relationship with Harlean after Jackie had married her.

For many years Johnny Roberts had resided in Palm Springs, California. The New York Mob had banished him to the west coast for some major infringement said to involve large sums of money. "I think what happened with him is he got himself in some kind of trouble," says Carl Davis. "He couldn't go back to New York. I think what they probably did was, somebody probably called out to California and said, 'We'd got to get rid of Johnny, so we want to send him to your area. We want to let you know he's coming. He still has our protection.'"

For some years he ran a night club in Los Angeles. Someone who knew him at this time says, "I know Johnny Roberts, he has a face like an ice cube – cold as ice. A person not to be messed with. Sepio was his real name."

After a long debilitating illness Roberts died on 14 December, 1994. This time he really was dead. He left a Korean born wife and two children.

Tommy Vastola has been in a New Jersey jail since October 1991 serving a seventeen year sentence which had been handed to him by the Federal Court. He has appealed his conviction as far as the Supreme Court. His attorney daughter, Joy, employs all of her efforts to have his convictions overturned.

In 1987, New York producer Dick Jacobs, who had been involved with most of Jackie's major hits, died. Years before he had been viciously knifed when he answered a knock at the door. His second wife had set him up and nearly succeeded in killing him. After his recovery he married for a third time.

Ernestine Smith, who as a young girl used to look out from her back porch and watch young Jackie singing and drinking wine with his friends, says for many years his old Shaker Gang cronies would get together. "They used to meet up on a playground on Westminster and they'd have a gang reunion," says Smith. "They had food and bring their kids and talk about old times. Jackie'd hang on the corner and sing with the guys...on the corner of Holbrook and Russell. They'd be in the alley singing and drinking wine. The alley is gone. It's Chrysler Drive [beside the freeway] now."

Two former senior gang members have become church reverends; Robin Pashe and Maurice Munson.

In May 1996 the court finally declared its decision regarding the split of Jackie's estate. Harlean was made the legal wife and thus heir. Provision was made for five of Jackie's children to be beneficiaries: Freda's son Tony, Harlean's son John, Lynn's children Thor and Li-nie, and Molly Byndon's daughter Sabrina. Also, deceased daughter Sandra's three children would split her share. There had been fifteen claimants. Originally Harlean won only over the estate in New Jersey, but there was no estate in New Jersey. Therefore a decision had to be made in New York, because that is where Jackie resided through most of his recording period and where Brunswick Records was located.

Freda never did manage to collect the many years of outstanding maintenance payments from Jackie prior to his collapse. She is owed a lot of money which should include interest. She estimates, "Mine is fifty thousand dollars now. Harlean owes too."

"I've got a copy of his earnings that were turned into Social Security," says Lynn Crochet. "There's one year he made ten thousand dollars. Another year $4,800. I know for a fact there were some years he made millions; from record sales and all the travelling he did." Her two children with Jackie haven't had the benefit of any of his earnings since September 1975.

"Here's two women fighting over a dead man," says Launa Toledo, "it's really sad. Jackie'd probably be sitting up there going, 'Look at you damn fools fighting over it. You dummies.' If either one of them would have given an inch. Let's face it, since Jackie got sick, half of his kids are gone."

At the 1984 Grammy Awards, as part of his brief acceptance speech, Michael Jackson, who had studied Jackie's stage performances, said simply: "Some people are entertainers and some people are great entertainers; some are followers, some make the path and are pioneers. I'd like to say, Jackie Wilson was a wonderful entertainer. He's not with us any more, but I'd like to say, Jackie, wherever you are, I love you so much."

From one legendary fan to another. Motown founder Berry Gordy co-wrote most of Jackie's earliest hits and was interviewed by *Goldmine* (3 March, 1995) about Jackie. "The most natural artist that I've ever seen in terms of dancing, vocals," he said. "His voice was the strongest. He could do opera, he could do rock, he could do blues and he created the most creative singer that I'd known. As I said in the book [*To Be Loved*], he never sang a bad note. Maybe a bad song, but never a bad note...one of the most talented artists I've ever seen. 'Cause I'm talking about all great people here. So when I say talented in another way, I mean he was the most natural.

"He was more dynamic live than he was on record. And he could dance, and do flips and splits and stuff like that. Different than Michael Jackson. Michael studied a lot of people who did a lot of things. Jackie did not study anybody but Jackie. Jackie was Jackie, the most natural, innate performer, probably, that I've ever seen. He had nobody to study that I know of. Jackie was an original. Probably the most original artist I've ever seen. And he should be rediscovered. Because he created stuff and he would wink on cue. I said it in the book. He could do things, do a spin, and then wink at the girls."

Finally, in his radio interview Norman N Nite asked Jackie about his audiences. Jackie replied: "Some people want to cry, some come to laugh, some to knock down, drag out, some come to plain listen; study. And it's a beautiful feeling; a beautiful sight to see."

Hopefully this book has helped reveal an artist who was totally unique. Trying, with words, to explain the magnificence of his honey rich, emotion racked voice is like trying to describe a Rembrandt painting to a blind person who has never seen. Jackie, known as "Mr Excitement", was destroyed by the career he had chosen. He would have called it *kismet* – fate or destiny. However he had thrilled and brought happiness to millions. Surely that is what he most wanted from his life and the rest of us should be grateful for that experience, because that's what it is; *an experience*.

CHAPTER EIGHTEEN

Tributes

HANK BALLARD

"Somehow I sat back and predicted these mishaps on some of these artists by the lifestyle they lived. You see fate has a way of dealing with people when they get on the wrong track, you know what I mean? You can't lose sight of who you really are. You can't get all tied up and addicted to commercial admiration. The pat on the back; being told 'You're the greatest' and all that. You've got to treat it for what it is; commercial admiration.

"You know there was only one Jackie Wilson. Mr Charisma! Jackie was...he was a monster...I remember Jackie out there making his debut with The Dominoes.

"Jackie was generous to a fault. His family missed out, but all the hangers-on got the money. He would go into the darkness of the ghetto and pull a guy out of a garbage can and give him money and jewellery. That's what he enjoyed doing. He didn't have any regard for the value of money, though he liked to have all these people around him all the time. I think 'yes' people are dangerous people; I call them Uncle Toms."

JERRY BLAVAT

"He was one of the true stars of this industry. In my opinion the great things Jackie did were 'My Empty Arms', 'Whispers', 'Alone At Last', and '(You Were Made For) All My Love'. That's when it took Jackie from the plateau and made people sit up and take notice. Jackie still lives with my radio show."

JOE BILLINGSLEA

"My personal opinion is that Jackie Wilson is one of the greatest artists there's ever been. Jackie would have been a much bigger artist, in the same mould as Elvis Presley, had he been a white artist. As a lot of people know, back then a black artist mostly played for black audiences. If Jackie had been given more of an opportunity to play to white audiences like Elvis Presley or other white artists of that particular time, he would have been a giant."

MARILYN BOND

"I saw Jackie so many times do rock 'n' roll and TV shows and I never got the full Jackie until just before his collapse. I went to the Flame Show Bar. Honest to God, the man was outrageous; he had everybody in the place off their seats. He was phenomenal...you just couldn't describe it."

RUTH BOWEN

"Jackie was a very private guy with his life. Of course there was a lot he didn't want people to know. He was a very proud man. He was happy with his last wife [Lynn], but not so happy with the other one [Harlean]; she made him a little miserable. Jackie, Aretha and Sam Cooke, we'd put them out on these packages...they worked together. Jackie was one of the sweetest guys you'd ever want to meet. A very sweet guy. There's not anything bad I could say about Jackie. He had a rough time, a rough life. His managers were not so nice. He was used a lot."

LYNN CICCONE

"I just want somebody to tell the truth about Jackie; the magnificence – incomparable as an entertainer. There's never been anyone like him."

DICK CLARK

"Having seen so many performers, people often ask me who stands out. Jackie Wilson heads the list. He was one of a kind. In person, or on record, there was only one Mr Excitement.

"It's a story that should be told because he was so influential. I'm so happy that he made his TV debut on one of my shows. He's an enigmatic figure that people need to know more about."

JOHNNY COLLINS
"A true solo artist, that is the epitome of what heaven and hell is to be, or is, or will be. When Jack walked out on the stage after having his ribs cracked, he sang as hard as he did when he was fine. The better the entertainer, the better the confrontation, the deeper the feeling. He was the most honest, but wasn't the best. He gave all he could give, that's more than most. That made him special. He was different.

"Entertainers start out as human beings and turn into something else. Boxing and music were the two most violent games there were. Jack wanted to be a pro. He did it both ways."

BILLY DAVIS
"He should be remembered as one of the greatest all round singers of all time in history, really, for the simple reason he could do so many things. He could have went classical, he could have went pop, he could have went rock 'n' roll, he could have went blues. And I can't think of any other artist with that type of range in his voice...that could do all of this. In my mind, he'll always remain the number one singer and entertainer. He was one of a kind. As a human being and performer, he was unique."

HARVEY FUQUA
"Jackie was the hottest male singer in his time. He paved the way, absolutely."

PERVIS JACKSON
"He was truly one of the hardest working entertainers in showbusiness. When you went to see a Jackie Wilson show, you saw a show. Every night was like an opening night. There was no let up. He had the knack of inspiring everyone to want to perform better. There was no such thing as the mike going out. At times, during a song, he would lay the mike down and could be heard all over the theatre. Ladies would line up to see the man but he had it so together the men would pack the audience to hear him too. He was a classic."

MARV JOHNSON
"Jackie has to go down as one of the most electrifying performers that ever went across the country. That barred none – Elvis Presley, you name it,

whoever – because Elvis Presley's influence was very obviously, to me, Chuck Berry and Jackie Wilson. "

JACK GIBSON
"Jackie was an individualist; he should be remembered more...if more people knew about him. Like Roy Hamilton; he's in that class; a real entertainer, who could really sing, who could capture everybody. It's like Little Willie John, they are just discovering him."

BB KING
"Jackie Wilson was one of the greatest soul singers in the business and we miss him greatly, but his music lingers on for all of us to enjoy."

GLADYS KNIGHT
"Those of us old enough to remember back ten or twenty years know that one man in particular had a lot to do with establishing the conditions we are enjoying today.

"When I think of Jackie, I think of pure entertainment. He was an unselfish performer and he gave his all because he truly loved his fans. His talent, tenacity, energy, and love for this profession was immeasurable. All performers could take a lesson from Jackie Wilson as to how to be the total entertainer. As a matter of fact, I did!"

PATTI LABELLE
"Jackie Wilson was the consummate performer. I remember standing backstage with the other girls in my group and watching all his performances when we appeared together on shows where Jackie was the headliner. He was magical."

SAM MOORE
"I know he should still be alive today...he didn't have to die! I am hurt and angry because even if he had to be in a wheelchair and couldn't sing a note he should have had the pleasure of seeing his youngest children and grands grow."

SIMON RUTBERG
These days Rutberg runs a small Jewish record store in Los Angeles where

the most famous rock 'n' roll songwriting duo in history, Lieber and Stoller, first worked when they moved to the city in 1950. Rutberg is Jackie's unabashed greatest fan.

"When I saw him last in Los Angeles, it was probably a year or two before he collapsed. He played this little club here and there were only twenty people, all white, in the whole place. He'd just come off this big tour in Florida, which was sold out every night.

"Once Jackie was playing the lounge at the Flamingo in Las Vegas, and The Jacksons were playing the big room and making millions of dollars. And yet The Jacksons went down to watch Jackie...they worshipped Jackie Wilson. Jackie used to take Michael Jackson on the road.

"There are great voices and great records, but you don't need a great voice to make a great record. There are great voices that will never have a great record. It's not they don't get airplay, it's because they are not catering...I didn't know Jackie as well as some, as much as I loved him and I'm totally unbiased. I do think he had the greatest voice in the world.

"To the people in the business, Jackie was very well liked. They also talked about him as 'the greatest'. Talent-wise he was. He was a star beyond being a star. I listened to Jackie almost everyday of my life since 1960. Yet, I can't tell you how great this guy was.

"On stage Jackie was amazing and it was so infectious. Talent-wise, there's no way to explain it. Anyone who has worked with Jackie says he's the greatest thing they ever saw. He'd come off stage looking like a wet rag. His shirts would be soaked. He would often get his clothes torn; if the women got their hands on him.

"Jackie would have been happy singing the Flame Bar for the rest of his life. All he wanted was to see the reaction of people and the applause. Jackie couldn't care less if there was only ten people and no microphone.

"Jackie was a kid; he became a star at nineteen. He had no real education. Tarnopol got him in a different circle. You've got to give Tarnopol credit. He could have been James Brown; thank God, he wasn't. People would have said, 'That's a good moving nigger.' He was a class act. Nat took him through the front door before a lot of other people. He was travelling in better circles. James Brown never played the Copacabana.

"But without Nat, there would have been no Jackie; at least not that way. Jackie had the talent, but would the next person have been able to recognise it? If he'd been pure rock 'n' roll, in two years he'd have been forgotten. They worked and developed Jackie and made him into a class act.

"If you're black they call you a soul singer. I hate that word. Jackie won all those NAACP [National American Association for the Advancement of Coloured People] awards, long before James Brown. They wanted to keep him as 'Our Jackie Wilson'.

"Marvin Gaye to me the most overrated. Otis Redding, I'm sorry, he can't sing. Wilson Pickett had a few good hits, but is no singer. Even Tiny Tim had a gold record. Al Green impressed me 'cause he had energy. He played directly to the audience. With Al Green, it's, 'Come on everybody, clap your hands.' I don't understand why they call him great. Al Green had nothing...he should clear his throat.

"Jackie didn't play to himself. He connected with the audience because of the emotion and his delivery of a song. He didn't just stand there and sing notes. He sang like he was singing to someone and everyone took it personally."

JOE STUBBS

"Jackie comes from the heart. He was one of the *baddest, meanest* singers I've known. And it gets to you. Something about Jackie when Jackie came out to sing, he touches you in all kind of ways. He could make you feel part of him. He makes you feel part of everything going on around him. He gives you every little feeling within words to make *you* feel. If you was a blind man, you would still feel what Jackie was doing, even though you couldn't see him, his moves and things..."

LEVI STUBBS

"From the moment Jack opened his mouth, the women went mad. He had a kind of magnetism. Women would just die, and men would love him. He was like them, one of the boys."

BILLY VERA

"To fully appreciate Jackie, you would have to see him twirling his mohair suit jacket above his head (he had already perspired clean through his black, custom-made shirt, which had ripped the full length of his back), jumping up landing in a split, with still enough breath to hit a note so high only a dog can hear it. In a micro-second, he's pulled himself up by his own collar, done a 360 degree spin, kicked the mike stand, and pulled it back by its cord so it lands in his right hand. The jacket ends up behind him (after he's teased the first six rows with it), and a few Elvis hiccups later, he's on his back, his head hanging over the edge of the stage.

"One would need a computer to figure out just how many syllables he makes out of the word 'be' at the end of 'To Be Loved'."

DON WALLER

"Wilson's stratospheric falsetto, his churchly phrasing and his uncanny ability to leap octaves within the space of a single syllable influenced such world class vocalists as Al Green, Van Morrison, Tom Jones and ex-Temptation David Ruffin.

"Exploiting both ends of his multi-octave range, Wilson swoops, dives and stops on a dime, climaxing with a show stopping cadenza in which he wrenches twenty-three notes out of the word 'for'. Hear it and know the meaning of soul."

DIONNE WARWICK

"He always gave his audiences pure excitement, and I believe Jackie was a major influence on all music. He was the innovator...with the dance, movements and energy you now see with Michael Jackson, Prince, and others. We all miss him but when I think of Jackie, I know we are all better for having had him as part of our industry."

WILLIAM WEATHERSPOON

"Everyone would like to have a gift like Jackie. He didn't reach his full potential, especially in the later days. Jackie was an all round singer. The quality wasn't as good on the recordings as Gordy would have produced. His tunes would have been well crafted, well written if he'd been with Motown."

HY WEISS

"He was a nice kid. Jackie was a nice human being. A happy guy. He got into the wrong hands. When he tried to leave Nat, Nat stopped him. They sat him down and taught him the *Bible*: 'Thou shalt not leave.' Still his career went pretty far.

"A lovely, lovely man; I liked him on a personal scale. How much more can you say? He was a great act, entertained millions of people and was a great human being. He came right out of the gospel. A tremendous, warm guy and it came out in his stage performances. He had religion in him. He was unique. He loved what he was doing and he loved it till the very end. That's why he couldn't cope with a lot of the stuff; with all the baloney. That's what frightened him. They robbed from the blind."

MARY WELLS

"He was an exciting performer. You know, you just can't come on after him. They had to take intermission. It was something phenomenal. He could do, you know, dance and flips. He was such a great singer, too, so he had it covered all the way around."

MARY WILSON

"Jackie was a performer's performer. He had the smile, the flash. That's what was just great. He would do this and the women would [screams]... 'aaah!' you know, 'Jackie'. And he'd fall down on his knees. And, God, he was that great...he was a great performer."

GEORGIE WOODS

"In the early sixties Jackie was number one – there was nobody bigger. He was pure electricity on stage, one of the greatest performers that ever lived. All those people he helped – you wonder where they are now. But you know how it is. If they can exploit you they are going to do it. This is the way our business is – everybody does it. They suck the blood from you and then leave you alone. They use you and then find somebody else to use. I think Jackie's a victim of being used by the wrong people."

Discography

All releases are for the USA, except where stated.

SONNY WILSON SINGLE RELEASES

(*JACKIE WILSON, lead vocals)

	DATE	LABEL	CHART POSITION R&B	POP
SONNY WILSON				
*Rainy Day Blues	1952	DEE GEE	/	/
Rockaway Rock				
*Danny Boy	1952	DEE GEE	/	/
Bulldozer Blues				

BILLY WARD AND THE DOMINOES SINGLE RELEASES

(*JACKIE WILSON, lead vocals)

	DATE	LABEL	CHART POSITION R&B	POP
Where Now, Little Heart	7/53	KING/FEDERAL	/	/
*You Can't Keep A Good Man Down				
*Rags To Riches	10/53	KING/FEDERAL	3	/
Don't Thank Me				
*Christmas In Heaven	11/53	KING/FEDERAL	/	/
Ring In A Brand New Year				
*Until The Real Thing Comes Along	12/53	KING/FEDERAL	/	/
My Baby's 3-D				
Tootsie Roll (with great Jackie backing)	3/54	KING/FEDERAL	/	/
*I'm Gonna Move To The Outskirts Of Town				

	DATE	LABEL	CHART POSITION	
			R&B	POP
*Tenderly *A Little Lie	4/54	KING/FEDERAL	/	/
*Three Coins In The Fountain Lonesome Road	5/54	KING/FEDERAL	/	/
*Little Things Mean A Lot I Really Don't Want To Know	6/54	KING/FEDERAL	/	/
Come To Me Baby Gimme Gimme Gimme	9/54	JUBILEE	/	/
*Above Jacob's Ladder Little Black Train	10/54	KING/FEDERAL	/	/
If I Never Get To Heaven Can't Do Sixty No More	2/55	KING/FEDERAL	/	/*
*Love Me Now Or Let Me Go Caveman	4/55	KING/FEDERAL	/	/
May I Never Love Again *Learnin' The Blues	7/55	KING/FEDERAL	/	/
Sweethearts On Parade *Take Me Back To Heaven (also two un-released versions on a 1995 CD release)	8/55	JUBILEE	/	/
*Give Me You Over The Rainbow	9/55	KING/FEDERAL	/	/
*Bobby Sox Baby How Long, How Long Blues	5/56	KING/FEDERAL	/	/
*St Therese Of The Roses Home Is Where You Hang Your Heart	6/56	DECCA	/	13
*Will You Remember Come On Snake Let's Crawl	8/56	DECCA	/	/
Half A love *Evermore	12/56	DECCA	/	/

	DATE	LABEL	CHART POSITION R&B	POP
Rock, Plymouth Rock 'Til Kingdom Come	1/57	DECCA	/	/
*One Moment With You *St Louis Blues	7/57	KING/FEDERAL	/	/
*To Each His Own I Don't Stand A Ghost Of A Chance	9/57	DECCA	/	/
September Song When The Saints Go Marching In	11/57	DECCA	/	/
Lay It On The Line *That's When You Know You're Growing Old	4/61	KING/FEDERAL	/	/

UN-RELEASED UNTIL 1977

(Yes I Can See) The Handwriting On The Wall		KING/FEDERAL – (GUSTO 1977)
I Need Someone In My Arms		KING/FEDERAL – (GUSTO 1977)
Deed I Do		KING/FEDERAL – (GUSTO 1977)

UN-RELEASED UNTIL 1995

*Stop! You're Sending Me	8/55	JUBILEE
*Come To Me Baby	8/55	JUBILEE
*Gimme Gimme Gimme	8/55	JUBILEE

BILLY WARD AND HIS DOMINOES (ALBUM)

BILLY WARD AND HIS DOMINOES   (DECCA Album Number 8621)

    *To Each His Own
    *St Therese Of The Roses
    September Song
    *St Louis Blues
    *When Irish Eyes Are Smiling
    'Til Kingdom Come
    *Evermore
    I Don't Stand A Ghost Of A Chance
    Am I Blue
    *Will You Remember
    Oh, Lady Be Good!
    When The Saints Go Marching In

JACKIE WILSON SINGLE RELEASES

	DATE	LABEL	CHART POSITION	
			R&B	POP
Reet Petite	8/57	BRUNSWICK		62
By The Light Of The Silvery Moon				UK 6
			(1986 re-issue) UK 1	
To Be Loved	2/58	BRUNSWICK	7	22
Come Back To Me				UK 23
I'm Wanderin'	5/58	BRUNSWICK	/	/
As Long As I live				
We Have Love	8/58	BRUNSWICK	/	93
Singing A Song				
Lonely Teardrops	10/58	BRUNSWICK	1	7
In The Blue Of The Evening				
That's Why (I Love You So)	3/59	BRUNSWICK	2	13
Love is All				
I'll Be Satisfied	6/59	BRUNSWICK	6	20
Ask				
You Better Know It	8/59	BRUNSWICK	1	37
Never Go Away				
Talk That Talk	10/59	BRUNSWICK	3	34
Only You, Only Me				
Night	3/60	BRUNSWICK	3	4
Doggin' Around			1	15
(You Were Made For) All My Love	6/60	BRUNSWICK	/	12
				UK 33
A Woman, A Lover, A Friend			1	15
Alone At Last	9/60	BRUNSWICK	20	8
				UK 50
Am I The Man			10	32

	DATE	LABEL	CHART POSITION	
			R&B	POP
My Empty Arms	12/60	BRUNSWICK	25	9
The Tear Of The Year			10	44
Please Tell Me Why	2/61	BRUNSWICK	11	20
Your One And Only Love			/	40
I'm Coming On Back To You	5/61	BRUNSWICK	9	19
Lonely Life			/	80
You Don't Know What It Means	7/61	BRUNSWICK	19	79
Years From Now			25	37
My Heart Belongs To Only You	10/61	BRUNSWICK	/	65
The Way I Am			/	58
The Greatest Hurt	12/61	BRUNSWICK	/	34
There'll Be No Next Time			/	75
I Found Love	3/62	BRUNSWICK	/	93
There's Nothing Like Love				
(both with Linda Hopkins)				
Hearts	4/62	BRUNSWICK	/	58
Sing				
I Just Can't Help It	6/62	BRUNSWICK	17	70
My Tale Of Woe				
Forever And A Day	9/62	BRUNSWICK	/	82
Baby, That's All				
What Good Am I Without You	12/62	BRUNSWICK	/	/
A Girl Named Tamiko				
Baby Workout	2/63	BRUNSWICK	1	5
I'm Going Crazy				
Shake A Hand	5/63	BRUNSWICK	21	42
Say I Do				
(both with Linda Hopkins)				
Shake! Shake! Shake!	6/63	BRUNSWICK	21	33
He's A Fool				

	DATE	LABEL	CHART POSITION	
			R&B	POP
Baby Get It (And Don't Quit It) The New Breed	9/63	BRUNSWICK	/	61
Silent Night O Holy Night (Cantique de Noel)	11/63	BRUNSWICK	/	/
Haunted House I'm Travellin' On	2/64	BRUNSWICK	/	/
The Kickapoo Call Her Up	3/64	BRUNSWICK	/	/
Big Boss Line Be My Girl	5/64	BRUNSWICK	/	94
Squeeze Her – Tease Her Give Me Back My Heart	8/64	BRUNSWICK	/	89
She's All Right Watch Out	9/64	BRUNSWICK	/	102
Danny Boy Soul Time	2/65	BRUNSWICK	25	94
When The Saints Go Marching In Yes Indeed (both with Linda Hopkins)	4/65	BRUNSWICK	/	/
No Pity (In The Naked City) I'm So Lonely	6/65	BRUNSWICK	25	59
I Believe I'll Love You Lonely Teardrops (slow version)	10/65	BRUNSWICK	/	96
Think Twice Please Don't Hurt Me (I've Never been In Love Before) (both with LaVern Baker)	12/65	BRUNSWICK	37	93
I've Got To Get Back (Country Boy) Three Days, One Hour, Thirty Minutes	1/66	BRUNSWICK	/	/

	DATE	LABEL	CHART POSITION R&B	POP
Soul Galore Brand New Thing	3/66	BRUNSWICK	/	/
Be My Love I Believe	5/66	BRUNSWICK	/	/
Whispers (Gettin' Louder) The Fairest Of Them All	9/66	BRUNSWICK	5	11
I Don't Want To Lose You Just Be Sincere	1/67	BRUNSWICK	11 43	84 91
I've Lost You Those Heartaches	4/67	BRUNSWICK	35	82
(Your Love Keeps Lifting Me) Higher And Higher I'm The One To Do It	7/67	BRUNSWICK	1 (1975 re-issue) UK 25 (1987 re-issue) UK 15	6 UK 11
Since You Showed Me How To Be Happy The Who Who Song	11/67	BRUNSWICK	22	32
For Your Precious Love Uptight (Everything's Alright) (Both with Count Basie)	1/68	BRUNSWICK	/	49
Chain Gang Funky Broadway (Both with Count Basie)	4/68	BRUNSWICK	37	84
I Get The Sweetest Feeling Nothing But Blue Skies	6/68	BRUNSWICK	12 (1987 re-issue) UK 3	34 UK 9
For Once In My Life You Brought About A Change In Me	10/68	BRUNSWICK	/	70
I Still Love You Hum De Dum De Do	2/69	BRUNSWICK	/	/

	DATE	LABEL	CHART POSITION	
			R&B	POP
Helpless Do It The Right Way	8/69	BRUNSWICK	/	/
Do Your Thing With These Hands	11/69	BRUNSWICK	/	/
Let This Be A Letter (To My Baby) Didn't I	4/70	BRUNSWICK	/	91
(I Can Feel The Vibrations) This Love Is Real Love Uprising	11/70	BRUNSWICK	9	56
This Guy's In Love With You Say You Will	4/71	BRUNSWICK	/	/
Love Is Funny That Way Try It Again	10/71	BRUNSWICK	/	95
You Got Me Walking The Fountain	1/72	BRUNSWICK	22	93
The Girl Turned Me On Forever And A Day	4/72	BRUNSWICK	/	/
You Left The Fire Burning What A Lovely Way	7/72	BRUNSWICK	/	/
Beautiful Day What'cha Gonna Do About Love	1/73	BRUNSWICK	/	/
Because Of You Go Away	4/73	BRUNSWICK	/	/
Sing A Little Song No More Goodbyes	7/73	BRUNSWICK	/	95
Shake A Leg It's All Over	11/73	BRUNSWICK	/	/
Don't Burn No Bridges Don't Burn No Bridges (instrumental) (with The Chi-Lites)	10/75	BRUNSWICK	/	91
Nobody But You I've Learned About Life	1977	BRUNSWICK	/	/

JACKIE WILSON ALBUMS

			CHART POSITION	
	DATE	LABEL	R&B	POP

1) HE'S SO FINE   3/1958   BRUNSWICK   /   /
Etcetera
To Be Loved
Come Back To Me
If I Can't Have You
As Long As I Live
Reet Petite
It's Too Bad We Had To Say Goodbye
Why Can't You Be Mine
I'm Wanderin'
Right Now
Danny Boy
It's So Fine

2) LONELY TEARDROPS   2/1959   BRUNSWICK   /   /
Lonely Teardrops
Each Time (I Love You More)
That's Why (I Love You So)
In The Blue Of Evening
The Joke
Someone To Need Me (As I Need You)
You Better Know It
By The Light Of The Silvery Moon
Singing A Song
Love Is All
We Have Love
Hush-A-Bye

3) SO MUCH   11/1959   BRUNSWICK   /   /
So Much
I Know I'll Always Be In Love With You
Happiness
Only You, Only Me
The Magic Of Love
Wishing Well
Talk That Talk
Ask
I'll Be Satisfied
It's All A Part Of Love
Never Go Away
Thrill Of Love

	DATE	LABEL	CHART POSITION	
			R&B	POP
4) JACKIE SINGS THE BLUES	4/1960	BRUNSWICK	/	/

Please Tell Me Why
Doggin' Around
New Girl In Town
Nothin' But The Blues
Passin' Through
Excuse Me For Lovin'
She Done Me Wrong
Sazzle Dazzle
Please Stick Around
Come On And Love Me Baby
Comin' To Your House
It's Been A Long Time

	DATE	LABEL	R&B	POP
5) MY GOLDEN FAVOURITES	8/1960	BRUNSWICK	/	/

Reet Petite (The Finest Girl You Ever Want To Meet)
To Be Loved
I'll Be Satisfied
Only You, Only Me
Talk That Talk
Ask
That's Why (I Love You So)
It's All A Part Of Love
Lonely Teardrops
I'm Wanderin'
You Better Know It
We Have Love

	DATE	LABEL	R&B	POP
6) A WOMAN, A LOVER, A FRIEND	11/1960	BRUNSWICK	/	/

A Woman, A Lover, A Friend
Your One And Only Love
You Cried
The River
When You Add Religion To Love
One Kiss
Night
(You Were Made For) All My Love
Am I The Man
Behind The Smile Is A Tear
We Kissed
(So Many) Cute Little Girls

	DATE	LABEL	CHART POSITION	
			R&B	POP

7) YOU AIN'T HEARD NOTHIN' YET   2/1961   BRUNSWICK   /   /
Toot, Toot, Tootsie Goodbye
Sonny Boy
California Here I Come
Keep Smiling At Trouble (Trouble's A Bubble)
You Made Me Love You (I Didn't Want To Do It)
My Yiddishe Momme
Swanee
April Showers
Anniversary Song
Rock-A-Bye Your Baby With A Dixie Melody
For Me And My Girl
In Our House

8) BY SPECIAL REQUEST   9/1961   BRUNSWICK   /   /
Cry
My Heart Belongs To Only You
Stormy Weather (Keeps Rainin' All The Time)
Tenderly
Lonely Life
The Way I Am
Try A Little Tenderness
Mood Indigo
You Belong To My Heart
Indian Love Call
One More Time
I'm Comin' On Back To You

9) BODY AND SOUL   4/1962   BRUNSWICK   /   /
Body And Soul
I Don't Know You Anymore
I Got It Bad (And That Ain't Good)
The Greatest Hurt
I'll Always Be In Love With You
Crazy She Calls Me
The Tear Of The Year
Blue Moon
I'll Be Around
There'll Be No Next
We'll Be Together Again

	DATE	LABEL	CHART POSITION	
			R&B	POP

10) JACKIE WILSON AT THE COPA   8/1962   BRUNSWICK   /   137
    Tonight
    Medley; Body And Soul / I Apologise
    Love For Sale
    And This Is My Beloved
    The Way I Am
    I Love Them All-Part 1
        1) What I Say
        2) Night
        3) That's Why
    I Love Them All-Part 2
        1) Danny Boy
        2) Doggin' Around
        3) To Be Loved
        4) Lonely Teardrops
    St James Infirmary
    A Perfect Day

11) JACKIE WILSON SINGS THE   1/1963   BRUNSWICK   /   /
WORLD'S GREATEST MELODIES
    Forever And A Day
    Take My Heart
    Pianissimo
    My Eager Heart
    Each Night I Dream Of You
    Night
    My Empty Arms
    (You Were Made For) All My Love
    A Heart Of Love
    Alone At Last
    You Thing Of Beauty

12) BABY WORKOUT   4/1963   BRUNSWICK   /   36
    Shake! Shake! Shake!
    The Kickapoo
    Yeah! Yeah! Yeah!
    You Only Live Once
    Say You Will
    Baby Workout
    It's All My Fault
    Love Train
    Now That I Want Her
    (I Feel Like I'm In) Paradise
    (So Many) Cute Little Girls
    What Good Am I Without You

	DATE	LABEL	CHART POSITION R&B	POP

13) SHAKE A HAND   7/1963   BRUNSWICK   /   /
(with Linda Hopkins)
     Swing Low Sweet Chariot
     Nobody Knows The Trouble I've Seen
     Yes Indeed
     Joshua Fit The Battle Of Jericho
     Old Time Religion
     Shake A Hand
     He's Got The Whole World In His Hands
     When The Saints Go Marching In
     Do Lord
     Every Time I Hear The Spirit
     Dry Bones
     Down By The Riverside

14) MERRY CHRISTMAS FROM   10/1963   BRUNSWICK   /   /
JACKIE WILSON
     Silent Night
     White Christmas
     O Holy Night (Cantique de Noel)
     The First Noel
     Deck The Hall
     Silver Bells
     Joy To The World
     It Came Upon The Midnight Clear
     Adeste Fideles (O Come All Ye Faithful)
     I'll Be Home For Christmas
     O Little Town Of Bethlehem
     God Rest Ye Merry, Gentlemen

15) MY GOLDEN FAVOURITES VOLUME 2   11/1963   BRUNSWICK   /   /
     Baby Workout
     Doggin' Around
     Baby Get It (And Don't Quit It)
     The Tear Of The Year
     Shake! Shake! Shake!
     My Heart Belongs To Only You
     Night
     Am I The Man
     Alone At Last
     The Way I Am
     Please Tell Me Why
     (You Were Made For) All My Love

	DATE	LABEL	CHART POSITION	
			R&B	POP

16) SOMETHIN' ELSE!! 6/1964 BRUNSWICK / /
Big Boss Line
Groovin'
Deep Down Love
Take One Step (I'll Take Two)
Love (Is Where You Find It)
Give Me Back My Heart
Squeeze Her Tease Her (But Love Her)
Be My Girl
Baby (I Just Can't Help It)
Rebecca
My Best Friend's Girl
Twisting And Shoutin' (Doing The Monkey)

17) SOUL TIME 4/1965 BRUNSWICK / /
No Pity (In The Naked City)
Danny Boy
An Ocean I'll Cry
Soul Time
Teardrop Avenue
She'll Be There
Star Dust
A Kiss, A Thrill And Goodbye
Mama Of My Song
She's All Right
Better Play It Safe
No Time Out

18) SPOTLIGHT ON JACKIE 9/1965 BRUNSWICK / /
Over The Rainbow
Pledging My Love
Georgia On My Mind
You'll Never Walk Alone
Rags To Riches
You Don't Know Me
What Kind Of Fool Am I
I Wanna Be Around
Until The Real Thing Comes Along
I Apologise
Lonely Teardrops (slow version)
We Have Love

	DATE	LABEL	CHART POSITION	
			R&B	POP

19) SOUL GALORE   2/1966   BRUNSWICK   /   /

    Brand New Thing-Part 1
    Three Days, One Hour, Thirty Minutes
    I've Got To Get Back (Country Boy)
    So You Say You Wanna Dance (Workout 2)
    Stop Lying
    Let Me Build
    Brand New Thing-Part 2
    Soul Galore
    What's Done In The Dark
    I Got My Mind Made Up
    Everything's Going To Be Fine
    Your Loss, My Gain

20) WHISPERS   12/1966   BRUNSWICK   /   108

    I Don't Want To Lose You
    My Heart Is Calling
    Who Am I
    Whispers
    The Fairest Of Them All
    (Too Much) Sweet Loving
    I Can Do Better
    Just Be Sincere
    Only Your Love Can Save Me
    To Make A Big Man Cry
    I've Got To Talk To You
    Tears Will Tell It All

21) HIGHER AND HIGHER   10/1967   BRUNSWICK   /   163

    (Your Love Keeps Lifting Me) Higher And Higher
    I Don't Need You Around
    I've Lost You
    Those Heartaches
    Soulville
    Open The Door To Your Heart
    I'm The One To Do It
    You Can Count On Me
    I Need Your Loving
    Somebody Up There Likes You
    When Will Our Day Come

	DATE	LABEL	CHART POSITION R&B	POP
22) MANUFACTURERS OF SOUL (with Count Basie) Funky Broadway For Your Precious Love In The Midnight Hour Ode To Billy Joe Chain Gang I Was Made To Love Her Uptight (Everything's Alright) I Never Loved A Woman (The Way I Love You) Respect Even When You Cry My Girl	3/1968	BRUNSWICK	/	195
23) I GET THE SWEETEST FEELING You Keep Me Hanging On Once In A Lifetime Who Can I Turn To (When Nobody Needs Me) People Don't Go To Strangers I Get The Sweetest Feeling You Brought About A Change In Me Nothing But Blue Skies A Woman Needs To Be Loved Growin' Tall Since You Showed Me How To Be Happy	10/1968	BRUNSWICK	/	/
24) DO YOUR THING To Change My Love This Guy's In Love With You Why Don't You Do Your Thing This Bitter Earth Helpless Light My Fire That Lucky Old Sun (Just Rolls Around Heaven All Day) With These Hands Hold On, I'm Comin' Eleanor Rigby	10/1969	BRUNSWICK	/	/
25) IT'S ALL A PART OF LOVE It's All A Part Of Love Only You, Only Me	2/1970	BRUNSWICK	/	/

	DATE	LABEL	CHART POSITION	
			R&B	POP

Night
For Once In My Life
People
We Have Love
Who Can You Turn To (When Nobody Needs Me)
Don't Go To Strangers
This Guy's In Love With You
(You Were Made For) All My Love
Alone At Last

26) THIS LOVE IS REAL	3/1970	BRUNSWICK	/	/

This Love Is Real
Don't Leave me
Where There Is Love
Let This Be A Letter (To My Baby)
Love Uprising
Think About The Good Times
Didn't I
Love Changed Her Face
Working On My Woman's Heart
Say You Will

27) YOU GOT ME WALKING	11/1971	BRUNSWICK	/	/

You Got Me Walking
What A Lovely Way
You Left The Fire Burning
My Way
Try It Again
Forever And A Day
The Girl Turned Me On
Hard To Get A Thing Called Love
Love Is Funny That Way
The Fountain

28) BEAUTIFUL DAY	3/1973	BRUNSWICK	/	/

Beautiful Day
Because Of You
Go Away
Pretty Little Angel Eyes
Let's Love Again
It's All Over
I Get Lonely Sometimes

	DATE	LABEL	CHART POSITION R&B	POP

This Love Is Mine
Don't You Know I Love You
What'cha Going To Do About Me

29) NOBODY BUT YOU	1976	BRUNSWICK	/	/

Where Is Love
You're The Song
Nobody But You
Just Call My Name
Just As Soon As The Feeling's Over
Don't Burn No Bridges
You'll Be Good For Me
It Only Happens When I Look At You
Satisfy My Soul
I've Learned About Life

AUSTRALIAN TOP FORTY CHART SUCCESS

REET PETITE	MARCH 1958	8
NIGHT	APRIL 1960	11
ALL MY LOVE	AUGUST 1960	24
ALONE AT LAST	NOVEMBER 1960	9
HIGHER AND HIGHER	OCTOBER 1967	5

Appendix

For Jackie's chart positions and his place in history to be put in context, listed below are the most successful recording artists of the period 1955 to 1982 inclusive, taken from *The Billboard Book Of US Top Forty Hits*. The list records groups separately from individuals.

SOLO ARTISTS

	Top Forty Hits	Number One Hits
Elvis Presley	107	18
James Brown	43	Nil
Marvin Gaye	39	6
(including 12 duets)		
Stevie Wonder	38	6
Pat Boone	38	6
Fats Domino	36	Nil
Connie Francis	35	3
Ricky Nelson	35	2
Neil Diamond	35	2
Aretha Franklin	33	1
Ray Charles	32	3
Paul Anka	31	3
Elton John	30	5
Bobby Vinton	30	4
Brenda Lee	29	2
Sam Cooke	29	1
Paul McCartney	27	7
Perry Como	27	3
Andy Williams	27	1
Nat King Cole	26	Nil
Frank Sinatra	25	2
Dionne Warwick	25	Nil
Gladys Knight	24	1

	Top Forty Hits	Number One Hits
JACKIE WILSON	**24**	**Nil**
Roy Orbison	22	2
Brook Benton	22	Nil
Chubby Checker	21	3
Bobby Darin	21	1
Neil Sedaka	20	Nil
Diana Ross	19	5
Johnny Mathis	18	1
Tom Jones	18	Nil
Wilson Pickett	16	Nil
Barbra Streisand	14	3
Chuck Berry	14	Nil
Bill Haley	13	1
Al Green	13	1
Otis Redding	9	1
Little Richard	9	Nil
Sammy Davis Jnr	8	1
Clyde McPhatter	8	Nil
Jerry Lee Lewis	6	Nil
Buddy Holly	4	Nil

Roquel Davis and Berry Gordy compositions recorded by Jackie Wilson

Etcetera	Roquel Davis/Berry Gordy
To Be Loved	Berry Gordy/Tyron Carlo
Reet Petite	Tyron Carlo/Berry Gordy
I'm Wanderin'	Tyron Carlo/Berry Gordy
It's So Fine	Albert Green/Tyron Carlo/ Berry Gordy
Lonely Teardrops	Berry Gordy/Tyron Carlo
Each Time (I Love You More)	Berry Gordy/Tyron Carlo
That's Why (I Love You So)	Berry Gordy/Tyron Carlo
Someone To Need Me	Berry Gordy/Tyron Carlo
We Have Love	Berry Gordy/Tyron Carlo/Gwen Gordy
I'll Be Satisfied	Berry Gordy/Tyron Carlo
Thrill Of Love	Berry Gordy/Tyron Carlo
Higher And Higher	Roquel Billy Davis and others

Bibliography

Many fine books, magazines and newspapers have been consulted in my research for this project. Some I have quoted from directly, and these are fully credited throughout; others provided general background rather than specific points.

Books

The Penguin Encyclopaedia Of Popular Music		Edited by Donald Clarke
The Blackwell Guide To Soul Recordings		Edited by Robert Pruter
Hit Men	(Vintage Books)	Fredric Dannen
Stiffed	(Harper Perennial)	William Knoedelseder
Find That Tune	(Neal-Schuman)	Edited by William Gargan and Sue Sharma
The Rolling Stone Illustrated History Of Rock'N'Roll		Edited by Jim Miller
Who Sang What In Rock'N'Roll	(Blandford)	Alan Warner
Temptations	(GP Putman's Sons)	Otis Williams
The Billboard Book Of US Top 40 Hits 1955 To Present		Joel Whitburn
Book Of Golden Discs		Gerald Morrell
To Be Loved	(Warner Books)	Berry Gordy
Chicago Soul	(University Press)	Robert Pruter
Mark Twain's Autobiography	(Viking Press)	Mark Twain
Death Of Rhythm And Blues	(Pantheon Books)	Nelson George
The Big Beat	(Schirmer Books)	John A Jackson
Showtime At The Apollo	(Da Capo Press)	Ted Fox
Dreamgirl		Mary Wells
They All Sang On The Corner	(Phillie Dee)	Philip Groia

Periodicals

Musician Magazine
Melody Maker
Downbeat
Variety
Michigan Chronicle

411

Detroit *Free Press*
New York *Sunday News*
Detroit *News*
Sepia
Jet
Goldmine
Rolling Stone
Big Town Review
Village Voice
Philadelphia *Tribune*
Philadelphia *Inquirer*
Hustler

Index

ALSO AVAILABLE FROM

SANCTUARY MUSIC LIBRARY

MIND OVER MATTER – THE IMAGES OF PINK FLOYD
£30.00/$39.95   by Storm Thorgerson   1-86074-206-8
DEATH DISCS – AN ACCOUNT OF FATALITY IN THE POPULAR SONG
£14.99/$19.95   by Alan Clayson   1-86074-195-9
LIVE & KICKING
£12.99/$19.95   by Mark Cunningham with Andy Wood   1-86074-217-3
BORN UNDER THE SIGN OF JAZZ
£14.99/$22.50   by Randi Hultin   1-86074-194-0
SERGE GAINSBOURG – VIEWED FROM THE EXTERIOR
£12.99/$19.95   by Alan Clayson   1-86074-222-X
HAMBURG – THE CRADLE OF BRITISH ROCK
£12.99/$19.95   by Alan Clayson   1-86074-221-1
LET THEM ALL TALK – ELVIS COSTELLO
£12.99/$19.95   by Brian Hinton   1-86074-197-7
JONI MITCHELL – BOTH SIDES NOW
£12.99/$19.95   by Brian Hinton   1-86074-160-6
GEORGE GERSHWIN – HIS LIFE & MUSIC
£9.99/$14.95   by Ean Wood   1-86074-174-6
THE QUIET ONE – A LIFE OF GEORGE HARRISON
£9.99/$14.95   by Alan Clayson   1-86074-184-3
RINGO STARR – STRAIGHT MAN OR JOKER?
£9.99/$14.95   by Alan Clayson   1-86074-189-4
CELTIC CROSSROADS – THE ART OF VAN MORRISON
£9.99/$14.95   by Brian Hinton   1-86074-169-X
**SEVENTEEN WATTS? THE FIRST 20 YEARS OF BRITISH ROCK
GUITAR, THE MUSICIANS AND THEIR STORIES**
£19.99/$34.95   by Mo Foster   1-86074-182-7
PETER GREEN – FOUNDER OF FLEETWOOD MAC
£9.99/$14.95   by Martin Celmins   1-898141-13-4
THE KINKS – WELL RESPECTED MEN
£9.99/$14.95   by Neville Marten & Jeffrey Hudson   1-86074-135-5